Opera Omnia

Volume II

Religion and Religions

Opera Omnia

I. Mysticism and Spirituality
Part 1: Mysticism, Fullness of Life
Part 2: Spirituality, the Way of Life

II. Religion and Religions

III. Christianity
Part 1: The Christian Tradition
Part 2: A Christophany

IV. Hinduism
Part 1: The Vedic Experience: Mantramanjari
Part 2: The Dharma of India

V. Buddhism

VI. Cultures and Religions in Dialogue
Part 1: Pluralism and Interculturality
Part 2: Intercultural and Interreligious Dialogue

VII. Hinduism and Christianity

VIII. Trinitarian and Cosmotheandric Vision

IX. Mystery and Hermeneutics
Part 1: Myth, Symbol, and Ritual
Part 2: Faith, Hermeneutics, and Word

X. Philosophy and Theology
Part 1: The Rhythm of Being
Part 2: Philosophical and Theological Thought

XI. Sacred Secularity

XII. Space, Time, and Science

Opera Omnia

Volume II

Religion and Religions

Raimon Panikkar

Edited by Milena Carrara Pavan

ORBIS BOOKS
Maryknoll, New York 10545

Founded in 1970, Orbis Books endeavors to publish works that enlighten the mind, nourish the spirit, and challenge the conscience. The publishing arm of the Maryknoll Fathers and Brothers, Orbis seeks to explore the global dimensions of the Christian faith and mission, to invite dialogue with diverse cultures and religious traditions, and to serve the cause of reconciliation and peace. The books published reflect the views of their authors and do not represent the official position of the Maryknoll Society. To learn more about Maryknoll and Orbis Books, please visit our website at www.maryknollsociety.org.

Library of Congress Cataloging-in-Publication Data

Panikkar, Raimundo, 1918–2010.
    [Religione e religioni. English]
    Religion and religions / by Raimon Panikkar ; edited by Milena Carrara Pavan
    — English edition.
        pages cm. — (Opera omnia ; volume II)
    Includes bibliographical references and index.
    ISBN 978-1-62698-130-0 (cloth)
    1. Religion—Philosophy. 2. Religions—Relations. 3. Christianity and other religions. I. Title.
BL51.P2613 2015
200—dc23

                                        2014045812

SERIES FOREWORD

All the writings it is my privilege and responsibility to present in this series are not the fruit of mere speculation but, rather, autobiographical—that is, they were first inspired by a life and praxis that have been only subsequently molded into writing.

This *Opera Omnia* ranges over a span of some seventy years, during which I dedicated myself to exploring further the meaning of a more justified and fulfilled human lifetime. I did not live for the sake of writing, but I wrote to live in a more conscious way so as to help my fellows with thoughts not only from my own mind but also springing from a superior Source, which may perhaps be called Spirit—although I do not claim that my writings are in any way inspired. However, I do not believe that we are isolated monads, but that each of us is a microcosm that mirrors and impacts the macrocosm of reality as a whole—as most cultures believed when they spoke of the Body of Śiva, the communion of the saints, the Mystical Body, *karman*, and so forth.

The decision to publish this collection of my writings has been somewhat trying, and more than once I have had to overcome the temptation to abandon the attempt, the reason being that, though I fully subscribe to the Latin saying *scripta manent*, I also firmly believe that what actually matters in the final analysis is to live out Life, as witnessed by the great masters who, as Thomas Aquinas remarks in the *Summa* about Pythagoras and Socrates (but not about Buddha, of whom he could not have known), did not write a single word.

In the twilight of life I found myself in a dark forest, for the straight path had been lost and I had shed all my certainties. It is undoubtedly to the merit of Sante Bagnoli, and of his publishing house Jaca Book, that I owe the initiative of bringing out this *Opera Omnia*, and all my gratitude goes to him. This work includes practically all that has appeared in book form, although some chapters have been inserted into different volumes as befitted their topics. Numerous articles have been added to present a more complete picture of my way of thinking, but occasional pieces and almost all my interviews have been left out.

I would like to make some practical comments which apply to all the volumes:

1. In quoting references, I have preferred to cite my previously published works following the general scheme of my publications.
2. Subject matter rather than chronology has been considered in the selection, and thus the style may sometimes appear uneven.

3. Even if each of these works aspires to be a self-sufficient whole, some ideas recur because they are functional to understanding the text, although the avoidance of unnecessary duplication has led to a number of omissions.

4. The publisher's preference for the *Opera Omnia* to be put into an organic whole by the author while still alive has many obvious positive features. Should the author outlive the printer's run, however, he will be hard put to help himself from introducing alterations, revisions, or merely adding to his original written works.

I thank my various translators, who have rendered the various languages I have happened to write in into the spirit of multiculturalism—which I believe is ever relevant in a world where cultures encounter each other in mutual enrichment, provided they do not mislay their specificity. I am particularly grateful to Milena Carrara Pavan, to whom I have entrusted the publication of all my written works, which she knows deeply, having been at my side in dedication and sensitivity during the last twenty years of my life.

R.P.

Contents

Abbreviations

Ex	Exodus
Gal	Galatians
Gn	Genesis
Heb	Letter to the Hebrews
Is	Isaiah
Jas	James
Jb	Job
Jn	John
Lk	Luke
Mk	Mark
Mt	Matthew
Nb	Numbers
2 Pet	2 Peter
Ph	Philippians
Pr	Proverbs
Ps	Psalms
Qo	Qohelet
Rev	Revelation
Rom	Letter to the Romans
Si	Sirach
Tt	Titus
Ws	Wisdom

Others

BC	Biblia catalana
BJ	Bible de Jérusalem
Caes.	Plutarch, *Caesar*
De sacram.	Ambrose, *De sacramentis*
Epist. ad Eph.	Ignatius Antioch, *Epistle to the Ephesians*
Fragm.	Heraclitus, *Fragments*
Fragm.	Philolaus of Kroton, *Fragments*
KJ	King James Version
Knox	Knox Bible
Met.	Aristotle, *Metaphysics*
NácarColunga	Nácar-Colunga Bible
NEB	New English Bible
NJB	New Jerusalem Bible
NRSV	New Revised Standard Version
PG	J.-P. Migne, *Patrologiae Cursus Completus*. Series Graeca, Paris, 1857–1866

Phileb.	Plato, *Philebus*
Phys.	Aristotle, *Physics*
PL	J.-P. Migne, *Patrologiae Cursus Completus.* Series Latina, Paris, 1844–1855
RV	Revised Version
Sum. theol.	Thomas Aquinas, *Summa Theologiae*
Theat.	Plato, *Theaetetus*

INTRODUCTION

The title of this volume, which recalls that of my 1964 book, deliberately underlines the ambiguity of the word "religion": in the singular, it stands for the constitutional openness of Man to the mystery of life; in the plural, it indicates the various religious traditions.

More specifically:

1. Human beings are not fully realized; they are unfinished, and in that sense they are "infinite." They are in a process of becoming, reaching out to be what they still are not. This goal, though not always and not necessarily, may be considered a better state.

2. Religions are meant to be *ways* leading people toward their fulfillment, however that may be interpreted and however the nature of the way or path may be conceived. A religion is the set of practices and doctrines (orthopraxis and orthodoxy) that one *believes* lead to liberation and perfection at the individual, collective, and cosmic levels. Every religion is a plan of salvation. Religion is thus defined by the function it intends to effect: to unite (*religare*) point *x*, the human condition currently obtaining, to point *y*, considered as a final state or goal of the person, humanity, or the cosmos. It is evident that what we believe regarding *y* will condition our experience of *x*, and vice versa. In other words, religion manifests itself as a path to salvation. Salvation is meant here in its broadest etymological sense: something that transforms Man into an integral, healthy, free, and perfect being—all notions, of course, that lend themselves to the most varied interpretations.

3. Many such paths of the past have become obsolete; others still survive. There is also a continual emergence of novel paths that strive for a better, and obviously different, way of achieving what traditional religions aimed at. Many of these paths do not call themselves religions, the reason being that this word implies heavy connotations associated with certain types of paths. It is clearly a semantic issue, and also a cultural and political convention, whether these paths should be called religions or not. However, these movements do make a strong claim to provide a genuine substitute for what they deem traditional religions have failed to achieve.

4. Humanity is currently in a *diachronic situation*. We live in various times, so that what happens to one part of humanity at a distinct point in time can correspond to what may have happened to another part of humanity at another time. For a determined path to function (as a religion), a certain degree of awareness is necessary, for without it this path would not actually *exist*, in that it would not even be considered a path. It follows that no ready-made solutions or universal answers can exist, since the issues themselves do not have a universal range. In this way, one

form of religiosity could constitute a suitable path toward human fulfillment at a certain historical moment and in a certain geographical location, while the same *religiosity* may produce deleterious effects in a different context or moment. Thus, statements regarding religion must take account of particular human contexts and may not be universalized by wholesale extrapolation. That is not to exclude that at a given point in space and time one religion may regard itself as the true way, and that others may be deemed untrue.

5. No religion, ideology, culture, or tradition may reasonably claim to exhaust the universal range of human experience. That is why *pluralism*, which should be distinguished from the mere coexistence of a plurality of worldviews, is a necessity of our times. Pluralism does not imply a super-ideology or a super-system; it does, however, imply an almost mythical trust that other perspectives also may be plausible.

6. The dialogue/encounter between religions, ideologies, and worldviews is a human imperative for our times. The "splendid isolation" of old would become today a miserable turning in on oneself, excluding any outside point of contact. Dialogue as such constitutes a religious activity, in the sense of point 2 above.

7. All human endeavors of this type (whether they are called religions, ideologies, humanisms, atheisms, or something similar) are engaged in striving for the perfection of humankind, although different notions regarding the nature of the improvement, and thus the means for its achievement, may be held.

If human communication has any meaning, if religion and atheism can reach a real level of exchange, if ideologies and worldviews are prepared to engage in dialogue in a noble and honest spirit of emulation, then all sides will have to try and speak a mutually understandable language and to agree, at least on the issue at hand.

Very often, criticisms of religions from outside are quite similar to those moved from within; the scale of values used is practically identical, even if the conclusion reached by an outsider may be to eliminate religion, whereas critics from within tend toward reform or cleansing. A certain atheistic humanism, for instance, and a certain current form of Christianity in the West are dealing with fundamentally the same problems, despite providing different answers and even if, evidently, their different ways of focusing on issues are undoubtedly part of the problem to start with. Both seek a solution to the human condition such as it is.

There is one last point I would like to emphasize. About thirty years ago I proposed the term *ecumenical ecumenism* for the genuine and sincere encounter between religions, modeled on the efforts made by Christian ecumenism (which attempts to reach a certain harmony between churches while respecting differences, and without accusing people of error in order to lead them back to one's own *truth*). Ecumenical ecumenism attempts to reach a fertile and reciprocal enrichment and to accept a critique of the world's religious traditions without overlooking the value of the unique role each one has. Just as the Christian confessions recognize a Christ over whom they hold no monopoly, a Christ who unites them all without requiring their complete leveling, so the distinct traditions of humankind recognize a *humanum* (variously interpreted as in the case of different interpretations of Christ) that is not subject to manipulation—that is, transcendent. While remaining faithful to this *humanum*, they can debate among themselves while attempting to approach the ideal.

I would conclude with a reminder that a further step is needed: to invite people of different creeds to come out in favor of a new *dialogical dialogue*, even when, for understandable reasons, they decline a particular religious label. If the world's traditional religions abandoned the monopolistic claim on what *religion* represents; if the modern *religions* agreed to join in a common effort, as many of today's representatives of religious traditions are actually trying to do; if, in other words, the common ground could be considered *religious* ground; if those paths that aim to improve the present human condition could join forces and make a reciprocal effort and this without hidden—*unconfessed*—arms (motives), then we could perhaps discover one of the fundamental and permanent duties of *religion*—and of *laicism*, by which we mean sacred secularism—which is helping Man reach his fulfillment.

*

The volume includes in its first section, apart from the book already mentioned, various articles that expand on the concept of religion from different viewpoints and develop some of the most universal aspects of religiosity considered as a human dimension. The second section deals with comparative religion and with the religious philosophy of the encounter, while the third includes more specific topics, among which are articles about the body and medicine, as religion rebinds (*religat*) not only Man to God but also the spirit to the body.

SECTION I

Part One

CIRCUMDATA VARIETATE
Ps 44:10[1]

---

[1]   Cf. Benedict XV, in *Acta Apostolicæ Sedis*, 1919, 98.

PRESENTATION

In our increasingly unified world the meeting of religions is inevitable. This triggers a series of issues, both for Catholics as well as also for all those who are open to spiritual and philosophical problems.

Thanks to the history of religions, today we know that there have never been a people without religion, or, in other words, that religion is a human phenomenon so integrated into society and the individual that, as Aristotle said, *homo est animal religiosum.*

In the work we are presenting, Panikkar, who is linked both to the Indian as well as to the European spirit, tackles the theological and philosophical problems that emerge in the present day from the contact between religions in his own particular way. There is no doubt that Christianity, especially, must show interest in this confrontation because, on the one hand, it cannot accept the syncretistic thesis of the equality of all religions and, on the other, its claim to universality can no longer be interpreted in the sense of exclusivity.

The author, as a Catholic and as a philosopher of religion, takes special care to show how all religions conceal an intimate dynamism and at the same time a historical evolutionary impulse toward a superior unity. In the context of this approach, he offers very interesting and stimulating considerations on the famous "notes" of the Church of God. In a universal and figurative sense, one could say that they also reflect four characteristic notes of the religious values present in religions.

Rome, on the occasion of the Second Vatican Council
November 6, 1963
FRANZ CARDINAL KÖNIG
Archbishop of Vienna

Preface—Dedication

This study was written in 1955 after the mature reflection of several years. However, it seemed advisable to let it lie for another five years, during which time the author not only consulted a great part of the vast literature that had since appeared, but also had the opportunity to compare the thesis of this book with the views of scholars and simple believers of other religions. He can therefore sincerely say that no line herein has been written that has not had the confirmation of the spoken word in friendly confrontation.

This study then is more than just dedicated to those who shared in the conversations that produced it. It belongs to them, and to them, with gratitude, it is returned.

Varāṇasī
March 19, 1960

Some time has passed since the author returned to Europe, and very often during these three years, he has considered that this book demands a much broader treatment, as well as the addition of numerous explanatory notes and a supplementary historical framework. In all, it would make the work more complete and accessible; nevertheless, the author has rejected this temptation, because his study of the meeting of religions would then have a very different character, and his intention is merely to make a plea in favor of a better understanding of religions, one that is not purely academic, but that includes the sacred meaning that religions demand in the cosmic juncture of our times.

Rome
November 1, 1963

THE STARTING POINT

INTRODUCTION

It is an undeniable fact that our age is groping for a world culture. The peoples of the world can no longer dwell in isolation; their lives are thrown together; they exchange ideas and exercise influence upon each other, sometimes deliberately, at other times unconsciously: a new synthesis is thus forged into being.

The several religions of the world no longer meet in the battlefield, nor only in the minds of a few scholars—the cultures of the world stand less than ever religiously and politically isolated. Instead they meet in personal contact, in the business of the city, in the affairs of the country, and in the strains and stresses of international relations.

The existing literature on this subject is as dense as a jungle, and perhaps for this very reason we often cannot see the wood for the trees. There are many excellent studies on the theme and we appreciate many of them, but we refrain from making any reference to them in an effort to approach the problem itself directly.

The following facts are incontrovertible: there is a plurality of religions, and every religious person feels the internal contradiction of such a fact because, ultimately, plurality means not only variety but also variance. That is why, on one level or another, people find themselves faced with the paradox that religion, which claims to be the highest truth and the supreme value in human life, seems to divide and be an occasion of contention rather than lead to unity and peace.

Ecumenism is today felt as one of the most pressing problems of religion. No religion can continue to ignore other religions and live in *isolation*. They are forced to coexist, but this *coexistence* is only the first step that leads to tolerance, and in turn to something deeper than mere tolerance. The way is then open for a sincere *dia-logos*, which constitutes the third step during which an interchange of their own *logoi* is reached. Only then is the way paved for mutual *understanding*. Only in this fourth phase is true *communication* possible, which produces mutual *enrichment*—sixth step—and finally *communion*.

We think that the underlying force in the present-day meeting of religions lies in the internal tension between unity and diversity, and that this polarity stimulates a vital historical dynamism: the existential growth of religion toward its fullness. To be aware of this fact seems to be of capital importance, for we, free human beings, can very well hamper, retard, and distort the course of history. The error lies in the two extremes: uniformism, singularism, narrow-mindedness, with its dangers of fanaticism and intolerance on the one hand, and eclecticism, vagueness, inefficacy, with its temptations of irreality, irreligiosity, indifference and spiritual death, on the other.

11

Unity

We would pose the problem straight away as follows: If religion is what it claims to be, namely, the path leading Man to his ultimate goal, it seems that there is—or rather that there must be—an everlasting and true religion underlying all the religions of mankind.

This religion, however, is not—and cannot be—a vague and common "religiosity," but it must be the true religion, living at the heart of all religions, incarnated, so to speak, in different forms of greater or less perfection, development, and purity. This "religion" within the core of religions, considered the truth-content of all of them, will be then responsible for inspiring an internal dynamism—not without its revolutions and mutations—leading all religions to this one religion.

We see a double reason for this.

The first is anthropological. An essential feature of Man as a whole—and of the human mind in particular—is that he cannot rest and find his fulfillment until he reaches unity. Where there is plurality and diversity, our human intellect must seek a deeper harmony and unity, either in a common denominator, or in a unique and profound identity, even if this manifests itself in a factual variety. Pluralism can never be the ultimate ground with which the human being can be satisfied. Even the mere recognition of a plurality involves a certain underlying unity. Otherwise plurality would not even appear as a multiplicity—of "being."

The second reason is of a quite objective and philosophical nature, belonging to the very essence of religion. For religion, in fact, has a threefold structure. It refers to

1. something *superhuman*
2. being the *end*
3. of *Man.*

In other words, the existence of religion requires three elements: *God*, whoever or whatever that may be; *Man* as he is in the entire mystery of his existence; and a *link* between both to serve as the internal or external path along which the human being reaches its fullness, or, in religious terms, by which Man attains God. This formal scheme seems to be common to all religions. Buddhism, for example—that paradoxical religion without "God"—in spite of a very different terminology and of its denial of ultimate substantiality to Man does not make an exception. There is also in Buddhism an Absolute: *dharma*; there is a goal: *nirvāṇa*; there is a path: Buddhism and eventually Buddha; and there is the phenomenical Man. Even polytheism recognizes an Absolute and, even more, that among the gods there must be not only a hierarchy but ultimately a deeper unity. Man is also one in his nature notwithstanding his diversity. Likewise the paths leading to God must ultimately be one. In other words, the core of all true religions must be in some sense one and the same. Otherwise they would not be paths leading the same *Man* to the same *end:* God.

Now, this kernel of all religions, properly speaking, could possibly be identified either with a full-fledged religion or simply with a germinal principle present in each and every specimen of the religious flora. The latter view indicates a transcendental or rather immanent unity of religions, and though it is a prima facie easier opinion, it presents two great difficulties:

1. The same seed may certainly produce different plants, yet all of the same species. The historian of religions, however, in spite of the best will in the world cannot overlook the existence of contradictory features in the several religions. Some scholars attempt to avoid this difficulty, either by dealing only with what they call the great religions—ignoring the more primitive forms of religiosity—or by viewing the unity of all religions as a formal and empty concept common to all of them. In the first case they abandon the strictly phenomenological study to introduce personal "cultural" valuations. In the second case, they bury the kernel so deep in the Earth that it can no longer be the living seed of any of them. It is not, then, a real core, but a mere abstraction in our mind.

2. The second difficulty is that this germinal principle would no longer be a religion, but at best the "identity-kernel" of all religions. However, the religious man does not live from the roots alone but mainly from the fruits of the religious tree. The mere seed cannot give him the shelter that he expects from religion as a living tree with its trunk, branches, leaves, fruits, and roots.

That is to say, the only consequent attitude of this hypothesis would be to deny and to minimize each and every religion, paradoxically destroying religion in the name of religion and substituting for it the pure quintessence of religion, which cannot nourish the polymorphous religious needs of Man, especially of the multitude. Even if we were to accept that this pith is the religion of the pure, we cannot forget that men are generally not stainless and sublime, that religion is meant for all, and especially, we would say, for the simple and poor, "blessed" by God.

Diversity

If, on the one hand, there must be a certain unity of all religions, and on the other hand, this unity cannot be purely transcendental and disincarnated, it remains to be shown that the unity looked for is an existential unity of a dynamic and historical character, that is to say, a unity in the making, not only in the lofty spheres of mysticism, but also in the concrete realm of human life. Unity, indeed, should not be confused with uniformity or totalitarianism. A living unity requires variety and diversity as equally important features.

We shall have to show, therefore, that there is a unity as well as a diversity and above all that the claim for unity does not lie primarily in the essential sphere, but in the existential realm. Obviously this unity is far from being reached, and yet it is there as a dynamic force. The aim of this study is to demonstrate that this dynamism is at work in our times and thus awakens our sense of responsibility. To be a conscious and enlightened religious person today means, among other things, to feel a concern for the religion or a-religion of our neighbors.

*

Had we to formulate our thesis in few sentences we would do it in the following way.

The relationship between religions is not one of *syncretism* (all of them are equally good and equally imperfect, that is, they are really equivalent) nor is it one of *exclusivity* ("my" religion is the only good and true one and all others are false), but of *inclusivity* (all authentic religions are on the way toward the only one and true religion, realizing it in different degrees, which may even include a difference in nature, the essence of religion). This inclusivity—which does not exclude a healthy religious emulation—is *not* of a purely *essentialistic nature* (of merely speculative ideas including one another because they are more general or more perfect) but it is an *existential concurrence* of a very definite *historical nature* (all religions having a place in the historical development of mankind, or, in theistic terms, in the plan of God calling humanity back to Him).

There is an underlying unity, not only of a quintessential but of an ontological and historical character, and a dynamic evolution toward a universal religion, not in the shape of a diffused and vague religiosity, but of a thoroughly human and universal religion.

Allow us, for the sake of clarity, to state our thesis in Christian terminology: if there is one God leading and calling mankind to its obediential fullness, that is, to Him, He is listening to all the prayers, and is the inspiration of all the efforts in Man's search for Him. If there is one Christ, as God's Son and Man's Brother, as the one and only Mediator between Man and God, He is really behind all *authentic* forms of worship and of religious life. He is the One who hears and grants the prayers of the African idolater, as well as the mantras of the pious *Sivaita*; He is the One who invites men to realize that they are a unique family and have a supernatural destiny to share the nature of God; it is He who instills the grace and the strength into Man so that he may grow more and more in discovering the true face of God, and consequently the true aspect of reality. Christianity can only claim to be the *true* religion if it accepts fully its catholicity, that is, if it recognizes that it is everywhere present where religious truth exists, regardless of the external garb. Christ—the real living Christ, God and Man, Beginning and End, Only-begotten Son of God and Firstborn among the creatures through whom everything has come to be—is not the exclusive monopoly of any *particular* religion, He is not captive in the walls of a single "confession," but is living in the true mystical Body of His Church. Catholicism, if true, cannot be a "confession." This means that Christ is all-embracing, that He includes and sustains everything that is ontologically not against Him; the kingdom of God grows up day and night like a seed planted in the Earth, without its guardian, the Church, being aware of it. It means that Christ is also living as the hidden Messiah or the unknown God, in the souls of all authentic religious men of all religions, and that, through the mysterious liberty of men, especially of those who have received the full Revelation of His Name, He is leading all religions—including the present state of Christianity—in one way or another to the only religion and ontological community of His Mystical Body, that is, to the real and true Catholic Church—where this last concept must be correctly understood.

Only too often people forget that the Church is a mystical reality, that is, an integral being with body, soul, and spirit; that she is, first of all, the inward kingdom of God on Earth, the pilgrim stage of the itinerant, "created" being on its way to the fullness, or, in Christian terms, to the Whole Christ. The Church is one with Him and by this incorporated into the Only One Trinity. And precisely because of this mystical, that is, integral character, the Church is also a body, a visible organism.

One last remark I would like to make before proceeding. It is extremely difficult to write on religion in a way acceptable to people of different faiths. In the past it was almost unthinkable; today, I am confident it is possible. Nevertheless the difficulty remains because it is a hard task to please alike the followers of the distinct religions. On the one hand, their mingling has increased their susceptibilities, and on the other hand, the danger of a cheap eclecticism has become more obvious. Even if you speak with the most correct orthodoxy of your religion while envisaging other believers, the people of your own fold become suspicious or feel certain uneasiness and even sometimes feel hurt by your language. And if you do not do so, the brethren of other denominations begin by not understanding, and end by misunderstanding you. In what follows, I do not put my Catholic faith aside; on the contrary, I only try to understand it as well as possible, and at the same time to make it comprehensible to others in trying to speak a common language in direct touch with the problem itself. How often in describing Christ my Hindu brother has told me that Christ is Kṛṣṇa and I have answered that Christ is certainly in Kṛṣṇa!

This personal confession was perhaps necessary, not only to dispel doubts about our intention, but also to allow us in what follows to be strictly philosophical, having discharged beforehand all possible extra- or super-philosophical baggage.

*

We call these pages a philosophical study because we should like to develop a philosophical line of thought along which a great majority of the serious thinkers about religion may dialectically agree. This implies a very painful, but very honest, limitation that obliges us to leave unexpressed many ideas that belong in a strictly theological context and can only find their place in another context. Our aim primarily is that followers of different religions find a "formal" agreement with the views expounded here by virtue of their philosophical coherence, though they may interpret them in favor of their own religion. The first condition of any believer is to have a profound respect for his own faith and the faith of others. But faith cannot be proved. We must stop at the threshold.

A philosophical study cannot say everything about religion, but it may clarify the issue a great deal by discovering the implications and exigencies of the relationship between religions. Our study aims at explaining a little bit the humble "and" that unites and separates "Religion *and* Religions." It is thus the study of the copulative and adversative "and" in the religious field.

Because philosophy is something more than pure dialectics it must refer to concrete instances and take the nature of Man into account; but because philosophy is less, or other than, theology, it will exclude faith and with it the claim of giving an exhaustive picture of the nature of religion. We shall remain in our "and."

On the other hand we could have also called this study "theological" because our philosophical analysis, precisely because it is strictly philosophical, makes room for a theological inspiration; in fact, we have already said that the leading thread of our investigation is a *religious* concern for religion. This concern could not be sincerely religious if it were not theological, that is, if it were not anchored to religion itself.

One more consideration along these lines may not be out place. One of the most hopeful signs of the revival of the true religious spirit among the followers of the different Christian confessions is the desire for unity and the sincere suffering because of their division. After more than a thousand years of a not too edifying history in this respect, there emerges in our times another type of relationship with "heretics" and "schismatics." The consecrated word for it today is *ecumenism*. It makes possible a dialogue of living ideas—the third step mentioned above—and it implies learning from one another. The inspiring force of this coming together arises from the singular source of our fidelity and love of Christ, which is inseparable from loyalty toward one's own "confession." Because of this, the dialogue's primary aim is at one's own "conversion" to a deeper and fuller Christianity without trying to "convert" others or to condemn them. This means that ecumenism makes possible for the first time—on this large scale at least—a meeting of Christians without falling into the two equally wrong extremes of syncretism and compromise on the one hand and of one-sidedness and exclusivism on the other. Of course, such an encounter transcends merely speculative problems, and it is full of dangers and hardships; it is an encounter of hearts and of persons and not just of disincarnated minds. It is based on prayer and faith, as well as on study and sympathy.

Our aim in this study is an enlargement of such an ecumenical spirit among all the religions of the world. Not only a Christian, but a human and religious ecumenism is the leading idea in these pages, a *Catholic ecumenism* as we have called it elsewhere. But the beginnings of such a purpose must be very humble. That is the reason why, instead of laying down the principles of such a universal ecumenism in a more or less a prioristic way, we would like to attempt here an essay that tackles the problems themselves without proclaiming any previous manifesto. Before laying down the motorable road we must first clear, by ourselves, a rough track by simply pushing through. We would ask those who climb the same religious peak later on in more comfortable vehicles not to take it amiss if our bridle path has not always taken the best shortcuts. We seek, in almost complete darkness but full of confidence, an *ecumenical ecumenism*.

It goes without saying that such a meeting of religions implies much more than cool speculation; this is why we would like to ask our reader to join us in prayer and share in our suffering. However, in these pages we must limit ourselves to a more modest enterprise of showing only the philosophical milestones of our itinerary.

*

After a double introduction of phenomenological and dialectical character we shall outline an integral concept of religion by pointing out its nine double-sided, constitutive dimensions. This will give us the necessary background to realize the complexity of the unity and diversity of religions under the several viewpoints through which we shall envisage the particular problem of our study.

1

PSYCHOLOGICAL APPROACH

A first contact, not with the problem itself but with the common people interested in the problem, as well as with the thinkers who have studied it, will lead us to discover two extreme psychological positions. We would call them the *centripetal* and the *centrifugal* attitudes.

The human mind has two main tendencies: one is inclined to immanence and to introspection; it discovers truth "inside," in the "depths," in the "kernel" of things. The other is inclined to transcendence, to extrospection, to look for truth "outside," in the "heights," in the "facts" that appear and are verifiable.

For our purposes, we shall call the first attitude *centripetal*, and the second, *centrifugal*.

Before we briefly describe these two attitudes we should remember that they are, first of all, psychological tendencies. In almost every opinion there is at least a grain of truth that perhaps another opinion has ignored or forgotten. Very often religious controversy is only a psychological duel, and so-called theological discrepancies are only a question of mentality—for example: can we speak of Hindu tolerance, or should we be speaking of the patience or wisdom of the Indian people? Is it Muslim simplicity or Arabic single-mindedness? Is it Christian superiority or Western mentality? Is it Catholic "realism" or Latin or Roman juridical sense? Indeed, religions as such belong to this world of ours, but they all also teach us to know ourselves before judging others. The problem of the unity and plurality of religions offers a striking example of the tremendous importance of the psychological approach.

We could describe at length these two attitudes and show how many of their representatives hold a particular view regarding the problem of religion and religions, not because they have studied it dispassionately but because they project into it the particular trend of their mind. You can ask a man what he thinks about colonialism, apartheid, American-Russian tension, atom bombs, modern art, European integration, and the like, and from the type of answers he gives you can immediately guess the religious attitudes he holds. We are not, however, going to describe pure psychological attitudes, but only their interpretation of our problem.

Centripetalism

People with this trend of mind will emphasize the need for the purification of every religion by pointing to the central message it bears. They will recommend a deepening of the true religious values as the urgent task of our days so as not to be swept away in the muddle and confusion of modern chaos. The true "religious" attitude, they will say, feels that it is better to have *some* religion whatever it may be than to have no religion at all; for example, a sincere Jew, a good Muslim, and so on is better than an unbeliever. The true religion is not so much the externals of my religion but its spirit and its intention. What really matters is not so much to be a Buddhist, a Hindu, and so on, but a *good* Buddhist, a *good* Hindu. It will be in that deep uncompromising goodness where we shall meet, say, the representatives of centripetalism.

This attitude presents two different features according to the culture, temperament, and ideas of its representatives.

Negative

This is the attitude of those who go to the center of a particular religion, because in it they find all that is needed for happiness on Earth and hereafter. It is necessary to preserve strict orthodoxy, they say, because otherwise one simply indulges in a kind of sweet, vague, and ineffective religious feeling, which apparently may make one feel oneself a brother to everybody, but in fact without any effective and concrete brotherly love for one's real neighbor.

This *negative* position stresses the purity of its own faith and the beauty and perfection of its own religion. Whatever the other religions may be—possibly they are wrong or at least not as good as one's own—let us earnestly follow our religion better. Whatever ways there may be of attaining the last end of Man, the only way for us and for our faithful is the singular path of our own religious tradition. All ways may lead to the same goal, but to attain it, we cannot just jump from one road to another or follow no way at all. We must truly and humbly follow our own. Only thus will our religion fulfill its mission and help us to bring peace to the world, and only thus will we attain our own salvation.

This is not necessarily a fanatical or narrow-minded position—though both dangers are there—but a very realistic and existential attitude, which can present a very humble and healthy aspect: I am content and satisfied with my own religion, so why should I change it or search without for that which I can truly find within? The only thing that I must do is to realize more fully the message of salvation that my own religion offers. Then, at the end, in the everlasting life I shall meet all the true followers of other creeds. Therefore I have no reason to try to change their faiths but only challenge them to be more true to themselves. We are too easily inclined to arrange the whole world, to see the speck of dust in our brother's eye and to neglect the beam that is in our own. The work begins at home, and the most urgent and important religious task is our own conversion. If I am really a devout and truly pious soul, at least half of the problems of the meeting of religions will not arise.

So, in broad terms, these are the arguments that the centripetal attitude in its negative aspect would argue.

Positive

The *positive* aspect of the centripetal attitude, while stressing the same need to concentrate all our efforts toward the better practice of our own religion, believes at the same time that by being better Muslims, better Hindus, better Christians—that is, by purifying our own faith—we shall meet together at the very foundation of all creeds. Religions are not the same, but there exists a kind of *transcendent* unity that can only be reached if we undergo this true *conversion* to the core of our own religious tradition. This attitude of mind also intends to contribute to world peace by preaching a true conversion to the inner depth of each religion by means of this positive centripetal tendency. Religions are the different garments of one and the same essence, and it is not the garb that saves us, but the thing-in-itself. Moreover, if our habits are an occasion for scandal it is better to throw them off and enter into the kingdom of heaven naked than to be cast into hell well clothed for our lack of understanding and charity.

While the first aspect emphasizes concreteness and efficiency, this second one puts the accent on universality and purity. A mystic temperament will be inclined to overlook differences and to minimize external practices and moral behaviors, while it also stresses unity, internal intentions, and ontological structures. Religions may not be the same, but after all it does not matter so much, because the soul of every religion, the main attitude of every religious man, is identical, the representatives of positive centripetalism will say. The religious truth lies in the depths of our own religion, and there, all religions meet; we need not go to the center of our *particular* religion, but to the center of *all* religions, they affirm, because there is only one center, which is the same for all. Just as a little knowledge of science may lead us away from God and a deep scientific knowledge will bring us to discover God again, so a little knowledge of religion may convert us into fanatics while the deeper religious urge will make us one with other people and their religions. This attitude, when exaggerated, may lead to the opposite one, as we shall see immediately; extremes meet.

Centrifugalism

The opposite position could be called *centrifugalism*. In the name of the same ideals of peace, human understanding, and salvation, it calls more or less for an abandonment of all particular and partial faiths, which, in fact, divide and separate human beings, say the followers of this attitude.

The true religion does not lie within the several confessions, which are to be interpreted rather as degenerations of genuine spirituality, but outside and above all existent religions, either in a purified religion of the future or in a suprareligious truth. It may be that for the past and even for the time being religions have played a role in the evolution of mankind, but we have to overcome all religious pettiness and provincialism and strive for the true "religion" of mankind, which shall hardly be comparable to the existing religions of today. Everything concrete is limited and particular; we should, thus, break down our tight compartments and become truly universal.

Such an attitude then would proceed on these and on similar lines.

And again, in this example we can distinguish between a positive and a negative *centrifugalism*.

Positive

This position maintains that the chance—if ever they have had one—for all religions is over. For thousands of years they have had the opportunity of bringing people together and establishing a world peace and culture, yet they have failed. It is time to realize that the true message of religion lies outside and beyond religion itself.

The *positive* centrifugalism is rather the radical negation of all religions either in the form of agnosticism and indifference, or in the form of atheism, if not irreligiosity.

Religions have been the cause of the divisions of mankind and are the opium of the peoples; therefore we must abolish all kinds and forms of rite, worship, and creeds because these by necessity are concrete and limited, whereas what we need is a universal spirit and an unlimited truth.

Man can be saved only in truth, and the truth is that there is no religion. The religion of irreligiosity will free Man of all superstitions and allow him to be truly himself and to reach the fullness of being Man. All religions are the same—they will affirm—because all are equally narrow and wrong. And yet we cannot deny that, ultimately, this is also a kind of religion and religious attitude.

Negative

Negative centrifugalism fights religions *in toto*, as narrow-minded and harmful human groups, but praises, at the same time, the excellence and necessity of religion, purified of all creeds, churches, rites, and confessions. It is urgent—they say—to end all religious monopolies and cliques in order to found a universal religion open to all people, so wide and broad that all temperaments, faiths, and convictions can be included in it insofar as they are not exclusivist and are prepared to get rid of their old adherences and be purified by the new universal religion of mankind. This new form of religion is only a certain religious sense and a peculiar religious experience of comprehension and tolerance.

The tragedy of religions—according to those who uphold this attitude—lies in their institutions and organizations. Priesthood, rites, creeds, churches, and confessions have imprisoned the religious worship of God in spirit and truth. Any kind of institutionalization of religion is a sin against religion and a curse on mankind. Yet, in spite of this, religion is the most noble and sacred thing on Earth, as it is the claim of the authentic human nature recognizing its connections with Reality, with the Absolute. And who can claim to put doors on the Earth? What a hideous blasphemy it is to make the Absolute, the boundless Godhead, prisoner of only one religious denomination and to limit God into the particularity of a single group! Every true religion transcends itself and points toward this pure religion of the spirit that cannot be pinned down, not even by words. Only the ineffable religious experience of the individual, beyond and above all religious allegiances, is the true religion. Such and similar utterances belong to this attitude.

Our concern now is not a criticism of all these attitudes. We had to describe them only in order to get a better understanding of the problem itself. Concrete examples of these attitudes can easily be found everywhere.

2

Dialectical Excursus

The Unity and Plurality of Religions

Before reaching the problem as such, let us analyze, by way of a second introduction, the mere dialectical implications of the unity or plurality of religions.

We shall begin by analyzing logically this statement: *All religions are the same.*

This expression, which regrettably is becoming a slogan for many, is an unfortunate formulation of a deeper truth. The statement as such is a contradiction in terms, for if "religions" are "the same," then there is only one religion, but if we can speak of "religions," then there must be differences to allow for the plural. If these differences are substantial, then there are several religions; if they are accidental, then there is only one substantial religion with many accidental garbs. But the external form does not make the religion, unless we mean by religion only the superficial and secondary features. No living religion would accept this because it would either mean that "all religions are religions," or it would imply a double—and logically forbidden—use of the same word: "All religions"—identified with the accidentals—"are the same" *religion*—understood as the unique core of all so-called religions. In other words, either the equality preached is fundamental and substantial and then there would be only one religion and we could not properly speak of religions, or it is secondary and accidental and then there would be many religions.

It is hardly necessary to insist upon this. Nevertheless, we can make it clearer still by means of pure logic.

"All religions are the same": but what do we understand by "same"? It can only mean either: "all religions are the same religion" or "all religions are the same thing," that is, the same "super-religion" or "sub-religion." The first interpretation is evidently contradictory for the reason already explained. If "all religions are the same religion" insofar as they are "religions," they are not "religion" at all. The second formulation amounts to saying that all religions are equal because ultimately they converge in the one and the same kernel, and this kernel would be the true and "same religion" of all religions. But then, whatever the truth-content the statement may contain, we have two different meanings of the concept of religion: the concept "religions" in the subject is understood as the several historical existent religions, and the concept "same" in the predicate is taken as the quintessence or kernel of the concept meant in the subject. This is to say all religions are *essentially* one, but insofar as they are "religions" they are precisely not the "same."

25

To follow the first interpretation implies a vicious circle that takes us right back to our starting point: to say that "all religions are *essentially* one" can either mean that "all religions are religions"—for "essence" is that which makes a thing be what it is, which is obviously a tautology—or that "all religions are different *forms* of the one essence of religion." This is precisely what is under discussion, namely, if there is a possibility of various religious forms, that is, of different numerical realities of the one essence of religion. This formula also allows for two interpretations: either all religions are really different realizations of the one essence "religion," that is, they are different religions, or all the many forms of religion are just irrelevant because "religion" is precisely only the "essence" of religion, which is what we must prove.

Dialectically, we can proceed still one step further and affirm that either *there are many religions* or that *there is only one*.

Within dialectical limits we can advance the thesis that the alternative "*R* is either one or manifold" will be solved by either one of the two different mental attitudes of human thinking: *essential* or *existential* thinking.

The Essential Thinking

Essential thinking will look at the concept of the religion, at the universal *R*, and it is evident that this concept "*R*" must always be the same. Otherwise we would have to speak of R_1, R_2, R_3, but not of *R*.

The essence of one concept must always be the same when we apply it to different numerical things. The concept "Man" indicates an identical essence "Man," because human nature is the same for all men. Likewise, there cannot be several essences of religion, but there can only be one, a singular essence of religion, although there may be many religions just as there are many men. If by *silver* we understand a definite chemical element with a precise number of elemental particles ordered in a definite manner, then there is only one silver. Moreover, false silver is not silver at all. It may look like it, but it *is not* silver. Thus, essential thinking will stress that there is *only one* religion because there is only one concept of religion, something that enables us to call a thing a "religion." This *essential thinking* can be *maximalist* or *minimalist*; each of these positions will interpret differently the statement, "*There is only one religion*."

Maximalism

The *maximalists* will say: there is only one religion and that is our religion, because only our religion fulfills all the essential characteristics of religion. All other so-called religions are false religions—that is to say, they are not religions at all but have only an appearance of religion, as false silver is not silver.

Minimalism

The minimalists will not deny that all existing religions fulfill the conceptual definition of religion. Therefore they will say that there is only one religion, which is the real essence of all existing religions.

They will say that there is only one religion that is the very essence of religions, multiplied in the several existing religious groups. They will not claim that *only one religion is true*, but that *religion* is true, and that this very essence is precisely that which enables us to call religion the multiple organized faiths on Earth. All are numerical cases, individuals, incarnations, more or less perfect, of the unique essence of religion.

The Existential Thinking

On the other side, *existential thinking* will not be concerned so much with the pure essential concept of religion as with the real existential things that call themselves religions; and consequently it will stand for the plurality of religions as the most evident and undeniable fact. Religion may be a system of thought and of life leading Man to God or to his liberation, or to his end, but, in fact, there exists a plurality of such ways. There are, thus, many religions. If we want to undertake a serious and realistic study of the problem without falling into utopian or idealistic theories—those who think in existential categories affirm—we must take things as they are in full, avoiding purely essentialistic abstractions. The concept of nation, for example, may always be the same, but Germany is not Argentina, and their national problems are not the same. Yet we are not concerned with studying the concept of nation but with the real problems and existential features of the German or Argentine people. The same applies to religions.

So far, we have tried to show that many apparently contradictory statements about the unity or plurality of religions are conditioned by the peculiar type of mind by which one confronts the problem, or rather by the special angle under which the problem is envisaged.

Of course, there must be something unique that allows us to call a religion "religion," but there must also be something different that permits us to speak of religions in the plural. In other words, religions can be many because there is *one* religion. Diversity implies oneness, otherwise it would not be diversity but sheer otherness. A reality is different from another insofar as it is a different reality, *another* reality. But as *reality* it must somehow be equal, otherwise it could not be a different *reality*. Thus, religions are the different specimens of one sole reality called religion. On the other hand, religions can be *many* only because the *oneness* of religion is not so absolute as to be exhausted, as it were, in a single religion. If the absolutely perfect religion existed there would be no room for any plurality, as the angel in Thomistic philosophy fills up his nature fully, leaving no place for different individuals.

But, of course, the problem lies precisely in the peculiar relation between unity and diversity in this temporal world of ours. Religion is not just one essence, nor is it a perfect existence. It is a complex human fact involving the cosmos and its revelation with God, but it is also a fact that concerns the temporal status of our itinerant being.

The Substantial and the Functional Thinking

We can approach our question with one of the attitudes of mind already described. We can also, in an attempt at philosophical integration, try to apply one or another of the above-mentioned psychological categories to the particular aspect of religion we are studying, or, what is equivalent, try to overcome the one-sidedness of each point of view by an integral study of the problem. However, before concluding this introduction, we must direct our attention to one of the most important epistemological features of our culture since the birth of the physical sciences in the West some centuries ago. We have called it elsewhere *substantial* and *functional* thinking.

One of the main characteristics of our times, which gives a very distinctive shape to our culture, is undoubtedly the birth of the physical sciences. They build the basis for technique, industrialization, and for most of the features of our times, providing also the basis for a type of universality that no culture has known since mankind's existence on Earth.

One of the starting points of this tremendous evolution lies in a humble, almost invisible change in the minds of European intellectuals of the late Middle Ages. It was a change of interest that carried with it a profound break in the very ways of our thinking. The interest shifted from the *why* to the *how*, from knowing the hidden "reasons" of things to discovering the effective "modes" of reality, briefly, from philosophy to science. In the first place, philosophy itself became almost a science and finally a handmaid to science. For a time, metaphysics was considered an obscurantist and unworthy remnant of the Dark Ages. Today, the equilibrium is on its way to being restored, although the impact of science not only on Man and his civilization but also on philosophy itself remains a positive conquest.

Science and philosophy are different, but not incompatible. The gnoseological instrument of science is a particular way of thinking that we could call *functional* thinking; what matters for science is not to *know* what things are, but how things *behave*, that is, their *function*. Philosophy, on the other hand, is concerned with the *substantiality* of things, with their *structure*, *essence*, and the like. As a matter of fact, this substantial way of thinking for many centuries was mainly interpreted in an almost *static* manner, so that there was hardly any place given to *dynamic* philosophical thinking. Substantial dynamism and philosophical thinking were considered incompatible, but in fact they are not, for the latter does not need to be only a merely static substantial reflection. The introduction of dynamic thinking into philosophy has been the good service done by science to philosophy, a fact that is of some importance for our subject. There are two ways of regarding religions.

The one way is concerned with the *static structure* of every religion, that is, its nature, its tenets, its static being as a thing that *there* is, its *truth-contents*; the other way is concerned with the *dynamic function* of every religion, that is, its real effects, what it stands for, the function it performs in human life, its dynamic being as a real force that *works*, its *truth-intention*.

Whereas the traditional minds look almost exclusively at the static aspect, modern minds stress, on the contrary, the dynamic feature. This has created certain uneasiness among several genuine religious thinkers. They provide another example of the "modern" misunderstanding between philosophy and science.

The important thing, according to the traditional stance, is what a religion *is*; what matters, answers the modern position, is what religion *stands for*. Consequently, a real and fruitful dialogue has often been doomed to failure, when the different perspectives had not been made apparent.

It is quite obvious that for static-substantial thinking religions are many and different. Moreover, for this epistemological attitude there is even little hope for any religious encounter because religions may coexist or merge into another, but not enter into any osmotic exchange, as it were.

For functional thinking, on the other hand, the problem of the unity of religions seems almost evident because religions perform, or at least claim to perform, the same function, thus they are *equi-valent*. In fact, this sort of mental thinking is only sensitive to the "valence" of things, that is, to their capacity of fulfilling a certain function.

The possibility of having philosophical thinking—substantial thinking—without reducing it to static thinking—that is, also including dynamic thinking—will allow us to overcome the gap between the two one-sided epistemological approaches. This shall later on be the foundation for our distinctions between the *static* (chapter 5) and the *dynamic* (chapter 6) points of view.

Until now philosophy has been more at home with the static substantial research, and in consequence philosophy of religion has been concerned mainly with the first set of problems; it was left to history of religions to deal with the second series of problems with the consequent tension between both disciplines. We think that the philosophical dynamic thinking we have mentioned may help to bridge this gulf and make possible a richer philosophical study on religion without falling into conflict with the history of religions or with the justified claims of a real philosophy of religion. In a word, we would like to reconcile the "science" of religions with the "philosophy" of religion, at least on a particular point in question.

The Great Dilemma

There is still a great problem that may receive some light from a dialectical introduction.

If every religion claims to have a message of salvation, it is bound to affirm that if you fall away from it you will not attain salvation, unless you then follow another path of salvation. However broadminded a religion may be regarding paths of salvation, it must recognize that the possibility of straying from the path, or the paths, exists. In simple words, the very message of salvation that every religion affirms to possess implies the recognition and the possibility of damnation in one form or another; otherwise, "salvation" would be an empty word. Every religion in singular, and the whole complex of religions must then face this great dilemma of salvation or damnation.

One of its most striking formulations is the known Christian dictum: "*extra Ecclesiam nulla salus*," that is, there is no salvation outside the church. In more general terms—for we do not wish to refer to a specifically Christian problem—only one religion, R, brings salvation to Man. What can this possibly mean? It can only mean, dialectically, the following:

Either you belong to R or you do not reach salvation. The whole issue now lies in determining who belongs to R; it is well understood that belonging to R is a *necessary* condition but not a *sufficient* one because one could well belong to R and yet not attain salvation. If belonging to R is incompatible with the allegiance to any other religion, then the dictum affirms that all members of other religions cannot be saved. This amounts to saying that the other religions are false religions and thus not religions at all. Logically speaking the conclusion is correct. Now, it seems hard to believe that any religion could make such a claim, for it could only be honestly held as true if the nonfollowers of that R were considered imperfect human beings, that is, deprived of certain necessary conditions that others hold. In the same way that God creates a manifold variety of creatures and gives them different ends according to the very nature they have received, so within the species Man there would be one class that has received as a gratuitous gift "salvation," whereas the other class has not. It would not be logically impossible for the human mind to justify such an inscrutable design of God, but unless one believes that God Himself has revealed such a thing, no human being can morally hold such a view. Yet there is something sufficiently revolting in such an assumption that we need not describe it further.

The only logical escape from such an incongruous conclusion is to admit the possibility of coexistence of both conditions: belonging to R and simultaneous membership in another religion R_1, R_2, and so on. If such is the case, the very conception of R—as a religion outside of which there is no salvation—must essentially differ from the common idea of religion as a sociological fact, for it would have to be said that R is a kind of super-religion containing the decisive element of salvation S, which other religions can also share.

S would be, as it were, the soul of religion.

The problem that now arises concerns the nature of this S. If religions are the instrument of salvation and S is the active element in them, that which makes a religion is the presence of that salvific S. This dictum then amounts to saying that outside a true religion—that is, a religion possessing the element S—there is no salvation and it would call R (church) the council of true religions.

Now a double interpretation is possible: a democratic equalitarian conception of R as a parliament of religions, or a hierarchic historical notion of R as the full depositary of S acting and present also in R_1, R_2, and so on.

Let us mention a concrete example to better visualize these two interpretations. Let us imagine that S is the advaitic intuition and that this intuition is considered possible within several or even all religions. The individual would then be saved by realizing that intuition and the role of religion would be to lead Man to such a realization. All religions would then be nothing but different ways to reach the same goal, and could meet in a parliament of religions in order to discuss their respective methods to make S more effective.

Let us now think of S as a divine grace identified with the Life of God given to Man through the one Mediator between the Godhead and the world, and that this Mediator is at work everywhere though He dwells fully on Earth in order to continue His work in the bosom of a concrete religion R, which without having the monopoly of S—as visible religion—offers to S its proper place.

Pure phenomenology and mere dialectics cannot go much further and do not solve a true and real problem in which the whole complexity of our integral existence is involved. We must try, therefore, to approach the problem with all the means we have at our disposal.

Religion

This second part of our study is only a premise that is necessary for the concrete problem we are faced with; it will soon be clear that, in a way, it can be considered our central question. In fact, we will only be able to say something about the unity or plurality of religions when we have a precise notion of what religion "is."

On the other hand, the particular perspective under which we envisage the problem of religion forbids our considering this analysis of religion as a systematic treatise on the question.

It is not thus our intention to give a thorough answer to this momentous problem on which almost all the vital questions about Man, reality, and God converge. On the other hand, we cannot skip it, nor avoid dealing with it because we cannot find an adequate way of tackling it, nor can we confront it through an a prioristic position.

3

What is Religion?

Method

The first thing we should mention before proceeding further is the double meaning of the word *religion*. On the one hand it means a particular *virtue* by which we pay to God our due respect and tribute. All of this can wrongly be identified with certain practices of . . . religion. And here the second meaning already emerges, as a group of religious practices that consist in just external acts, manifestations of the spirit of *religion*, which in this case means *dharma*, charity . . . in other words, that bond which, while transcending time and space, already binds Man and God together and yet is anchored to the Earth.

Both meanings are indeed connected, for every orthodoxy will claim that the normal means for reaching the "religion-end" is the religion-cult, regardless of whether the latter is external or merely internal. We should not forget this double meaning of religion, though we shall be referring to its ontological and integral meaning.

The proper method of approach for a philosophical study of religion seems to consist in two stages:

1. Knowing the facts.
2. Interpreting them.

Knowing the Facts

In order to know what religion *is*, we must learn what religions *are*; that is to say, we need to understand *religious facts*.

These facts are, on one side, of a *historical* nature and on the other side of a *mystical* structure.

The historical approach again presents the double perspective: the individual, of *personal facts*, and the historical, of *sociological events*. To know what religions are, we must come to consider the particular history of the religious Man, as well as the sociological and institutional history of the existing religions. But if the phenomenology of religion wishes to be an authentic knowledge of the religious phenomena, its method must be a very particular one; that is, it must possess a special organ to grasp the characteristics of the religious facts.

35

In other words, the nature of the religious phenomenon is much more complex than a simple historical fact. Just as the "integral fact" of dance cannot be caught by means of a "deaf" phenomenology that only takes into account visible movements without factoring in rhythm and music, which are the soul of dancing, similarly a pure rationalistic approach to religious facts would not understand, and perhaps would not even "see" these very facts, in spite of the exactness of an external description.

The religious *fact* is not just an empirical *thing*, which we can see with the photographic camera of our eyes or even our reason. It does not need to be irrational and much less unreasonable, but nevertheless it is not a simple fact that we can understand by reason. Love, for instance, cannot be "caught" by pure reason, and there is no religion without an element of love.

The only realistic and true method of approaching a *fact* depends on the very nature of the fact, and this is only patent when we use the appropriate method to detect it. It is not a vicious, but a vital circle, which, like many other aporias, can only be broken by life itself overcoming it.

The fact of "color," for instance, requires a visual method to catch it, whereas an acoustic method would not detect it. This means that we must approach religious facts, like all other facts, with our whole being and observe, first of all, which parts, faculties, and so on of our being are affected by it and then proceed to examine the "impressions" received. Just like a "deaf" man will not perceive acoustic facts, neither will an a-religious scholar grasp the very essence of religious facts. Ultimately it is undoubtedly true that the philosophy one has depends upon the kind of man one *is*.

Interpreting Them

In the second stage of the approach we are able to know *how* religions appear and what religions *claim* to be, but we must proceed further and deeper in order to know what religion *is*. For this second moment—and we have seen that in some sense for the first one also—both philosophy and theology are involved: theology is nothing more than the integral human effort of understanding religion from within—in Christian terminology, the expression *fides quærens intellectum*, meaning that faith rests on a rational basis and that the intellect integrates faith in our attempts at understanding.

The interpretation of a fact means—properly speaking—the integration of "impressions" that we have received from the fact into an intelligible frame, so that, inserted as a part of higher whole, it may have a *sense* for us. This intelligible frame is, on the one hand, already there to receive the fact, and, on the other hand, modified, enlarged, corrected, and so on, every time a new "fact" comes in.

The intellectual interpretation or rather explanation of religious facts constitutes the philosophy of religion.

Philosophy of Religion

Philosophy of religion, in the sense of the objective genitive—the philosophy of an object called religion—is indeed a part of philosophy. On the other hand, philosophy of religion, taken in the sense of the subjective genitive, is the philosophy contained in religion or the philosophy that religion has. In this case you could develop a certain philosophy of religion—a certain philosophical intelligibility of religion—acceptable to those who do not share your total philosophy. This would not be a philosophy of religion, but could lead us to a wider mutual agreement.

Yet the difficulty lies in the language we use. As an example let us examine the dependence of Man on God since this is a central problem of every philosophy of religion. We think that this is also the case with Buddhism, for example, though a Buddhist would never speak in these terms, for neither Man nor God is a reality for him. The Buddhist will speak in different words about the same problem, which constitutes the core of his religion. Call God the Absolute, *Śnya* (the Void), or *Nirvāṇa*; call the realization of Man's dependence the discovery of *anātman* (notself) or *anityam* (impermanence); call Man the bundle of obstacles that prevents full realization and you will have expressed in other terms what we are trying to describe. Indeed, the interpretation and explanation will differ widely, but the disagreement does not lie on the ultimate level.

We cannot undertake here this double task—of knowing the facts and interpreting them—which has been so abundantly and effectively done by many authors. In what follows we must take this knowledge for acquired as we shall draw conclusions from it. After all the preliminary work of the past century in trying to understand the religious phenomenon on a world scale, and after the attempts of the first half of the century to elaborate the new "sciences" called "phenomenology of religion" and "comparative religions," the time seems ripe for a "philosophy of religion."

We hope that the present study may contribute to the introductory chapter of the philosophy of religion and thereby help to clarify the nature of religion and shed some light on the problem of the relationship between religions.

Our line of thought then would proceed in the following way.

Man is in total *dependence* on God, whether He be called the Absolute or by any other name, whether considered as Immanent or Transcendent, or both, whether taken as personality or not. This dependence is not only an initial one, but also a present and future one, that is, Man is *currently* depending on God, and his goal in this life is to be united with Him—his personality being identified with Him by means of the realization of the Self, of partaking in His Life, or however it may be expressed. This dependence is not a simple external tie with a divine master, but something that penetrates into the very essence and existence of our being itself. Furthermore, this dependence is not just temporal but also constitutive in the line of being itself. It is our being as being that depends on God, the Being. We *are* insofar as we depend on Him, that is, *we are dependent* on Him, since this very peculiar dependence is what we are. Every being depends on Him, but human dependence is of a specific and particular nature.

This dependence that constitutes our very being is also the very ground of our *becoming*. Properly speaking, animals and material beings *change*, but they do not *become*, as Man does; they may perhaps in some sense grow, conserving in the folds of their temporal existence the relics of the past, but this they do without really assimilating their past in their present and thereby building up with time an indescribable unity. Other creatures are not historical beings as Man is.

Man's dependence on God in his becoming means an "existential" link with God not only at the beginning but also at the end of his being, as well as during his ontical pilgrimage of becoming that which Man has to be. From Man's side this implies a *conscious* and a *free* becoming; without these two moments of consciousness and freedom, there is no religion.

All other beings in one way or another also come from God and return to Him, but they have no religion. Only Man has two characteristic faculties: intellect and will. In other words, only Man is *conscious* of this dependence and thus able to *collaborate* in attaining his goal. The totality of means—truths and deeds, ideas and facts, contemplations and actions—by which a man makes his way back to God is religion; the existential way by which Man comes to God, or reaches the integral fulfillment of his being, is religion. As Man is an intellectual being as well as an active free agent—whichever way this liberty may be interpreted—religion for every man implies a doctrine as well as a praxis, that is, an *ethic* (in its exact philosophical meaning). Moreover, because Man is a pilgrim on his way back to God, the principle and end of his existence, the very *way* by which he goes can also be called religion.

In one sense religion is the most personal and intimate thing, for it is my own personal, ontological way to my fullness. In another sense, it is the most universal and common thing, for that which distinguishes Man's nature is precisely his *specific* being as pilgrim who must arrive at a certain goal; Man is that particular being that alone has religion. Religion can thus be considered the most adequate category to define Man: *animal religiosum*. And again, religion could be called the most immanent reality of Man for it is his thirsty being, his hopeful structure, his very becoming, his potentiality, that constitutes the core of religion. But in another sense, it is his most transcendent, and even extrinsic, characteristic, because Man's movement toward God would make no sense and would be a useless effort if God had not previously descended toward Man, if He did not call, if He did not reveal Himself, or if He did not show the way and lead Man along his path. Religions would be an empty wish or an impotent cry; better said, longing and clamor would not even be possible if the Only Source did not impel us to do so. This complementary polarity is an essential feature of religion. Now, as a matter of fact, several groups of doctrines and practices gather men together under one religious denomination and teach a set of truths and laws of action which must be realized in order to attain the goal of life.

This consideration brings us nearer to the problem in a much more realistic way than any of the approaches mentioned so far.

In this way we can look at religions and analyze them from two different points of view:

1. From the first point of view, we can consider them as an *objective* or rather "objectivized" human value. By this, then, religion appears as an assemblage of rites, doctrines, beliefs, experiences, and so on that we classify under the name of *religious phenomena*. Religion here becomes a kind of cultural value, which we have to study and to understand as such. It is considered a human product and it belongs, like any other cultural value, to the arts and crafts of which human nature is capable.

2. From the second point of view, religion appears as a *subjective* human feature that is the source of all religious manifestations. Here religion appears to be an anthropological element and cannot be understood unless we discover the religious dimension of Man himself.

This second point of view leads us further into the understanding of religions. Yet we cannot proceed a priori or begin by this second viewpoint as has sometimes been done, for the path we have to follow for the anthropological study is that of phenomenological analysis. On the other hand, this perspective is not simply a gathering of the results of the first approach, or a drawing of the consequences of it, but has its own specific and distinctive method. Even if we preferred to start from the first point of view, the second approach also has its *proper* consistency, which we have elsewhere called *ontonomy*.

The philosophical reflections and the numerous phenomenological studies of our times on the problem of religion allow us to undertake this second, more synthetic and philosophical point of view without forgetting the first or indulging in philosophical a priorisms.

The first thing we discover, when we try to proceed on this path, is religion as a form of *consciousness* of my dependence, of my *religatio*[1] on God, inspiring the means I must follow to reach Him, that is, to become that which I should be—to realize the Absolute. Religion is not only the reality of dependence (*ligatio*) but also the consciousness of that dependence (*re-ligatio*); it implies a sort of consciousness, a certain self-awareness that inspires, determines, informs the actions and "duties" of life. The consciousness may be of different kinds, from a deep mystical awareness of my divine origin, end, and being, to a dry and sober conviction that I am a creature with an absolute destiny—and therefore must perform some particular acts of life in a certain way. The influence of this consciousness in the field of our human life can also be of different types: from a total and pervading consciousness that all my work, activity, and life has to be accomplished in His presence and that everything

---

[1] It is well known that the word *religion* has had three different etymological interpretations:

(1) from *re-eligere* (Augustine) as the effort and the choice Man undertakes in order to be again connected with God, to restore the connection which was lost with original sin (*egressus a Deo, peccatum originale, effectus immanens redemptionis, regressus ad Deum*); (2) from *re-legere* (Cicero) as cult and honor Man gives God as his Master, Principle, etc.; (3) from *re-ligare* (Lactantius) as link and specific—constitutive—tie between Man and God.

that I accomplish—my salvation, my actions, and so on—are for His glory, to a pure external religion that asks me only to execute some determined rites but has no other influence in my life. Every man has his own religion insofar as he is Man, for every man recognizes, in one way or another, that he is an itinerant being who, therefore, has not yet reached fullness and needs to strive toward his goal.

The second thing to add, continuing on this anthropological approach, is that religion has not only the just mentioned ontological dimension of our being but that it possesses also a complex sociological structure that tells us the definite goal of our life and leads us to it, giving us all the means we need to attain it. That is to say, religion is also a sociological dimension of Man, and as such it is not only anchored to the individual, but also to society.

We can then say that the concept we form of religion depends on the idea we have of Man—and vice versa. For religion claims no more than to lead Man to his goal, which is his definitive being, and thus the nature of religion depends upon the very structure of Man himself. Because Man is not a mere individual, religion is not merely an intimate thing; because Man is an intelligent being, religion also has an *intellectual* side; because Man has a will—and a free will—religion also presents an ethical *aspect*; because the human person is not pure spirit, but a sentimental being, religion also has an emotional dimension, owing to the cosmic ties of Man with the universe, material and spiritual, religion has *cosmic* features; as Man is simply a being, a reflection, an image, a participation, of the Creating Being, religion is founded on this *ontic* character of reality as the expression of the deepest structure of Man; and, finally, owing to the fact that Man is a historical being, different from God and yet not separate from nor outside Him, religions present an *immanent-transcendent* polarity arising out of the *ontonomic* structure of our being; or, in other words, from a different perspective, since Man is a temporal being with an eternal destination, so religion shows also this polarity of a *temporal* and an *eternal* structure.

These several aspects of the one and the same thing are based on the very nature of Man himself, for religion is an anthropological fact. Man *is*; he is a unity of spirit and body with three different aspects: *cognitive, volitive,* and *emotional.* And he is simultaneously a social *being* with ties—*religatio*—not only with society but also with the *material cosmos* and with the *spiritual universe.* Moreover, we must bear in mind that he is not properly an "is," nor even exactly an *I.* But rather he is a *be-ing,* a be-coming, a *not-yet-being,* a *participation* of the real IS; he is rather a *you* than an I, than the I. He is a temporal being with a *tempiternal* destiny. Because religion involves the whole of Man, it directs and inspires these nine dimensions of human existence.

In order to proceed with some accuracy in our approach to the complex problem of the unity or plurality of religions, we must distinguish therefore these nine dimensions in the very nature of the complex reality that we call religion.

4

The Multidimensional
Nature of Religion

In order to be complete, that is, to be a perfect link—*religatio*—of Man with the absolute, a religion must be a multidimensional reality, in such as way that if even one of the aspects considered is lacking, we cannot properly say we have a complete religion, but only a partial representation of it.

Yet it should also be noted that the different existent religions in the world do not need to differ in all aspects to be distinct. It may be only one factor that sets one religion apart from another.

Obviously we do not intend to give a classification of all existent religions according to their specific features, for this has already been done many times. We intend rather to describe the real aspect of every religion—which in the factual religions may be more or less developed—basing our study on the nature of Man, that is to say, starting from the anthropological foundation of religion. Since religion is the integral link connecting Man with his absolute destiny, the nature of that link will depend upon the real structure of Man himself. This ninefold dimension of religion is valid for every religion and yet does not say anything directly about the truth-content of any religion. We shall, however, remain within the limits of pure philosophy while we examine the aforementioned content.

Our point of departure, thus, is anthropological, understanding anthropology as the integral wisdom about Man. The nature of religion depends on the structure of Man: this philosophical statement is not only anthropological, but it is also in agreement with the religious belief of nearly all religions, namely that religion has been *given* by the very Godhead to Man. The first thing God handed down to Man was Man himself, his nature and the religious structure of his being, which is the first basis for receiving any revelation as well as for having any religion. Religiously speaking our anthropological foundation is nothing but the ontological counterpart of God's Will toward Man, for his first Will toward us is that we are what we are, that is, that which He has made us to be.

For lack of a better word and in order to stress the fact that each of these aspects represents a constitutive ingredient of religion, we have used the word "dimension."

One remark however should be advanced here before proceeding further. Although the word "dimension" properly refers to a homogeneous set of properties, in this case they are not, for obviously the nine features do not lie on the same level and, although they are all integral parts of religion, they are not equally important.

Therefore they should not be compared out of context. The same could be said of the dimensions of Man, as being, as individual, and as social entity, as these three features do not belong to the same level. In fact, Man as a living being cannot be logically classified. Therefore, for the sake of clarity, we shall keep using the term we have chosen and we will speak of nine "dimensions."

Summarizing, we can divide the matter as follows. Man is a being in the making, an itinerant being—foundation of religion. To begin with, Man *is* (I dimension), but properly speaking he is just be-ing, on the way to be, *he is not yet* (VIII), he *is* a *temporal* being (IX). His being can be considered in relation to himself, as an individual person, or in relation to others, as a social person. In the first case he is *intellect* (II), *will* (III), and *sentiment* (IV). In the second he is *social* (V), *telluric* (VI), and *cosmic* (VII).

All this may be resumed in the following scheme:

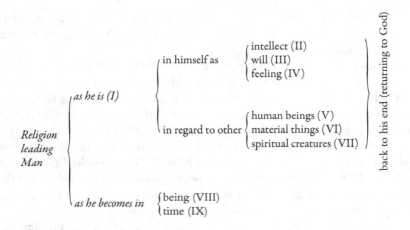

Let us now examine a little more closely these nine dimensions of religion.

The Ontic-Mystical Dimension

In order to describe the first and most important dimension of Man and consequently of religion, we said that Man simply *is*. The human being is neither his mind nor his will, his body nor his soul. I may think *with* my mind, but it is not my mind *who* thinks. I may live, thanks to my soul, but I *am* not my soul and it is not my soul *who* is. I *am* always something beyond whatever predicate I may join to my *am*. Whatever I may be, I *am*; whatever I may have, I *am* the deeper and previous unity of all that I have. Whatever parts I may consist of, I *am* not just those parts. My being is not the mere addition of the elements I might discover in myself. On the other hand, however frail this unity of mine may be and whatever distinct hierarchy my elements may possess, wherever my deep and real being, or I, may dwell, I am not only the purest element or only the deepest layer of my being. I *am* neither my pure I, my naked substance, nor all the things I *have* (my accidents). I am simply a *being*, whatever this being may consist of, or even be. This is acceptable not only to Christianity and to Hinduism including its vedantic form, but also to Islam and to Buddhism, though the latter may reject our way of putting it. The most nihilistic Buddhism will surely agree in saying that I am nothing of what I have because I *am* precisely *no-thing* and yet this *nothingness* that I am supposed to be is what has to be saved, realizing—in Buddhism—its ontological inconsistency, that is, its nothingness. Unless this our non-being is liberated, salvation is not reached. Liberation may be here understood as dissolution, but nevertheless it is our "that thing that we are" that has to be saved.

Precisely because every religion wants to help Man realize his being; because every religion intends to lead the itinerant being that Man is, to its end, to the Absolute, to God; and precisely because religion has a claim on the whole of Man, every religion claims not simply to possess some truths, but to be definitively true, that is, to be based on the ultimate structure of the human being and to derive its tenets from a primordial and vital attitude toward that which Man *is*. Every true religion is more or less directly connected with this unutterable conception about the very end of Man, his ultimate status, his ontical goal. Here is the fountain source of faith, as the substantial conviction of things to come,[1] that is, of that which Man shall *be*.

It is not necessary, of course, that every religion should have a definite and clear intellectual picture of this. Most of the existent religions have it as their hidden source and implicit foundation. But here lies the root of every religion. This root as such is always invisible and unutterable, and very often unconscious.

No one can express in words or concepts this ultimate kernel of Man and of religion. We can only attempt to describe it negatively and symbolically, being aware that any negation is only the conceptual form of an affirmation and every symbol is the veil of the very truth that it reveals. Real nakedness would be fully invisible and it could not even be intuited.

We are still here, not yet in the realm of the reflex consciousness or on the level of the awakened experience, although we must try to give an outer description of that inner reality.

We can distinguish two sides of this one basic and fundamental dimension of religion: an inner side that could be called *ontical* and an outer side that I would propose to denominate *mystical*. In other words, the objective and subjective aspects of this first dimension.

---

[1] Cf. St. Paul, "Fides est substantia rerum sperandarum, argumentum non apparentium" (Only faith can guarantee the blessings that we hope for, or prove the existence of realities that are unseen) (Heb 11:1).

The Ontical Side

The ontical side of religion converges with the ontical aspect of Man. Human beings may be principally intellect, consciousness, but they are not only that and they are not ultimately and primarily that. When we speak about the *ontological* aspect of Man we mean his ultimate inner being, but always as it appears, as it reveals itself to our *logos*. We presuppose—and probably rightly—that the *logos* is the organ of being, the discoverer of being, and that we ourselves are open to ourselves, thanks to our *logos*-constitution. This *logos*, which *is*, on one side, our most specific nature and, on the other side, our most characteristic instrument of awareness, is responsible for our consciousness and for our experience and also for any kind of knowledge. But we are not completely transparent to ourselves, we are not *noēsis noēseōs* (absolute self-consciousness) in Aristotelian terms; we are not pure *logos*, or if we prefer, our logos is not pure. Essence and existence, as well as the ontical and the ontological aspects, coalesce only in God. That is why we feel justified in speaking of an *ontical* side prior to any *ontological* structure.

I am not only my consciousness or the experience of my being; I am not even that *which* I find or discover in this my consciousness or experience; but I am that out of which my very *logos* springs, *that* from which my consciousness emerges. I am a being, *I* have a being—in some sense or other—that grows up, that moves to an end, that follows an internal development, that gravitates, so to say, according to its structural law whether I am aware of it or not, whether I agree with it or not. This growth and this movement may be interpreted in the negative way as stripping off and ridding oneself in order that the Non-Self may be liberated, or in the positive way as the purification of the Self. On this ultimate level on which we now stand these interpretations are equivalent. We may then express the ultimate anthropological truth and the first ground of any religion: Man *is* a becoming, his being is an itinerant being (*gatiμ*, "movement"), a not-yet being. We do not mean to say that he is going somewhere, but that he is a *going* itself, whether he may know it or not, admit it or not. Man has an ontical dimension, which is "what it *is*" with absolute priority to Man's faculties or to Man's powers.

What is meant by the *ontical* dimension of Man is this: his pure and simple being without being touched or tinged by any conception or awareness of it. Man has an ontical structure, he is a being, a special being with specific constitutive laws, with an *ontonomy* that makes him what he is and conditions what he *shall be*. We cannot say anything about this ontical dimension unless we convert it into its ontological translation. We can be aware only of its *existence* as the hidden source of all our actions and thoughts.

We shall not—we cannot—say anything of this *Urgrund* ("primal source") of our being. It is not even an *ex-sistence* but pure *sistence*. It makes even less sense to discuss "about" it and to describe it as created or noncreated, as equal or not equal to the Divinity. Could we not wait for a while—the period of our life here on Earth—before speaking about it? The creature cannot enter into that *Grund*[2] of the soul, in the words of Meister Eckhart, but must remain outside; when the "substantial touch" is there, as St. John of the Cross would say, there is not even touch. But already we are speaking too much. . . .

The Mystical Side

This ultimate and fundamental aspect of our being also has an outer side: the objective aspect has a subjective correlation, as it were.

I am, or perhaps better and simply *am*, whatever this *am* may be, or I may think, or feel, or will about it. Now, in some sense, I not only *am*, but at the same time, in the same act, I know, I feel, I am aware or conscious—all words here are imperfect and false—that I am. If I were not aware in some way of the kind of *am*—of being—that I am, I would not be *this* kind of being that I am.

That is to say, I am a being with the characteristic property of being aware that it *is*. Indeed this being does not "know" exactly *what* it is, but it "knows" that it *is*. This self-awareness it possesses is a certain being-consciousness.

Moreover, this first and original self-, or am-awareness, or being-consciousness, can have different shades of meaning: it be either a purely formal and empty aware-ness, or one that is filled with varying degrees of content about the nature, the reality, of myself, of my *am*. The former case is the necessary condition for being a normal Man with normal faculties; in fact, without some being-awareness, no human person can properly be called a *person*, "illud quod primo cadit in intellectu est ens" (Being is that which is first known to the intellect).

In the latter case my being-awareness contains varying degrees of intuition, experience, knowledge, faith—no word is exactly correct—of my being as being of myself, as that which *is*. This is what is meant by the "mystical aspect" of this first dimension of Man and of religion.

When the human person is aware of this peculiar experience of the being, as *be-ing* (*ens*), then the proper mystic dimension of Man appears. Every being has an ontical structure insofar as every being simply is; but only Man—in our world under the moon—has an experience of it and suffers the *impression* of the Being, of being *of* a Being (see the *pati divina*, of all mystical traditions).

This experience is beyond any division in soul and body, intellect and will. I do not "know" myself as intelligent or as free, as body-soul compound, or even as Man, but as *being* in a very concrete and at the same time transcendent way. I "know" myself as my *being-me*—the real mystics refer to this "self" as *thou*; it is neither the knowledge of a part of our being, nor the formal being-awareness, nor a kind of intuition of God, of the Being, but a kind of consciousness, of primary and original consciousness by which we are immediately aware of *our* being not as ours—because

---

[2] Properly the *grunt der Sêle* that Eckhart speaks of in his German works and that he identifies with *vünkelin* (*Funklein*), the *scintilla animae*, the *abditum animae*.

ultimately it is not "ours"—but as *ens*, as be-ing, that is, as be-ing *from* (God), *in* (God), *for* (God), or as be-ing *be-coming* God. We discover, or rather we realize ourselves though it is not properly an intellectual intuition, but a kind of ontic *touch*, thanks to which we enter into contact with *our* being, as the divine particle or the divine seed that we are. "Creatura in Deo est divina essentia" (A creature in God is the divine essence), says Thomas Aquinas.

This experience is completely ineffable because it is the dark light of the hidden reality that we are—outside time—or that we shall be—at the end of "our" time; it is the extra temporal awareness of my definitive being; it is the dark ray of consciousness of my final state, it is my seeing me (myself) as a seer, knowing me (myself) as a knower, my grasping me (myself) as (in) God.

It goes without saying that this self-experience has little to do with the so-called ontologism, that is, with the intellectual-intuition of the Absolute Be-ing. This is so for two reasons: first, because this intuition is not—and cannot be—an intellectual intuition, and second, because the being we experience is not primarily God, but our *own* being, though this expression is an unfortunate one for I am not the possessor of "my" being, I have no being of my "own." It is not an autonomous being, severed from the Being that we discover, but our being as (being) *from, for, in, of,* and *through* the Being. We touch God as He is *in* ourselves, so to speak, or, better still, we are aware of ourselves as a part, spark, creature, relation . . . of the Absolute Being; we suffer the God, the part of God, the aspect of God, the love of God, the creation of God . . . that we are.

It is, as I have already mentioned, an ontonomic *experience*.

We must point out that the word "experience" is not taken in its philosophical nor in its mere psychological or even sentimental sense, as a kind of personal feeling, but in its anthropologic-metaphysical sense, as the word itself connotes: an existential passing through, through a door (*porta*), being at the same time on this side of the threshold, at some distance and in some tension (*ex*) in order to observe, to be aware of that test (*experientia*) that is going on within us.[3]

The ultimate reason of the possibility of this mystical experience is precisely the special structure of our ontic being; because we are as we are, because reality is as it is, we can have this awareness of being. Utilizing Christian terminology we could say that we can have this awareness of our definitive being, this anticipation of our goal, because it is really present *in hope*, and hope transports us beyond and above the temporal status. The mystical experience transcends time.

This mystical experience does not always bubble up to the level of our intellectual consciousness, but when it does, it does so only in an indirect way, through an ontological translation. Moreover, among those who "feel" the internal reality of these "living waters" in their being, only few are capable of finding an intellec-

---

[3] *Experientia* comes from *ex-perior*, from *ex-* and the root *per*, equivalent to the Sanskrit *par* (*pi-parmi*) "to conduct," the Greek *peraō*, "to pass through" (see the Latin *porta, peritus, periculum*), the German *fahren, er-fahren*, and the English *fare, ferry*.

tual expression for that experience and translating it into the language of *darśana* (school), or philosophy, or theology, or religion.

Some of the great religious prophets of mankind seem to have had that experience and the skill to translate this experienced reality into words, formulating laws of conduct for their followers. From this fact we can understand that the religious acceptance of the prophet by the faithful does not depend only on an external correspondence with his predications, but also on the internal discovery that everything that the prophet puts in the light of people's consciousness belongs to the common human experience, even if it does not manifest clearly and consciously in the majority of people. "I saw you under the fig tree" (Jn 1:48): these words were for Bartholomew the internal criterion for recognizing the Messiah.

This mystical experience can be more or less complete and profound, and its expression more or less consistent and congruous with the intellectual laws of our spirit. However, as pure mystical contact with the absolute truth and with the ultimate structure of our real being, it is one and unique.

We should consider this experience a divine grace rather than a human power that Man possesses; although this distinction, important as it is, should not make us forget that after all, every human faculty is also a divine gift.

We could also adduce here the "modern" distinction of Catholic theology between a natural and a supernatural experience of this kind, which undoubtedly clarifies the issue a great deal, but this would lead us far away from our proper field.

Suffice it to say that the experience of which we speak here is an experience of the ultimate reality—of Man—which is at the same time an experience of the Divine. With this we do not discover God as He is in Himself, but certainly as I am in Him, because He and I are one—and no analogy can break the unity of being. We experience that God is One and that we are one part, one aspect, one manifestation, one spark, one creature *of* this One. In mystical terms, some would say: I experience that I am He; others, on the other hand, would prefer to say: He is the I, and my-self only His *thou*.

Every religion has this ultimate and transmystical dimension as the hidden fountain of its further teachings. The several creeds, morals, and so on represent the translation of this dimension into concepts or laws. By saying this, it is obviously not ruled out that inadequate translations may exist or that the central experience was not fully "grasped," but it is not our office here to pass judgment on this.

We cannot describe the nature of this experience, not only because it is ineffable, but also because its very translation in human terms requires the choice of a terminology specific to a particular religion. Let us, however, suggest, in Christian terms, what is meant by this first dimension of religion. Needless to say, using Christian terms does not mean that we are describing a Christian experience.

According to a classical *dictum* of Christian theology, "after" creation there "are" more *beings*—in existence—but there is no "more" *being* at all. The real being, the "quantity" of being—so to speak—has not been modified; neither can it be modified. Creation cannot hurt the absolute perfection of God and cannot be therefore at His level—to admit this would be falling into pantheism—but must be *māyā*, *relatio*, *creation*, that is, something *of* Him, *from* Him, *for* Him, *in* Him, without being Him—whatever our *appearance* may be, whatever we *may be*—but without being either something separate, apart, independent of Him. We must discard the monist position, because the creature is not one with God, but we must also avoid the dualism that accentuates otherness and places Man outside of all relation to God. Here lies the *advaitic* solution.

This means that God dwells in the most interior of all beings, that He is the most intimate and ultimate supporter of all created things. Things *are*—are *beings*—insofar, and only insofar, as they are *in*, *from*, and *through* Him.

Of all creatures Man has, among other things, the special characteristic of being aware of himself, and this self-awareness goes together with free will. When a man reaches the ultimate stage of his being he touches God, he enters into contact with his inward dweller and dis-covers the ground of his own being—in time, by means of symbols, in darkness, till the light dawns. . . .

It may be that for this experience Man has to be pure and invaded in a very special way by divine grace; it may be that a full awareness of our reality cannot be reached here on Earth; nevertheless this experience—up to a certain point—is the beginning of religious life as the participation of God's Self-knowledge, as a new light descending upon us and letting us look through "reflections in a mirror" (1 Co 13:12) into the ultimate Reality. In this connection it is clear that though religion has a doctrine and tends to develop a full religious doctrinal system, both things are not identical.

Christianity claims to be the religion of Christ, for example, but he did not write a single statement, nor did he propound a full and developed doctrine or a closed religious system; Christianity as religion is much more than a doctrine. A little child baptized at birth does not know anything about the doctrine and yet he is a Christian and member of the Church. The native religions of Africa, to take another very different example, are undoubtedly religions—what else could they be?—and yet most of them do not have a proper doctrinal system.

It would be a mistake to identify the limited words in which religious doctrines are expressed with transcendent mystical experience. We do not refer to the obvious fact that there are correct and incorrect translations; we refer to the possible mistake of forgetting that a doctrine is only *a* translation, that is, a translation, a trans-porting of one absolute integral sphere to another, namely the intellectual, which, being in itself perhaps also absolute, cannot be fully comprehended by any human being on Earth, because the fullness of the *intellectual intuition* lies beyond our natural power. The mistake would then lie in one of the two extreme attitudes: in confounding *orthodoxy*, on the one hand, with *monodoxy* (in identifying religion with a closed and monolithic doctrine) or, on the other hand, with *metadoxy* (of making religion fully independent from and indifferent to any doctrine).

An example will make it clearer. It is almost commonplace among Catholic theologians today to accept the doctrine of creation ex nihilo as a fundamental

Christian dogma. Indeed, the dogma is not the Aristotelic-Scholastic formulation or even the *conception* of creation, but the *res significata* as Thomas Aquinas himself points out. The thing-in-itself meant by that dogma is the real dogma. Moreover, this dogma could be transcended in a threefold way without being a Christian heterodox opinion.

First, by finding another doctrine, that is, another formulation which, while remaining loyal to the thing-in-itself, could explain the same Christian truth. And this is not a priori impossible. If, for example, Indian metaphysics could allow us to enlighten the same *fact* from another standpoint, then we would have the same dogma in another metaphysical formulation. Christian theology is not a sort of unique supernatural metaphysics. In the hypothesis we have proposed, owing to the real historical character of Christianity, this other formulation would have to be existentially integrated into the doctrine of the Church; that is, it would have to be recognized by her as such in order to become a dogmatic expression, for a Christian dogma is never a private or an isolated formulation.

Second, by finding not another point of view, but another deeper truth in which the former one is included, so that "creation" is not negated but integrated into a deeper, or more precise, or more total, consideration, which without being a negation of the former dogma becomes its fullness and completion. In this way the monotheistic idea of the Old Covenant is overcome and not negated by integrating it into the Trinitarian dogma of the New Testament. A true Christocentric attitude for which the whole nondivine being is nothing but a *Christophany* would not need to overstress the autonomy and substantiality of a pure creation (*natura pura*). Everything has been made by the *Logos*, and "creation" would appear only as the temporal projection *quoad nos* of a *part* of the "creative" process.... In other words, Genesis 1:1 would be included and overcome in John 1:3.

Third, overcoming the dogma would be possible by transcending all formulation. In the ultimate ontic-mystical dimension, it makes little sense to speak of creation or noncreation, as any "created" concept is unfit to express either the mere ontical side of our being or the pure mystical experience of the roots and depths of our being.

I, as a Christian, may believe in *creation* and you, as a Hindu, may not. I mean to say that this difference of doctrine, important as it is, is not absolutely ultimate, and the fact that you do not believe while I do might well be due to the same reason: because we want to stress and to express one and the same experience. Perhaps it is because we want to stress the same transcendence and immanence of God that the Christian expresses it by the doctrine of creation and the Hindu by the negation of creation. This means that it is not impossible that we both have the same unutterable experience of our relation with the Supreme, but that the differences become manifest when we translate this lived reality into concepts. In this point, we seize two completely different expressions because our mental background and the conceptions from which we draw our thoughts are distinct.

It is obvious that we cannot say that both *doctrines* might be true; we do not say that there is not a doctrinal gap that has to be discussed and solved; nor do we say that formulations or dogmas are irrelevant and much less that they are simply expressions of internal feelings—this "modernist" interpretation is the ruin of any revelation and of any real religion. We only say that from merely different doctrines we cannot *conclude* the existence of distinct experiences, aims, or even intentions. That is, we cannot infer from this a divergence in our ultimate "experience" of reality, but neither can we say that there is identity.

We may refer in this connection to the common objection against any *apophatic* attitude. If you say that the truth is unspeakable, unfathomable, beyond thought, feeling, and so forth, how do you speak about it, and how do you characterize, even if negatively, this transcendent Being? Evidently it is not sufficient to say that we do not assert anything positive, because any negation implies two things.

1. It implies an affirmation: when we say "A is not B," we imply that "A *is* not-B." Even when we try to negate any attribute of God (*neti-neti*), we are affirming that He *is* neither this nor that, He is not-adequate to any human conception.

2. Any negation implies some cognition about the negated object. We can verily say God is *not* because we know something about Him, namely, that He, in a sense, *is* different, above, beyond, etc., all that "is." This is the reason why we cannot do without dogmas.

It is true that we neither know nor feel anything about the ultimate nature, structure, being of the Absolute, but we grasp, surmise, believe, experience, realize something of It simply because we are a *part* of It—beam, spark, creature, effect, and so on. It is a good sign that we do not possess any word to express this kind of consciousness or awareness, which is the real mystical experience. Reality is above, outside, and beyond all our forms of knowledge but it is not above, outside, and beyond ourselves. That is why *we can*, though improperly and negatively, speak of it. The mystical dimension is a real one, if not the most real one. We are precisely that which we cannot speak out; our speech is nothing but a babbling and chattering.

The importance of *myths* and *symbols* belongs mainly to this first, indiscriminate sphere.

The Dogmatic-Doctrinal Dimension

Man is not only an individual with an ontic instinct that guides his being; he is also an intellectual or, if we prefer, a spiritual being with two definite features that we usually call *intellect* and *will*. If religion has to lead the whole Man to fullness, it will also have to provide the answer for his intellect and the response for his heart.

With the will, Man can love, aspire, desire, long for, and perform all kinds of active (centrifugal) movements to God and to the outside world. With the intellect, he can understand, grasp, see, comprehend, and perform all kinds of passive (centripetal) movements by which God and the outside world come to him, are received in one way or another.

By the harmonious use of both faculties—that is, by performing the corresponding acts of this twofold structure of Man, or in other words by willing what he knows and knowing what he wills in a concrete situation—Man feels and experiences the full set of human emotions and feelings. Intellect, will, and sentiments form the trilogy of the human faculties. Here we need to deal with the first one only.

Man possesses many organs of knowledge—faith, intuition, reason, imagination, and so on. Knowledge as such—merely to know—is not an end in itself, but it is a means to being—though perfect knowledge is an end in itself because it is identical with perfect being. The ultimate function of knowledge is not merely to reflect reality or simply to make us aware of it, but to develop the human being and let him acquire his final status by means of intellectual assimilation—to know is to assimilate being.

The individual is not left alone to discover reality, including his own self; he is not a kind of monolithic monad that has to begin absolutely afresh to discover from utter nothingness everything about God, about this world, and about himself. He is born in a community and in the midst of history with a past gravitating from within upon his own nature. This means that religion, being a personal intellectual discovery, is not an individualistic affair even in its intellectual dimension.

Religion appears here as the Weltanschauung, as the *darśana*, worked out by Man's ancestors and seniors, conveying to the individual the doctrine, the truths, and the dogmas that will help him to realize his being, to reach his goal. Religion, in this connection, is that set of intellectual truths which Man must "know as being true" for his salvation, for attaining his goal, for filling up his being, as it were.

By "know as being true" we mean to know from within, that is, to realize and to be convinced of the truth conveyed by those statements. The *religious doctrine*, Weltanschauung, or *darśana*, is not just a "scientific" and "objective" picture of the world with no subjective commitment. It is not satisfied with a noncommittal acceptance of several sets of formulations or with a purely theoretical acknowledgment of a doctrine, which does not affect us personally. It requires a vital and sincere conviction of the righteousness of the religious conception, not necessarily as an intellectual system, but simply as the truth referred to by the religious doctrine. In other words, the religious Man has faith in several vital *truths* of existential importance for his life; thus, religious doctrine requires something *more* than mere rational agreement: it requires a deeper and integral human conviction of the truth of that doctrine.

No religion is a mere school of thought, but every religion has a body of doctrine more or less developed, a set of fundamental truths—what religions call dogmas—which contain the message of liberation or salvation for Man. When a religion demands consent to its doctrine, it does not do so because people need to believe the doctrine per se, but because those dogmas are considered to be for that religion the intellectual translation of the truth. Only by adapting his life to truth and realizing it will Man be able to reach truth. Not the dogmas but the truth that they claim to contain will set us free and bring us salvation.

When Islam says you must believe in Allah, it does not mean primarily that you must sign your adhesion to a definite formula. It means rather that only by being vitally convinced of the existence of the only One and True God will you be able to

lead a worthy human life—of divine Sonship and human brotherhood—and fulfill
the purpose of your own existence.

Religious dogmas are not just philosophical formulations or universal statements; they are not merely the expression of a philosophical doctrine. The Hindu
dogmas, for example, are not written down in a book, yet Hinduism has a doctrine
and fundamental dogmas even if they are not explicitly formulated or stated with
authority. The dogmas of Hinduism are everything that can be said expressing
what Hinduism specifically is. The *mahāvākyāni*, that is, the fundamental sayings
contained in the *Upaniṣad*, for example, are the dogmas of vedantic Hinduism. As
we have distinguished an inner and an outer side in the first dimension of religion,
likewise we can make the same distinction between an *objective* and a *subjective*
aspect of this second dimension.

The Dogmatic Side

According to all religions—and contrary to a certain way of speaking that seems
to have lost the sense of the sacred—we call dogmas the fundamental intellectual
statements of religion.

It is hardly necessary to point out that when we use the noun "dogma" and the
adjective "dogmatic" we do not by any means indulge in the pejorative use of these
two words that has been their fate in the nonphilosophical English language, where
they have come to mean exactly the opposite of what they intend to convey. Dogma
(in Latin *placitum*) comes from the Greek verb *dokeō*, which means "to seem," and
its first translation is *opinion*. Indeed, in Greece its meaning was, on one side, the
technical opinion of the physician, philosopher, scientist, and on the other side, the
democratic decision of the Senate.

In both cases the underlying significance was that of a poised and carefully
considered opinion that imposed itself on the people by its own character though
not evident by itself, but acceptable because of the legitimate authority it came from.

In the last period of the Hellenic culture the main tenets of the philosophical
systems of the great thinkers—who were supposed to have founded a philosophy of
salvation—were called *dogmas*. After this, the word was adopted by the Christians
to express a fundamental truth that brings salvation because ultimately it does not
rest on any human authority but on divine Revelation.

However, we are not concerned now with revaluing any word but only with
explaining the objective side of this second dimension of religion.

1. We observe that although the formulations of the main dogmas may differ,
almost all religions recognize the same fundamental truths: there is one Ultimate
Reality, which is the origin and end of all beings, and It is Good and True; there is
a moral law here on Earth that prescribes the behavior of men; this human earthly
life is only a transitory status, and so on.

Sometimes there is only an apparent discrepancy: for instance, *some* forms of
polytheism are not incompatible with the existence of One Supreme God, of whom

the minor gods are either mere particular symbols, or superhuman beings participating in one of the aspects of the Divinity and are useful or harmful auxiliaries for the human world.

At other times there is no discrepancy because dogmas may refer to different levels. The Christian Trinity, for instance, does not contradict the Muslim Unity of Allah or the Jewish Uniqueness of YHWH. The Christian dogma of the Trinity claims to give us a glimpse of the interior life of the only One and Unique God, and for this very reason it is not a tritheism and does not introduce any kind of pluralism in the Unicity of God; it just reveals something of the divine simplicity.

And yet at other times there are certainly dogmatic differences that may be perhaps transcended and benevolently interpreted, but that cannot be denied. For example, rebirth is a dogma of Hinduism that cannot be reconciled with the Christian dogma of the personal and unique destiny of every human person. In such a case the unity ought to be sought beyond the dogmatical formulation, by digging down to that deeper level where error cannot dwell and by trying from there to explain how the wrong formulation came to be a seeming translation of a deeper fact. In this particular case it could very well be that these two dogmas do not refer to the same subject, but denote in one case a transpersonal continuity and in another a personal uniqueness. Nevertheless, as dogmas they remain different and even opposite.

A special feature of the dogmas of all religions is their claim to be of sacred or even divine origin. A dogma is not a human truth reached by means of our reasoning, but it is a given truth, a superhuman revelation that is to be understood, realized, and even reasoned about as far as possible, but whose origin and authority are always divine.

No one has the right to establish dogmas, except God. No founder or prophet of any religion has ever laid claims to personal human originality; they always speak in the name of God and, incidentally, hardly ever formulate a dogma.

In summary, dogmas are the fundamental religious truths considered by every religion as sacred and divine, upon which the full development of the religious doctrine is based.

2. The dogmas that each religion has represent a need of each religion itself, in that they express the fundamental truths of its faith. For religion is meant to be the path of salvation not only for the few who can understand an elaborate intellectual doctrine, or for the fewer who can realize the mystical experience, but also for the ordinary man, for the simple people who have neither the time, nor the capacity, nor the opportunity to peer into the intimate experiences of Reality.

Religion must be a sublime and profound message, but at the same time a simple one. It cannot be based on any difficult or esoteric doctrine; it cannot demand a particular intellectual or even cultural development. A Gospel will always be a message to the poor, glad tidings for the simple.

We need hardly point out, on the other hand, that the real dogmas are not to be exhaustively identified with the merely human formulations of them, though neither can they be separated from these formulae. Each real dogma is a theandric symbiosis between a divine spiritual message and a human intellectual structure.

Dogma is not its formulation alone, but without the intellectual expression there is no dogma. Dogma is not the empty formula, nor is it the unexpressed content; it is the unity of both, the incarnation of a divine truth in human concepts, building up a living unity that can only be understood from within, that is, by faith. That is why it is so easy to criticize dogmas from outside and to ridicule their intellectual frame. But such a criticism does not touch the dogma.

The Doctrinal Side

The human person cannot help being an intellectual and more particularly a rational creature. The human intellect cannot help but unify the received or elaborated dogmas and its own personal experiences, within a congruous doctrinal system, within a *darśana*, a Weltanschauung, a philosophy or a theology.

Let us remember that we are ascending from the deepest levels of our being toward the realm of the intellectual and even rational light. All three subdimensions discussed up to now were far beyond the proper level of our specific human form of intelligibility. That is why all that we said so far can easily be misunderstood if there is not the good will to understand and the deeper love to realize our own personal religious adventure.

We mean by doctrine a more or less systematized body of intellectual truths expressed in a *reasonable* way—even if this conceptual expression does not explain the entire content of faith—so that a general understanding about the main tenets of a religion is possible.

Every religion develops its own peculiar doctrine as the intellectual translation necessary for the human assimilation of the religious message. Moreover, it is necessary for every religion to have a certain doctrine.

The relations between religion and religious doctrine could be summarized in the following statements.

1. Every religion develops its religious doctrine not because of any moral imperative or apologetic instinct, but because of an internal necessity of the human mind to bring to the realm of reasonable intelligibility all that lies in the depths of human existence.

2. The existence of a doctrine, in spite of the danger of confusing it with the dogmas or of overshadowing the first dimension of religion, is not an imperfection but it is a good and even necessary condition for the full growth of religion.

3. A completely developed doctrinal system is not absolutely essential for a religion. There can well exist a religion of pure disconnected dogmas and of simple laws of action without a rational or an intellectual elaboration of them. Moreover, the doctrinal system cannot be a closed one, for by its very definition a dogma always leaves a door open to transcendence. Nor does it need to be a spotless and almost self-evident rational exposition.

Dogmas may well be a constant challenge to the human mind, which is not always capable of reconciling in a rational way complementary, opposite, or seemingly incompatible dogmas—*brahman* and the world, liberty and grace, *śūnyavāda* and dharma.

4. No religion is essentially connected in a *positive* way with a *definite* doctrine. Hinduism as religion is not to be identified with the *advaita* doctrine or even with vedānta. Hinduism itself has survived in spite of deep doctrinal changes through the ages and is alive in the most different doctrinal systems. Christianity can be expressed in an Aristotelian system or by a Neoplatonic doctrine or by any other adequate doctrine. Islam was equally strong if not stronger before its medieval theological doctrine evolved. We could speak, therefore, of (1) the *greatness* and (2) the *weakness* of every doctrine.

• Since human nature is social and intellectual, the doctrinal side of a religion is very important, for it speaks directly to these two sides of human nature. An unutterable mystical experience can hardly be conveyed naked—stripped of all doctrinal coating; the striking affirmations of a set of dogmas may be very difficult to accept and even to understand. On the contrary, an elaborated doctrine appeals to our intellect, can be easily grasped, gains without difficulty our assent, and works on an intelligible level that is accessible to the majority of mankind. Unlike faith, as St. Paul would point out, a religious doctrine is a systematic explanation of the whole of reality seen from the point of view of a religious faith. It presents a more or less intelligible system about God, Man, and the world, and from accepted truths leads us to more or less complete and congruous knowledge. A doctrine can be expounded and can be convincing. Moreover, a doctrine is universal because every human being has a minimum of intelligence for certain doctrinal understanding.

• On the other hand, the weakness of every doctrine lies in its limitations, in its provisionality or nonultimateness, and in the great danger of its being identified with religion itself.

Every doctrine, being a human intellectual effort to a comprehensive view of Reality, is limited not only by the boundaries of the human spirit but also by the limitation of a particular point of view. Every doctrine tries to be as universal and as comprehensive as possible, but cannot help possessing certain viewpoints, points of departure, and starting assumptions from which all other things are considered. Thomism and Scotism within the most pure orthodox Catholic scholasticism, for instance, accept the same dogmas and claim to be the doctrinal development of the same faith, and yet they are two different doctrinal systems.

Every doctrine is nothing but the intellectual—we do not say rational and still less rationalistic—expression of one religious faith. Doctrine is neither religion itself nor is it identical with revealed or accepted dogmas. It is merely their intellectual exposition. No doctrine, as such, has saving power; no pure doctrine can be a substitute for existential and integral religious realization. "And though I have the power of prophecy, to penetrate all mysteries and knowledge, and though I have all the faith necessary to move mountains—if I am without love, I am nothing" (1 Co 13:2). And finally the *more* perfect a doctrine is, the greater is the danger of identifying its views with the absolute truth and with religion itself. "Knowledge puffs up" (1 Co 8:1), says Christian Scripture, and the believer is warned: "make sure that no one captivates you with the empty lure of a 'philosophy'" (Col 2:8). The failure of the *Konklusionentheologie* of Cartesian inspiration within Christianity should be a warning example.

5. The relation between religion and religious doctrine is *one-sided* and *negative*. This means that every religious doctrine is dependent on the religion that it intends to explain, but not vice versa. It means also that the following of one particular doctrine does not imply the sharing of the religious life of which that doctrine claims to be an expression. There may be doctrinally orthodox Catholics who are bad Catholics or perhaps not Catholics at all.

On the other hand, the negation of a particular doctrine may imply, though not always, the abandoning of the religion that professes such a doctrine. This is the sphere of orthodoxy.

It has already been pointed out that the doctrinal side is an integral part of religion and that these limitations do not alter its important place within this second dimension of religion. If religion, on the one hand, *is* not a doctrine, it *has* a doctrine. If religion cannot be reduced to the realm of ideas, neither can it be expelled from this realm, which constitutes one of the most important elements of the human being.

We should by no means volatilize religion with the excuse of keeping it safe from human struggles. In other words, religion is not an abstraction.

The Ethical-Practical Dimension

Man is something more than an intelligent and knowing being. He is also of a volitional nature; he not only knows, but also wills and loves; he not only "realizes," he is also moving toward and striving for "realization." Religion not only teaches what or where truth is, but also leads us to that very truth, and is concerned with *how* to reach the goal of human life.

Religion, therefore, has a fundamentally dynamic character, which in some sense is its most striking feature, for the aim of religion is salvation, and salvation is not only an intellectual affair but is also and primarily an existential goal.

Religion is much more a practical endeavor than a theoretical school. It is true that this practical side will be internally dependent on the theoretical one, but nevertheless theory or doctrine alone could never exist without this other essential dimension of religion.

We should mention here a very important point for the meeting and understanding of religions. If religions were exclusively based only on dogmatic principles and not on ethical grounds, sincere dialogue between believers of two different religions would be almost impossible. If truth for you was one disincarnated thing and for me it took another chemically pure opposite view, we could only meet in a duel-to-the-death armed with our mental powers. No coexistence would be possible, nor the basic human trust that makes the endeavor of trying to convince one another a honest enterprise. Were I to disregard this ethical dimension of religion when facing an atheist or a convinced monist or a sincere believer of another faith, I could not find any human common meeting-ground. We would instinctively regard our partner as a freak. The religious encounter of several faiths only becomes a religious endeavor if based on this ethical level of personal honesty. I may disagree theoretically with my partner, but we are each convinced that both are striving for truth and have this common ethical attitude of mutual respect, of fair play, of a single honest aim to reach understanding and promote the common cause of peace, religion, humanitarianism, and first of all, of truth. It is precisely the sincere meeting with believers of other religions that greatly helps us to enlarge not only our intellectual horizons but our ethical basis.

In the realm of ideas we may not agree with one another, yet we discover a deeper existential communion in our human ethical endeavor. We discover one another as persons. One of the two may be wrong, but both can be good and honest. Sincerity is, in this respect, more than an intellectual endowment. It is a moral virtue, the foundation of any religious encounter worthy of the name. Moreover, the moral ideas may differ—as we shall see—for already ideas belong to the previous intellectual dimension, but the fundamental ethical attitude may very well be the same. Any honest and happy marriage of persons of different religions could give us an example of what we mean. The ethical dimension touches precisely this deep aspect of Man and of religion.

It belongs to the nature of religion to lead Man to his goal, and for this it not only shows the truth but also provides the means by which Man will arrive at the goal. We can call these means Cult, Laws, Sacraments, Rites, and so on, but we cannot here enter into this important chapter of the philosophy of religion. Let us only distinguish an inner and an outer side of this third dimension of religion.

The Moral or Ethical Side

The end of Man and his goal in the intellectual sphere is called *goodness*. The same reality can be envisaged as truth and goodness insofar as it is realized by our intellect or reached by our will.

Every religion claims to help Man to realize the truth and also strives to aid him to reach and realize goodness. In this respect, religion is the path to the ultimate Good, and the means to reach the end of the journey, that is, the means for achieving the integrity of Man's being. This properly constitutes the moral or ethical side of religion.

Morals, according to religion, are not simply the set of laws people must follow in order to attain salvation, but rather that very path of life that leads to the fullness of Man and that lies at the origin of every law.

The deistic period of European culture has left in the mentality of some people of our generation a vague impression that morality is fully independent of any dogma and even of God, and that morals are only concerned with some kind of sociological and external rules that allow people to live peacefully together. This conception, however efficiently it may work for giving "moral" counsels to our civic behavior, is not adequate enough for the religious idea of morals.

Morals are not rooted in the good manners taught us by wise men. Morals are founded in the very nature of Man and are the practical and concrete translation of the fundamental law of Man's becoming.

"Thou must not hate," for instance, is a moral principle not primarily because to hate hurts your neighbor or deteriorates the social order, but because to begin with it hurts you, because it does not "become" you, for you have to be-come, to grow up, and hatred destroys the ontical becoming of yourself. Moreover, you ought not to hurt yourself because you are not the absolute master of yourself. You belong to Another, another Self who has care of you, and has called—created, destined . . .—you to be—to be what you are *supposed* to be (sub-posed, placed under). Egoism thus does not enter into a genuine moral attitude.

Man is a pilgrim being, and his being is not exclusively knowledge or intellect. Religion is there to lead Man to his full being, and for this it does not only enlighten his mind but also guides and helps him on his way to becoming. Morality is the aspect of religion that deals with this existential growth.

How can the human person—we do not say the individual—reach his fullness? What is the *way* leading Man to his end? This is the fundamental moral problem. It appears from here that the answer is dependent on what Man and Man's goal is. Moreover, this moral *way* is not an external path on which Man has to walk in order to reach his destination. Man himself is on the way; he is the itinerant being that has to complete the way in himself; he is in some sense the very way going up or down, but in any case going toward the end of the way that is the end of himself.

In a certain sense, this third ethical dimension is deeper and closer to his being than the second intellectual dimension, which considers Man as a knowing being. This is only true in a certain sense, however, for Man is essentially an intellectual, namely, a spiritual being, and the end of his becoming is by no means independent of the perfection of his own intellect.

This ontic, this essential growing is what is meant by the ethical side of every religion: the effective guidance of Man in order to enable him to achieve his being.

With this as the ultimate aim, religion proceeds to the formulation of the moral laws: love God and thy neighbor, follow thy *dharma* without looking for reward, and so on.

It is obvious from what has been said that moral laws are internal and personal, as distinguished from the social laws of a state, for example. The latter regard the external order and are established for the sake of the common good or the well-being of others. For that reason they are compulsory. The former are intended for the person and his salvation; and, therefore, they are free and cannot—not only ought not to—be enforced. They are internal laws of my becoming. The fact that any person is ontologically connected with others and that, therefore, the law of my becoming has a communitarian side is again another problem.

Religion points out these laws and attempts to give Man the necessary means to fulfill them in order that he may realize his own being.

It is commonly said that it is precisely here that almost all religions coincide. But to say this leads all too often to looking for a religious unity on the moral level, overlooking any other difference, and reducing religion to morals. This view has also led to replacing religious instruction by moral instruction in educational institutions, where students belong to different religious communities, for—they suppose—religions may differ and are not universal, whereas morals are unique and are really a science acceptable by everybody.

We should not deny the greater agreement of many religions on ethical principles, and we should furthermore stress that the ethical dimension of Man as well as of religion may be a very important starting point for a fruitful religious confrontation. But we should carefully avoid the above-mentioned danger of identifying religion with morals or, rather, of reducing religion to morals. Nor is this all: two other points are of relevance here.

1. The identity between the ethics of the several religions is not as *absolute* and, especially, not as deep as a prima facie view may lead us to believe. Here we have perhaps the opposite of what we have discovered in the case of religious dogmas. There, under an apparent difference, we may sometimes discover a deeper agreement. Here, under a seeming identity, we sometimes find deep discrepancies, unless, of course, we reduce morals to rules of external and practical behavior to which hardly any religion will agree.

To begin with, no moral doctrine or practice of any religion is independent of the dogmatic elements of that religion. The practical way by which Man will reach his goal and attain his fullness depends entirely on what his goal *is* and what his fullness consists in. The moral laws for the growth and development of Man's being are just an expression of the nature of his being. In other words, the foundation for the goodness of a human action—a moral action—depends on the truth that such an action realizes. Indeed, human conscience has its own *ontonomy*, and I can discover the good by means of my own conscience without implying that my mind has reached the corresponding truth. But morals as the norms for right conduct rely on dogma as the expression of ultimate truths. My conscience can only find a justification of its "feeling," inclination, or moral judgment, if it arrives at an intellectual ground based on a truth discovered by the intellect.

Certainly—to illustrate this by one example—almost every religion has a moral precept of the kind "thou shall not kill." Moreover, almost every human conscience discovers in itself such an injunction. Yet this is not all, nor is it sufficient to allow us to identify two moral systems. The field of agreement of this precept is not much wider than the prohibition of killing a friend without any motive. We become conscious of the moral precept as such when we enter into conflict with some other opposite inclination of ours and then we are forced to ask the reason for the precept.

Why should I not kill the person who comes to kill me? Why should I not kill the enemy or the suffering old man whose existence in this world seems to have no meaning at all? Does this precept extend to every form of life or only to human life? Is it really possible to live without killing? Does the precept include not doing other kinds of harm to other beings? Is harming another ever justified? Is there a hierarchy of harms and of being which allows and perhaps even commands to kill or to do harm in order to save higher values or more perfect beings? It is obvious that the answers to all these questions depend on the theoretical doctrine of the meaning of life, the purpose of existence, the hierarchy of being, the rights of authority, the nature of the common good, and so on—all of which transcend by far the ethical level, being the answers grounded in the doctrinal sphere, and depending on the vision one has and on the belief one holds.

2. On the other hand, the ontonomy of the moral conscience should not be minimized. That is to say, the human person possesses in his conscience an organ of judgment and of discrimination between good and evil. Every religion will agree not only on the general ethical law that "the good action should be done and the bad one avoided," but will also have a certain immediate judgment of what is good and what is evil. This healthy moral conscience is an important personal and existential bridge of communication between persons of different religions. Yet history proves and experience confirms that this moral judgment relies to a great extent on the theoretical ideas, namely, on the dogmatic views of every individual.

Practical agreement or utilitarian compromises are sometimes very necessary, but are not enough. Two reasons lie at hand: the first is that the morality of any action lies not in the material act, but in the intention of the doer; for example, if you do not kill just because of the police or because of hell, or because of social environment or pressure you cannot say that you are a perfectly moral man, and you may find endless strategies to eliminate your enemy without killing him. If you do not sterilize people or assist at abortions just because it is not done in your society or the conflict has not yet arisen, you cannot say that your ethical behavior is equal to that of those who refuse to do it on ethical principles.

The second reason is that morality lies not only in the intention of the doer—this intention being what has to be purified or clarified or brought to an agreement, or disagreement, with the moral principles of other religions—but the morality of an action also has a certain metaphysical element in itself that tinges, as it were, the action to its near core. To act morally it is not enough to have the intention of performing the moral act if you do not fulfill its ontological conditions. An example may make this clear. Christianity claims that the factual and real end of Man is not his "human" or created fullness but his supernatural and gratuitous divinization. For Christianity, therefore, a Christian action is not just an action that is not "bad" according to "human," natural standards, but an action that leads Man, however remotely and indirectly but efficiently, toward his ultimate supernatural end. To act morally for Christianity it is not just to add a "Christian" complement to any action but to elevate that action to the specifically Christian supernatural sphere. Christian morals do not aim at forming just an "honest" man, but a "saint," a "child of God" in the sense Christianity understands these concepts. Thus a mere equality in the intention does not justify speaking of the identity of the moral laws of the various religions.

An altogether different problem concerning this example of Christianity is whether the non-Christian acting with right intention according to his conscience is not also lifted up by the grace of God to that supernatural sphere. But we are not concerned here with exposing religious doctrines. To illustrate this last point we could equally have used the example of the moral actions within the caste in Brahmanism.

In this context we realize that we cannot minimize the importance that almost all religions place on rites, sacraments, and sacrifices. Liturgy, in one word, is not just a ceremonial that can be dispensed with or changed altogether. Liturgy has an outer ceremonial appearance, but the core of liturgy is the cult given to God not only in the *form* God desires—according to each religion—but with the only *contents* that can really reach God and fulfill our being.

The room for superstition, exclusivity, and Pharisaism is only too obvious. We should take care, however, not to reduce religion to pure humanism in our efforts to correct such abuses. The justification of liturgy is not in saying that *God* wants only this form of worship or prefers it to another one. The religious justification lies in the belief that the particular form of worship of a particular religion reaches God because of its ontological conditions. The interpretation of these conditions differs from religion to religion, but the underlying claim is the same.

The Practical Side

The help religion offers Man for attaining perfection by means of the moral law is not only internal, theoretical, and personal, but also external, practical, and organic, for the human being is not only pure will but also "weak flesh," not merely an imperfect creature tending toward perfection, but also a rebel and hesitating "willy-nilly" fellow.

Religion tries to provide the opportunities and facilities for the moral way, within the framework that history and society have made possible. Here is the place for the many religious regulations that have only this auxiliary meaning. They are aids to the carrying out of our duty, a kind of human support for our weak and bad hours and, on occasion, for development and organic growth in our bright moments.

Religion is not a pure theoretical doctrine or ideology, but a practical endeavor and realistic pattern for the ordinary human being. Religion puts in a concrete and common way the high demands of the mystical insight. As an example, every religion affirms that prayer, a life of prayer and meditation, is necessary to lead a worthy human life so that Man can reach the real level of his being, that is, liberation. But religion does not stop here. It points out to the people how it is to be done and the minimum necessary for such a life. So Catholicism in the most definite way says, "Once a week, and precisely on Sundays, all Catholics have to share in the most high and holy Sacrifice of the whole of creation to God reenacted in the Mass." Islam, Hinduism, and others offer additional examples.

Penance and abstinence are necessary to reach the goal of human life. Religion, thinking realistically and having a concern for the majority of the people, does not let this remain as a general counsel or a simple statement, but points out very concretely how and when to perform this minimum requirement.

Of course, to confound religion with these little rules or to think that religion does not teach other things than these limited regulations is to misunderstand the very essence of religion. On the other hand, the danger of pure formalism and the slavery to the letter is also obvious. These practical regulations, however, are also a part of religion that is not just a pure and superhuman doctrine but a very realistic, integral, and earthly reality.

Only too often followers of religious confessions confer on this subdimension of religion an exaggerated importance that overshadows the other elements.

Another dangerous example of this abuse and degradation is not only the religious formalism and Pharisaism already mentioned but also the magic character of some religious forms. In fact, magic exists in many degrees; from the belief in the formal physical-psychic-supernatural form of causality—that is, the belief that a *pure* physical act has an automatic and unavoidable effect on the psychic and, especially, on the supernatural sphere—to the idea that in order to achieve our being we must perform certain acts that by themselves will produce salvation. Between these extremes there is a vast gamut of intermediate stages of which every religion should be well aware.

This aspect of religion, however humble and material it may seem, however dangerous it may appear due to the peril of overgrowth and of inflation in the popular levels, is an essential element that cannot be dispensed with.

The examples of the great religious men throughout history should be illuminating in this respect. Here again we have an important point of contact among religions in spite of many other differences even on this very ethical dimension. Yet it is a fact—which modern syncretists and overspiritualists should bear in mind—that a *Śaṅkarācārya*, or a John of the Cross—to put only two examples of mystical natures who might seem to be more inclined to overlook the lower dimensions of religion—never believed they would have no need for the ritualistic side of religion. A *Rāmakṛṣṇa* in our modern times may have been syncretistic, may have thought that all rites are secondary, and may have had experiences quite revolting to other believers, yet his religious instinct showed him that the essence of the rite could not be dispensed with.

The Sentimental-Emotional Dimension

Man's powers are not only pure mind and sober will. Encroaching upon both and sharing in the nature of both there is a third human power of the utmost practical importance for the concrete shaping of human life on Earth: the realm of feelings.

We do not need to deal here with the anthropological problem regarding the nature of feeling—that is, whether the human spirit is a trilogy of intellect, will, and feeling or ultimately only a duality without the latter—because this question is irrelevant to our case. Whatever feelings ultimately may be, it is an anthropological fact that they play a great role in daily human life. If religion has the mission to lead Man toward his goal, and Man is led not only by his reason and his will but also by his feelings, religion will have to offer something in response to the human world of feelings. The question is a very delicate one, for a small exaggeration in any sense will break the balance and poise of Man and of religion.

It would be totally erroneous to reduce religion to a sentimental human affair, but it would also fall short of the truth to eliminate the realm of feelings from religion altogether. Religion is not just a sentiment but also provides an answer to the sentimental aspect of Man and offers a means for the formation of the human heart, an indispensable element for the harmony and entire development of the human personality.

For the sake of methodology we shall distinguish between an *internal* aspect of Man as an emotional being and an *external* response of religion filling up Man's sentimental capacity.

The Emotional Side

Man is an emotional being. He may be moved by convictions and be determined by his will, nevertheless in practice—and this holds for the greater part of mankind—he is led by his own feelings. Moreover, short of his emotional fulfillment Man remains unbalanced and unhappy. A cold and merely intellectualistic religion would never take hold of the entire Man.

This emotional bias of Man is so strong that religious virtues like piety, devotion, love, surrender, adoration, and so on—which by no means belong primarily to this dimension—have come to design almost exclusively the emotional aspect of religion—as mysticism at not too distant times was held to be synonymous with metapsychical experiences. One thing is to fall prey to an emotional overstressing of one's religious attitude, reducing religion to pure emotion—"where no belief, no relief"; another thing is to eliminate the emotional side from religion altogether. It is a phenomenological observation that an emotional type of spirituality goes hand in hand, paradoxically enough, with a certain religious "juridicism."

It is not only the popular aspect of religion that demands such a dimension, as if it were a concession to a sort of human emotional weakness. It is also the very nature of Man that makes this dimension of religion one of the most important features from a sociological standpoint. If religion were not incarnated, as it were, in the emotional sphere of Man it could hardly be spontaneous and be present everywhere with that kind of presence which, without disturbing the intensity of human earthly life, strengthens it with a deeper sense of transcendence.

All along these pages we have been pleading for an integral conception of religion against oversimplifications. In spite of the possible exaggeration and real dangers of this dimension of religion we cannot but emphasize the humble importance of the emotional side of religion if we have to overcome the temptation of the mere theoretician and of the a-religious student of religions. Religion is indeed far more than a mere sentiment, but being an integral anthropological reality it cannot be reduced to a disincarnated essence or to an ideal or idealistic construction. It is this sentimental dimension that tinges this most sublime element of the human being, his religion, with humanity and spontaneity.

In fact, human life on Earth is much more than willpower and acute mind. Man needs the concrete and warm touch of the sentimental world. Moreover, the ties that relate Man to the Earth and to the other nonhuman beings—without which Man would be a kind of intellectual robot—are mainly of a sentimental nature. Also his relations with God need a warm and personal touch that, only when an authentic sentimental life is integrated in his spirituality, can find a proper channel and a harmonious expansion.

The Sentimental Side

Man's sentimental urge is so great that it tinges almost every human endeavor. In the same way that our material cosmos hardly ever presents substances in a chemically pure state, the human world hardly ever shows a human reality free from emotional concomitances. Perhaps the first step of phenomenology of religion is the discovery of this sentimental aspect of religion. Religion appears in fact, prima facie, not as a set of doctrines or of rules of conduct, but as a complex framework of rites and ceremonies that *seem* to be there just to fill up the human appeal for a fully developed sentimental life.

In a second moment, phenomenology of religion discovers that the sentimental aspect is just an aspect and even a kind of outer veil of deeper dimensions. Nevertheless it cannot altogether explain away sentiments from religion.

Fear, anguish, nostalgia, but also joy, trust, love, and the like, seem to be originally all religious experiences, or, we could also say, human experiences intrinsically connected with religion. Even what we today would rather call profane or secular experiences seem to be a metathesis from the religious or sacred sphere. Leaving all interpretations aside, the presence of religion in the sentimental world of Man is an undeniable fact. The great sentimental moments of Man, birth and death as well as human marriage and love, appear to be his most religious moments.

The sentimental factor of religion is so striking that this has been the origin of the theory that considers religion as the projection of the sentimental world of Man. We would rather say that it is because Man is so fundamentally a sentimental being that religion has such a great part in his sentimental sphere.

The thirst for the infinite and the longing of the human person for perfection and completeness comes ultimately, in theory, from an ontological movement of his whole being expressed in the dynamism of his mind and his will. Yet, in fact, this ontological desire is wrapped up in a sentimental set-up that has not only the upper hand but that tinges the whole of that constitutive thirst of the human being with the particular colors of each human temperament. It is not only the ultimate philosophical analysis that discovers the contingency of Man. On a more effective and universal level—though also more superficial—it is the human sentimental life longing for fulfillment and desiring a fullness that it cannot satisfy here on Earth that leads Man toward God as the very goal of his desire. The whole thematic is too well known as to require further explanations.

Within every religion are one or various devotional trends that stress this dimension. We have already noted that the real and true mysticism lies elsewhere, but many a manifestation of mysticism and above all the devotional aspect of religion have their place here.

The agreement of religions on this point is a very great one. Almost all religions recognize the existence of this human sphere and the important part that religion plays in it. They generally agree also in saying that this is not the most fundamental tenet of religion, important as it is. The differences are rather of accent and of hierarchy of values, leaving the contents and interpretations of such feelings aside.

The Ecclesiastic-Sociological Dimension

Man is not a solitary being, either as a matter of fact or as a matter of nature. Certainly he is a person, but he is not strictly speaking an individual, that is, a separate, disconnected being, ontologically severed from others. He depends on others—and others depend on him—for realizing his personal goal. The end itself of human life has a communitarian character. In consequence, his liberation is neither a *purely* individualistic affair, nor a mere isolated salvation. Heaven is not, strictly speaking, precisely private amusement, and the conception of *nirvāṇa* is the strongest reaction—eventually excessive—against an egoistic idea of the ultimate end. I do not realize *mokṣa* alone, nor is eternal peace a state of aloof and individual bliss. Human beings are different persons, but human nature is *one* here and hereafter.

This communitarian dimension of Man and of religion does not destroy the other aspects of Man and religion, nor the unchangeable and intimate destiny of human persons.

It belongs to the mature nature of Man and of religion to find the equilibrium and via media between the extremes of individualism and communism. In philosophy and religion as well as in politics this is one of the most difficult tasks of human life on Earth, especially in our times.

This dimension again sheds some light on one of the most painful experiences of a good number of pioneers in the field of religious understanding. Here, patience and courage are the most needed virtues. Because religion is not just my private affair, I must have the patience to wait or to go not so rapidly as to disregard the rhythm of things or of others. Because religion is not my private affair, I do not have the right to be discouraged by those who may not understand or by those who may persecute me. Religions have lived isolated from each other for centuries, and misunderstanding has very often become chronic. The remedy would be worse than the malady if, disregarding the present status quo, the elite interested in harmony among religions should create a new religion for the few and a new creed for the "broad-minded" and "nonbigoted." Yet they cannot and have not the right to give up the ideal of bringing religions together and to a closer understanding.

As in the aforementioned dimensions we may also distinguish here an inner and an outer side of this fifth dimension of religion.

The Ecclesiastical Side

Ekklēsia, the *ecclesial* aspect of religion, does not mean here organization but rather *organism*; it does not mean the external arrangement of a membership, but the internal structure of a fellowship.

It is not a part of our task here to develop all the internal ontological threads by which people are connected to one another, but only to point out that religion in one way or another must develop this ecclesiastical aspect. For example, prayer, vicarious suffering, preaching, service, mutual love, and so on are all religious categories also pertaining to this aspect.

Human life on Earth has a constitutive unity. We are all launched in one and the same adventure, and even in my very striving for my goal, my efforts extend to the very limit of mankind itself, that is, in performing my duty I do my personal and particular task as a part of the whole and for the welfare of the whole.

A part of the whole has been entrusted to me and that is *me*. The law of *karman* has not only a vertical dimension and is not only a temporal link between past and future; it also has a horizontal dimension and is a spatial link between the people.

Religion, whether organized as a body or not, recognizes the interweaving of human efforts and the supra-individual responsibility and effects of personal actions.

I may have my own, personal, and even individual religious views and may try to follow my intimate and unique religious path; nevertheless, if I am truly a religious soul I shall realize that my path is only a *part*—with many *particulars*—of the general universal path of mankind. I shall also constantly discover in my own path crossings of other paths and the mingling of other tracks from which I receive influence, impulse, and direction, and on which I also effect modifications.

Every religion is communitarian not because it looks after more than one individual, but because it is aware of the profound unity of human beings. Should we imagine that religion is only an individualistic affair, we would then be blind to many a religious manifestation and would miss an essential feature of religion.

True religiosity is never an individualistic and selfish attitude, and for the same reason religion manifestly shows a communitarian character. The reason for this *ecclesial* dimension is again the integral nature of Man.

An aspect of modern culture at times gives the impression that Man is a mere individual having only external relations with others, whereas in fact he is properly a person, having constitutive inward relations not only with God but also with his fellow beings. Fellowship is not a human luxury or a product of a refined civilization, but an exigency of our very being, a constitutive feature of our person. Because Man is a person and a person is a supra- and trans-individual reality, religion being personal is communitarian, social, and *ecclesial*. Another extreme would be to dissolve the person in society or in collectivity and to ignore the specific "personal" and untransferable value of the human being.

Phenomenology of religion shows us this essential ecclesiastical feature. Moreover, in one sense or other, every religion—insofar as true religion breathes in it—has a certain claim not only over the whole man, but over the whole of mankind, even though very often a particular religion may appear to be a particular aspect of a general solution, a concretized form of a more universal religion.

In fact, some religions have limited this universality, mainly because of the following three factors:

First, ignorance of the outer world beyond the large or small enclosure of a racial, geographical, historical, or cultural unit.

Second, a practical need for peaceful coexistence and prudence, where spreading beyond their limits would endanger their own possibility of continued existence.

Third, the more or less explicit conception that the other gods are inferior deities and the other races, nations, communities . . . are not worthy to share in the privileges of their own "superior" religion.

This ecclesiastical subdimension is more than a simple communitarian idea uniting the followers of one religion. It is the expression of the very community of nature and the destiny of mankind.

In spite of individualistic trends, every religion in one way or another deals with something other than individual salvation, because after all, this salvation is not an individualistic disconnected fate, but an organic and ecclesiastic fact. That is the deep reason, for instance, why religions always have a special place for ancestors; this is not only due to psychological motives, since these psychological sentiments are rooted in the consciousness of an ontological community of nature and of destiny.

Nor is this all. Religion is not just something for modern Western Man, with his highly developed sense of individuality and personal consciousness. Religion is for the Man of all times and all cultures. It is a known fact that human beings have not always had the individual sensitivity of modern Western culture.

The so-called primitive, as well as many other cultures, offers us examples of group consciousness and of collective experience that imply an altogether different way of "living" the human personality.

The Christian dogma of original sin presents us an example of what we are saying. If Man were just an individual, that dogma would be sheer nonsense. The different rites of initiation also belong to this chapter of religion. Initiation is not only the awakening of a new relationship with God, but especially the integrating of a person into a religious community which believes that as a body it is carrier of an effective message of salvation.

Each religion is thus, to some degree, a church, that is, an organic body, a living organism that maintains and contains the religious message for the peoples to come or the individuals to be born or to be educated. Only in the community and by the community can an individual grow up to the full stature of his being.

This implies a certain body of traditions and regulations that can dangerously proliferate but that nevertheless belong to the essence of religion.

The Sociological Side

Human beings are not held together only by the unity of their nature, but are also united by the bonds of history, geography, and race. I am not a pure individual. I am also son, or daughter, father, neighbor, professional, citizen, national, and so on; I belong to a family, to a group, to one sex, to a city, a nation, a profession, to a certain time and culture, and so on. If the little groups darken the greater ones, if my being a national makes me forget that I am a man, if my being of the human species leads me to despise other, inferior creatures, then these particular groups are a source of trouble and abuse. But within their own limits these connections with smaller units are essential for my being a definite and particular creature.

Religion does not deal with the abstract man or with his pure nature. Religion wants to be the way or the message of the ultimate truth for the concrete and historical human being. It speaks a certain language, adopts a definite character, and puts on a particular garb according to the circumstances of space, time, race, and culture.

Moreover, as the historical existent Man is a person integrated in a definite sociological frame. His religion cannot be a vague or subtle abstraction, or something foreign and distant, but must fit into that sociological structure in which he lives. Even when revelation comes and God "speaks," He speaks a language somehow intelligible to the prophet or seer. Even His most universal message need not only to be grasped in a definite language and garb, but also to be expressed in forms and concepts or images with a definite concrete meaning.

In fact, many of the diversities of the several existent religions are simply socio-logical differences. It is obvious that one and the same religion in different circum-stances of culture, history, time, and space will take completely different forms that can be seemingly interpreted by an outsider as an absolutely distinct religion. The study of this sociological subdimension is of the utmost importance for the mutual understanding of the religious problem today.

Every religion is deeply rooted in the concrete human situation of Man in time and space and brings forth out of that specific situation the ideas, rites, customs, institutions, and so forth into which the higher aspects of religion crystallize. All these manifestations can change as they are not absolute. But in one way or another, religion needs such a garb. The vestments can be different, but religion is not a naked thing and must be always clothed in a sociological dress. Without such it cannot even exist.

Any living religion must possess this external sociological shape that also implies, not only the concreteness of a living organism, but also the necessity—and danger—of a real organization.

We are not concerned now in condemning the abuses or in describing the dangers of overemphasizing this external and sociological aspect of religion, but only in pointing out that it also belongs to the nature of religion. The known discussion in Indian Christian circles of whether a Christian in India should call and consider himself a Hindu-Christian or an Indian-Christian could offer a suitable example here.

The most important aspect of the relationship between religion and culture belongs to this subdimension of religion in a very special manner. It suffices for our purpose just to mention the problem without entering into it. Regarding our particular problem, however, of the relationship between religions, a few brief considerations may prove useful.

1. We have already warned the reader against the culturalistic conception of religion, as if religion were one cultural product among many. On the other hand, religion is not only a great cultural factor, but culture is also a great religious factor. Both belong together and are sometimes almost inseparable, especially in such cultures in which the distinction between the sacred and the profane does not exist.

This means that we may distinguish one from another but we can never separate one from another. If we were to say, for instance, that Hinduism is just the product of the soil of India under the rays of the sun in India, or, in other words, that it is the integral response of the children of India to the calling of the Absolute, this description would hold good also for Indian culture since, in fact, any cultural encounter with India is a religious encounter. It is not very consequent to grant that one could accept Hindu culture while rejecting at the same time Hindu religion unless a secularized Indian culture appears as something that, although this is not yet the case, would always be the product and child of Hindu religion. Assimilation of Indian culture means at the same time assimilation of Hindu religion.

2. The meeting of cultures always implies the meeting of the religions of those cultures, and if a cultural synthesis should take place, this would also imply a religious synthesis. The basis for a mutual religious understanding in our times has undoubtedly been brought forth by the ever-growing cultural exchange that is taking place in our world.

This could be put in another way. A religious encounter is doomed to fail if it is not a cultural encounter at the same time, for religion without culture can hardly subsist and indeed cannot be communicated. Yet a dialogue of religions is more than a mere cultural symposium.

3. Some religions are essentially bound to a particular culture, whereas others can subsist in, and also inform, several cultures. It is a striking paradox that the more historical a religion is—Islam or Christianity, for example—the more it seems to transcend a definite cultural set-up. When a religion is essentially bound to a culture, every cultural mutation implies a religious conversion, every cultural evolution represents at the minimum a religious crisis. The so-called primitive religions offer us many instances of this.

4. There are cultures incompatible with specific types of religions and vice versa. It cannot be denied that the contemporary communist world has developed a very

definite type of culture that is obviously so far irreconcilable with Christianity. Also, it seems that some of the existing religions today are not able to subsist within the frame of an industrialized culture.

5. These and similar considerations lead us to the conclusion, important for our study, that the meeting of religions is not just a pure "religious" encounter, that the living exchange among religions is not a purely "spiritual" affair or a mere academic endeavor, but an integral human event following the development and movements of history. In other words, the encounter of religions is not the product of the desire of a few intellectuals or of a handful of wishful-thinking religious souls but a historical imperative. This amounts to saying that the perspective under which we should envisage the problem of religion and religions is not a merely theoretical viewpoint but a reflection on the philosophy of history and an effort to discover the signs of the times and the dynamism of the present cultural-religious constellation.

The cautions and lessons for a missionary religion like Islam or Christianity could easily be expounded in this context, but to do this falls outside the scope of our study.

The Corporeal-Cosmological Dimension

The fifth dimension of Man and of religion does not exhaust the ontological communion of Man with other beings. Man is not only united in destiny and being with the whole of mankind, he is also connected and linked with the entire cosmos. The entire universe is a unity, and though Man has a very special place and role in the cosmos, he is, nevertheless, not only a spectator of it but an actor in it as well. In simpler words, he forms part of the universe. The whole created world we could, eventually, say is a unity and has a certain unity of destiny. Man and the world belong together, and the one is not without the other. Moreover, because this world, like Man, is created by God, or proceeds from Him and is sustained by Him in whatever form, it also goes back to God in one way or another—in the way proper to its own specific being.

This amounts to saying that this cosmos of ours is not Man's physical platform; it is not just a companion to Man during his terrestrial journey, but the world shares also in Man's destiny. In fact, hardly any religion has forgotten this connection, and the so-called primitive religions in particular act here as a constant reminder to the dangers of the more "spiritually" developed "higher" religions.

This cosmic-material aspect of religion, which indeed represents a constant danger in religion—heaven a place of sensual pleasure, the external rite valid on its own merits, fulfillment of the mere "letter" in the commandments, and so on—is, however, a constitutive feature of religion that cannot be dispensed with. In fact, nearly all existing religions have reacted against an exclusively spiritualistic conception of Man and of religion. Even if not all religions have had a positive notion of the human body, all religions have nevertheless dealt with it and paid attention to it. It is a matter for Christian meditation that St. Paul did not call the church the reunion of Christians, or the soul of Christ, but the "body of Christ." The same is true in Buddhism.

From the point of view of ecumenism, this apparently irrelevant feature may prove successful in providing the right atmosphere for a religious encounter. This cosmic consciousness will bestow on us automatically, as it were, a sense of proportion and a serenity that we all need in religious controversies. It will give us a kind of cosmic humility and an awareness that a religious ecumenical encounter is not a meeting of gods or a senate of "great" people of the Earth, but just a coming together under the sun of a handful of people aware that they have a body, are very limited in all aspects, and are humble inhabitants of a greater world following the cosmic rhythm detected in the palpitations of our heart and in the decisions of our free will.

We can here distinguish again between an inward and an exterior aspect.

The Corporeal Factor

We have already emphasized the integral nature of religion that has a concern for the complete human being. The human person is not only his *ātman*, his soul, his spirit, but also his body; that is, he has material ingredients. Religion stands for the salvation of the whole man and not only of a part of him.

It may well be that whereas some religions overstress the material elements, others are focused on the more spiritual nature of Man; however, in fact, all religions have to give an account of both, and even those that dismiss the present body as irrelevant are forced to postulate another subtle body and cannot avoid admitting, at least, some connection with the gross-body. This gross-body may be the carrier of the former or the prison, instrument, appearance, form, or matter of the soul and, as such, its peculiar existence will have to be taken into account.

The part that sacraments, symbols, *saṃskāra*, and rites play in all religions has not only a sociological meaning but also a particular relevance for this corporeal dimension of Man.

Properly speaking, Man *is* not his body, but he *has* a body and, besides, this body in which he is "incarnated" exerts an influence upon him. Man is not independent of his body, and the corporeal and material actions are means for his purification or vilification.

The agreement of religions regarding this point is almost unanimous. The differences lie in the doctrinal principles and in the interpretation of this subdimension, but almost every religion will agree that it cannot ignore the body and that the corporeal and material elements of Man must also be incorporated into religion. In other words, every religion pays attention to the body and to the material means by which Man has to work out his salvation. Indeed, from the extreme attitude of getting rid of the body down to a coarse, magical materialism there is a great distance. No religion, however, is so unconcerned with the material ingredients of Man as to ignore them completely.

The Cosmological Factor

Man is not only in communication with his body; he is also in communion with the whole universe. The attempt of religion to save Man is not least of all a cosmological adventure. The cosmos is not indifferent to what happens to Man, so to speak; and vice versa, the destiny of the universe has a repercussion on Man. Both are interconnected.

Religion has a cosmological dimension because, though religion is primarily interested in Man, it cannot neglect, first, that Man is interested in this cosmos and, second, that Man is not complete without the cosmos. There is still another, more strictly religious reason for this cosmological interest of religion. Religion, we said, is interested in Man in order to lead him to his end and fulfillment. Religion, therefore, cannot overlook the other side of the relation, namely God. That is to say, religion is interested in God, and the divine adventure with the world is not only a human event, but a cosmic process. Religion, leading Man toward his union with God, also brings him into communion with the universe. Religion automatically enlarges the horizon of Man and makes him aware of his connections with the rest of the universe. Besides the sonship of Man with God and his brotherhood with other men, religion makes him discover his fellowship with the whole cosmos.

We do not need to linger long over this subject, which is so important to a complete philosophy of religion. We may just mention the importance of this subdimension for an understanding of religion in our times and for bridging at least momentarily the gulf between traditional religions and modern science.

On the one hand, science purifies many a religious idea that, being true perhaps in what it wants to convey, remains false in its factual formulation and in the antiquated cosmological presuppositions on which it is based. The impact of science on the Christian interpretation of the Bible, for instance, cannot be minimized. The effects of science on the traditional beliefs of Hinduism, to cite another example, are also obvious, and for some are so alarming that they represent one of the greatest challenges Hinduism has ever had to face.

On the other hand, the cosmological aspects of religion may appear as the rope of salvation for science itself. It is an undeniable fact that the first impact of science on Man distracts him, even if does not separate him from religion. Science will again find its *ontonomical* place in the religious world or at least make its peace treaty with religion when religion rediscovers its cosmological dimension that alone can integrate science, put it in its place, and lead the scientific Man to a fuller discovery of a reality beyond the scientific sphere. Science and religion both speak about the cosmos and are interested in it, though from two very different perspectives. Both meet there. If religious cosmology is prepared to be more scientific, science will also be ready to become more religious. The place of *Man* in the cosmos is ultimately a religious issue.

Whatever this relation may be, religion cannot do without a certain vision of the universe—this belongs to the doctrinal dimension—and without relating Man to the universe and the universe to Man. Religion is not science and cannot decide the scientific value of scientific hypotheses, yet it cannot do without a cosmological dimension that requires the scientific collaboration of each epoch in order to express the cosmological substructure of the religious message in a way that is understandable to the people of that epoch.

In spite of the dangers and difficulties of the Christian theory of the assumption of all things in God (*apokatastasis*), the Hindu conception of the cycles of time (*kalpa*), astrology, alchemy, and the like are not just speculative excretions of little value, but are representations more or less pure of this constitutive dimension of religion.

The Angelic-Daimonical Dimension

If only for the sake of a certain completeness we should mention this dimension of religion here.

Man lives within a society, and he is an inhabitant of the cosmos with which he has deep exchanging relations in the most diverse manners; yet Man is immersed in still another invisible and supraworldly universe: the world of the spirits.

The struggle for the salvation of Man that is the incumbency of religion is more than an individual, personal, and cosmic affair; it is a part of a colossal adventure in which the world of the spirits is also involved. The religious salvation of Man is an event in which angels and devils, good and evil spirits are also at work.

It would amount to an abandonment of religion to deny this fact. The weakening of the sense of religion in modern times about which some modern thinkers complain and others rejoice finds here a very sensitive touchstone. Indeed the symbolic, mythical, and unscientific way in which almost all traditional religions clothe this aspect of reality makes it difficult for the modern mind to accept in toto the religious picture of the invisible spiritual cosmos, but no religion can abdicate from its belief that Man is not alone in working out his salvation, and that he is not the only existing spiritual being.

It is beyond the scope of this study to describe at length this spiritual realm and to show that to throw away the baby with the bathwater is not a feasible solution. It may suffice to offer here this general consideration.

It is only too obvious that the belief in the existence of spiritual beings has been one of the causes of the many evil by-products of religion: superstition, magic, fear, inhuman practices, and so on. It is also an undeniable fact that human evolution and especially scientific progress have succeeded in convincing Man that the picture of the animistic world is no longer acceptable. Yet the triumph of reason, of science, and of modern humanism is not strong enough to destroy the reality of the spiritual world in which Man has always believed and still believes, though perhaps in different forms.

Our main point is this: We started by saying that the claim of religion to give an integral answer to the existential problem of Man must be based upon anthropological grounds. We would like to point out that the existence of the spiritual world is also an anthropological fact. It is not perhaps detectable by means of mere reason, it may only be acceptable by faith, but it is somehow discernible by that integral human wisdom for which our times are again groping. Poetry, art in general, even medicine, besides depth-psychology and philosophy, are discovering again that it may well be that Man is not alone in the realm of the spirit. We do not mean the existence of other beings in the astronomical world, we refer to the other realm of the angelic and daimonical world that not only witnesses the human struggle for salvation but also interferes in it.

Caution here is not enough. Angelology and demonology have to be rethought and reshaped. We are neither propounding any interpretation nor discussing the value of any of the similar doctrines of the several religions. We are just trying to expose three ideas:

1. *Phenomenologically*, the traditional and almost universal belief of religion in a world of spiritual beings cannot be dismissed just because of the many aberrations that were interwoven with such a belief.

2. *Anthropologically*, there is an open field of research to investigate whether the effects of such spirits can be detected. And we may add that the present trend of our culture is moving toward this realm of research.

3. *Religiously*, no man in his noble effort to modernize and reform his religion should forget that this belief is an ingredient of his faith, however different the interpretation and formulation of the fact may be expressed. He should not give up his faith on this point too easily. Perhaps this will provide a guiding factor even in the scientific and anthropological investigations of the near future. Indeed he should cleanse this belief of all the excrescences of the past.

There is also a double aspect here. We should like to describe these two aspects in Christian terminology only for the reason that in comparison with similar doctrines—that of Hinduism, for instance—it appears to be more demythologized and hence more comprehensible to the modern mind.

The Angelic Aspect

Man is one of the beings working out his salvation and going back to God. Beyond human time—and hence within a certain contemporaneity with Man—purely spiritual beings are also going back to God. Because of the unique cosmic adventure of the whole creation there is an interrelation between Man and the spiritual world just as we have seen that there is also an interconnection between Man and man, and between Man and the material cosmos. Because the relation here is between a purely spiritual being and incarnated spirit, the relationship is personal, free, invisible, and the priority or initiative belongs to the more perfect partner, namely the angel. The latter help and inspire Man, or, in other words, effect upon him a spiritual gravitational attraction—force—that helps him to realize his goal.

As religion opens the understanding of the believer so that his relationship with God may be what it has to be, similarly religion opens the eyes of its follower so that he may discover these superior beings and the influence they exert upon him without jeopardizing his liberty.

Religion would say the opposite of what an incredulous phenomenology would affirm. It is not that religion shackles people with a fear of spirits; it is rather that religion tries, more or less successfully, to free Man from the fear of spirits by teaching him how to deal with them.

The Demoniacal Aspect

The human journey toward salvation is not an automatic process. Human freedom means that Man can fall short of his destiny. The demons are spirits that have failed in such an endeavor. Their gravitational influence is therefore negative; they play the role of tempters of the human race. Because religion recognizes an Absolute above such spirits, a God who is God of the evil spirits, temptation is always subjected to the will of God and therefore never exerts a total influence upon Man, who thus does not fall as an impotent prey to the demons. Moreover, one of the roles of religion is to strengthen the human being in his fight against the devils and to provide him with the means by which he can overcome the trial and emerge victorious from their temptations.

It is an unpopular side of religion indeed, especially among those who are no longer "popular," that is, common people, and it is very often with reason that the elite rejects childish or materialistic or just untenable ideas about the demoniac world. Yet sometimes its unpopularity comes from being a constant reminder to Man of his insufficiency and a call to him to humility and caution. Certainly it requires a religious spirit to recognize that Man is subject to influences of higher beings and that he must be in friendship with God if he is to overcome the temptations to which he is exposed.

The Immanent-Transcendent Dimension

From the point of view of a philosophical analysis the seven dimensions already mentioned appear to us as the main characteristics of religion. That is to say, analyzing philosophically some of the religious *facts* under the light of the nature of Man, or, if we prefer, analyzing the religious *data* and understanding them as derivatives of the very anthropological structure of our being, we discover that sixfold structure of religion: Man is an *intelligent* person, a *free* agent, a *sensible* animal, a *social* being, and a part of the *material* and *spiritual* universe. Now, we should try to submit religion as such to a kind of philosophical *synthesis*, that is, we should consider religion as a whole, trying to understand it under the light of our ultimate philosophical categories. In this way we discover a new dimension that does not lie on the same analytical level of the former ones, but on another different synthetic stratum.

Man is a religious being, or in other words, his being is religious and this religiosity is not an external aspect of his being, but belongs to his very nature. His being, his human being, is a contingent one, or as we have already stated, an imperfect one, an itinerant being, a *not-yet-being*, a being in the making. But precisely because the religious nature of Man is not an accidental feature, religion shares in this peculiar character of the human being itself.

To make these statements clear, we should state the ultimate metaphysical categories under which we see the being of Man and, in consequence, the ultimate nature of religion.

If there is a God—and in one way or another all religions affirm this conditional—He is properly speaking the only Being and all other beings *are* insofar as they *participate* in Him. Moreover, they are and they can only be *from*, *with*, and *through* Him. Each being is only a spark, a beam, a part, an image, an appearance . . . of Him.

We cannot avoid using a definite terminology, but we still hope that the majority of philosophers of religion, even if they express this problem in a different way and interpret it with minor divergences, could agree with what we mean to say. It is not difficult, for instance, to see that even a so-called atheistic religion like Buddhism would agree with what we intend to say, though it would use quite a different terminology, speaking not of "God," of "being" or "participation," but of "Absolute," of "void," of "pure succession," "states of consciousness," and so forth.

To put an example of the different kinds of language one may use to express a determined thought, here is a sentence expressed in Christian terminology: *we are-not-yet* (our being is a real be-coming, we *are* what we shall be, our *are* is a *shall be* and we shall be God); the same affirmation according to Hinduism would have a completely different accent: *we are-not-yet* (our *are* is only Brahman; insofar as we *are*, we are Brahman and insofar as we are *not-yet* Brahman, we *are* just a *not-yet*); according to Buddhism this sentence would have a totally different intonation: *we are-not-yet* (there is no *are* to be or to be-come, there is a pure unsubstantial *yet* that is *not*). Therefore we can say that *we are-not-yet*, we are *not-yet*, we are-*not*. But in all cases there is an *x* moving toward an end, the flux of an *x* toward a *y*. What is meant is that *x* is a function of *y* and that religion is precisely that solution which claims to fulfill the equation $y = f(x)$.

Or in simpler words, religion is a fundamental dimension of the human being. It depends not only on the nature of Man but also on the nature of God, so to speak, for Man himself depends entirely on Him. This means that an integral anthropological study of religion would not be complete if we sever the nature of Man from God, if we simply take Man as an *autonomous* being with only external or extra-ontological relations with Him. This leads us to say that the nature of religion does not depend on the autonomous nature of Man but on his *ontonomous* structure of being *in*, *with*, and *through* God. Or in other words, the essence of religion ultimately depends on the nature of God.

On the other hand, as Man is not quite God, but has a peculiar and specific nature that absolutely depends on God—whatever God and whatever this character of creatureliness might be—and as God is not exhausted in Man, so to speak, but is something more, besides and above Him, religion presents this typical feature of polarity as a kind of bridge depending, on one side, on the nature of Man, and, on the other, on the nature of God. We know that ultimately religion depends only on the Absolute, because Man himself is nothing but a certain relationship to It. But this relationship is not discovered if we look only at Man in himself without realizing that he is only the human term of a complex situation. That is why religion presents this character of polarity, that is, a dependence on both the nature of the Absolute manifested in the Will of God and the nature of Man manifested in his response to that Will.

Let us consider briefly this special polarity, describing both sides of this dimension.

The Immanent Side

Religion is a human dimension, rooted in the depths of Man's nature. Religion quiets not only that which has been called the religious feelings or instincts of Man, namely, his need for self-surrender, for superhuman love, and so on, but it also answers the most profound thirst of the human being for its fullness and perfection.

Religion fits so well as an answer to all the professional human longings that it can easily appear as a kind of projection of such desires into an artificial or man-made God, "invented" in order to fill up that emptiness that every human being experiences. On a metaphysical level this is not altogether wrong. Human nature is not complete and has in itself the dynamism for projecting, for throwing in front of itself, the very end of its existence. Hope, in theological terms, is a constitutive ingredient of our being. However, this leap to the transcendence out of its own immanence is in itself the effect of that very transcendence.

Or, in simpler words: Man constructs for himself a God, because God Himself has made Man so. Those philosophers that speak of God as being made in the image of Man are only ontologically formulating the classical argument for His existence. Man "re-creates," "discovers" God in himself and, out of himself, simply because God has "created," has "discovered" him so. He discovers the God he wants and needs, because he has been made a "God-wanting" and a "God-needing" creature.

Religion is an immanent feature of Man to such an extent that he does not need to go outside to discover God and religion; he has only to penetrate into himself and to listen to his own ontological hope to find the divine ground from which he has emerged. This God, who may exist outside, is also inside his being and speaks to his most profound nature from within. The God from above and the religion from without meet, in the religious Man, with the God from beneath and the religion from within. Moreover, he recognizes the God from above and accepts the religion from without because he feels, discovers, experiences . . . , because he *believes* that this is the very God he belongs to and this the very religion of which he is in need. Man has a thirst for God and a need for religion because this thirst and this need are constituents of his very being.

What we are looking for, *ultimately*, in all our wishes, tendencies, and struggles is nothing else but God. What we are in need of, *ultimately*, in all our urges is nothing other than the ontic growth of our being, that is, religion.

Religion answers as a final instance to all human needs, because it is the answer; it comes to meet all longings of men, because it is the very way to human perfection. This human perfection, as a fact, is split up into an almost unlimited number of fragments, and each fragment has an autonomy that makes possible a certain development of a particular value at the cost of damage to the whole.

Secularization is precisely this, a historical process that breaks the—religious—unity of Man for the sake of his partial perfection. Modern culture with its wonderful partial achievements is perhaps one of the most striking examples of this in the history of mankind.

The integration of all human values into the religious unity of Man, in view of his ultimate and harmonic perfection, is without a doubt one of the most urgent tasks of our times. Up to what point this is possible or merely the desire for a lost paradise is again another problem. Creation, fall, redemption, and resurrection are the Christian milestones of such an itinerary.

We should not lose sight of our pilgrim status and be too optimistic regarding the quenching of human urges here on Earth. Religion is not yet human perfection, but is the way, the integral way, toward the fullness of Man, toward his divine fulfillment.

A very important aspect of religion, which has baffled more than one "modern" scholar, appears here. One of the deepest roots of religion is precisely that part of Man called today the unconscious. Man is a wayfarer, a pilgrim not only in body and in the upper part of his spirit, but also in his amorphous psychophysical structure, in his unconscious magma. Religion, taking hold of the entire human being, leads and directs those unconscious depths of the human being like a magnet.

This explains not only the well-known fact laid bare by depth-psychology that a person without an appropriate degree of religion gets his spiritual bowels upset and lives in danger of falling into one of many pathological perturbations, but it also explains why many of the practices and devices of religion refer and belong to these unconscious strata of our being.

For centuries Sanskrit, Latin, Arabic, Syriac, and other liturgical languages have quenched the religious thirst of the masses in spite of the fact that they do not understand the meaning of the words employed; a simple *amen* is sufficient for them.

Indeed, the whole point of the unconscious is that it ceases to be such at the moment it is thought or spoken of. In such a moment a liturgy in an archaic language, for instance, will not suffice, but up to that moment it was quite in order. The practical problem increases when you have several strata of the population involved in the same issue. A first, but always provisional step is to provide translations or books for those who can read, but this cannot stop the movement once launched. This is just an example.

In the same way that a healthy man takes the necessary food and does not care about his metabolism anymore, so a religious man has the confidence in the structures of this world and of his being that they will work according to a plan—which he has not previously established—provided he does his share in it. To put it in other words, religion gives Man the confidence that God is working within and that He knows best.

Obviously the boundary line between confidence and presumption, between trust and carelessness, between surrender and fanaticism, is often only too vague. Nor is this all. History shows us an unmistakable progress in self-consciousness, in the reflective mood of our mind. Man asks more and more immediate *whys*; Man becomes more and more reflectively conscious of himself, especially of his being detached from the tribe, group, caste, society, family, and so on.

The increase in religious defections in monastic life, or the increase of divorces or even of suicides, is not a sign of an increase in human wickedness. Those things until now were in the unconscious and were almost impossible to imagine. Children have always passed through times when they have felt parental authority a heavy burden, but only today do they show a personal individualistic reaction that may lead to a break of family links, a thing that was unthinkable and subjectively impossible in other times.

Because God, the unconscious, and the unknown are hidden values, they have often been indiscriminately taken for one and the same thing. With the dispelling of technical ignorance and the increasing of reflective consciousness it seems as if the place for God were diminishing—as if He were only there to cover the holes of our ignorance. Many religious crises are an outcome of such a process, which after all is the crisis of innocence: it has the appearance of an offer of enlightened answer to why the prayer has not been answered, the temptation not overcome, the perfection not attained, the promise not kept, the love not returned, the knowledge not sufficient, and so on, because we "discover" the second causes working better and more efficiently than the first cause. Let us adduce as an example the cases in which the scientific fact seems to explain something that up to the present day would have appeared as miraculous, the historical fact that contradicts a common belief—say, for instance, that of the Christians some time ago that Man on Earth could not be older than seven thousand years—the psychological fact that explains things up to now taken for granted, or "unscientifically" accepted. All this lets science appear as a better and more efficient substitute for religious beliefs. Thus, the process of pushing down the realm of the unconscious appears to be connected with a displacing of God to an ever increasingly remote corner.

Meditation offers us a typical example of the role of the unconscious in religion and of the changing attitude of our modern mind. For thousands of years the ideal of a certain type of meditation was to plunge again into the unconscious, with the underlying—sometimes also unconscious—idea that there we do not offer resistance to God and that there, God is and acts and takes care of us. We do not think of Hindu and Buddhist meditation only, but of Christian contemplation as well.

Modern times, having discovered the unconscious—and thus having wounded its unconsciousness—put the ideal of meditation not in abolishing thinking deeply on one subject, they insist on concentration and afterward on examination of conscience, resolutions, decisions, discovery of a line of conduct and of a purpose of action, and so on. Meditation becomes exactly the opposite of what it was before: no more a plunging into the unfathomable depths—here God and God alone may take care of us—but the effort is laid in making the unconscious merge into the consciousness, so that we may not be deceived and led astray by the former. Doing this, we take religion out of the realm of the unconscious and relegate it to the sphere of mere consciousness. It would sound preposterous for some people today to put the ideal of worship in the *practice* of contemplation without *knowing* about it, as the Christian Fathers of the Desert did. The present reactions within Christianity, for instance, or the renewal of monastic life are just efforts to regain this unconscious dimension of religion. To worship is not to know that I worship. To worship, and at the same time to know it, can be perfection, but also a hindrance if it distracts, or worse, if it replaces the worship.

We should now close this digression by briefly pointing out our main argument. The unconscious, in one way or another, also belongs to religion and is "unconsciously" led by religion toward the fulfillment of its functions. Moreover, the unconscious, though not alone in this respect, offers us an example of the immanent side of Man as a working place of God, who is the other pole of religion.

The Transcendent Side

Philosophy of religion—when authentic and unbiased—discovers that religion is not only founded on the nature of Man, but also on the nature of God, that religion is not only an answer, but also a call, not simply the *complement* to our shortcomings, but the *supplement* to our own "nature."

In other words, Man does not know his own existence exhaustively, he does not understand his own thirst, he is at a loss with his own longings, he does not reach the end, the depth, or the summit of his own being. He is still itinerant, on the way, and religion appears not only as the implicit, immanent answer that fulfills the structure of his essence, but also as the explicit, transcendent calling of his life.

Almost all religions without exception—in one sense or other—claim to be not man-made constructions but God-given solutions. This transcendent dimension belongs essentially to the very nature of religion. For each person the discovery of his religious path undoubtedly passes through a certain immanence; nevertheless no religion, and certainly not the authentic personal spirituality of a great religious soul, stops here. The exclusive immanent interpretation of a certain "modernistic" mind is the very destruction of religion itself. The transcendence must also be there, regardless of the manner in which this transcendence may afterward be interpreted.

Three considerations will help us to the understanding of this transcendent side. The first is a *phenomenological* one, derived from the very fact of the existence of religions. The second is *metaphysical*, drawn from the nature of being. The third is *dialectical*, taken from the logical exigencies of the existence of God.

1. As a fact, religion does not appear as a pure human activity toward perfection or toward God. It appears, rather, as an open human passivity vis-à-vis God's activity, which is calling us, exacting us, commanding us, loving us . . . in order that we may go to Him and so attain our destiny—namely, perfection, bliss, and so forth. The first factor of every religion is the activity of the gods. In every religion we have *revelation* in one form or another, *incarnation* in one way or another, *sacraments* in a great variety of rites. The value of them may be very different, but their presence is a proof that the existential character of religion cannot be explained away as human construction. Religion is not a human "hobby" but a divine concern. Religions are more God's business than Man's affair.

2. Man is not a mere logical being, and his future, therefore, is not simply the inexorable resultant of given forces. His end and the existential goal of his life can be surmised and even known in general terms, but the factual and definite end, the concrete fullness of his being is logically unpredictable because it is not logically given in his present. I may discover that I have to be truly *my-self*, that I have to reach perfect *happiness*, that I have to know *reality*, that I have to become *God*; but I do not know and I cannot have a concrete knowledge about the true nature of this my-self, happiness, reality, and God until I reach that state in which those things are given to me, that is, unless God Himself, the Absolute Itself manifests them to me, reveals them to me and, at least, discloses for me the existential and definite meaning wrapped in those concepts. Moreover, not only the existential and concrete nature of the end of my life is unknown to me—because it is not the mere conclusion of a syllogism—but also the means and, above all, the strength, the grace, the power to reach it do not depend on me alone. If God does not help me to reach my end I will not reach it. Certainly, this help of God is given in my own being; after all, I am His being, His own, much more than I am *my* own property. However, this divine strength, this power, this will, this grace is, again, not a kind of blind necessity gravitating upon my being, but is a real and vital, free help of God—free because all that the Absolute does is done utterly free by definition (not of the Absolute, but of Liberty itself)—which depends, in consequence, not on me, but on Him.

3. If, on an ultimate level, we are not able to know what Man *is* and much less what he *will be*, a fortiori we are not able to know what God is and what He has called us *to be*. Any authentic religious attitude respects not only the liberty and the initiative, so to speak, of God, and realizes that the future of Man is not the end of an automatic process, but also recognizes that the destiny of the human being depends on God and, thus, that we can by no means deduce dialectically the concrete destiny of any individual. Neither can we logically infer what He wants from us *in concreto* or how the potentialities of our being are meant to be developed—*by* Him and in consequence *in* themselves.

Neither can we, and much less can our minds, limit God nor set boundaries to His Being. Nor can we know—speaking a language that is not to be interpreted anthropomorphically—his "plans" for us, "beforehand," or His "Will" concerning us. The Absolute remains always absolute, unconditioned, unlimited, free; it can act as it acts, as it "likes," and there is no "reason," no "motive," no "ground," no "anything" beyond it.

This means that we cannot have a closed and finished idea of religion, that we cannot a priori say what religion is ultimately or looks like unless we "know" it from God Himself, and even then, our "knowing" can only be a humble "faith" in fear and in love, in confidence and in symbols.

The first important consequence of this is the constitutive openness of religion, or in other words, the constant readiness of religion to listen to God, to conform itself to His Will. Again, putting it in different terms, this transcendent subdimension of religion amounts to the acceptance not only of the development and growth of religion, but also of its expectant character. Religion is essentially eschatological, not simply because it is concerned with the ultimate things, but also because it is always expecting the coming of the Lord, the manifestation of God.

We could develop this idea at length, but it will suffice our purpose just to mention a direct consequence of this character—which every authentic religion shows—of a real dependence on the Will of God. This consequence is the concept of conversion.

Religion is constantly open to con-version, that is, to a deepening into its own nature and the consequent changing conversion meaning a going into the depths of oneself again and again in order to discover a fuller truth within. Religion is an open reality. It can never be a closed system or a static organism. The moment a religion is closed in itself, it does not admit influences from above or about, the moment it considers itself perfect, and thus no longer perfectable, it becomes not only deaf to the voice of the Spirit but also barren, and it could well cease to be a religion. Religion owes an allegiance to the past and to the present; religion is bound by tradition and by its present commitments, yet religion is linked above all with God, with the living God who has the initiative and who has not yet closed His chapter of Providence for men. Religions, like individuals, must always be ready for conversion. Let us add immediately that conversion does not, and cannot, mean a changing over to another religion, but means a conversion to God. However, the way of that conversion to God may sometimes pass through another religion.

The recognition of the transcendent keeps religion free from stagnation and from being self-centered and self-sufficient, but paradoxically that transcendence ties religion to the Earth and binds it to the concrete destiny of Man.

Perhaps this is the reason why this transcendent side of religion is the deepest and most mysterious dimension, and at the same time the most concrete and striking—the first outcome of this subdimension being *historicity*. Religion does not deal primarily with symbols or with ideas, but with men, with concrete, existing, historical beings, whatever the interpretation of history or even of Man may be. Moreover, religion is not a vague consciousness of God, but a definite and existential way to Him. And this God—be He an infinite, groundless, and unutterable Being beyond all human conceptions—appears, manifests, descends, or incarnates Him-self in historically existing forms and speaks "through" Prophets and Signs. Religions claim to know His Will, His Doctrine, and have something from Him in their doctrines or commandments, Scriptures, or traditions. Christianity goes to the furthest end in its claim of "having" God Himself in the Eucharist.

Religion is a historical reality, and it is as essentially historical as Man. After all, religion is there to lead this historical being which is Man to his real—suprahistorical—end. Historicity is an essential feature of religion.

·It looks, prima facie, like a paradox, but it is nevertheless true that precisely this historicity is the best bulwark for this transcendence. Precisely this character of religion as a free historical manifestation warrants the absolute liberty of God and His superiority and independence vis-à-vis Man. It is He who reveals Himself to whom He wants and for a purpose He alone knows. It is He who speaks through the Prophets, here in one language, there in another; He who here forgives, there punishes; here warns with His Justice, there lavishes His Mercy on us; here hides Himself under the veil of an impersonal Law, there manifests Himself almost indiscriminately in the whole of nature. A living religion always has a living God. What are miracles, after all, if not this constant, historical intervention of the Divine into Man's daily life? All religions claim to have miracles to their credit, since a religion as such could exist only with this living and historical contact with the Divinity.

This historicity-character also shows the transcendence of God—and of religion—because it leads us to discover the origin and the formal justification of religion not in the nature of Man, or in his reason, nor in any philosophy, but in the very nature of God, in His sovereign and absolute design-will with Man.

Of course, this character of historical reality does not overshadow the complementary feature of religious immanence and of trans-historical reality of God and of Man's destiny. Some religions will stress this historical character less than others, but insofar as they are religions—and religion—they cannot abolish it altogether. For example, Hinduism among the misleadingly called "great" religions does not stress very much the historicity of the facts of its mythology, but sees them principally as symbols meant to convey to us attributes of the Attributeless, which otherwise would be out of the reach of the ordinary man. However, the symbols as such exist in history and are historical realities. It may be that for some Kṛṣṇa is not the son of Devakī and the disciple of Aṅgirasa, but the living figure of the Bhagavad-gītā; for that culture and religion he is more than a mere idea, he is a *historical symbol* even if as a human person he never existed.

While other religions may stress the "symbolic" character of their historical tenets, Christianity, for cultural and historical reasons, stresses the historicity of its Founder, never forgetting that the historical Jesus is a real man—the son of Mary—as well as the Son of God. Unlike any other human birth and being, he *had* a human nature, but *is* not a human person. He is identical to the suprahistorical Christ, alive yesterday, today, and in all eternity, the origin and final end of all creatures, the one by whom everything has been made, and also identical to the sacramental Christ living in the hearts of all who love Him, and present in the supratemporal and yet historical reality of the Eucharist.

Transcendence does not only connote independence and historicity, but also revelation and even incarnation. The Divine can only descend and be incarnated because it is above Man and without flesh.

The most common form of God's intervention in Man's life is His "coming down" in the form of "speaking" to us, "revealing" to us what He likes to unveil, and this, not in order to magnify Himself or to humiliate us, but for the sake of healing. His words are always a message of salvation. But we cannot foresee His revelation, or limit it, put conditions to it, or deduce it. It is the free act of His good pleasure to which we have to listen and accept. Religion is the conductor of that divine revelation.

In one sense, God speaks to everyone; moreover, every man is in some way a *divine utterance*, and the whole universe is a *word* of His *Logos*, as it were. This threefold speech, which is a *psychological* inspiration, an *anthropological* illumination, and an *ontological* locution does not exhaust His communication with Man nor exclude the need for His *religious* word in direct revelation. Revelation is not only possible; it is a fact that all religions acknowledge. Prophecy is an essential particularity of religion itself. The prophet is the man who hears, sees, perceives divine revelation and transmits it to his fellow beings.

The Temporal-Eternal Dimension

We should mention the last dimension of religion, which is closely connected with the previous one and which follows it almost as a corollary, and yet has a consistency of its own.

We have already said that Man is a temporal being. If our main argument, based on the anthropological foundation of religion, is right, we have to say that religion is also a temporal reality. In fact, time belongs to one of the most important religious categories. There are religions without a clear-cut idea of God. There are some with hardly a concern for morals or such, and so on. I do not know of any religion for which time is not a main concern. A nonmetaphysical religion may not agree in saying that Man has to reach the fullness of his being or that the Absolute is the Being. It will, however, accept that Man is inserted in time and that his destiny is to transcend time, in one way or another, and that the Absolute is either eternal, or timeless, or somehow above or beyond time.

Birth and death are just two moments *in* or *of* time, and no religion can bypass this problem. In fact, salvation appears in almost every religion as a redemption of time.

It is an almost impossible task to summarize in a few lines so important a chapter of religion. We shall proffer only a couple of ideas in order not to leave void this extremely relevant dimension of religion.

Without entering into philosophical discussions on the nature of time we may say that the science of religions discovers not only that religions deal with the problem of time but that the problem of time as such—that is, the very consciousness of time and its implications—is primarily a religious problem. There is indeed a philosophical as well as a psychological and a scientific problem of time, but originally, and we would like to add principally, the category of time is a religious category.

Time, in fact, means not just succession or change, as a naturalist or a scientist with a very specialized eye would see it.

Time, above all, means the peculiar mode of Man's existence—faced with birth, death, and resurrection—and of all other living beings faced with a similar dialectical or vital process. Time is not directly opposed to rest, changelessness, and the like but to a timeless mode of existence that some would call eternity.

Every religion shows here, again, the double polarity that we already know.

The Temporal Side

Religion aspires to lead the temporal Man to a timeless or to a supratemporal state. Religion is precisely the bridge between these two worlds, and therefore claims to be temporal like Man, on the one hand, and supratemporal like God, on the other. An almost common feature of religion is that the extra-temporal factor is somehow integrated or linked with the temporal existence already here on Earth. Religion brings the eternal down to Earth, as it were, lets it be discovered—or believed—that the eternal already "begins" here and is contemporary with the temporal. Moreover, the *nityanityāvastuviveka* (the discrimination between the temporal and the eternal)[4] is again one of the first conditions for our authentic religious life.

This relationship can be interpreted in very many ways indeed. The different types of spirituality of many religions find here their theoretical foundations: the goal of human life is to cross the river of temporal existence and to be inserted into the eternal.

We find three different types of spirituality according to the three interpretations of time, or rather, of the relationship between time and eternity.

1. Time is just an illusion or merely appearance, so that the end of Man is to overcome—or to deny—time and the whole of temporal existence in order to realize, to discover, to plunge into the eternal.

2. Eternity or the definitive state of Man is beyond—almost after—time so that eternity follows time, and when the latter ends, the second enters into force.

3. Time is neither the stage previous to eternity, nor the mere illusion of a nonexistent reality, but is a real process, a real growing up, an ontical becoming *by* which

---

[4] Cf. Òscar Pujol, ed., *Diccionari Sànscrit-Català* (Barcelona: Enciclopèdia Catalana, 2005), 467–68: "*nitya*: eternal, permanent, indestructible; *anitya*: a-eternal, transitory, perishable; *viveka*: discernment, discrimination; according to the vedānta this discrimination is a reflection which consists in knowing that only *brahman* is lasting, while all other things in the world are perishable."

and *in* which the itinerant being *trans-forms* its mode of existence and reaches its definitive state. We shall come back to this third via media a little later.

The Oriental religions show a tendency toward the first type of spirituality; so-called primitive religions, to the second. Christianity offers a typical example of the third attitude. And yet no religion is completely void of tenets referring to the other points. Our division is not an exclusive one, but rather one of a spiritual emphasis. No religion, for instance, totally forgets that the eternal state is somehow dependent on the works and actions performed during temporal existence. No religion would, on the other hand, put temporality and eternity absolutely on the same level so that the everlasting life could be considered just as another temporal existence, and so on.

It is also noteworthy that every religion deals very seriously with time and is directly concerned with it, whether it be just to deny it, or to transcend it, or to let it be transformed or informed by another principle. Time may be the obstacle, or vehicle, or the means for reaching the religious end of Man, but it is always one of the main concerns for religions.

Another consequence of the temporal dimension of religion and connected also with its historicity is the temporal growth or evolution of religions.

Because of this second subdimension—that is, the eternity-character of religion—religion instinctively offers a resistance to and shows a mistrust of any temporal change in its structure. And yet history proves that religions follow the temporal evolution of Man and not only show signs of youth, maturity, and old age, but also that they adapt themselves to the various conditions of the temporal evolution of the individual and of society. In fact, one and the same religion in two different "times" would look to an outsider almost like two completely different religions.

The Everlasting Side

One of the greatest proofs of the genuineness and authenticity of religion is not only its adaptability to the times but more especially its fidelity—in spite of the inopportunity, or unpopularity, or even sad consequences on the purely human level that such a loyalty may carry with it—to what it believes to be the untouchable deposit of everlasting values—of which a religion feels itself to be the guardian.

In spite of the lack of flexibility and of intelligence that sometimes such conflicts show, the cry of "*non possumus*" that every honest believer is bound to utter when the temptation of a worldly compromise menaces him belongs to the most serious and grand pages of the history of religions.

Religion owes loyalty not only to the present Man but also to the man of all times—and very often what appeared to be religious stubbornness has afterward proved to be a profound honesty that has preserved for later generations what the optimistic reaction of a former one wanted to destroy.

Religion is for Man, for the temporal man living in this world, and yet it cannot forget that it stands precisely for the everlasting and supraworldly values of that very temporal man. A religion may at times stress its otherworldliness excessively, but no authentic religion can forgo this, its most specific feature. A totally worldly religion would not be a religion at all. The kingdom of God may be interpreted in the most diverse ways, but every religion has a kingdom of God that is distinct from the realm of Man at the present time.

Obviously the interpretations that religions give to the definitive and supratemporal status of Man differ widely. The difference, however, is more doctrinal and sentimental than concerning the thing itself.

In connection with the above-mentioned via media, in the conception of time we wish to introduce a concept that may prove of some use in the clarification of this important religious issue. It is the concept of *tempiternity*.

The consequences of what is meant by such a word seem to us to be also relevant to the mystical problem as such, but we shall restrain ourselves from doing more than sketching this concept, having only our particular context in view.

If eternity is the proper mode of the divine existence—of the "duration" of God, one could add for brevity's sake—if *eviternity* is the angelic mode of permanence, *temporality* is the specific human way of being—that is, of being temporal, namely, in time during the earthly pilgrimage. Temporality is a purely philosophical category that expresses the way of human existence here on Earth. What happens to Man when he leaves time and enters into everlasting life? With perhaps very few exceptions religions in general do not agree in saying that Man merges in such a way into God that he completely ceases to be. Everlasting life does not exactly mean eternity; the divinization of Man does not need to be interpreted as a total disappearance of the creature, and yet the mystical dimension of religion is constantly there to remind us that any human end short of a total divinization and oneness with the Absolute is not what Man is longing for or worthy of God Himself.

The problem could be put like this: What happens to Man once his time is exhausted or fulfilled?

Temporality is the human dimension of Man during his permanence on Earth. What happens with it once Man has finished his pilgrimage? It is here that we could introduce the concept of *tempiternity*.

The main characteristic of human temporality is the gathering up of the past into the present, as it were, so that the human temporal itinerary is not just a walk along the path of a temporal evolution but the assimilation of the past into the present and the ontical growth by means of this peculiar temporal accumulation. This temporal being that is Man does not leave his past behind but carries it with him. This growth finishes when time is over. Time has played its role and disappears from Man; Man is no longer temporal. But the everlasting Man is not just, because of this, eternal; his temporal scar remains. Temporality has given way to this peculiar and definitive mode of existence that we call *tempiternity*.

Man is full, he is fully divinized, he shares in the Godhead without any limitation yet his mode of existence is not eternal, nor is it temporal but *tempiternal*. He has no past and no future, he lives in a perfect actualized present, but he "has had" past and future. He *is* God, we could say, but he *was* not God before, whereas God was always God and has never had any "before." Man has *become* God. God does not become God—but Man does. Temporality is no more time, has no more change, nor potentiality, yet it is not just eternity. It is rather a theandric existence.

From a Christian point of view we would add that the above-mentioned tempiternity is the peculiar mode of the theandrical existence of Christ—and of the whole Christ also, once united in the *Logos* with the Father, so that really there shall be only God in all.

We surmise that without any need of such a terminology, most of the religions on Earth point toward this everlasting state of a man, of being one with the Absolute and yet conserving somehow the relic of "having been," "having reached," the Absolute.

We must, thus, emphasize the polyhedral nature of religion. Religion, for example, has a *personal* aspect and an *impersonal* one, in the same way that it has a *conscious* one and an *unconscious* one. The list is not finished, and we could add other aspects, such as the *historical* and the *geographical*, but we are satisfied with having touched upon the most important dimensions.

*

Summarizing, we can say that a study of religion cannot overlook this ninefold aspect, existing in every religion and belonging to its integral nature. The great danger in the noble aim of bringing together the several religions of the world lies in the one-sided consideration of this complex theandric fact which is religion. If, for instance, we consider a religion without the first ontical dimension that is disclosed to us in a mystical experience, we shall have no religion at all, but only a dead body of rites and doctrines. If we take the first aspect into account, ignoring the second intellectual dimension, we shall have not a religion but rather a pure, ineffable experience. Taking the first with the third and fourth dimensions we would have an arbitrary system of cult and behavior. If we overlook the eighth aspect of religion as a divine manifestation, we shall miss the actual reality of religion and deal only with our own concept of it, and so on.

On the other hand, we must again stress that these nine dimensions of religion do not all have the same importance, nor are they on the same level. We accept the term "dimension," always bearing in mind the heterogeneity of the different dimensions. Religion is then characterized as a *heterogeneous nine-dimensional theandrical fact*.

When we say *theandrical* we want to give equal stress to the human and the divine aspects of religion. Short of this balanced view we should fall either into a mere "naturalistic" conception of religion, leveling down the divine initiative to our needs, ideas, and preconceptions—we grant and allot to God the place He has to take and the role He has to play—or we should fall into a superstitious and unnatural idea of religion as the whim and caprice of a *mere* transcendent God amusing Himself with men. Religion as the *very* link between God and Man can only be properly conceived by taking both factors into account. Religion is a *theandric* fact that can only be understood if we regard Man not as an isolated, self-sufficient being, but as the mysterious and wonderful meeting place where God and evil, spirit and matter, individual and community, person and universe, struggle, come together, and meet. "Quid est homo, quod memor es eius" (What are human beings that you spare a thought for them [Ps 8:4])?

Religions

If religion is what we have intended to describe, we should now investigate how far and to what extent the several religious creeds of the world fulfill this integral conception of religion, and examine the problem of their unity or diversity.

Dealing now with the problem of religions we must consider, before anything else, the serious question of their authenticity or inauthenticity.

We have until now presupposed that we are dealing with religions, that is, with authentic religions. However, we cannot discard a priori the possibility of inauthentic forms of religion. We do not refer here to the truth- or untruth-contents of religions; some religions may have a richer truth-content than others, but nevertheless be authentic religions. For example, according to Christianity, Judaism is not a false religion, but a pre-Christian one that, without denying its fundamental tenets, finds in Christianity its implementation and fullness—let us recall that the Christian exigency of death and resurrection implies that it is the same thing that rises again. Yet, it is possible to find inauthentic forms of religion, and as a matter of fact, the history of religions shows us examples of them.

This inauthenticity can be of two different kinds. A religion as such can be inauthentic or it can have only inauthentic *forms*.

Obviously we are not concerned with this second possibility, which being important for each religion does not affect our study of religion as a whole. Superstition and Pharisaism are two of these inauthentic forms that may creep into any religion. Superstition is an abuse of something right; it is a faith shifted to an object or an action unfit to sustain that faith. It is a degeneration of belief, but the underlying attitude of faith may not be wrong.

Hardly any religion can boast of not having inauthentic forms that the weakness of human character has attached to it. Moreover, the inward vitality of each religion could in some way be measured by this incessant process of cleansing its imperfections and impurities and getting rid of its extinct forms. Pharisaism, though it can well cause the death of a religion, is nothing but a transfer of the religious attitude from the essentials to the nonessentials, from the spirit to the letter. However, the attitude as such is fundamentally a religious one. We can hardly overestimate the tragedy of Pharisaism, but this now is not our point.

Yet there is also the possibility of truly inauthentic religions, that is, not of degenerated forms within a religion, but of a corrupted religion.

An inauthentic religion could be a false religion in the full sense of the word—that is, it would not be religion at all. It would be something with the appearance of religion, but not fulfilling the essential function of it. History shows us diabolical and prostituted pseudoreligions that in some times and in some places take the appearance of religion and mislead men into fanatical or inhuman degradation. Generally speaking, this integral inauthenticity does not last long. Human nature and divine grace are both factors of such great importance in shaping religion that they do not permit a complete triumph of such irreligiousness.

It is clear anyway that we have not to deal here with the imperfections of religions, nor with the nonauthentic religions, but with those that undoubtedly are truly religions. It is among these that the question of unicity or variety arises.

We should recall here what we said in the introduction regarding *substantial* and *functional* thinking, which will provide the basis for the distinction of the two following chapters.

We would like to do justice to both sides and to deal with these two aspects separately. We recall again the synthetic character of our study, which allows us just to contrast the problems without submitting them to an exhaustive analysis, which would require a monograph for each paragraph.

5

THE STATIC CONSIDERATION

The static consideration of religion presents a manifold aspect. The static structure of religion can be envisaged from different levels and perspectives. Here a distinction is important. Either we can observe and study religion *from a particular point of view*, or we can see and consider *a particular point of view of religion*. The *first* approach is not only permissible but also necessary, as our human mind needs to work mainly in an analytical and partial manner. The two requirements are that the viewpoint be a correct one and that it be completed by complementary points of view.

The *second* method is also permissible and not wrong provided it is conscious that it is not studying the whole of religion, but only an abstraction of religion, a part, a dimension of it, that needs to be integrated—and thus corrected and modified—into the total concept of religion.

We intend here to follow the first way, that is, to study religion as a whole, though from several particular points of view. These particular viewpoints will not allow us to *judge* religion but will permit us to *compare* religions, which is our present task.

Similarities

The first and staggering discovery of the relatively recent science of religions was the finding of striking similarities among almost all religions of the world. The whole of the nineteenth century is full of this amazement: scholars with a Christian background began to discover that the doctrine of grace was not to be found in Christianity alone. They began to surmise that polytheism had a monotheistic source, that love for the neighbor was a Buddhist doctrine also, that the tradition of the fall of Man was not an exclusively Jewish feature, that the myth of the flood was almost universal, that the theory of sacrifice was everywhere more or less the same, and so on. Some ventured the theory that common features were remnants of a primitive revelation, others spoke of the identity of human nature as being mainly responsible for identical religious creations, others put forward the idea of a unique God inspiring several religions, and so on.

Christianity was fearful of losing its specific character of uniqueness, and Christian scholars began to stress the profound difference between the apparently similar institutions in Christianity and elsewhere—the Greek mysteries cannot be compared with the Christian mystery, the *Logos* of Plotinus has nothing to do with that of

St. John, Christian charity is essentially different from Buddhist *karuṇā* or Hindu *bhakti*, Christ cannot be matched with any other *avatāra*, and the like.

Neither side, either that of stressing the similarities or that of putting the accent on the differences, was led by merely philosophical or scientific interest. The science of religions began in the West with the aim of disproving the exclusivity claimed by Christianity. Christianity, in turn, organized a corresponding defense by denying the existence of real similarities.

It cannot be denied that it was a surprise for the nineteenth century in Europe to discover that other religions were also good and beautiful, a fact that was used as another weapon in the internal religious struggles of Europe.

We are now far away from such an attitude. Neither do non-Christian scholars utilize the science of religion to attack Christianity, nor do Christian thinkers fear that the true uniqueness of Christianity is jeopardized by the existence of other religions and by their similarities with Christianity. Rather they see in these similarities, following the trends of the Patristic age, an argument for the universality of their religion.

It goes without saying that we are not concerned here with such discussions, as we are trying rather to contribute to a Catholic ecumenism that is not frightened by any fact.

The truth is that not only do religions present deep and wide similarities but they show an inwardly unifying dynamism.

We shall mention here just the headings under which a detailed study of the similarities of religions could be undertaken.

Formal Structure

We can begin by saying that all religions have the same formal structure with only slight differences, that is, that all of them possess the essential notes that allow us to apply to them the formal concept of religion.

This formal structure is not only the minimum required to build up a concept, but it extends its identity far beyond. In one way or another, all religions possess the ninefold structure maintained before. In one manner or other, sacrifice, priest-hood, adoration, prayer, God, world, and so on, are religious categories found in all religions. The contents may diverge, but the formal frame is the same.

We do not need to insist any longer on this point, which has been sufficiently clarified by the modern science of comparative religions.

Formal Teachings

The main formal teachings of all religions are also almost identical. That is to say, all religions in one way or another recognize the positive values of truth, goodness, love, and so forth, as well as the existence of an Absolute, of a moral law, of the acknowledgment of the provisionality of this life on Earth—as we live or see it—and so on.

Of course, this formal identity does not imply a material equality. The contents given to what is God or what is love may differ, but nevertheless a long set of formulae could easily be written down, which all religions would approve of and recognize as their own, although the interpretation or the significance or importance given to each of them may be very different.

There is no need to linger on this subject, which should be obvious to any student of religions.

Religious Spirit

Along with the formal teachings there is something akin to them that, in one way, groups all religions together and, in another, differentiates them from one another.

All religions have what we could call a religious accent. A religious teacher, regardless of the religion he adheres to, is easily recognizable and distinguishable from a scientific, philosophical, cultural, or political teacher. There is something that breathes in all religions, which may be called a religious spirit. And today, with the growth of irreligious outlook and a profane civilization, that spirit is even easier to detect. There is little doubt that the conflict between religion and irreligion in our times brings to the consciousness of the various religious creeds, not only their divergences, but also their many points of agreement.

Our task here is not to enumerate or to study the elements of the religious spirit. However it is clear that a certain sense of the divine or transcendent, a conviction of the provisionality or the nonabsolute character of our life on Earth, a recognition of the existence of some superindividual, and in some sense superhuman and transcendent, basis for moral law, etc., are elements of this religious accent. We could eventually call it the sense of the sacred.

On the other hand, the various religions accentuate one or another aspect of the religious spirit. In fact, we find religions that put almost the whole accent of their faith on one particular point with the danger of forgetting the other ingredients of religion. This accentuation of a particular point has often been the cause of misunderstandings and rivalries among the followers of different confessions. The various religious sects of Hinduism offer us an example of what we mean.

This diversity in the accentuation explains the reason for the appearance of several schools of thought or of spirituality within one and the same religion.

This religious accent has also very often served the scholar of philosophy of religion as a criterion for the classification of religions. We could characterize, for instance, a religious faith according to a particular accentuation on the fear of God, human brotherhood, cosmic compassion, asceticism, sense of the transcendence, love of God, and so on. The only weakness in such classification is that the deeper unity among religions and the underlying completeness in every religion are easily overlooked. One religious school or sect can place its accent on one or another of these points and even give preeminence to one of them; nevertheless, the deeper existential and living reality of full-fledged religion always takes into account the complementary aspects of its central features. Buddhism, for example, could be called the religion of universal and cosmic compassion, but although this accent may be almost overwhelming at one particular moment, Buddhism also contains, implicitly, the idea of human brotherhood, of love, and so on.

Divergences

Material Teachings

Though the formal features of religions are close to one another, it is in the contents and interpretations of these features that religions begin to differ.

It could be said in some sense that differences arise where religion begins to be the work of Man. If we consider only the religious projection of human *existence*, then even the diversities can easily be bridged. However, religion needs a human elaboration, and unless a very special divine help comes from outside, history proves, and our personal experience confirms, that not only error is possible, but also that diversity of opinions and doctrines appear.

In fact, divergences exist among religions. Whereas one holds a personal God, others only accept an impersonal Absolute; whereas one believes in the unicity of each human being, others sustain a kind of spiritual communism of souls and persons; whereas some religions do not make any ultimate difference between God and the world, others do, and so on.

How far and how deep these differences are is a particular problem in each case. Sometimes the gulf is wider than it looks—for example, between the belief in metempsychosis and the faith in a personally unique and nontransferable reward destiny. At other times the distance is not so great—for example, in the gap between the impersonal Hindu Absolute and the personal Muslim God. On other occasions the doctrinal differences are only distinct levels of profundity—for example, the divergence between the Muslim unity of Allah and the Christian Trinity of God.

Whatever difficulty of harmony there may be, the fact persists that the various religions of the world have different doctrines.

It is not wrong for followers of different religions to meet together in order to try to bridge the gulf and to search not only for understanding but for truth; on the contrary, it is an imperative coming from the deepest urge of religion itself. The authentic religious disposition is an attitude of loyalty, sincerity, and humility. We shall come to this point later.

Cultural Practices

As deep, at least as the doctrinal gap, is the practical order. Though formally speaking, the practices and ways of living and of worship of every religion may have the same external frame, nevertheless the way to fill up this frame is peculiar to, and different in, every religion. We have already mentioned that this aspect of religion is a fundamental one.

Moreover, these practices are and must be in some way exclusive. Hindu temples are meant only for Hindus, and this is perfectly comprehensible. The orthodox Hindu does not need to despise the outcast or other believers, but his temple was built and is meant for the particular form of worship of a particular group. Only baptized people are allowed to take part in the Christian mysteries, though the priest may offer the Sacrifice for the salvation of the whole world, and today the nonbaptized may passively witness the Christian liturgy. It is again not because of a sense of exclusivity or disregard for others, but due to the existential concrete nature of the Christian sacrifice, which is not a spectacle to be seen but an action to be performed for which a psychological preparation—instruction, doctrine, and so on—is required, and an ontological transformation—baptism, grace, and so on—is needed.

There are many ways of worship, and there are numerous paths leading or intending to guide men to God. We cannot mingle them indiscriminately, neither can we say that they are all equal or at least equivalent. They are simply different, and philosophically speaking we cannot judge them, as is the case with the doctrinal aspect, saying that one way is better or more fit than another, except in the extreme cases of antinatural or antihuman practices. Philosophy may discuss whether the Sufi doctrine is more or less perfect than the Jain doctrinal system, but it cannot decide whether God hears more readily the prayers held in a mosque or in a Shivaite temple. Pure philosophy is obliged to assent to a kind of status quo, saying that for the Muslim it is better to go to his mosque and for the Shivaite to his temple.

Philosophy cannot decide in favor of these forms of worship, nor can it defend utter indifferentism. Only a superior instance could—can—really decide which is the form of worship God wants from mankind, or which concrete path the individual should follow. Unless this revelation is heard, everyone must remain where he is, with full respect for other forms; but this respect implies also intangibility and distance. To violate the sacred enclosure of religion—of the temples—for the sake of enlarging or purifying religion is a very unreligious act, which brings with it the destruction of religion itself.

The most important part in cultural practices is, of course, the *spirit* in which they are performed, and this spirit does not differ greatly from one religion to another. The spirit of prayer, for example, is what matters, whatever the words or the actions may be. Certainly, we must adore God in spirit and in truth, yet the truth is that we are not pure spirits, but human, concrete, historical beings ontologically connected with our fellow men, especially with those who are close to us in space and time. The truth is, furthermore, that God wants me to adore Him in a particular way, which is my way and which my religion tells me is God-given. Unless reasons of paramount importance convince me that the Will of God for me lies in another direction, I should follow the traditional way of my historical coordinates.

Pure philosophy cannot bridge the gulf and must recognize its limitations. Philosophy could eventually prove that one cult fits better than another on certain anthropological grounds, but it cannot prove the greater effectiveness of one cult compared to another, nor that the cultural paths should be reduced to a unity.

We should warn the reader here again not to minimize the cultural differences. Cult is not ceremony, and to want to find religious unity, overlooking the cult as if it were a matter of mere external forms of worship is to harm the very cause of religion. To destroy the cult of a religion is to suppress that religion, for cult is the specifically religious action, that is, the action that links Man with God, the action that bears the fruit of eternal life. When the *Upaniṣad* shifted the accent from the external cult of the Vedic sacrifices to the internal cult of the act of knowledge they did not destroy Hinduism but changed it radically, the implication being that the action that begets salvation is not the cosmic sacrifice but the intellectual sacrifice. This knowledge of reality is not a secularized awareness of the nature of things but *Brahma-jñāna*, or the wisdom about God that can only be obtained by the given intuition into the truth of the revealed formulae.

The whole of religion is summed up in the cult. This brings us to our next paragraph, namely, that cults are different insofar as the existing religions as a whole are different.

Factual Existence

Religions as they exist in fact are different or, perhaps we should say, separate. One religion may have great similarities with another, but every religion is an existential unity unto itself. This definite existence is what constitutes a religion. Religions are not abstractions, ideas, or ideals but human realities, having a soul and a body. Muhammad might have taught the same doctrine that Christ preached and may have recognized Him as the "greatest" Prophet; nevertheless he did not teach men to join Christianity but to embrace Islam. Buddha's teachings may not differ from the most pure Hindu tradition, but nonetheless Buddhism is a different religion from Hinduism. The quintessence may be the same, but religion is not a bi-distilled liquor. It is an integral reality.

It is not too uncommon to find among people engaged in the noble quest for the understanding of all religions—very often unconsciously—an almost rationalistic and even sometimes a practically atheistic point of departure. This mental attitude considers the various religions as pure human facts and tries to discover their common features at the same time, trying to transcend every religion because they are considered too narrow. In one sense this attitude destroys religion. It implies that all religions are the same because ultimately all are equally wrong.

There would be only one unique and universal religion that would not be religion at all, but only a vague religiosity and, of course, not any of the existent religions. Trying to unify and simplify religions they would found a new one, as has already happened more than once.

This attitude implies not only a kind of rationalistic analysis of all religions and an extremely rational examination of all of them—they must pass through the examination board of our reason—but it indulges also in certain atheistic presuppositions. If religion is the totality of means binding Man to God, that is, the ontological path of mankind to the Absolute, and if this God exists, then religion must be given, directed, inspired, in some way, by God Himself. He would have cared for the way in which men are to go to Him, and if we deny the personality character of the Absolute nonetheless there must be an attraction from this Absolute, an internal structure of reality or a constitutive law of nature that provides Man with the means of realization; this is his religion.

That is to say, if God is, He will surely look after men; if the Absolute is, it will attract the relative to it; if the Transcendent is, the way to it is a discovery and not an invention. In other words, our conception of religion cannot be an irreligious one; it cannot disregard the point of view of God; it cannot disregard the primacy of the Absolute, the initiative of the transcendent; it cannot forget that religion is not merely a human manipulation but also a divine inspiration.

The intention of bringing all religions together cannot overlook the undeniable fact of the existential diversity of religions. Moreover, we must beware of doing harm to any religion or of destroying any of them for the sake of religion. Respect for religions, however "primitive" they may be, is a fundamental tenet of religion.

If we want to bring all religions together, we cannot be satisfied with detecting only similarities, discovering only common features and a similar religious spirit.

We cannot reduce religions to a disincarnated and devitalized "spirit," but we should strive to let all religions evolve from within toward a fuller and more catholic religion. Setting out from the real situation of each believer, we should try to discover and to accelerate this internal dynamic convergence that is still at work. This is what we still have to explain. Moreover, we should not *want* to bring them together if they do not belong together. We should not try to unify them if they are not somehow already one. In other words, the zeal for the unity of all religions should be a genuine religious zeal, that is, an obedient and a docile auscultation to the Will of God, to the exigencies of the Absolute, to the very nature of the Transcendent and not just a human idea and a private good intention. There is no gain for the cause of the unity of religions simply in postulating this unity, overlooking the factual diversity of these differences.

Ecumenism must begin by suffering because of these differences. It should proceed by finding out their deeper common urges and it could very well culminate in the religious effort of bringing that unity nearer to reality. The unity of religions is more a mission than a fact, more a goal to be reached than an end that has already been achieved. Man is a pilgrim, and the religious pilgrimage of the ecumenical-minded man of today is a painful way of the Cross through the many stations where the Savior is still falling down and is being despised. Some will attack us as eclectics and even traitors, others as cunning propagandists and shrewd fanatics. . . . Even so we shall proceed on our pilgrimage.

6

The Dynamic Convergence

Religions are not only static realities, fixed structures in human life, but also dynamic forces, active factors not merely of human culture but of the human being itself. We remind the reader of what we said regarding *functional* thinking. We do not speak in this chapter about the truth-*content* of the different religions, but about their truth-*intentionality*. This is what a religion stands for: the completion, the perfection, the assistance of the human being in reaching fullness—in a transcendent sphere since, obviously, this end is not reached within the appearance of our earthly life.

There must, then, be a functional equivalence between religions, because they all share the same intention: to guide Man to his goal, and in this function they cannot be substituted by any other; in fact, if religions do not fulfill this function of salvation, then this function will not be fulfilled at all, for the performing of such a function is what defines religion.

That is why every religion must recognize that where it does not perform this function of saving Man, either other religions with better or worse chances will have to perform that function, or Man will not be saved at all. There is no other alternative because to say that those who make no appeal to the saving power of their own religion can be saved by merely following their personal good conscience amounts to saying that the other religions are the instrument of salvation, because the geometrical place, the existential room for this "good conscience" is precisely religion not excluding the "other" religions. It cannot be retorted that the "other" believers are saved because of their good conscience and in spite of their religions; this would be neither possible nor fair because the "good consciousness" to which we appeal to justify their salvation refers to the attitude that the follower must have in regard to his own religion. In fact, if God saves a bona fide Buddhist, He saves him *through*, *by means of*, and *with* his Buddhism, and not *in spite of* this Buddhism. Every religion offers Man the necessary means to achieve its ultimate goal. Every religion possesses in itself the "sacraments" through which salvation is attained, and this is not in conflict with Christian theology.

To think, then, that Man can be saved outside of any historical religion—to put it more exactly, *despite* this religion—is theologically and psychologically wrong; theologically because this places all religions, except one's own, outside of divine Providence, which seeks the salvation, or fullness, of all men; psychologically because Man, despite a certain form of individualism that was born but a few centuries ago and only in a certain part of the world, is not an isolated individual who can be separated from his cultural, philosophical, or social world, disregarding his collective consciousness. In order for religion to fulfill its function of being a means to salvation, everybody needs "good faith" in their own religion, whatever this may be, because faith is the necessary condition for the fulfillment of this salvation—"your faith has restored you to health" (Mk 5:34), said Christ to the woman who suffered from a hemorrhage for twelve years—but it must be a faith intrinsic to the very environment of the faithful, not one that disregards this. Indeed, if the believer in the most true religion does not have *bona fide*, not even he will be saved despite belonging to the most excellent religion. Belonging to a determined confession is not enough to attain salvation, even if it is considered the best confession, because authentic religion is not exhausted simply in an act of obedience to determined external practices, nor is salvation attained as a guaranteed fact by virtue of a special external rite. If this were the case, the meaning of salvation would be found in the realm of magic.

The most rigorous sacramental *ex opere operato* of Catholicism, for example, is not a magic ritual, and we know today that many of the so-called magical religions only look so to the outsider who has not realized the spiritual and living link in which the follower of that religion believes. Magic exists and is certainly an excrescence of religion, but it is not a religion. Again, we cannot say that only individual conscience has objective exigencies and also it is molded in the collectivity and precisely in the religion of the community. Natural conscience, for instance, tells us that we must honor our father and mother, and strictly speaking, the manner of this homage is irrelevant. Nevertheless, for an individual peasant of China in the last century, this universal voice of the human conscience took the shape of all the ritualistic cult to parents and ancestors of the China of Confucius, so that he could hardly fulfill his duty—of conscience—without following the particularities of his religion.

If we observe the various religions of the world under this aspect we shall be inclined to admit that in some sense they are different ways to one and the same goal because God could hardly leave the whole of mankind groping in darkness toward Him or bestow His Light exclusively upon one particular group. He may have given a special assistance to one people or another, but this preference cannot contradict the divine Justice, which not only lets the sun rise for the just and the sinner, but which also gives to every man who comes into this world the necessary light—means—to attain salvation.

We can say, therefore, that, in spite of all the undeniable static differences that exist among religions, every authentic religion shelters an existential and real way to God for those who *bona fide* follow it. We can speak of a real *dynamic convergence*, or if we prefer, of the *functional unity* of religions.

Each religion is not objectively equally perfect or objectively equally fit to lead Man to God; each way is not objectively the same; there are shorter and longer ones, better and worse and also apparent and false ones.

Each authentic religion has existentially the *function* of leading men to God, and so each religion performs this function for the people who with good conscience and pure heart follow the path of any authentic religion. We say "authentic" because we do not discard the possibility of a mere false religion, a schism of hatred and resentment, a reaction against something holy or against nature and human conscience.

The member of any religion following the prescribed law for his being, crystallized in that religion, will reach the goal of his life—and this existential mission is the most important feature of religion. If it is true—and it can hardly be denied—then we can truly accept the functional unity of religions. This is a very important question that has to be considered with some accuracy.

Dynamic convergence does not mean substantial identity, but a certain functional equivalence. This equivalence should be valued precisely in the function of the concrete historical situation of Man. This historical situation is not something irrelevant and accidental to the concrete Man, since historicity is one of the constitutive dimensions of Man. Hence historicity must also be an essential feature of religion. It is within this frame that the functional unity of religions has to be understood.

Not only Man, but religion as well, is conditioned by history.

This functional unity of religions is a function of *space* and *time*, the two main categories of our human earthly existence. Man on Earth is bound to space and time; he is both limited and expressed in space and time. Likewise religion as human reality has a spatial and a temporal structure that we should not overlook in our hurry to discover the supraspatial and supratemporal aspect of religion.

This double spatio-temporal structure of the human being manifests itself in two levels, which we must distinguish though we cannot separate them completely as they are mixed and intermingled.

On the one hand, the human person is a product of history, and thus personal religion has a historical dimension. On the other hand, mankind as such is also a historical phenomenon, and thus religion on Earth must have also a historical character. The answer that religion provides for Man is not just an intemporal elixir disconnected from Man's temporal existence, but a concrete temporal milestone in mankind's existential pilgrimage.

Man is a historical being. This means, first, that Man is in a peculiar sense a product of history—that is, he lives in and from a historical heritage, he is influenced by his surroundings, his culture is handed down to him from the land where he is born, and he belongs to a certain limited space, and so the one and the same human nature appears to be different in almost all profound accidents of its substance according to the spatiotemporal coordinates of its being. History has shaped the tastes of Man, his very concepts, his way of life and manner of looking at it. Accordingly, religion shares in this historical diversity and changes along the more or less profound human historical variations. It is quite clear that even one and the same religion could not have the same form in the stone age and in the electronic age. Nor is this all. The historical dimension of Man is deeper than that; it is something more than an accidental cultural garb or a spatial difference. Human nature is the same throughout the ages, but this identity is neither a material nor a static one. It is an ontic dynamic identity like that existing between a person when he is a child and when he is an adult. It is a historical identity.

It is not that the man of Cro-Magnon as a matter of casual fact did not have a radio apparatus, it is that he *could not* have it; not because he *did not* possess the skill to construct one, but because *he could not* possess that skill. It is not that the people of Israel had not known *God*, the Father of Jesus Christ, it is that they could only have known YHWH as He revealed Himself to them—and this in spite of the fact that YHWH is one with God the Father, just as the Herzian waves were circulating over the Earth also in the times of Cro-Magnon.

Time and space are not just two external containers of Man's life, they are two constitutive dimensions of the concrete Man, *his* time and *his* space making up an element of his very being. The religion of the adult is the same and yet has not the same features as the religion of the child. The religion of Man is also a function of history because only when it is temporarily homogeneous with the concrete Man can it fulfill its function of answering to the particular religious need of the particular individual.

This leads us already to the second historical dimension, which is also full of consequences for our problem.

Not only man as an individual is a historical being; mankind as a whole also has a temporal existence. This evolution is neither that of a straight ascending line nor that of a single line. Mankind presents ups and downs and different temporal coefficients may coexist. The diversity of religions corresponds to the enormous variety of human historical levels. The multifarious variety of Man does not destroy the unity of the human family; likewise, religion offers the diversity we see because of its essential link with the concrete Man living in the most diverse situation. And yet mankind is one, and religion also has a functional unity that is linked with its historical mission to the temporal Man. A colorless uniform religion for the colorful polyhedral Man would not do.

This does not mean, obviously, that all the differences of religions are just historical varieties. Religion—like Man, precisely because both are historical—is also a free agent and can develop forms of existence that are at variance with its own nature. Besides, as we have already stressed, religion is anchored in God, not only in Man.

But this means that . . .

1. We should no longer commit the common mistake of judging other religions from without, that is, from our own point of view and our own categories, disregarding the concrete historical stage of the people who practice the religion in question.

2. Underneath the apparent diversity of religions there is a certain—not exhaustive and certainly not mathematical—proportionality between the historical factor of a people and their religion, so that there is a certain equality between religion and people, which allows us to speak of the functional unity of religions.

3. Just as there is a historical growth and a historical evolution of mankind, so is there a historical dynamic convergence of religion. The religious quest is, on the one hand, one of the strongest factors in producing such a growth and accelerating such a way toward unity, and, on the other hand, an effect of such a historical dynamism of mankind.

4. In the same way that the course of history is free and the temporal development of mankind depends on many other factors, one of them being human freedom, the religious evolution of mankind is a historical process that is under divine Providence, yet is left to the free evolution of Man and free decisions of the people who have an awakened religious conscience. Religion presents a dynamism toward unity; the *functional* unity of religion in itself seeks a deeper *substantial* unity, but this is neither an automatic process nor an exclusively human achievement. Yet Man as a free agent can—as a moral person ought to—collaborate in this historical upward movement of mankind and of religion.

We shall now review some of the aspects of this dynamic convergence of religions. A simple enumeration will suffice for our purpose.

Historical-Cultural Factors

We have already seen that religion exists for Man and not Man for religion. Man exists for God, and thus living for God, he is for himself, for he really *is* only when he has reached the divine status of his very being. Religion is that very path leading Man to God; but this way, if it has to be a real way, cannot be an impracticable ropeway inaccessible to the majority. It has to be a possible route for the concrete Man living on Earth under the most varied historical and cultural conditions.

Religion, therefore, needs a historical-cultural form, which is something more than a mere external garb. Religion must be as available and accessible to the savage and primitive as to the cultured and sophisticated man. Religion is a reality not only for the twentieth century, but it is, and it was, a reality for the human being living seven thousand or seventy-thousand years ago.

Man is a historical being, and in consequence religion is also a historical reality accommodated to the historical, that is, the concrete existing Man. That is to say, the "primitive" Man must have a "primitive" religion; any other would not be religion for him at all.

Could the Arabs of Muhammad's time more readily accept and understand a religion other than Islam? Has not Hinduism grown up as a kind of "natural" fruit of Indian civilization, so that its strength and weakness are mingled with Indian culture itself? What God would have been more fitting for the Jews of the Old Testament than YHWH? Were the religions of Africa not in tune with its degree of culture?

This historical diversity thus carries with it a religious variety. If religion, though being rooted in culture and history, is an original and anthropological fact, it must go beyond culture and history, and, in consequence, historical or cultural divergences in religion do not justify and much less consecrate forever the existence of several religions. Sometimes, in fact, what we call different religions may be just the same religion in two cultural manifestations, or else they may be different historical religious forms, the antagonism of which is only justified as long as those two cultures are really still separate. Several religions of Africa, for instance, though they are separate religions, can hardly be called anything else than different cultural manifestations of one and the same religion. In this case the functional unity of religions is so strong that they appear rather as a confederation of religions. Another interesting and striking example is offered by the religions of India—which, by the way, may offer an explanation for the attitude of many an Indian scholar applying this very scheme beyond the boundaries of Hinduism. On the one hand, Hinduism cannot be called a religion; it is rather a bundle of religions of the greatest variety. Yet the functional unity is so striking that it is fully justified to speak of *Hinduism*. Indeed, in the highest forms of Hinduism there are also doctrinal differences, but in the majority of the forms we have only to deal with cultural and historical differences of the most variegated colors, yet all performing the same function and more or less accepting a certain, again, mainly historical and cultural frame.

In our times all kinds of particular frameworks are breaking down; not only as a matter of fact, but also of necessity, the various cultures of the world are coming closer together. This contact is very often superficial and only material, but our technical civilization has made the contact unavoidable. We cannot as yet foresee how far this contact is also a convergence of cultures, but undoubtedly the contact is there, and with it, the contact of religion becomes deeper, at least for these genuine religious spirits who are longing for unity and searching for truth. This fact widens our views and opens doors to mutual and self-understanding, as the learning of a foreign language not only enriches our cultural outlook but also deepens the knowledge of our own mother tongue. We are no longer able to condemn as barbarous what is foreign.

But there is more. For the first time in human history the world is becoming a human-geographical unit. We are not prophesying a political unity or a cultural uniformity, but nevertheless mankind is conscious of its unity, which is awakening to a very specific world consciousness.

Religions are also deeply engaged in reflecting upon themselves and trying to maintain their own boundaries, but the frontier incidents today happen more in the hearts of the believers and inside the nonexisting wall of our towns than along the geographical or historical limits of different cultures and religions. The "holy war" begins to be holy and ceases to be war because it becomes a *struggle for holiness*. Only the holiest shall conquer.

If we consider now from this historical point of view the development of all religions of mankind, we must be very cautious and humble in our conclusions, especially regarding the old stages of history in which other categories were at work. However, some points seem to be incontrovertible.

Cultural Homogeneity

There is a kind of homogeneity between the religion of a certain human group—country, race, civilization—and its cultural situation. We cannot say that religion is simply a cultural outgrowth, but we must endorse the fact that religion takes the cultural forms from the place where it lives, so that there is a vital exchange between the culture of a determined group and its religion. Moreover, perhaps, the first cultural factor is religion itself, so that between religion and culture there is a living exchange and a deep intermingling. Properly speaking, culture is nothing other than outer-side of religion, for while religion intends to perfect the substantial kernel of Man, culture tries to perfect his human faculties. That is why very often culture appears as a kind of secularized religion.

Religious Heterogeneity

On the other hand, religion is never a mere intracultural event. It has always something transcendent, something foreign, and it always created a certain tension with its proper cultural surroundings. It always offers a secret—and sacred—resistance to being swallowed by culture and to being considered as one of many cultural factors. Religion is never completely of this world, even when it boasts of being worldly. It is interesting to note that the kind of atheistic religiosity we witness in our times is perhaps more world-denying than any religion, for it has shifted the otherworldliness not to another world that nevertheless is acting and somehow present amidst us, but to a *future* world in the same horizontal line as ours. Consequently this type of spirituality is much more a matter of future-world than is the religious spirituality that holds a supratemporal presence of the transcendent life. Culture aspires to perfect Man as he appears on Earth, trying to develop all his faculties harmonically. Religion welcomes this perfection and contributes to it, but nevertheless stresses a deeper and transcendent perfection, the fullness of the substantial being. Owing to a tragic existential situation—the Christian will say, due to original sin—these two perfections do not always go hand in hand; that is, you can enter into the realm of God crippled and blind in one eye and on the other hand conquer the whole world and lose your soul.

Historical Relativity

Relativity does not mean relativism, but inwardly relationship. This is the case with the relativity of religion regarding history. There is an internal relationship between both.

Let us describe this connection from a purely religious point of view. If God exists and leads men to their end—namely, to Him by means of religion—the particular religion that a human historical group has must be adapted to the spiritual situation of such a group. There is something true in the sarcastic commentary of the "enlightened" Greeks of the golden age, that if cows were to imagine or were to worship God they would worship Him in the form of a cow. There is something correct in this, namely that if God had to speak to cows and wanted to be worshiped by them, He would speak a "cowish" language and appear to them in some way acceptable, "intelligible," tangible for cows, not because God is a Cow, or simply a projection of the "imagination" of a cow, but because only something of the nature of the cow can appear, can uplift and can enter into relation with cows.

We see in the world a rich variety of historical cultures, from the most "primitive" and "savage" forms to the most "refined" and "sophisticated." Man living in these different stages must, however, have the possibility of realizing the final goal of their existence, and this is the role of religion. We cannot say if all this diversity of cultures is desired or not by God, and besides it is irrelevant to our question. We merely acknowledge that such differences exist, and we then see that if there is, as the attracting goal of human existence, Man has to have a real possibility of reaching this goal, whatever his culture may be. The geometrical place of those possibilities is religion, though the externals of religion will be very different according to the distinct historical cultures. The Godhead looking after men in all the human diversities that history teaches us "speaks," "attracts," "appears" each time in the peculiar forms of these cultures. As long as a particular, "primitive" tribe, for example, has not come into contact with any other superior form of religion, it will find in its "primitive" religion the salvation that other people find in another, "higher" religion. We do not say that this "primitive," and let us suppose imperfect, religion saves the human person. It is always God who saves the human person, even in the "highest" religion, but it is *in* and *through* that religion that the individual is saved. It is a different case altogether when this "primitive" man discovers the shortcomings of his faith and meets another, "superior" form of religion. Then his conscience compels him, not to betray his tribe, but to fulfill his religion and to fill up the gaps of his existence by adapting that new religion that can appear only as a fulfillment of his previous one.

But as we have already stated, the historicity of Man is not only a cultural diversity, it has a deeper aspect that alone will give us the clue to the dynamic convergence.

Historical-Ontological Dynamism

In spite of the personal individuality—or rather, together with it and complementing the human individuation—mankind is a unity. Not only all men have the same destiny and are alike, but humanity itself as a whole constitutes a certain unity. Moreover, this unity presents a peculiar historical nature. Not only is Man a historical being in the sense that his past emerges from the past in his present and both are "historically" stored in every now moment, but mankind itself is a historical "nature." We know very little about the laws of its historical growth, as the clue to it lies in the transcendent end. We can, however, discover some formal characteristics of a certain importance to our question.

Very often the quest for the deeper unity of all religions has taken refuge in a kind of transcendent identity disregarding, on the one hand, historical diversity and, on the other hand, historical dynamic convergence. To take shelter in the transcendent in order to defend the unity of all religions is not only to destroy religions but also to deny unity. It is a lack of historical patience and in a certain way pride to believe that they have already reached the transcendent and are where we all *shall meet*. It is equivalent to saying that in the darkness all cats are black.

We can surmise and forestall this convergence from two points of view: by inductive considerations on the factual evolution of religions, and by deductive reasoning about the nature of God, history, and mankind.

Inductive Consideration

This inductive method offers another threefold perspective; a *psychological* introspection of the authentic religious mind, a *phenomenological-sociological* study on the actual evolution of the different faiths, and a *theological* reflection on the meaning of the actual diversity of religions.

Psychological Reflection

Let us suppose I am an orthodox Muslim trying to understand the fact of religious diversity today.

On the one hand I cannot help suffering due to the actual divergences and feeling the scandalous situation that the most high and holy human value, religion, is separating and dividing mankind instead of uniting and harmonizing men. I will strive with all my force to collaborate in any effort to change such a situation.

On the other hand, as I am convinced of my faith and I am an orthodox believer I cannot give up the religious tenets of my faith. That brings me very close to the attitude of trying to convert the other confessions to my own faith.

Stirred up, first of all, by this desire of unity I will try to study and to know other creeds better, and then I shall discover how much they have in common without overlooking the differences. I shall realize also, if I study without bias, that not only other faiths have great similarities and deep converging points, but also that other confessions have developed some aspects of religious life or of religious doctrine that could enrich my own religion positively without destroying it.

However, if I am an authentic believer and a humble worshipper of the true God in whose hands the future of mankind lies and whose loyal instrument I try to be, I shall discard not only any kind of violence, forced conversions, and immoral means, but I shall also reject any kind of pride in having the true religion and any sort of appearance of superiority, though this may not always be easy. I shall pray the Almighty and All Merciful to hasten the day when He will be recognized, sung, and loved by all people, and I shall try to serve His projects by living my religion with intensity and devotion and by being a living example of love and surrender to Allah, trying to convince other people of this one and only way.

But then I shall not exclude the possibility of being convinced myself of a better way if this exists, though I do not believe so at the moment. Here arises a very delicate problem of conscience. I cannot reach any fruitful religious dialogue with any other fellow men if I do not get rid of the patronizing attitude of a man who possess the full truth and considers others only as heretics or heathens. That means that I must search with others, discuss with others, share with others their longings and anxieties in order to rediscover along with them the truth that I possess in my religion. On the other hand I owe a loyalty to my religion that is much deeper than that, that cannot be shaken by pure intellectual reasons. I shall admit that, even if they defeat me intellectually, I am not for that reason going to change my religion. From within I understand the attitude, which is unintelligible from without, of my religion, which forbids its members to participate in any such discussions and to make such a compromise, which is either a betrayal of their own faith or a rationalization of it. It is not due to "reasons" that I believe, though I can give reasons for my belief, and I can prove that my faith is not unreasonable, that is, against reason. This is my problem of conscience. I cannot level down my faith in my religion to a mere dialectical game. Again I must agree that my partner from his own point of view finds himself in the same position. This gives me the clue to my puzzled conscience.

I am convinced. He is convinced. I am not prepared to yield even if I am convinced of intellectual error. I shall then have to reconsider my system and try to find a solution. I shall have to enlarge the doctrinal scope of my religion, but I cannot betray the existential, historical, and living connection with my past, my tradition, my religion, and my God *only* because my reason—not my conscience—finds some invincible difficulties. But this is exactly the position of my partner, and I cannot claim without immorality that he should do what I am not prepared to do. This means that I am going to try to convince him, but I am not going to make him change his religion. I must find within myself, he must find within himself—and our mutual help is of great value in our common search—we must find in ourselves the growing point, the common basis, the deeper level, the living faith out of which I can accept and be convinced of all that I accept from him, and vice versa. We shall grow together, and I cannot predict whether he will come out more enriched than I. It is not a question of a one-sided victory. Even if I accept his view, even if our contact has transcended the intellectual field and had been a human encounter, even if I am on the point of conversion, to Christianity, for example, my conversion will only be real and moral if I do not betray my previous faith, but fulfill it. Only if I find in Christianity—to continue with the example—all that I had and all that I was longing for in Islam can I become a real and true Christian.

Only with such dispositions can the encounter be moral and fruitful.

What does this attitude mean? It means that we are really converging, coming up and not giving up or spoiling our being or betraying our religion. It means that even if I am converted to another faith, I shall provide the leaven within my own kin, which will cause my own religion to grow broader, more universal, and closer to the other one, to its higher values. It means that I shall be a living factor in this historical convergence because if I am loyal to my convictions we shall all necessarily come closer not only to a better mutual understanding, but to a greater unity.

Moreover, in spite of all our private opinions, and our individual limitations, truth in itself is still so bright and powerful that somehow it directs many a sincere dialogue and imposes itself in a very discrete and particular way. We must remember that this is still a psychological reflection. Speaking with a Buddhist, for example, I discover that because God—this tremendous, undeniable reality—is simply discarded as irrelevant, it has been said that Buddhism is an atheistic religion. The purely static and essential mentality will accuse Buddhism of atheism or of imperfection and falsehood because it does not give account of sin, to give a second example. But I find that "speaking" with a Buddhist about sin, I induce him, so to speak, to elaborate for himself a doctrine of sin and to discover not only its reality but also its place within Buddhism.

I learn also in this dialogue that God is the silent background and the underlying unquestioned reality of Buddhism and that at the time when the Buddha had to take a position concerning the reality of God, he did not deny his existence. So our dialogue—and this exchange began in the living contacts of men of different religions—helps Buddhism to be more complete, more perfect, more developed. Of course, I do not make the Buddhist a Muslim but our dialogue brings him closer to the truth, and only in truth can we, shall we, meet. It goes without saying that this dialogue moves two ways only under the guidance of the truth in which we both believe, and that I shall also learn from the Buddhist his sense of contemplation, his calmness, his detachment, and so on.

Sociological Observation

Not only in the minds of the awakened or among the few leaders is such dynamic convergence found, for, sociologically speaking, the same phenomenon is observable on a large scale. The religious people of all denominations also play a very important role here.

If we cast a rapid glance on the evolution of the various religions of the Earth from the most remote times, we discover a kind of historical growth in the sense that they widen their limits and come closer to each other. This does not mean a mere dialectical evolution or an amorphous equivalency of all religions, but it simply signifies that there is a certain historical convergence, a certain law in the very core of each religion, that every religious soul will easily accept as belonging to the divine providential plan for religion.

The historical fact is that almost all religions begin by being a very particular and limited religion, reform, or confession and evolve into a bigger and bigger universality, due to a kind of historical and theological imperative. Well known, for instance, are the origins of ancient religions that grew up in outlook and doctrine due to or along with the political achievements of the group, clan, tribe, or race. Such political expansion transforms religion itself, sometimes helping it to acquire its full size, so to speak, at other times converting it into another religion altogether. Islam would be an example of the first case, and the religion of the Romans of the second.

Hinduism offers us another instance of historical growth. With its amazing flexibility and capacity for assimilation and integration, Hinduism began as a pure, particular, and limited religion of the newcomers to the Indian subcontinent and developed itself into a huge faith, embracing almost all diverse racial and cultural groups of India.

Moreover, when a religion does not meet the challenge of the times and does not grow according to the historical imperative, it dies or remains barren, narrow, and full of resentment. It may be that even then it is still the last consolation of the defeated and being so still fulfills its role, but it disappears with the last man of that particular unfortunate human group. Pre-Columbian America furnishes us with some such examples.

This historical growth is not always eclecticism or infidelity to primitive purity. It can simply be a homogeneous development. Let us take the example of Christianity. Christ's message, or at least the church's, claims to be universal and not bound to any race or culture, but the universality de facto is a historical event that can become a fact only with the development of history itself. It is not that the personal genius of Paul transformed Christianity from a Jewish sect into a universal religion, though it was mainly he who received the "Christian" mission to enlarge the *factual* Jewish boundaries of Christianity. Christ himself before the redeeming act of the cross hardly overstepped the limits of Palestine in his preaching; it was only after the refusal of Israel and the culminant act on the cross that the time had come for a universal expansion.

Even the consciousness of the church matures; for example, the prevalent opinion of the Christians in the Middle Ages concerning non-Christians was less open and favorable than it is today. The ultimate doctrine may have been the same, but the existential consciousness has changed, and even the doctrine has undergone development. From the exclusivity of YHWH in the Old Testament to the revelation of God by Christ in the New Testament there is a gigantic step; and from the beginnings of Christianity down to our times there is an increasing consciousness of universality and, therefore, comprehension and assimilation of outstanding values.

Let us only adduce, for instance, the different interpretation made by Christian popular consciousness of that Christian principle according to which "there is no salvation outside the church." We could find almost all kinds of interpretations, from the most terrific exclusivity to the most open broadmindedness, as is the present theological interpretation.

Let us mention briefly still another example. It is often said that the Christian missionary effort in India for many centuries did not succeed in the way the missionaries had expected. And this is true. They wanted to change the Hindus into Christians, and only a very small minority did change, but undoubtedly Christianity in India has changed and is changing Hinduism itself, not precisely toward a preconceived idea of a certain type of Christianity but to begin with toward a better and more purified Hinduism. Christianity has helped Hinduism become a better Hinduism and has made Hinduism reflect upon many of its features and discover that they—the Hindus—also had that which the Christians claimed to possess, except that it had been forgotten or was potentially hidden—let us say, a sense of social justice, human equality, personal dignity, and so on.

With little doubt it has to be a two-way traffic if a real encounter between these two religions is to take place. In fact the Hindu impact upon Christianity cannot be denied, and perhaps through Indian Christianity it also extends beyond these boundaries. Another amazing example of this assimilation is the history of the Christian holidays. We refer not only to the more or less extraordinary cases like Buddha being in the Roman Calendar of the Saints, but to the most general practice by which Christianity has been able to assimilate very many values and to adapt itself to different cultures, incorporating them to a higher religious unity. Not only was Easter a Jewish feast—this, after all, according to Christians, was nothing more than a prefiguration of the resurrection of Christ—and Christmas a "pagan" holiday in honor of the sun, and not only did the harvest festivals become Ember days, and so on, but this process is still visible in the Christian holidays of the Philippines, for instance, where the non-Christian elements are still quite visible. The efforts of the church in India not to sever herself from the Indian people by trying to Christianize all Hindu festivals is another example. We could also mention the case of the Chinese New Year and other holidays. Only recently the Church in Rome decided that the First of May, Labor Day—and in practically the whole of Europe a pro-communist celebration—should be the feast of St. Joseph the laborer and the labor holiday for all Catholics.

It is not within our scope now to deal with details of historical problems. We can say, however, that the history of religions detects a certain growth and also a certain convergence among the several religions of the Earth. Whether this convergence points toward a definite unity and whether this growth is, or has always been, a right one, are two different problems altogether that are outside the field of our historical sketch.

The Logico-Phenomenological Aspect

We mentioned already en passant that the growth toward unity is not only a historical but also a theological imperative. The phenomenology of the sacred has shown us, almost with complete evidence, the tremendous polarity to be found everywhere between particularism and universality. On the one hand, the God of the tribe is unique, special, particular, concrete. On the other hand, any particular divinity is somehow implicitly and potentially the universal God, God of Gods at least, if not the only one because all others are—dialectically forced to be—either sheer nothingness or aspects, manifestations, or just names of the recognized God. This dialectic is not exclusive to the primitive religions. The same is to be found also among the great religions. Again Judaism is not the only example regarding the conversion of a particular deity into a universal God. In the same way that phenomenologically human love implies timelessness—there is no meaning in saying, "I love you for a couple of days"; the *always* is implied in any act of true love—similarly the idea (experience, realization) of God demands oneness. My God can only be such if He is somehow unique, better than or superior to . . . the other divinities.

There is thus a general process of unification that has its roots in that potential universality of every religion that tends to assimilate everything good found elsewhere, considering it as belonging to its own proper religion. We need not quote St. Justin's saying that all that has been said by other peoples that is good and true belongs to Christians by their own right, or Islam's saying that every human person is born a Muslim and that society makes him fall away if he is not brought up in a Muslim community, or Buddhism's speaking of the universal mediatorship of the Buddha, or Hinduism's claiming a right over all these upon whom the law of karma gravitates, and so on. We would prefer to use two living examples of our present times. Some of the most sublime features of Hinduism are its eschatological character and its openness to the transcendent. These two features do not fit very well within the modern frame of a secularized society, and, in fact, people from the West have criticized Hinduism for being a world-denying religion.

The normal reaction of its representatives has been not that of fortifying their positions by showing that his world is provisional and fades away and that Hinduism stands for the eternal, but it has been instinctively a reaction of that "accusation" and trying to find stepping-stones on which to build and to prove the world-affirmative character of Hinduism. The task should not be very difficult, for Hinduism contains in fact *artha* (wealth) and *kāma* (desire) and many other elements from which it is easy to prove that it has also a concern for this life. What interests us here is not justification of Hinduism, but its attitude of being willing to change its accent and to become more consciously universal by contact with other religious mentalities. No religion will ever admit something from outside if it does not discover the seed of such within.

Another typical example of this process of growing from within and universalization is offered by the religious philosophy of Śrī Aurobindo. He can by no means be called a Christian philosopher, as he is a Hindu reformer. Yet, in fact, all the main ideas and best motives of his endeavor were of Christian origin: the value of the body and even of the flesh, evolution, historical divinization of Man and recapitulation of all things without destroying, abandoning, or denying the lower strata of reality, and so on. Indeed, all these ideas can also be found in the Hindu Scriptures. Aurobindo developed them from these without copying Christianity or even borrowing a single concrete idea. Only the inspiration, the élan came from outside; the rest, however new, was found within. Vivekānanda offers us another similar example.

This problem is important enough to allow another very concrete example. The sharp and old criticism by Protestantism of the ideal of monastic life in Catholicism is only too well known. The historical reasons are also obvious: degeneration of the ideal in many cases and anachronism or lack of true adaptation to the times. No possible discussions could convince Protestantism of the opposite. Protestantism by developing a kind of "monastic" life from internal exigencies has rediscovered by itself all those values of obedience, world detachment, and so on that it used to criticize in Catholicism.

In a nutshell, the process is this: I am convinced of the truth and goodness of my own religion. This amounts to saying that I stand for a certain universality, for truth and goodness are universal. On the other hand I see very well the concreteness and peculiarity of my own religion, which I can only envisage as one form of religion containing not the partial truth but the total truth in a particular way. Now, if I happen to discover some other value outside, I must say that, one way or another, that value was also within my religion, and I shall look for and eventually discover the seed, the growing point, on which I can base and justify my acceptance of that value.

What we are expressing here as a conscious process is indeed quite often an unconscious movement.

Deductive Reasoning

Not every kind of deduction has to be an apodictic one. Thus, our essay of deducing something out of certain principles is only an attempt to make more comprehensive the central problem of our study, but is by no means a rationalistic one, leaving no room for similar or even perhaps opposite deductions.

We shall say only so much: If God is one and mankind is a unity, and if Man and mankind have a specific historical nature, it seems very comprehensible that Man's religion should be only one or, more accurately, that religions should converge toward a unity and climbing toward the Only One.

This unity of mankind is first of all transcendent and eschatological. We have already stressed a certain transcendent and eschatological oneness of all religions in their functional unity, but the unity of mankind is also historical. This means that already here, in their pilgrim stage, men are somehow one. It means, further, that also here, on Earth, mankind is growing into its fullness along a historical line; that is to say, mankind is engaged in a divine adventure that is happening not simply "along" time but *in* time and *through* time. Every human person in some sense bears in this adventure the whole burden and responsibility of humanity; every human person is a child of the past and a father of the future, but the past gravitates upon him and the future emerges from within him—*in hope*—molding what has to come. No man is an atom, a disconnected particle having only an isolated relationship with God; every man is a bridge, a window, an electronic field, a counter of reception, an irradiation, a mirror reflecting not only God but also the universe. Not only does God pervade everything, but there is also an ontical communion of beings.

If there is one God leading all men to Himself, and the roads for men are religions, it seems that the nearer mankind comes to Him the closer together will religions come. At the fullness of time they shall be one as He is calling us to be one with Him. Whether this "time" is just a terrestrial horizontal date of a historiographical future or a "vertical reign" is a great mystery that here we do not dare to scrutinize further.

God is present in all religions. He is worshipped in thousands of forms. But this variety is not pure anarchy. Religions themselves present a dynamic movement toward the only one and true religion, and all efforts of the truly religious spirits of our times are directed first of all to purifying and to cleansing the existing religions of the imperfections of human weakness and of the limitations of human history.

The first duty of a sincere religious spirit is to love and to live in his own religion, and in many cases to transcend it. The right word for it—in spite of the misuses it has suffered—is *conversion*, that is, deepening, going back to the kernel and turning into the inside of one's own being and of one's own religion—discovering the eternal truth of the mystical dimension of one's own existence and of one's own religion, and emerging or rather being raised again from there to the new and authentic personal religion that does not exclude the allegiance to an external existent religion. After all, the most essential acts of the virtue of religion by which we adhere to a religion are, in the words of Thomas Aquinas, the internal and personal, that is, incommunicable acts of our deepest being.

It goes beyond the limits of our study to show in detail how all religions present a transcendent dynamism toward the only one true religion. To be a better *Muslim*, a better *Hindu*, according to the common formula, can sometimes signify abandonment of Islam or Hinduism . . . without abandonment of all that is good and true in these religions—that is, being *really* Hindu, *really* Muslim, and thus even a *better* Hindu, a *better* Muslim.

This movement toward unity is rooted in human nature, lies in the heart of all religions, is in the mind of the awakened spirits of today, is a historical characteristic of our times, and, above all, is a calling, an extrinsic and supernatural calling by the only one God who, looking after all beings and leading every person toward salvation, is gathering to Himself, so to speak, all the fragments of the universe.

On the one hand, unity does not mean centralization, uniformity, abolishment of all human colors and varieties—*circumdata varietate*—but, on the other hand, neither does it mean a kind of vague and unreal anarchic common ground of certain principles without any binding force. Unity means the existential and real oneness of God, faith, and communion, expressed and living in a diversity of rites, doctrines, and cultures.

Accordingly, it seems to us that the true attitude with respect to the plurality of religions ought to be neither that of *centripetalism* nor that of *centrifugalism*, but one of a via media whose symbol could well be not the straight arrow coming in or going out but rather the *spiral line*. True religion is to be found neither exclusively in the center, in the pure heart of all, nor in the periphery, in the escapism of an indefinite future, but in the integral and concrete reality of complex human existence.

This spiral line has a center and a law of growing. It maintains its contact not only with all realms of the human being but it touches also all existent religions of the world, which very often form some of the spires of this cosmic spiral.

This *realistic historical* attitude does justice to the very raison d'être of all religions and tries to integrate them not in an empty eclecticism or in a mere disincarnate and bodiless pure spiritualism, but in a real and existential catholicity as the fullness and dynamic convergent point of all religious confessions.

We have not to escape and run away from the existent religious confessions in order to find the true religion, and yet we cannot remain in the static middle point of one of them. We must go forward and upward in space and time, perhaps through painful purifications, advancing through many spires, touching the shores of many religious lands and being always connected with an invisible center that leads and drives us toward the true universality without our losing contact with the real human historical concreteness.

Let it be repeated that if our ideal of the unity of religions has to be something more than a mere dream of idealistic intellectuals, then this catholic religion cannot be only an idea or an abstraction, or the colorless and shapeless distillate of all existent religions, but a living, definite, and concrete religion with enough vitality and historical and universal roots to assimilate all sparks of truth, goodness, and beauty spread over all the world religions. It cannot be a human construction but a divine work-piece. It cannot be a race monopoly or a special, limited doctrine but must be a universal love, a human community, a living God in man and mankind, a real mother church, being herself holy and yet embracing also sinful and weak, poor and humble people.

We cannot but pray and perform our daily duty, trying meanwhile to be better Muslims, better Hindus, and indeed much better Christians.

*

Summarizing we can say that religions show an internal constitutive evolution toward the only one religion, and all contribute to the richness of the true catholic one, the only leading force being God calling from above and attracting through truth, goodness, and beauty the man of goodwill.

There may be lights of many colors in the world of religion, as has been said, but they all proceed from a pure white beam.

According to Christianity, this white light would be the living Christ enlightening every man who comes into this world.

The different colors come out only when that white light is incident on the prism of human nature and takes on different wavelengths. This would mean that unless all the colors revert again in a new white beam, all are partial, though one may have a higher degree than the other. The inverted prism that restores human nature to its fullness, according to Christianity, is the church. The claim to be a catholic religion amounts to saying that that religion has not a particular color, but is the white light.

Yet again we could apply another common metaphor: there may be many rivers flowing into the sea, but there is only one sea. And, despite first appearances, it is not the rivers that fill the sea, but the sea that supplies the water to the rivers. Similarly, the many religions may be the different ways humanity attempts to reach its end, but it is this End that inspires, attracts, and supplies everything that moves on Earth. Ultimately every longing, every wish is a desire of the Infinite, and every knowledge, every experience, is a discovery of the Absolute, though imperfectly, partially, and in some sense erroneously. One is not only the end but also the beginning of everything, the sustainer and supporter of all that is. If Man's fundamental impulse is the desire of goodness, we can say that every man who pursues his own pleasure is, unconsciously, erroneously, but ultimately in search of God, and that every passion is a deformed and degenerated love for the Absolute that attracts and calls him; we can also affirm that every religion is a human, cosmic, and sociological movement toward God, and that this movement has God behind and within it. From here we cannot draw the conclusion that every religious form is perfect and stainless or need not be corrected, rectified, reintegrated into a higher order, but certainly it implies that in every religion there are the divine waters running down to their Origin, and that there is God, leading the course of the rivers toward the universal sea. How far man-made constructions detain the "natural" course of the waters is again another question, but nevertheless, the God-made "nature" of the human Earth presents a natural slope that impels the waters down to the sea.

The geography of the human Earth is history, and only this historical geography can reveal to us the meanders of these rivers, the circuitous journeys of the tributary streams, the human channels, and the artificial ponds of still waters.

This shall be our last consideration.

7

THE HISTORICAL CHALLENGE

We have gone, so far, a long but not very promising way. We have tried to show that, in spite of undeniable and serious differences, religions present a certain historical dynamism that not only permits us to speak of a certain functional unity of all religions but puts us on the track to the discovery of an existential concurrence of religions toward unity without destroying the rich and complex variety of religion.

We can now proceed still further and investigate whether this unity in the making is somehow visible, and whether we can detect where this synthesis is taking place.

We have also stated that philosophy can help us reach, perhaps, the halfway point. We must attribute this to two distinct factors, both of essential importance.

The *first* is that along this unifying dynamism there are also forces of disintegration at work. The future of mankind and of religion is a constant historical challenge, and it is this which is at stake. Mankind is an open battlefield, and this battlefield is not always that which Hinduism calls *dharmakṣetra*. We still believe that the positive forces are superior to the negative trends. History, however, warns us of a too uncritical optimism. Even this history of religions does not always show a positive development, and the example of religions with their splits and quarrels is perhaps the biggest stumbling block to the fulfillment of the religious mission on Earth. We may still believe that the prodigal son may come back one day to the mansion of the Father, but sometimes the behavior of the elder brother is even more alarming than the debauchery of the younger. In short, nobody possesses the clue to the mystery of history.

The *second* reason is based upon the radical insufficiency of mere philosophy in religious matters. In one word, we cannot avoid stumbling upon the fact and reality of faith. Philosophy can limit the place of faith and can push it far off, into its proper place, but cannot eliminate it altogether. There is an ultimate realm that is precisely the core of religion in which faith alone is competent and philosophy must stand on the threshold. This is also the reason why this study is insufficient and demands another theological study on the subject. This latter would help to go deeper into the problem and to make one's position more clear, but would hardly help those who do not share the faith of the writer and could be only of secondary, or of a posteriori, use in an ecumenical encounter. We are afraid that some readers may find our pages already too theological.

We shall now proceed with this last part of our argument, which deals directly with the historical existence of Christianity.

Among the religions of the world there is one that always introduces itself
with a striking, rather scandalizing, claim of uniqueness. This is Christianity, and
even more precisely Catholicism. This uniqueness, inside and outside the Catholic
faith, has been often understood as a kind of exclusivity and a damnation of all
other religious forms. We could easily answer that this monopoly is philosophically
untenable and theologically—that is, from the very standpoint of the Catholic
doctrine itself—false.

On the contrary, the singular position, the claim of uniqueness of Christianity,
is to begin with, a historical fact and an affirmation of the greatest importance for
a philosophical study of religion.

We remind our readers that we have discarded any kind of apologetics and we
ask the Catholic reader not to draw hurried conclusions about our remarks here
on catholicism.

We do not need to linger very long over this to prove that uniqueness is not as
such a positive criterion of truth, and on the other hand, this singular position can
be interpreted in many ways, not always favorable to Christianity.

We are rather concerned with the philosophical understanding of the claim to
uniqueness itself. First of all, uniqueness can be given two almost opposite meanings: an *all-excluding unicity*, as the number 1 is unique and excludes all multiplicity
and any other number, or an *all-including uniqueness*, as the mathematical infinite
is unique because no number fulfills its properties and is equal to it.

The very name of the Catholic religion inclines to presume that the uniqueness of
its claim is of the second type, for as it is known, *catholic* means universal, ecumenical,
all-embracing, whole; or, with perhaps even greater accuracy, we can derive it from
the Greek *kath'holon*, which means tending to, aspiring to universality, to fullness,
to perfection, to totality, to integrity, to wholeness. Moreover, the absurdness alone
of the first meaning of uniqueness leads to believe that the Catholic religion cannot
seriously claim that all other religions are false. This would amount to saying that
they are not religions at all, as false silver is not silver, and, in consequence, have
no religious values, and are devilish, wrong, ignoble, and wretched, for they call
themselves religions without having a right to it and so delude and deceive their
followers, who deem to follow a sure path of salvation.

In fact, the Catholic religion itself has stated from the very beginning down to
our own days that the catholicity it claims is that of the second type.

From our philosophical point of view we are rather interested in the *dialectical
implications* of this claim and in the *historical meaning* of the universality, without
indulging merely in a religious controversy. For our purpose, we repeat, whether
this religion is Catholicism or any other is not the point.

Dialectical Implications

Any religion, *R*, that claims to be not only true but also to possess the full truth
and to be unique in its universality must fulfill and accept a set of pure dialectical

implications similar to those we have already mentioned in the introductory part of this study.

When we say implications, speaking of existential objects, we must nevertheless stop somewhere; otherwise we would never be able to make any statement, since, ultimately, everything is somehow implicated in everything. We would like to mention only a few of such dialectical necessities, having in view the central problem of our study.

Fullness of Religion

If R claims to be a catholic religion, this can only mean—if it has to make any sense—that it is the *full*, true religion or, in other words, that it is the *fullness of religion*.

This means to say that R and only R fulfills the full meaning and realizes the full function of religion. All other religions may be performing the same function but only provisionally and with regard to a certain epoch of history or group of mankind. This R is not yet the infinite, but it is close to it and is tending toward it, so that all other religions are a lower number that covers a multitude of units—members, functions, truths—but they are overcome by an ever-greater number.

An R claiming to be universal without, in an absolute sense, being so—as historical facts prove—can only mean by this claim, or rather the only true meaning a philosopher can discover in it is . . .—that it is the most perfect of all religions, not primarily in a moral sense, but in an ontological one.

This perfection means the fullness of its being "religion." It would then be *religion* as such, whereas all others would be *religions*.

Presence

We must discard any kind of religious competition: the meaning of that fullness cannot but be a sort of personal or moral superiority. It cannot mean, for instance, that Christians are better than Buddhists, lest we deny human liberty and we limit God's freedom of the conferring of His grace and the calling to the highest perfection to only a certain group of people. In a concrete existential sense it does not mean either that R is by all means and in all respects and times better than R_1 or R_2.

That R is the fullness of religion implies that R is somehow present wherever there is *a* religion; otherwise it would be *a* religion along with others, a little better or even much better, but not *the* religion as such—that is, truly catholic. The fact that R is the religion demands the presence of R wherever there is religion. It means not only that R is a greater number than R_n, but also that R can fulfill all the properties of R_n because without being exhausted in R_n and much less identified with it, it is present there.

R is within R_1, and similarly R_1 is in R. This has not necessarily to be interpreted as a kind of participation or historical influence, because the presence we are concerned with is an ontological presence. If R is *the* religion it is present wherever there is any religion.

This presence is rather of an open and dynamic nature, the meaning of it being that this religion is the working place from which God directs his activity—in other religions also—or rather the specific dwelling place of the saving power of God, which Christians would simply call Christ.

Immanence and Transcendence

This catholic R, due to its fullness and presence, must possess a very peculiar characteristic of *immanence and transcendence*. It is like any ever-greater number n that is immanent in the concrete number n_1 we may choose for a definite mathematical operation, and yet n transcends n_1. Likewise the presence of R in R_1 neither exhausts R nor makes R coalesce with R_1. Moreover, this catholic R needs to have this very dynamic, bipolar character of being immanently present and yet transcendent regarding the concrete *manifestation* of R itself. That is to say, this catholic religion is not only immanent and transcendent with regard to, let us say, Hinduism but also with respect to the existent form of Christianity itself. Otherwise, it could not fulfill the first and second conditions of fullness and presence. If we identify, in an absolute and static way, R with R_1, then it could not be present also in R_1, R_2, for R_1 is R_n and not R_1, R_2, etc. Nor could R_1 be the fullness of R. We should assume for this that R_1, R_2 are pure nonentities, that is, not religions at all, which is untenable. In other words, R's claim of catholicity implies that it cannot be *statically* identified or *exhaustively* equaled to any existent religion as it stands in a particular, frozen moment of history. The moment we identify R with R_n we make any growth and evolution impossible. If R_n has already reached its full catholicity it can neither expand nor assimilate; it should condemn a priori not only any other religion but also any effort of growth within itself.

Supradoctrinal Nature

Thus, R cannot be identified with any static reality. It cannot have a fixed and crystallized, static, immutable doctrinal body, as long as human history lasts and Man strives and struggles here on Earth. In other words, its catholicity can only be a universality in principle, *in potentia*, a fundamental ecumenism but not *in actu*, not a finished and already attained catholicity. R is tending to the infinite, but the infinite number does not exist as number, as actual essence. This R need not be an abstraction; it can be really and concretely present in R_n, but this R_n, is, properly speaking, a dynamic, living, growing religion tending to R, containing somehow R, but not identified with it.

In other words, R is not limited to any system and not exhausted by any doctrine. R must be *supradoctrinal*.

Existential Mission

This does not mean that R_n has no right to be called catholic. It points out only that this R_n is catholic insofar as it tends to R. It does not mean either that R_1, R_2 . . . can only reach R passing through R_n, but it means that the way to R is R_n and that R_1, R_2 . . . can only reach R passing through an R_m that shall be the existential *status* of R_n at this moment: $m = n + q$, where $q = 1, 2, . . .$ This is the real meaning of conversion.

R_n must somehow contain R, we said, but this "somehow" is precisely the reversal of the statement. It is R, the R immanent and transcendent, the R that is more than an essence or a doctrine, which contains R_n, that makes R_n be practically, functionally, existentially R. That means that R_n cannot have, as we said, a fixed, frozen doctrine, but that R_n possesses, or rather is possessed by, an existence, by a living principle, by a divine seed, by an incarnated *logos* that living in R_n and present also in R_1, R_2 . . . makes R_n the stable organic and normal abode of His action. Taking again our mathematical metaphor, we could say that though the number n we take for our infinitesimal calculus is not the actual infinite, the infinite must, so to speak, be acting and present in it and must lend to n all its properties for that particular mathematical operation we are dealing with; that is, n must be an ever-greater number.

R_n would be like R_1, R_2 . . . or simply a little better if it only possessed a mere adequate doctrine, a more efficient morality, and so on. If R_n is catholic it is because the catholic principle abides in it, because the living God possesses it or perhaps better utilizes it as His instrument of union and as His leaven of catholicity and light of universality. R, or as we have seen R_n, can only claim to be catholic if this claim is not its own, but the Voice of the One and Universal God, who has at least allowed the existence of so many religions and whose ways are inscrutable to any human mind. Not even the Son of Man knows the hour (Mt 24:36) of the concrete historical designs of the Father; perhaps because God has so high a respect—a divine respect—for the reflection of Himself, that is, His creation, that He has left the destiny of the universe to its immanent working forces. R must not only be divine, but it must be entrusted with the divine mission of gathering together all the fragments of this world of ours. The divine *ātman* must dwell in it in a very peculiar way, which we can with little doubt foretell will be one of service and of love.

For this, our last point, we must drop back again into the inexorable exigencies of human history.

The Historical Meaning

Any historical religion's claim to catholicity can only be a historical claim. On the other hand, only a historical universality has a concrete human and integral meaning.

To affirm that there is one universal religion because all humanity is one and from the very beginning has been in search of God, and that this quest for the Absolute is the essence of all religions, is to beg the question with regard to the unity of religions indulging in one-sided essentialist thinking. This kind of "universal religion," as the Romantic epoch of European culture used to refer to it, is so universal that it is no longer religion; it is only the common distillate of the most contradictory statements and the shapeless atmosphere of a vague religiosity. In fact, neither Christianity nor any other religion, not even the "natural religion" of the Romantics, vindicates such a pure formalistic universality. What religion claims to give is not a vague and formal advice of "follow your own urge," but the full, concrete, and integral answer to such a universal and religious thirst.

No one contests that thirst is universal; the question is who possesses the living waters to quench this thirst and where they are.

To this question the supposed religion that claims catholicity must give an answer.

We are concerned with giving a philosophical interpretation of this historical ecumenism and with drawing conclusions relevant to our problem. We are going to develop this line of thought under the inspiration of the religious and historical fact of Christianity and its catholic doctrine, but we repeat that ours is a purely philosophical reflection, concerned with understanding the problem of the unity and plurality of religions. The questions are these:

1. What is the meaning of a historical catholicity?
2. What are the consequences of such for the various religions of the world?

1. There are two main ways to understand the universality of a particular religion without destroying the integrality of the very religion, without reducing religions to a mere disincarnated "universal message" or an "everlasting essence."

The *first* method is to follow a mystical way, which tries to overcome the appearance of time and to dip into real time, which is discovered through the very tenets of that religion. An important sector of the present theology of history within Christianity tries to get rid of what I have called elsewhere *egochronism* (centering time on my ego), and doing this tries to prove the universality of Christianity, centered in Christ, the beginning, middle point, and end of world history. This way, however, does not seem fit for the present purpose. Buddhism could also offer us a similar example.

The *second* way is the purely historical one, without further theories on time and history. This path seems to be of some relevance for our problem.

The almost popular historical scheme of Christianity looks roughly like this:

Not only is mankind one, but humanity has a definite *historical* origin from a single human couple, who had, of course, only one religion and that was, in some sense, a perfect one toward which any existent religion has to turn if it wants to become *the* religion of Man.

Owing to what Christians call "original sin"—which in some way or other is also recognized in almost all religions—Man lost that perfect religion and had to find his way to God on a different basis. With the multiplication of men came also the varieties of that single, let us say "fallen," religion.

God had never abandoned His creation and was continuously inspiring, attracting, and leading men to Him—though, due to human divisions, weaknesses, and sin, these varieties of religions began to differ more and more in essential points. Nevertheless, His "Providence" awakened from time to time and elected and selected men and women, religious prophets, whose principal task was not precisely to create new religions but to purify the various religious confessions on Earth. History gives us abundant notice of these *ṛṣi* prophets and saints all over the world down to our present times. With the course of time and the intercourse of human and superhuman good and bad factors—the whole universe being a single divine cosmic adventure—these various religious confessions lost connection with one another, forgot their common ties, and crystallized in what we call today the various religions. Besides this general Providence of God inspiring his saints everywhere, there was a special assistance to a certain people charged with a very definite mission. That assistance continues down to our days upon the religion that has inherited the fulfillment of that mission. And this mission is none other than to assemble again the children of Man who were and still are scattered and divided and to recall them to the perfect unity of the universe and lead them toward the union with the living God. It goes beyond pure philosophy to prove the truth of the presuppositions of such statements and to recognize in Christ the cosmic Messiah and Redeemer of the whole universe. We are only concerned in trying to find the meaning of such a claim of universality and the consequent relation between religion and religions following from it. The very boldness of such statements has great appeal to an unbiased philosophical mind.

We could have presented this historical origin of mankind without reference to Adam and to original sin, and the main argument would have remained the same. Mankind from wherever it may have come and however it might have originated forms a certain historical unity; whatever evolution it may follow, mankind is not an empty word; and the religion of mankind can very well make definite, historical sense.

Whatever the ultimate truth about Christianity might be, philosophy of religion suggests to us a solution akin to the Christian one.

2. The relationship among religions for a philosophical phenomenology studying the historical facts of the various religions is neither that of an utter independence with no other tie than a fundamental unity—each religion considered as more or less good and as fulfilling more or less its function, all of them meeting in a transcendent sphere—nor that of an absolute interdependence or subordination, so that one is the best or the most perfect from which all others are derived—each religion being envisaged as a kind of heresy of the perfect one. On the contrary, the relation taking into account the historical development of religions and of mankind seems to be an organic, historical relationship of the kind claimed by Christianity.

In fact, there is no leadership among religions except the leadership of service; there is no dominance except the reign of love; there is no conquering save the conquest of truth. Only that which offers a purer and more disinterested service, which gives a higher love, which recognizes a brighter truth, only that will lead, reign, and conquer—in a much higher sense than the worldly meaning of these words—without any effort or ambition for power, honor, and glory. The history of all religions is the most striking proof of this. It is not a question of predominance or influence, but of comprehension and stewardship. The failures of many other approaches are still visible.

The sign of the true mother is the renunciation of the possession of her child provided he is kept alive. It is the royal privilege of the true religion as well as the prerogative of the higher truth to renounce partial statements and lower or one-sided formulations when mere central questions are at stake.

The panorama of the world religions does not appear as a kind of great scandal and failure of God—as certain good Christians are often inclined to imagine—nor as a sort of natural and obvious human condition—an idea that many Hindus, for example, cherish—but as a historical dynamic, and nevertheless dramatic situation of growth and accomplishment.

The philosophical and historical vision of religions on Earth is not precisely the optimistic naïve picture of a colorful and harmonic symphony, it is rather that of an existential and wonderful chair of thousands of voices crying, yet singing and expecting the manifestation of the children of God. The whole of creation is united if not yet in a single love, certainly in a unique hope: hope of salvation, of becoming, of being.

Philosophy can also foretell that arguments and "apologetics" here will be of little value, for what counts ultimately in human life is example, service, comprehension, love, truth.

If one of the existent religions claims to possess such catholicity, let it try to fulfill this claim. Nothing worthwhile in the others will suffer or disappear. It will be for them a historical growth and a new life within a more capable frame. And not a few changes will occur in the Catholic religion itself. This movement cannot be an imposition from outside, a compelling from without. It has to be an authentic growth from inside, a true enrichment from within, indeed a real increase, a veritable conversion! But who is going to trust another religion in such a *crucial* experiment? The most that that Catholic religion can expect is that the peoples be in an expectant mood, without much faith, with a little hope and open only to real love.

This historical challenge has a personal side that could be described as follows: I must strive to discover the truth, to perfect my religion, to convert myself, to live as a witness of the divine Light that enlightens every man who comes into this world. But it has also a sociological side: we must meet, know, learn from each other, love one another, live in intense communion with men, our brethren, and *God*, our Father.

Moreover, this diversity of religions appears as one of the most important historical forces; it appears as one of the main dynamic factors for the uplifting of humanity, for the transcendence of our laziness or narrow-mindedness, for the sanctification of ourselves and the world. It gives to this world of ours the necessary tension, the required level-difference, to overcome ourselves and to overcome the Earth. It is, of course, on the other hand, an almost dangerous potential that could launch the most hideous wars and catastrophes if not used properly, if not understood in the right way, if not handled with a humble love. "Corruptio optima pessima!" (Corruption of the best is the worst of all).

I would dare go a step further and say that for the present state of humanity we could hardly expect anything better than the present situation. The premature crystallization of a unique religion before the unity of mankind had been achieved would represent an irreparable loss of values and an impoverished Catholic religion. The present situation is the situation that we and our ancestors have merited, and it is a good one for our present state.

No religion should die without having said its last word, as Rudolf Otto once said. No religion should disappear without having handed over its sacred fire to a higher and more comprehensive religion.

The variety of religions bears upon the divergence of our human race. It is not the ideal state insofar as besides variety there is also variance, but it is the realistic historical present that no one has the right to ignore in the—unreligious—hurry of achieving a synthesis that requires a proper maturity and that has its own rhythm. As long as that Catholic religion is not capable of interrogating without suffocating the other religions, the colorful picture of the present day is in a sense the best situation. As long as the catholicity is not capable of containing the most opposite tensions in a higher harmony of a tunic of many colors—*circumadata varietate*—the truly religious spirits will have to strive among themselves and with others in order to enlarge the premises of the common mother. In her bosom must be a place for the mystics of the Ganges as well as for the hermits of Mount Athos, there must be room for the contemplatives of the Himalayas as well as for the activities of the modern cities, Sinai and Mecca; the plains and rivers of Africa; the smile of the Buddha; and the dances of the God of the jungles, the wisdom of Confucius, the Hellenic measure, and the modern sciences. All have to find their place in the only religion that claims to be the servant and the bearer of the message of salvation for humanity.

We have not yet reached that stage. We are still excluding one another, and like the man of Cro-Magnon who *could not* fly, we still *cannot* do anything but exclude one another, yet with hope and with regret. With the regret that we have to do it in order to be loyal to ourselves and to our times and with the hope that this our humble loyalty is a positive factor in the dynamism toward that catholic, universal religion to which we all already in spirit belong.

8

THE ONE, HOLY, CATHOLIC, AND APOSTOLIC RELIGION

The religion of our faith is the only one that can be the *one* religion. Man is passionate for unity; he cannot live without reaching it or at least striving for it. He, himself, is nothing but a spark of the divine One. The underlying longing of all religious efforts from all times down to the present day has been this thirst for unity, a thirst that sometimes has been abused by utilizing bad means of compulsion and violence of which the history of religion is so full. But there was always something positive behind it, and this ontological hunger for unity is impossible to renounce without committing the highest form of suicide.

When the intellectuals of our times speak about the unity of religion they are not, they cannot be, altogether wrong. Religion ultimately is only *one*.

The religion of our love is the only one that can be the *holy* religion.

Holiness is the proper value of religion; it is its peculiar prerogative. Only God is holy, and a religion leading us to God must be holy.

When the followers of all religions humbly try to climb the path of sanctity, they are doing more for the union of all creeds than is done by all the attempts to indiscriminately sweep away all differences.

We can only follow a religion of love, because ultimately we are craving for sanctity. The sanctification of ourselves and, through this existential way, the sanctification of our own religion will bring religions together, will unite them in the truly central point of human existence: Holiness, that is, God fully in Man. We have been called to become God. Very often we do not know what this means or what divinization is like, and we are tempted to quarrel on the basis of our little knowledge instead of realizing what is undoubtedly the concrete and infallible way to reach the goal: true sanctity.

The religion of our hope is the only one that can be the universal religion, the *catholic* religion. We can no longer expect salvation from private methods or partial remedies. Our epoch has discovered the historical and geographic unity of the human race and is tending toward the realization of a higher cultural unity—not uniformity—and cannot put its hope anywhere but in a catholic religion.

We must enlarge our views, without letting them become vague; we long for real brotherhood in deed and in truth and not only in language or in a clannish isolation. With little doubt the existential evolution of all creeds is toward a better catholicity. No religion can claim *perfect* catholicity as long as there are outsiders, as long as not everyone feels at home within it.

All true and authentic believers of all religions have the implicit *faith* in *one* religion, the craving *love* for a *holy* religion and the living *hope* in a *catholic* religion. *Unam, sanctam, catholicam . . .*

Et apostolicam! The religion of our life can only be a concrete and historical religion. We can only *live in* an apostolic religion and *by* it. We can only lead a complete human life in an incarnated religion, which is something more than a mere creed or a pure idea or ideal. Human life is historical and religion must be historical—that is, must have a historical shape and a historical basis. It cannot be an abstraction or a pure dream. It must have a Body to incorporate also the flesh and blood that we are. It must present not only a Message but a Messenger, who sends his ministers to be such, that is, servants of the others.

We can live only in a full *religion*, divine, transcendent, holy . . . but also human, immanent, and for sinners—we would add: composed of sinners with the humble desire to become saints. Everyone can dream up for himself a holy and catholic religion and even imagine that this is the only one, but religion is not a matter of dreams or of imagination, but of human and plain tangible reality.

We cannot invent religion. We must certainly discover religion, but this discovery that we have to work out and to make again and renew is at the same time something that exists before us, and above us—that is given to us and causes our very personal rediscovery of it, and of ourselves.

The religion we need for our human life is not a simple ideal or a mere good wish or any man-made construction but a God-given solution, a God-given answer not only for our individual problems but also for those of society and for our ancestors. It must be a historical religion with a historical mission, with a divine authority—not human—that is, one that at the same time transcends history.

Apostolic means that religion is sent by God for the real man, not for the human "nature" or for "mankind" in the abstract, but for me, for you. . . .

This apostolic religion, because it is meant for the existent man, not only does not rebuke sinners, but must accept and console . . . and forgive them. Thus, these sinners may invade and even stain the external purity of that religion, but it must be so divinely anchored and so humanly rooted that it will not fear and will not cast off the mediocrities, the little men. It is a religion that gathers the poor and the rich, saints and rascals, geniuses and simple, vulgar people, along with the educated and the illiterate "primitive" and savages. The apostolic religion will have to preach the simple and common message of Life, which sometimes the "elite," the "intelligentsia," will find hard to accept. Unfortunately, priest craft and Pharisaism throughout the history of religions have been the enemies of the true prophets of God and of the real spirit of religion.

This apostolicity must be definite, concrete and thus limited and subject to all human weaknesses and temptations, but needs also to be broad, universal, and thus without boundaries and above all human pettiness and selfishness. It will have a certain human shape, but it will not exclude anyone from its prayer, its care and—if we understand the concept well—its jurisdiction. If it has a hierarchy sent by God, this cannot be only for a part of the world, for he who is not against it is for it. Priests and ministers of this religion cannot regard themselves as being pastors and servants only for their own "flock." If they have received a mission for the whole world, they cannot exclude anyone and must be really there for every man.

I would dare to say that the implicit confession of faith of any good believer—*bona fide* in the full sense—of any religion is really directed toward the one, holy, catholic, and apostolic religion. And this faith, with hope and the life lived according to it, saves him.

What is this religion in the concrete? Where is this religion to be found, or when will the seed of the Word of God grow to its visibility and greatness so that the birds of the sky can repose in its *many branches*? Philosophy cannot give the complete answer to these questions, at least not what we call by that name today. But philosophy can begin asking and teaching us how to ask, how to pray for an answer. The answer, if any, can only be given by the requested. And He will show us *what* it is, *where* to find it, and *when*, the *una sancta, catholica, et apostolica ecclesia*!

Epilogue

Whoever might have had the patience to go carefully through these sometimes rather condensed pages will have understood—we hope—the main purpose of our study.

We could try to summarize it again in the following points:

1. Religion must be taken in its full complexity as a theandric fact and should not be reduced to one or two characteristics that we personally think important according to our ideas or liking.

2. Just as any kind of true love has in itself the note of perennity—to say "I love you for five minutes" or "for five years" has no meaning, though, alas, not every love is everlasting—likewise, the philosophical analysis of religion shows that ultimately religion has unity as a fundamental note. Plurality of religions can only have provisional meaning. Either the plurality is for the time being—that is, only for a certain time, which can be, of course, more or less durable and even cover the whole extent of our earthly, but provisional, existence—or the plurality is there only because religions have not yet reached their maturity and perfection.

3. The increasing claim for unity of religion that we detect in our times is a healthy and positive sign of human vitality, and it is a religious truth. But we want to warn against the temptation of "spiritualizing" such a unity, reducing it to a transcendental or mystical sphere which would amount to destroying religion and not reaching any unity. Religion would then have dissolved before reaching that purely transcendental unity—like the man who died just when he became accustomed to living without food.

4. That unity of religions lies in the very human realm of religions themselves—that is, in history—and we have tried to show that there is almost a historical-dialectical process that brings all religions together and prepares the ground for a truly single religion. This process is, of course, still open, and we have only described it rather philosophically instead of having recourses to a substantiated historical study.

5. Because the only way to give a full expression to one's thought is within an organic, though open, system, and in this case within a religion—because that religion also offers to us the most striking and daring example of such an inherent claim of all religions—we have chosen Christian terminology and background in order to express the dynamic evolution and integrating dialectics; but our aim was to describe sincerely a philosophical process without any afterthought of Christian apologetics. We hope that followers of other religions can fully agree with us regarding the formal structure of our reasoning. If they consider their own religion as the true catholic religion, the present writer shall be more than content, for this

authentic zeal will stir up that necessary spiritual emulation that we all need in order not to sleep on the way, or to be Pharisaically satisfied with our own ideas that are stagnating in our own clan.

6. This was the whole intention of our effort, to induce people to face the most tremendous religious challenge of history: the meeting of religions under the accepted leadership of God and within the recognized fellowship of men.

Part Two

9

MEDITATION ON MELCHIZEDEK

Apellatus a Deo pontifex iuxta ordinem Melchisedek.
And was acclaimed by God with the title of high priest of the order of Melchizedek.

Heb 5:10

Melchizedek, the "king of peace," appears quite suddenly in the biblical horizon—we do not really know where he comes from: he simply emerges from the Earth!—and permeates Christian spirituality; from ancient times until today, this enigmatic figure has always captivated the church's attention. The reason for this great interest must be attributed to the profoundly mystical and theological sense of his personality. In this study I would like to outline, albeit roughly, a partial aspect, a simple fragment of the theology of Melchizedek:[1] what is the meaning of the order, the line, the mode, the *taxis*, the *ʿal-dibrātī*, by virtue of which God has designated His Only-Begotten Son priest forever?

The Facts

Sacred Scripture

Unlike other Christian themes, that of Melchizedek does not derive from tradition or from the life of the church. Rather it has a scriptural origin, that is, it comes directly from the Bible, and it is imposed, so to speak, from above, by the sacred authors. The only passages that speak directly of Melchizedek are the following:

Old Testament

The figure of Melchizedek only appears in two places, and in both of them, quite abruptly.

---

[1] To justify the main idea of this study, cf. the following biblical passages: Gn 20:3–7; Dan 2:21; 2:28–29; 2:37–38; 4:22; Is 6:9–10; 45:1; Nb 22:5ff.; 23:7–10; 23:18–24; 24:2–9; 24:15–24; Ac 14:12ff.; 16:8–16; 17:23; Rom 1:19–20; 2:9–10; 2:14–15; 11:16–19; 12:1ff.; 1 Co 10:19–29; Ph 4:8; Tt 2:1ff.; Col 3:22–25; Ep 6:5–8; Heb 5:6–10, etc.

1. *Genesis 14:18–20.* Abram, who had not yet received the name of Abraham—this is relevant—returns victorious from the war, and "Melchizedek king of Salem brought bread and wine; he was a priest of God Most High. He pronounced this blessing: Blessed be Abram by God Most High, Creator of heaven and earth. And blessed be God Most High for putting your enemies into your clutches. And Abram gave him a tenth of everything."[2]

2. *Psalm 110 [109]:4.* After revealing the Messiah's royal dignity, this messianic psalm, quoted by Christ himself and studied in the Epistle to the Hebrews, states, "Yahweh has sworn an oath he will never retract, you are a priest forever of the order of Melchizedek."

New Testament

Only Paul speaks explicitly of Melchizedek, in order to connect him to Christ and his Priesthood.

1. *Hebrews 5:5–6; 5:10.* The entire text discusses priesthood, and the priesthood of Christ in particular: "And so it was not Christ who gave himself the glory of becoming high priest, but the one who said to him: You are my Son, today I have fathered you." And in another place it says, "and was acclaimed by God with the title of high priest of the order of Melchizedek."

2. *Hebrews 6:19–20.* "This is the anchor our souls have, reaching right through inside the curtain where Jesus has entered as a forerunner on our behalf, having become a high priest forever, *of the order of Melchizedek.*"

3. *Hebrews 7:1ff.* This chapter, entirely dedicated to Melchizedek and to Christ, is considered the crucial point of the epistle and the nucleus of biblical priesthood doctrine. It has also been said, always with regard to this text, that one cannot obtain a global idea of Christ's priesthood without understanding his relationship with Melchizedek.

*

Melchizedek, king of Salem, a priest of God Most High, came to Abraham when he returned from defeating the kings, and blessed him; and Abraham gave him a tenth of everything. By the interpretation of his name, he is, first, "king of saving justice" and also king of Salem, that is, "king of peace"; he has no father, mother, or ancestry, and his life has no beginning or ending; he is like the son of God. He remains a priest forever.

Now think how great this man must have been if the patriarch Abraham gave him a tenth of the finest plunder. We know that any of the descendents of Levi who are admitted to the priesthood are obliged by the Law to take tithes from the people,

---

[2] Biblical quotes are from the New Jerusalem Bible (NJB).

that is, from their own brothers, although they, too, are descended from Abraham. But this man, who was not of the same descendant, took his tithe from Abraham, and he gave his blessing to the holder of the promises. Now it is indisputable that a blessing is given by a superior to an inferior. Further, in the normal case it is ordinary mortal men who receive the tithes, whereas in that case it was one who is attested as being alive. It could be said that Levi himself, who receives tithes, actually paid tithes, in the person of Abraham, because he was still in the loins of his ancestor when Melchizedek came to meet him.

Now if perfection had been reached through the Levitical priesthood—and this was the basis of the Law given to the people—why was it necessary for a different kind of priest to arise, spoken of as being *of the order of Melchizedek* rather than of the order of Aaron? Any change in the priesthood must mean a change in the Law as well. So our Lord, of whom these things were said, belonged to a different tribe, the members of which have never done service to the altar; everyone knows he came from Judah, a tribe that Moses did not mention at all when dealing with priests.

This becomes even more clearly evident if another priest, of the type of Melchizedek, arises who is a priest not in the virtue of the law of physical descent, but in virtue of the power of an indestructible life. For he is attested by the prophecy: *You are a priest forever of the order of Melchizedek*. The earlier commandment is thus abolished, because of its weakness and ineffectiveness, since the Law could not make anything perfect; but now this commandment is replaced by something better—the hope that brings us close to God.

Now the former priests became priests without any oath being sworn, but this one with the swearing of an oath by him who said to him, *The Lord has sworn an oath he will never retract: you are a priest forever*; the very fact that it occurred with the swearing of an oath makes the covenant of which Jesus is the guarantee all the greater. Further, the former priests were many in number, because death put an end to each one of them; but this one, because he remains forever, has a perpetual priesthood. It follows, then, that his power to save those who come to God through him is absolute, since he lives forever to intercede for them.

Such is the high priest that met our need—holy, innocent, and uncontaminated, set apart from sinners, and raised up above the heavens; he has no need to offer sacrifices every day, as the high priests do, first for their own sins and only then for those of the people; this he did once and for all by offering himself. The Law appoints high priests who are men subject to weakness; but the promise on oath, which came after the Law, appointed the Son who is made perfect forever.

Liturgy

At least since the fifth century, the Church, in the Canon of the Mass of the Roman Rite, makes explicit reference to St. Melchizedek—as he is called as of the Roman Council of 860—and his priesthood. In all the other rites Melchizedek also holds a preeminent position and is remembered in a great number of ancient prefaces next to Abel and Abraham. There is a feast specifically dedicated to him, as saint, and even today, the first part of Mass in the Greek-Syrian Rite receives the name of Melchizedek—the second is called Aaron and the third, Christ.

An *epiklesis* of the Gallican Church calls the ceremony of Mass "ritu Melchisedek summi sacerdotis oblate." Another *epiklesis* of the Mozarabic liturgy identifies the offering of the Christian sacrifice with the oblations of that "type" of priest, that is, Melchizedek. The meaning of the *lex orandi* in the Church is always the same: the "king of justice" is considered as he who has offered God a worthy and pleasant sacrifice, in the same line of Christ and ours.

Roman Canon

After the consecration, the priest asks God to once again accept the sacrifice of His Son, because Mass is not just the repetition of a previously accepted sacrifice, but rather it supposes our real and temporal incorporation into this sacrifice. Every *re-presentation* of the act of Christ entails that He make Himself truly present in space and time, and consequently, this *new* act requires a new acceptance by God, so that *this* Mass may be incorporated to the sole oblation of His Son. And it is precisely at this moment that the priest recalls the continuity between Abel, Abraham, and Melchizedek: "Look with favor on these offerings and accept them as once you accepted the gifts of your servant Abel, the sacrifice of Abraham, our father in faith, and the bread and wine offered by your priest Melchizedek, a holy sacrifice, a spotless victim."

Tradition

From the beginning, the Fathers of the Church have considered the "mysterious" figure of this king and priest not only as a "type" and precursor of Christ, but also as a representative of divine priesthood on Earth since the creation of the world. We could quote, among others, Justin, Tertullian, Clement of Alexandria, Augustine, and others.

The language of the Fathers is quite bold and transmits the full conviction of the cosmic significance of Melchizedek and of the catholicism of Christ, who frees us from the uselessness, the ἀνοφελές, of the Old Testament. Thus, for example, St. Ambrose writes, "Take in what I now say. The mysteries of the Christians were before those of the Jews. . . . Where did the Jews begin? From Judah, the great-grandson of Abraham. . . . So they are called Jews from the great-grandson of Abraham, or from the time of the saintly Moses. . . . In Abraham's time, when he collected three hundred and eighteen well-appointed men, and pursued his enemies, and brought his grandchild back from captivity. Then, returning a victor, there met him Melchisedech the priest, and he offered bread and wine (Gen. 14:18). Who had the bread and wine? Abraham did not have it. But who had it? Melchisedech. He then is the author of the sacraments" (Heb. 7:1–2) (*De sacram.* 4.10).

Must we quote John Chrysostom as Greek representative of the Early Church Fathers? "[Abraham] would not have given tithes to a stranger unless his dignity had been great. Astonishing! What has he accomplished? He has made quite clear a greater point than those relating to faith which he treated in the Epistles to the Romans. For there indeed he declares Abraham to be the forefather both of our polity and also of the Jewish. But here he is exceedingly bold against him, and shows that the uncircumcised person is far superior. How then did he show that Levi paid tithes? Abraham (he says) paid them." And Theodore declares that he was not "the priest of the Hebrews, but of the Verb."

The theology of priesthood in the Middle Ages was also directly connected to this man who "has no father, mother, or ancestry; and his life has no beginning or ending," as can be seen in, among others, Peter Lombard, Bonaventure, and Thomas Aquinas. All Scholastic theology agrees on this point, and it comments that "the sacrifice that Christians throughout the world today offer to God was first established in the meeting of Abraham and Melchizedek—according to the words of Saint Augustine."

History

What we could call the ecclesiastical tradition is not the only one that mentions Melchizedek, as he also appears in the writings of many philosophers and heretics, in apocryphal writings, rabbinical literature, and elsewhere.

This mysterious figure is interpreted according to the main tendencies of each time period or to the personal convictions of each writer. Hebraic literature, for example, attempts to connect him to Noah and points out that Shem had been circumcised. Philo offers a purely allegorical interpretation of the king of peace, in the interest of his conception of the *logos*. Similarly, for gnosis, Melchizedek is considered an intermediate power in the process of cosmic emancipation.

Legend

We find, throughout the Christian era, typical and interesting stories that refer to this most singular personality. There is no reason, in principle, to neglect these legends even though sometimes they may seem like myths. Their meanings are profound, and the symbolism they contain shows us aspects of the mystery of Melchizedek without which we would have great difficulty understanding him.

Perhaps the best-known story, which is recurrently found, though with many variations, is the one narrated in the Eastern Book of Adam, in which Melchizedek is presented transporting Adam's dead body to Calvary; in this way, he participates in Adam's priestly function and becomes his connection to Christ.

Melchizedek has also been interpreted as a "cosmic spiritual energy," like an "angel" (Michael, in particular), and even as the "Holy Ghost." Even today we can read, with a certain interest, a legendary account of the life of this priest of the First Alliance in a text not much later than St. Anastasius, which is part of his apocryphal works.

The Interpretation

Physical Continuity

The totality of the Christian message represents something new, previously unknown, and its irruption doubtlessly entails a profound change of course in history. Christianity is not only the development of a "natural" religion, and its doctrine is not a certain kind of sublimation of Greek theories or of pagan mysteries. Yet this *innovation* does not destroy the complementary *principle of continuity*.

The people expected Christ, but he did not come to abolish the Law or the Prophets. In fact, he has been active since the creation of the universe; everything has been created by Him, in such a way that, in a sense, Christianity exists since the beginning of time.

Furthermore, given that humanity, along with the whole of creation, forms a unity, there can be nothing either completely new or isolated on this Earth. Christ himself, Son of God, had to have a Mother in order to be Son of Man. History never restarts absolutely *ab novo*, and a "human being created" by God is at the same time fruit of his parents. Everything and every process that takes place in the world has its origin in previous beings, and at the same time they influence other beings. A new nation is only the result of a preceding historical reality; a discovery always derives from known facts; new sects or religions constitute the reformation or the fullness of others that have preceded them, and they adopt a form that is in consonance with the place from which they emerge.

Christ is the only priest of the New Alliance, but his priesthood, because it is new and supreme, constitutes the continuation and fullness in the temporal order of the priesthood of the Old Testament, and in even greater measure, the continuation and perfection of the priesthood of the First Alliance.

The divine adventure—*oikonomía*—of humanity with God, its Creator and Redeemer, has been the object of at least three testaments. The first is the alliance with Adam, or cosmic testament of God and Man, that of his very being: *Let us make Man. And Man was made son of God.* This testament has, so to speak, two clauses: the first comes from the fall of Adam, and the second is constituted by the promise—it is the Proto-Gospel—after original sin. There are many points we are ignorant of in regard to this second clause. They belong to the mysterious relationship between God and Man in the course of history. We only know some of them: the promise made to Abel, the pact with Noah, the illumination of the Buddha, the inspiration of Confucius, the intuition of the ṛṣi, etc.

The second testament is the gift of circumcision, the alliance—*berit*—with Abraham: *You will be Father of the chosen people! You will be Forefather of the Messiah!*

The New Testament is the completeness of both, the alliance of God with all of creation in the person of Christ, the Mediator: *You are my Son, my beloved!*

However, Christ is not only the Messiah of Israel; nor is he the successor of the sons of Levi in the priesthood. He, High Priest of the New Testament, does not belong to the priestly dynasty of the house of Israel; rather his title belongs to the line of the high priest of the primitive testament, who is no other than Melchizedek. It is significant that the devil, through the possessed man of Gerasa, calls Jesus Son of God Most High—ὑψίστου—which was the title of the God of Melchizedek.

This continuity can also be seen in the mysterious meeting between Abraham and the priest-king. Many of the legends that relate Melchizedek to Adam, Noah, Shem, and others begin here.

Abraham has been separated from his people and sent to a new land to become father of countless generations and backbone of the people of God. A new testament is about to take effect. God wants him to assume responsibility not only for his own people but also for the entire world. That is why belonging to his own lineage is not enough; he needs, in addition, a special link with the rest of humanity; he needs the blessing of the priest of the old alliance, because he must be something more than the representative of his own race and father of the chosen people. The mission of the people of Israel is not only the salvation of Israel, it also includes the whole of humanity. Salvation, in fact, comes from the Jews—*salus ex iudaeis*—but is not only *for* the Jews. This link that unites him to humanity is what is reinforced by Melchizedek, since Melchizedek is certainly a figure—*figura expressissima* (St. Bonaventure)—a "type" of Christ, but, however, continues to be a historical and real person. In fact, he was God's priest and his priesthood was real—a priesthood that was not only accepted but also instituted and desired by the Almighty. The New Testament shows us the reason why this continuity was established and the way in which the king priest blessed the father of the nations so that this blessing could remain among them.

Do we have to remind today's generation what a blessing means? A blessing—a fact that is found in all religions—is a psycho-physical reality that in itself proves the deep unity that there is between the material and the spiritual worlds. How could a spiritual gift connect itself to a material object if they were not both absolutely heterogeneous? A blessing is a spiritual reality that descends upon a material object and remains there. A blessed object contains something that an object that has not been blessed does not possess, and this "something" remains; it impregnates its very matter and it bestows a new value on it. Something that has been blessed carries with and in itself a spiritual content.

Abraham was blessed thanks to coming into contact with that uncircumcised and unknown priest who most likely came from Mount Carmel, the sacred place of the Canaanites, and who in one way or another had maintained the continuity of the priesthood since the beginning of the world.

Melchizedek does not have an esoteric, or pseudo-gnostic, meaning, and his personality should not be interpreted too whimsically, as, for example, the ancient sect of the order of Melchizedek did, or as modern falsifications of a perverted spirituality tend to do.

The "king of peace" priest has a specific, physical function to perform, and even if his mission in itself is transcendent, it also continues to have a defined historical meaning: meeting with Abraham in order to restore the bond that united him, from the beginning, to the universal and general priesthood of humanity. God has never forgotten his creation, and in choosing the people of Israel and bestowing upon them a special mission on Earth, he has not forgotten to connect them to the rest of the world, so as not to leave the rest of the nations of the cosmos aside.

Pastoral Continuity

Physical continuity does not mean the negation of *moral discontinuity*, just as *pastoral continuity* does not intend to abolish *practical discontinuity*; the only goal of both is to complete the beginning, or better said, the fact of Christian *innovation* by means of the principle of *constancy*. We are fully conscious that both belong to different categories, and we do not aspire to question the rupture, the innovation, the restoration or, if you wish, the revolution of Christianity. We only wish to point out another aspect of the problem.

What does it mean for Abraham, who is to become the cornerstone and living symbol of the oath of YHWH to his people, to accept the blessing of a "pagan" and offer him tribute by recognizing him as more important than himself? If we think in terms of the spiritual climate of absolute exclusivity that characterizes the Old Testament—of the jealous God of Abraham, Isaac, and Jacob, who does not tolerate any other God, that is, any other form of worship different to that which He has so minutely established—we will only discover an orthodox response that is reminiscent of similar paradoxes that appear in the Old Testament and, more often, in the New.

This fact has the same meaning as the prophecy of Balaam's donkey or as that expression with which Jesus forbids his disciples to do evil, to launch any kind of excommunication against those who perform miracles in his name, even if they are not his followers, because "anyone who is not against us is for us." It has the same meaning as the Master's reprimand to Peter, the visible head of his church, when—with a final residue of intolerance—he wants to discover the nature of the privilege reserved for the preferred disciple, who had to *remain* until the return of Christ.... It means, in short, that Christ already was before Abraham, that He is the *alpha* and the *omega*, beginning and end, in which all things subsist and thanks to which everything has become.

There is only one High Priest in the new alliance, because in the end of time, in the fullness of time, there is only one priest: that of the Redeemer. The priesthood of the Law, the priesthood of the sons of Levi, has accomplished its mission, which has objectively been abolished from the moment it has not known how to recognize and welcome the Messiah.

Melchizedek, however, embodies the priesthood of the first alliance between God and Man, and his priesthood—although containing many strains—still remains in pre-Christian religions; Melchizedek is the priest of the Almighty, and in a certain sense, all true priests of the only God in the multiple religions of the Earth participate in the priesthood of this first testament. The priests of all religions, despite their imperfections and the possible disfigurations of the authentic figure of Melchizedek, are, because of their priesthood, priests of *Elyōn*, the ὕψιστος, the sublime and transcendent God.

And this seems to be the meaning included in so many documents of the Church, among them the data of the Council of Trent and the encyclical of Pius XI to the Catholic clergy, when they recognize the need for and the authenticity of the priesthood for the human species. The legitimate priesthood of the so-called natural religions derives from the eternal Divinity, and independently of whatever Melchizedek's personal excellence might have been in the performance of his particular functions, he was, in fact—and this is important—priest of the only and identical God.

The religions of the world may have flawed doctrines, bad aspects, and even diabolical influences, but insofar as they are religions, they foreshadow and announce Christianity, and their priests are truly priests according to the order of Melchizedek: mediators, chosen men, chosen from among others for the salvation of their brothers, in order to perform sacrifices and oblations for the sins of humanity.

Thus, a true Christian approach to the deep level of an ontological relationship cannot be established considering the other as a competitor or an enemy who has usurped a place that does not belong to him, but rather it must be performed by means of the Christian path of service and of love. We will have to act in the opposite way of how the prodigal son's big brother did; we will have to imitate Christ, who came to serve and not to be served, and we will have to be willing, whenever necessary, to receive "peace" from our "pagan" priest brothers, in order to accept that which they can still offer us, in order to establish continuity and integrate them in the plenitude of their own priesthood, according to the order of Melchizedek.

The day when the climate of understanding is strong enough for Christian priests to receive "peace" from non-Christian priests, or by the same token, the day in which these priests are willing to give us, to transfer to us, all that they have and possess and we, Christian priests, are ready to receive it, that day we will be much closer to the path that leads to one flock and one shepherd. . . .

There is no need to say that this blessing of peace does not imply a Christian obligation but rather a Catholic embrace. It is also clear that a blessing is not, strictly speaking, exclusively a priestly act and that after the inversion of the purely terrestrial values that Christ carried out, the hypothetical blessing of a "gentile" to a Christian does not mean that the non-Christian is better, but that the most important has become the servant, and that the first has learned to be the last and is simply prepared to assume the responsibility and continue in a more complete way than his brothers had begun, in the order of desires and of hope. Did Christ teach us something different? Did not He, Immaculate Savior, let himself be circumcised and allow John to baptize Him in order to fulfill all justice? And Mary, the Immaculate, did she pose any objection to going to the Temple in order to undergo the rite of purification? This is not about deceit or about acts that are lacking in sincerity, but about sublime examples of the Catholic spirit which, on the other hand, cannot be separated from the whole of its testimonies. Furthermore, between the sixth and tenth verses of the fifth chapter of the Epistle to the Hebrews, in which Melchizedek is mentioned, Sacred Scripture introduces one of the most extraordinary texts that refer to Christ, a text that corroborates this interpretation. He, the Son of God, the Only Priest, offered up prayer and entreaty, with loud cries and with tears, for the salvation of the world; he learned obedience through his suffering and achieved perfection in his being to the point of becoming cause of eternal salvation. It would have been enough for the disciple to behave like the Master!

Catholic priests, heirs of the priesthood of Melchizedek, not only do not scorn true priests from other religions, no matter how "primitive" these may be, but they also consider them brothers who participate in one sole priesthood, precursors of Christ, custodians of the eternal order of Melchizedek, in the highest summit and supreme fullness from which God the Father established at once and for all Christ, His Son. This does not translate into a canonical *communio in sacris*, nor does it in any way justify the approval of or the indiscriminate participation in religious practices. The king of Salem most probably belonged to the Canaanite people, a nation cursed by God, but this did not prevent him from being the priest of the only God.

We are not exclusively referring to the respect that any truly consecrated soul deserves, nor to the reverence that is due to people of goodwill and the best intentions, but rather we are talking about the consciousness of an ontological community, of a source for the pastoral attitude that neutralizes the much too human and much too frequent temptation of considering oneself the "other," "pure," "superior," because of having received a vocation that addresses a higher service.

Christianity is not exactly a religion different from others: it is the conversion and the perfection of all religions. Christ does not exclude, but in Himself includes and embraces everything; He does not come to destroy nor to demand the help of His legions of angels, but to perfect and to redeem. He has urged us not to blow the wick that flickers. As there are sacraments of the old alliance—similar to the sacraments of the Old Testament—there is also an authentic and true priesthood from the beginning.

The Order of Melchizedek

The Epistle to the Hebrews does not especially emphasize the priestly *acts* of Melchizedek—since it is well known that neither his blessings nor the gift of bread and wine, despite their Eucharistic symbolism, contain in themselves anything that is essentially priestly—but rather the *person* Melchizedek, or more exactly, the *order* of the priesthood of which Melchizedek was a living example.

This order is superior to the Levitical order, and it is part—and up to a certain point, the base—of the Christian order, which can never be reduced to a devitalized, impoverished, and "supernaturalized" order. The authentic Christian order is found in the same "line" as Melchizedek, and he perfects it.

What is, then, this *taxis*, this "mode," this "disposition," this "semblance" or "way of being," this "ordinance" or this simple "line," according to which Christ is the supreme and everlasting High Priest, and which has been called "order of Melchizedek"?

The Epistle to the Hebrews is the letter of the "testaments." The word *diathēkē*, which is used thirty-three times in the New Testament, appears seventeen times in this short letter, and the concept it wishes to express appears in even greater measure if we consider the intimate relationship between the *diathēkē* applied in the two Testaments and the *taxis* of Melchizedek, which refers to the first alliance. Both words express ordinance, disposition, order.

We know that this "mode" is very special, that it possesses all the characteristics of greatness, and that it is enveloped in the Divine Mystery. It is Melchizedek himself who descends in order to find Abraham; he, who has no father, no mother or ancestry, who has no beginning and no ending, who is like the Son of God—*aphōmoiōmenos*—and who remains priest forever.

Christian tradition has seen in all of this the sign of the grace of Christ, of His free "coming" and of the natural human impotence to elevate itself to the supernatural order, which does not come from the body or from the will of Man, but rather is born directly in God. However, God's grace will always be present while the world exists because Christ was already before Abraham at the very beginning of creation; He is not only the Only Son, He is also the firstborn of all creatures.

It is not necessary to penetrate deeper into this particular Christocentric aspect right now. Suffice it to say that Adam was already included in the order of grace, integral and supernatural, and therefore, the reality that God originated was not simply "nature" but rather "super-nature."

Melchizedek, though, in the capacity of representative of the order of the cosmic priesthood, no longer belongs to the initial state of Adam because Adam's nature is that of a fallen man and belongs to the factual-existential condition of humanity before being transformed by Christ. His state is neither supernatural, because it is a fallen state, nor purely natural, since "pure nature" has never existed. This is why we say *existential order*, the order of any human being after the fall of Adam, the order that demands to be newly elevated in order to recover its lost plenitude and that suffers because of its incapacity of becoming free unless a Savior comes to aid.

Melchizedek, the *automathēs kai autodidaktos* (he who learns from no teacher but himself), as Philo calls him, is the priest of existential fallen creation that yearns and cries out for God, waiting for the redemption of every creature. His is the existential order of humanity, the order in which Christ Redeemer is incarnated. Christ did not assume a pure, Adamic nature, but a real, factual, and existential nature, with all of its shortcomings, except for the stain of original sin; in a certain way, according to the bold Pauline expression, He himself became sin in order to erase sin, to destroy the sting of sin itself.

The historical form of Christ's priesthood is not that of Adam's before the fall, nor that of God's chosen people who received circumcision, but that of the line of Melchizedek, the cosmic priest of the fallen creation that needs to be redeemed. This is precisely the line of Christ, the second Adam, who came to redeem Man from the conditions in which he finds himself upon the Earth and, for this reason, is the authentic and true line of the priests of the old alliance. Melchizedek is the priest who does not know Christ, even if they are part of the same line; he is the priest who offers wine and bread without knowing the symbolism that lies behind them; he is the priest who dares to bless God's chosen one, he who has no father and no mother; he who does not know from where he comes or to where he goes, who comes from the Earth, who has no ancestry, nobody knows his origins, and nevertheless is a figure of Christ, whom he will purify, redeem, elevate, and in this way complete his priesthood.

The Catholic priest is not, strictly speaking, a priest, because the new alliance only has one priest; but he is a qualified minister of the only Priest from where his priesthood derives and in which he participates. As such, he not only participates in the supernatural power of Christ High Priest, but he also participates in His perfect priesthood, and he forms part of the order of Melchizedek in a much fuller sense than that of the pre-Christian priest, because the former obtains from Christ the plenitude of everlasting priesthood, while the latter receives from Melchizedek a temporal priesthood, a fallen figure, although authentic and true priesthood.

The Bible uses the term priest, *kohen* (of uncertain etymology), for the first time here. Strictly speaking, then, there is only one priesthood: Christ's—if we consider it in its fullness—or the authentic priesthood of Melchizedek—if we refer to its *minimum* or to its existential *status* before Christ.

There is a line of continuity between Adam and Abel, and between Abel and Melchizedek. This is where separation occurs. With a specific goal, Melchizedek addresses his blessing to Abraham and makes him take part in his priesthood, which will develop especially in the sons of Aaron, Moses's brother. However, Melchizedek, the king of justice, does not join Abraham's descendants, but again disappears—surely in order to newly transmit his blessing, by means of which God, doubtlessly, has conferred the priesthood to his brothers, to the other "gentiles," sons of God, and thus the priesthood continues through time in the person of the true priests of the Almighty.

Likewise, this double order—that is, the line from the first Testament and the order of the old alliance—meets again in Christ, the Only High Priest of the New Testament. Christ, furthermore, by joining the line of Melchizedek, closes and seals the line of Levi. All things converge in Christ, and everything that is subject to the effect of time participates of Him.

However, in the mystery of time, in the development and growth of the Mystic Body, traces of Aaron's priesthood remain in all those Jews who are still (*bona fide*) ministers of YHWH. Moreover, there are still traces of numerous pre-Christian priests who find themselves in the existential line of the priest king, without father,

mother, and origin, emerged from the primitive ages and rising in the cosmic beginning of the world, in the priests, or more accurately, in the ministers of the diverse
religions that exist.

We are not here interested in determining up to what point the true character
of the order of Melchizedek has been preserved in the diverse religions of the Earth,
nor do we aspire to deny the existence of shadows and the possibility of aberrant
forms of priesthood. We only wish to emphasize that this line still exists and that
the priests of all religions who truly deserve this name participate, in one way or
another, in the priesthood of Melchizedek; and also that in his name Christ, High
Priest, by means of the priests of the new alliance, offers to his Father God in each
Mass a holy sacrifice, an immaculate victim to which all offerings are joined, *pūjā*,
rituals, sufferings, sacrifices, and prayers of this world.

"May the contrite soul, the humbled spirit, be as acceptable to you as the burnt
offerings of rams and bullocks, as thousands of fat lambs; such let our sacrifice be
to you today, and may it please you that we follow you wholeheartedly," says the
liturgy, in the words of Daniel (Dn 3:39–40).

10

THE INVISIBLE HARMONY

A Universal Theory of Religion or a Cosmic Confidence in Reality?

Harmonia aphanēs phanerēs kreittōn.
Invisible harmony is stronger than the visible.

Heraclitus, *Fragm.* 54

In the first part of this chapter I examine the reasons that direct modern Western scholarship to search in the direction of a universal theory of religion. In the second part I submit the "universal theory" to a critique. In the third I attempt to offer an alternative.

A general remark at the very outset is called for. I am fully aware that there is no East and no West, no monolithic Christianity, nor standard Hinduism, that human traditions and even human beings themselves are much more holistic than most of our intellectual disquisitions tend to assume. In every one of us looms an East and a West, a believer and an unbeliever, a male and a female, and so on. Every human being is a microcosm, and every human culture represents the whole of humanity. The true *ātman* of (in) every one of us is *brahman*. Buddha-nature lies at the bottom of every being. We all are called upon to share divine nature. Hence, the level of my discourse is directed at detecting predominant winds, leading threads, the dominating Zeitgeist, on the one hand, and the deeper structures of the human being and of reality on the other.

I encompass under the notion of "universal theory" all those efforts at reaching a global intellectual understanding, be it called "ecumenical Esperanto," "world theology," "unified field theory," or even a certain type of "comparative religion" and "ecumenism." The common trait here is the noble effort at reducing the immense variety of human experiences to one single and common language, which may well respect the different dialectical forms of expression and of life but which somewhat subsumes them all and allows for communication and understanding on a universal scale. The universal theory assumes that a certain type of rationality is the general heritage of humankind, and even more, that it is the one specifically human trait.

It assumes we are human beings because we are rational creatures, reason being our last appeal; thus, the same reason theoretically has to be capable of solving all the problems that plague our human race.

The gist of this study is a challenge to all this. And yet the alternative is not solipsism on the one hand or irrationalism on the other, as if we could only be respectively victims of a depressive individualism or of a shallow sentimentalism. I have already hinted that a whole anthropology and metaphysics are here called into question. The raising of such problems should be the concern of cross-cultural studies, if they really want to be cross-cultural and not simply window dressing with more or less exotic or less known ways of thinking.

The reader will have noticed that I do not mention the usual names of sociologists, anthropologists, and philosophers dealing with the traditional problems of evolutionism, structuralism, synchronicity, and the like. Is there a common human nature? Does evolution, on the one hand, or structuralism, on the other, offer a basis to understand our phenomenon? Although it would have been very instructive to take a position in any one of the contemporary discussions, I have opted for not entering into these scholarly debates for two main reasons. The one is that to do it properly would require an almost independent study as long as the present one—and this has already been done several times.[1] The other and more important reason is that my perspective claims to be more cross-cultural and "metaphysical" than such studies usually are, for they by and large remain within the problematic of today's (and yesterday's) Western scholarship.

I am not now criticizing a particular theory of an individual scholar or a school. I am submitting to analysis the sense of the enterprise itself. However, because of the very holistic character of our being, our theories also are more comprehensive than we generally imagine. Thus, if my criticism is answered by showing me that what I am saying is precisely what others wanted to say, because it was already implicit or taken for granted in their minds, I shall then be glad to have elicited this clarification.

Analysis of the Intent

Continuation of the Western Syndrome

The thrust toward universalization has undoubtedly been a feature of Western civilization since the Greeks. If something is not universal, it looms as not really valid. The ideal of humanity of the Greeks, the inner dynamism of Christianity, the feats of the Western empires, the emancipation of philosophy from theology in order not to be tied to a particular confession, the definition of morality by Kant, the modern cosmological worldview, and so forth all are explicit examples claiming universality.

---

[1] As a single example, useful not only for its contents but also for its rich bibliographical references (mainly German, English, and French) see Lluís Duch, *Religió i món modern: Introducció a l'estudi dels fenòmens religiosos* (Montserrat: Abadia, 1984).

Plus ultra was the motto of imperial Spain, and following it the Spaniards could reach America. World government, global village and global perspective, planetarian culture, universal net of information, world market, the alleged universal value of technology, democracy, human rights, nation-states, and so on all point to the same principle: universal means catholic, and catholic means true. What is true and good (for us) is (also) true and good for everybody else. No other human civilization has reached the universality that the Western one has. The way was prepared since the Phoenicians, prefigured by the Christian empires, and made actually geographically possible by the technocratic complex of present-day civilization.

To be sure, this feature is not totally absent in other civilizations, but it is not so prominent, so developed, and so powerful. The belief in being the best, which the Chinese culture had, is different from the belief in being universal and thus *universalizable*, exportable to any place and time.

Further this feature is not altogether negative. Yet it is ambivalent and often ambiguous. The destiny of the West rises and falls with this basic thrust. It is visible in the Abrahamic religions, without excluding Marxism and liberalism, cosmology, and the universal economic system. Proselytism as well as messianisms and expansionisms of all kinds also imply a conviction of representing universal values that thus impels those who are charged with this burden to share, communicate, convince—and ultimately conquer (for the benefit of the conquered). This feature is also visible in the psychological makeup of *Homo occidentalis* and is clearly detectable in the very spirit of Western philosophy. The "once and for all" of the Christian event (see Heb 7:27) and its claim to universality are perhaps the clearest manifestation of this spirit. From the point of view of the history of religions we may say that only the Western gods (YHWH, Allah . . .), which like most divinities were tribal deities, became the universal God—and this to the extent that Christianity even renounced a proper name for God—or accepted the Jewish one. Most religions have a proper name or proper names for God or the gods. Christianity uses the common name "God," although the New Testament makes a distinction between *Theos* and *ho Theos*. In a word, the power of the West is linked with this thrust toward universalization. It has produced glorious results and also deleterious effects. But this is not my point now. My only point is to detect this specific trait.

To be sure the Chinese Son of Heaven or the Indian *cakravartin*, the Buddhist *dharma* or the Confucian *li* have an inbuilt claim to unbound validity and Nāgārjuna's philosophy has an equivalent pretension when it criticizes all possible *dṛṣti* or world-views. But in most cases that universality was more of a metaphor and an expression of power and grandeur than an a priori. It was often a sense of superiority, not of universality. There is something democratic in the belief of being universalizable. Which monarch in history, to give another example, has claimed to have universal jurisdiction over the world without even the intention of conquest, as did the Renaissance popes? What philosopher begins thinking by inquiring about the very conditions of absolute possibility, as did Kant? Heretics have been butchered in Asia and Africa because they were judged to be harmful and had to be punished, but not because truth was considered to be one and they had to be saved, as in the Inquisition. In short, there is here something special in Western civilization. "Everything that exists, exists therefore because it is one" (Omne quod est, idcirco est, quia unum est), said the synthetic mind of Boethius (PL 64.83b) speaking for the West. This *unum* is not the Vedic *ekam* and much less the *Upaniṣadic ekam evādvitīyam* (CU VI.2.1), which are surrounded by *asat*, Non-Being (RV X.129.2). This thirst for universality forms part of the Western myth. Yet it is difficult to prove this, because we discover only the myth of the others, not the myth in which we live.

A long story (of thirty centuries!) in short: The very trend of looking for a "universal theory," even if expressed with all the respect and openness possible, betrays, in my opinion, the same *forma mentis*, the continuation of the same thrust: the will to understand, which is also a form of a will to power and thus the felt need to have everything under control—intellectual in this case.

I have not said that this feature is wrong. I have only situated it within a particular context and submitted it to an initial analysis by sociology of knowledge. It is not accidental that this need for universalization is felt precisely in the West and more especially *today*.

This *today* should be clearer than the preceding general reflection on the character of the Western mind. Probably in no other time of human history have we had so much information available regarding the way in which our fellow human beings live and have lived. The time is gone when the *oikoumenē* could be the *mare nostrum*, when the languages of the human race were believed to be seventy-two, and true religions only those of the "peoples of the book," when we could speak of Christianity on the one hand and lump together all other religions. We are now submerged in an avalanche of data. How to proceed in this jungle of information? The need for intelligibility becomes imperative. We cannot live as if we were self-sufficient, in our own little corner. "The spirit of the Lord *fills* the world" (Spiritus Domini replevit orbem terrarium) (Ws 1:7), sang the Christian liturgy at Pentecost. Now radio and television waves fill the whole world.

I am saying that in the present situation of the world we cannot have the innocence of the Amerindian tribes assuming that the others worship more or less the same Great Spirit and are governed by similar cosmic feelings. We need knowledge and knowledge of the other for survival and for self-identity. The thrust toward a universal theory is very comprehensible indeed. Join to this the desire to understand the other—and even ourselves better—without committing the past blunders of intolerance and fanaticism—and we all rejoice in this mood. The intention is more than justified. My doubt is whether it offers the proper remedy.

Inasmuch as we generally learn more from other areas when the subjects are too touchy for our own skin, I may cite simply as an example the ideal of the physical sciences. It was Einstein's dream—and his drama—to work toward a "unified field theory," as he called it. In it, the set of laws governing gravitation and those governing electricity should find a common mathematical formula. Faraday had succeeded in "converting magnetism into electricity," thus unifying those two groups of phenomena.

Einstein later unified gravitation, time, and space. No wonder that the next step should appear to be total unification. Yet we are still waiting for the formula. Perhaps not even in mathematics and physics can all be reduced to unity—think of Gödel and Heisenberg. We should be alert to this warning.

In short, my suspicion is that the drive toward a "universal theory," be it in physics, religion, or politics, belongs to the same Western thrust. And I repeat that this trait, in spite of its often bitter results and today its menacing danger, is not altogether negative and that at any rate we have to reckon with it as probably the most powerful force in the world today.

But I also insist that this thrust is not universal, and thus not a proper method to deal with human problems, both because it is not truly a universal *theory*—rationality is of many kinds—and more importantly, because no theory is *universal*—rationality does not exhaustively define the human being. Moreover, the phenomenon of religion is certainly not exclusively theoretical.

The Unavoidable Search

The important thing for us is not whether Einstein's lifelong search will fail or not, or whether a universal theology of religion convinces or not. The important thing is to realize that Western culture apparently has no other way to reach peace of mind and heart—more academically referred to as intelligibility—than by reducing everything to one single pattern with the claim to universal validity.

I could put it facetiously by describing the plight of the drunk coming home in the early hours of the morning and looking for his lost house key under a particular streetlight. Asked by the police whether he was sure he lost the key there, he answered, "No, but there is more light here." We look under the only light we have.

Now, my whole enterprise here consists in showing that there are other street lights in the city of humanity and that the Western light is not the only one we have. Obviously, the response is to say that it is not a question of a Western light, but that it is the human light of reason, the sole source of intelligibility, and that unless we wish to break off all human intercourse, commerce, and communication, we have to accept that single light. Pushing the example further I would suggest that to find the key to the house of wisdom we had better rely on daylight and that only the superhuman light of the sun may be the common light for the entire universe and not the artificial streetlights, be they of the gas of reason, the electricity of intuition, the neo-gases of feeling, or whatever. Yet, what if it is at night that we lose our key? But I am not now pushing a theological argument.

Without identifying Descartes with our drunk, I may recall the logical fallacy of the father of modern Western philosophy: everything that I see with clarity and distinction (remember, under the light)—that is, all evidence—must be true. I may concede here, for the sake of argument, that it may be the truth. But from this it does not follow that truth is *only* what I see with clarity and distinction. Evidence may be our criterion of truth, but first I cannot a priori assume that what I see with clarity and distinction you also will see in the same way. Second, truth may be wider, deeper, or even elsewhere than what I, or even we, see with clarity and distinction. Here we must recall the Western philosophical paradigm that was present since the beginning: "Humanity is the measure of all things, how those which exist do exist and those which do not exist, do not exist" (*Pantōn chrēmatōn metron anthrōpon einai. Tōn men ontōn hōs esti, tōn de nē ontōn hōs ouk estin*), as Protagoras said (reported by Plato, *Theat.* 151e–152a).

This is not necessarily sheer humanism, as it is often said. It can also be traditional theology, for even if God speaks, God will have to use human language and be ultimately dependent on our understanding of the divine words. My quarrel here is not with *anthrōpos*, with humanity, or even anthropocentrism—although I would contest this; my quarrel is with *metron*, with the drive to measure everything—and to extrapolate, with the thrust to want to know everything, because it is assumed that everything is knowable. Ontologically said, thinking does not need to exhaust Being. Now, under those Western assumptions, the move toward a "universal theory" is a welcome move to put a certain order among the many worldviews. Within that framework it may be the best way of expressing it. But Reality is richer. The "divine darkness" of Gregory of Nyssa has not had a follow-up in the West. It became the "dark night of the soul" in St. John of the Cross, and faded into the unconscious of modern psychology, after the lightning of Meister Eckhart.

This is my point. Granting that a hypothetical universal theology of religion were possible, it would be a very positive contribution to understanding the phenomenon of religion *only* for those who live within the cultural process in which all those words make sense, that is, for those who in one form or another subscribe to the myth of history, who accept the *intellectus agens* (*nous poiētikos*) of Aristotle and the Arab philosophers, the Cartesian intuition, the Kantian critical revolution, the Marxist analysis, or an absolute monotheism. This is a very impressive and powerful club, but it is not for everybody. To be sure, nobody now consciously wants to circumscribe the others to their own ways of thinking in order to reach universality. In short, the striving for a universal theory is *one way* of expressing the manifoldness of the human religious experience, but it is just one way of doing it. It has a formal value. It expresses the genius of the West. However, we do not any longer want intellectual colonialisms.

I should not be misinterpreted. The effort at a universal theory is a noble enterprise. It is also a fruitful one. So many misunderstandings are overcome when we search for a common language; collaboration is made possible, and religions are purified of so many excrescences, narrow-mindedness, and fanaticisms. It would be totally mistaken to interpret my critique as not being a constructive one, as not aiming at the same goals and going in the same direction of mutual "understanding," tolerance, and appreciation. It may appear that I am also searching for a universal myth although it would not be the same. Myth emerges and cannot be concocted; myth is polysemic and irreducible to one interpretation; myth does not support any particular theory.

What I am against, ultimately, is the total dominion of the *logos* and a subordinationism of the Spirit—to put it in Christian, Trinitarian terms—or against any form of monism, in philosophical parlance. And yet I am against all this, I repeat, without ignoring the function and power of the *logos*, this fellow-traveler of all reality, coextensive with it, but not exhaustively identifiable with it.

Let me sum up my misgivings before I engage in a more positive critique. The search for a "universal theory" indeed fosters dialogue but runs the great danger of imposing its own language or the frame within which the *dia-logos* has to take place. It claims to be a *lingua universalis*, which amounts to reductionism, to say the least. Second, it assumes that religion—or in a broader sense, human traditions—are, if not reducible, at least translatable into *logos*—and probably one kind of *logos*—and thus gives a supremacy to the *logos* over against the Spirit. But why should all be put into words? Why is not acceptance without understanding—as I read the Christian symbol of Mary (Lk 2:19–51)—also an equally human attitude?

Critique

The Question of Pluralism

I have the impression that most of those who speak about pluralism and fill it with a positive meaning are not sufficiently aware of the far-reaching consequences that it entails: the dethronement of reason and the abandonment of the monotheistic paradigm. It is like those who speak grandly of tolerance of others without taking into consideration that the real problem of tolerance begins with why and how to tolerate the intolerant. "The tolerance you have is directly proportional to the myth you live and inversely proportional to the ideology you follow."[2] This could be the law of tolerance.

Pluralism in its ultimate sense is not the tolerance of a diversity of systems under a larger umbrella; it does not allow for any superstructure. It is not a supersystem. Who or what principles would manage it? The problem of pluralism arises when we are confronted with mutually irreconcilable worldviews or ultimate systems of thought and life. Pluralism has to do with final, unbridgeable human attitudes. If two views allow for a synthesis, we cannot speak of pluralism. We speak then of two different, mutually complementary, although apparently opposite attitudes, beliefs, or whatever. We do not take seriously the claim of ultimacy of religions, philosophies, theologies, and final human attitudes if we seem to allow for a pluralistic supersystem. In that case, obviously, we all would like to be pluralistic and not so narrow-minded as the Muslims, Catholics, Marxists, or whoever who still think that their analyses or views are ultimate, at least within their respective horizons. It is easy to be pluralistic if the others abandon their claim to absoluteness, primacy, universality, and the

² Raimon Panikkar, *Myth, Faith, and Hermeneutics* (New York: Paulist Press, 1979), 20; Panikkar, *Opera Omnia*, IX.1.

like: "We pluralists have allotted each system its niche; we then are truly universal." This, I submit, is not pluralism. This is another system, perhaps a better one, but it would make pluralism unnecessary. We have a situation of pluralism only when we are confronted with mutually exclusive and respectively contradictory ultimate systems. We cannot by definition logically overcome a pluralistic situation without breaking the very principle of noncontradiction and denying our own set of codes: intellectual, moral, aesthetic, and so forth.

In other words, to assume that Hindus or Catholics are so dull as to be either fanatics or blind to the fact that the other also has the same or similar ultimate claims is to do an injustice to the self-understanding of the best minds of those religions. They know well that the claim of absoluteness, for instance, is a scandal to the human mind and that it does not entail disrespect of the other or straight condemnation of other views. There exist in the world today well-balanced and thought-out absolutistic and mutually irreconcilable positions. And when we have to deal with sufficiently long-standing traditions, we cannot reasonably be satisfied with the proleptic attitude of a vague "hope"—I would rather call it expectation—that in the future our dissensions will fade away or find a solution. They have lived too long for us to believe that one fine day the Vaishnavas finally are going to recognize that the Shivaites are right. This pious hope—without irony—is a very healthy attitude as far as it goes.

Christian ecumenism offers a good example: what was considered impossible at one time became a fact a couple of decades later. But this model cannot so easily be extrapolated, for not everyone necessarily shares the conviction that history is the locus of reality or has a central point of reference, like Christ. In other words, an interdisciplinary study is not yet cross-cultural.

There is even more. A pluralistic system as such could not be understood. Pluralism is only a formal concept. Sensible persons cannot understand how on Earth there are many who think that all is matter, or that there is a God, or that the inferior races or less intelligent persons should not serve the superior ones, and so on, if they happen to have firm convictions in the opposite direction. And yet we are forced by circumstances to coexist with such worldviews or systems. No overarching is possible. Either there is God or there is no God, either the individual does have ultimate value or does not, either the cosmos is a living organism or it is not. Despite all our sympathy and effort to understand, we disagree with the other; we cannot even understand how the contrary opinion may be reasonably held. We may have our personal interpretation and interpret the given examples, for instance, as false dilemmas. It remains, nevertheless, a fact that the others may not share our belief in a *coincidentia oppositorum*.

In short, there are a few fundamental human attitudes at the very basis of different human traditions that are mutually irreconcilable. I am an animist, and you are a positivist scientist. Our two visions of the world cannot be both true. Or can they? The question of pluralism belongs to that ultimate level. And we should not take this lightly. Is it allowed to torture one individual who otherwise will not speak in order to save fifty thousand persons who are going to be blown up in the next few hours? We cannot say yes and no or withhold an answer, for that would already imply giving one.

What this example contains in a time capsule is the situation of the world, today. My hypothesis may be right or wrong, but I am not off the track. Such is the seriousness of the problem of pluralism. We cannot postpone to an eschatological happy ending the solution of all antinomies, nor can we rely on the last scientific or theological discovery of some guru telling us what to do. By that time, not the fifty thousand of my example but millions of our fellow beings will have already starved to death or been killed in fratricidal warfare.

The problem of pluralism is paramount and has many facets. One of them is the question of good and evil. For my purpose I shall concentrate on the central issue of truth. What happens to it in the face of so many disparate ultimate convictions? Let us assume that we have exhausted all the provisions and cautions at our disposal. We know that the context is essential, that different perspectives yield different visions, that temperament, culture, and the like vouch for bewildering diversities. As long as the lines of dialogue are open, as long as the other does not draw the ultimate conclusion, there is no need to speak of pluralism. We are still struggling to find a common truth. We speak, then, of a dialogue of tolerance, of difference of opinions, and even of competition of worldviews in the human arena. We all recognize a legitimate multiperspectivism. The question of pluralism appears only when all those doors have been shut, when we return to ourselves and then have to take the decision to *écraser l'infâme* or to allow ourselves to be overrun by evil, either to tolerate ultimate error and evil, or to fight it, even succumbing to it.

If the history of humankind is a succession of wars, and if war today appears so terrible, our issue of pluralism is not alien to this human predicament. What is the place of the philosophies underlying the Hitlers and Stalins in a "pluralistic world-view"? There is no "pluralistic worldview"; there are simply incompatible worldviews.

One of the presuppositions of the universal theory is that all problems are theoretically soluble. I am in complete agreement with the effort to try to solve the problems, and with patience, goodwill, and intelligence much can be achieved. We should go on trying again and again, untiringly. But we have to recognize two facts. One is that the partner may break off relations, stop the dialogue, become dangerous, oblige me to make decisions. And this is not necessarily because of some evil design, but because of the inner logic of the system. Not all who waged wars were criminals, not all who preached crusades were corrupt, not all those who believed in the inquisitions and slaveries of various types were subhuman—although now in our age we could not justify such acts or attitudes, which today should be condemned as out-and-out aberrations.

Now, there is no guarantee whatsoever that all human problems are—should be—theoretically soluble. This is probably not the case, even in mathematics, let alone in the complex existential situations in which contradictory human views are embedded. The universe may not have the logical coherence assumed by the spirit of Laplace or even by the belief in a monotheistic Deity for which nothing is unintelligible. These are already religious presuppositions that not every human tradition shares. Would those who think differently from us have to be excluded from a universal theory?

A second fact we have to take cognizance of is of another nature altogether. It is the unexamined presupposition—it has been taken for granted, "presupposed"—that the truth is one rather than pluralistic.

The pluralism of truth is a much more serious and disturbing hypothesis than the obvious recognition of *perspectivism* and *relativity*. To admit that truth depends on the perspective should not offer any difficulty, although on that ultimate level the problem emerges as the question of what is the most adequate perspective in order to have the most accurate vision of things. And this obviously cannot be again another perspective without a *regressus ad infinitum*.

The *relativity* of truth, once it is distinguished from *relativism*, should also not be difficult to accept. Relativism destroys itself when affirming that all is relative and thus also the very affirmation of relativism. Relativity, on the other hand, asserts that any human affirmation, and thus any truth, is relative to its very own parameters and that there can be no absolute truth, for truth is essentially relational. The latter case is the reverse of the former. Relativism destroys itself if we affirm it. Relativity on the other hand is presupposed in the act of denying it. Any truth actually relates to an intellect. The concept of absolute truth has to relate to an infinite intellect.

The pluralism of truth goes a step further. It asserts that truth itself is pluralistic, and thus not one—nor many, for that matter. Pluralism is not plurality. To affirm that truth itself is pluralistic amounts to averring that there is no one all-encompassing or absolute truth.

The pluralism of truth is based on two fundamental assumptions: the *first* is anthropological; the *second*, theological or philosophical. I should prefer to stay in communion with all those traditions that do not make the split between philosophy and theology.

The *first* assumption is the recognition that each person is a source of under-standing. *Person* here means not only any subject of rights as an individual or a juridical person; it also includes collective units and especially cultures as historical entities.

I am not necessarily resurrecting the Augustinian illumination theory of knowl-edge or subscribing to any subject/object epistemology. I am saying only this: Each person is a source of self-understanding. What a person is has to take into account the self-description and definition of the person in question. I am another person and have no right to superimpose my parameters and categories of understanding on others. Or, rather, if I do, the understanding I impose would be my understanding of the others, not the understanding of the others as they understand themselves, that is, as the understanding of their self-understanding. When the Hindu tells you or the Bantu tells me something that to us sounds preposterous, we have no way of passing any other judgment than that to us it sounds unacceptable for such and such reasons, apparently not accepted—or seen—by the other. However, we cannot reduce it all to objective statements. We are dealing with personal convictions, not with objectifiable events.

This almost obvious fact has been often dimmed by the influence of the natural sciences, which deal mainly with objectifiable phenomena and even more precisely with measurable entities. There is, for instance, a relative universality, at least in elementary mathematics, so that $2 + 3 = 5$ may appear as a universal truth independent of any source of understanding besides the objective intelligibility of the statement. Without discussing the nature of mathematics, suffice it to say that this is not the case when dealing with human affairs. And this happens even in applied mathematics. If $3 + 2 = 5$, everybody should agree in exchanging three canoes plus two women for five pounds sterling. And if it is replied that the quantities have to be homogeneous, we should then be inclined to agree to exchange two acres of land plus three houses for some other two acres and three houses (of the same price) outside the tribal country—and wonder why those "savages" of Papua New Guinea make such a fuss at being relocated or why the Israelis could not go elsewhere or the Palestinians for that matter. The fact is that neither land nor house are measurable entities. Each being is unique, that is, incommensurable.

Be this as it may—although it is not off the track—we may easily agree that the self-understanding of a particular culture is, in a certain sense, an ultimate and has to be taken as such without a reductionist twist to our ways of judging things. This is an epistemological statement. I am in no way saying that the Aztecs did well in performing the human sacrifices they did just as I am not saying that some countries today do well in trading arms or in building atomic arsenals. I am saying that unless we understand the inner logic of a person and consider that person to be a source of self-understanding, we shall not understand that person, which will remain a permanent irritant among us.

If each human being qua human is endowed with self-understanding, so is each culture because it possesses a specific vision of reality, a certain myth as the horizon within which things and events are discerned. Now, to privilege our understanding of reality and reduce all other perspectives to our own, even if we accept the data of the others, does not seem a proper method of dealing with what humans think about themselves and the universe, unless we reduce the human being to a set of scientifically detectable data.

If each person is a source of self-understanding, if humans are beings endowed with self-understanding, then we shall not be able to understand humans without sharing the self-understanding of the person(s) concerned. In that sense, an objective anthropology makes no sense. Human beings are not objects, but subjects. It would be methodologically wrong to treat humans as scientific objects.

Religions deal mainly with the collective ultimate self-understanding of a human group. The truth of religion can be gauged only within the unifying myth that makes the self-understanding possible. If we want to cross boundaries, we will have to share in some common truths brought forth in the common endeavor. But we should not project the truths of one religion over against an objective screen of truth in itself.

Even if such an objective truth were to exist, we could not apply its canons in order to understand the self-understanding of a tradition that does not recognize them without distorting the issue. We may eventually condemn a religion as a human aberration, but always judging with our standards.

If the first assumption is anthropological, the *second* is theological, or rather, metaphysical. It contests one of the most widespread beliefs in the West as well as in the East, namely, that Reality is totally intelligible, that the *noēsis noēseōs* of Aristotle, the *svayamprakāsha* of the Vedantins, the self-intelligible and omniscient God of the Christians, the total reflection of many spiritualist philosophers, is really the case. It contests the ultimate belief of every idealistic monism: that there is a Being or a Reality that encompasses all that there is, and that this Reality is pure consciousness, absolutely self-intelligible because all is transparent to the light of the intellect all is pervaded by *cit, nous*, mind. I am not contesting that *logos, nous, cit*, or by whatever name we may call this dimension of the real is a fellow traveler of reality or coextensive with Being. I am only contesting that Being is totally reducible to it. What I am saying is that Reality has other dimensions—Matter, for instance, or Spirit—which cannot be reduced to *logos*, word, *vāc, nous*, mind, consciousness, *cit*. Consciousness is Being, but Being does not need to be only Consciousness.

One of the philosophical implications of this view is that there is no being absolutely identical to itself. Self-identity would imply absolute (total) reflection: an *a* identical to *a*. Each being, not excluding a possible Supreme Being, presents an opaque remnant, as it were, a mysterious aspect that defies transparency. This is precisely the locus of freedom, and the basis of pluralism. Thinking, or the intelligence, covers the totality of Being only from the exterior, so to say. Being has an untapped reservoir, a dynamism, an inner side not illumined by self-knowledge, reflection, or the like. Spontaneity is located in this corner of each being—its own mystery—which is unthought, unpremeditated, and free, even from the structures of thinking. The mystery of Reality cannot be equated with the nature of consciousness. There "is" also *sat* (being) and *ānanda* (joy), the Father and the Spirit. They may be correlative and even coextensive with consciousness, probably because we cannot speak or think of the one without the other, but certainly they cannot be all lumped together as ultimately one Single "thing." This is one of the consequences of what I call the theanthropocosmic or cosmotheandric insight. From all this follows that there is no absolute truth, not only because we mortals have no access to it, but because Reality itself cannot be said to be self-intelligible unless we a priori totally identify Reality with Consciousness. The Absolute is in the Relative. Something can be absolutely true, but this is not absolute Truth. Truth is always a relationship, and one of the poles of the relationship is the intellect that understands the thing in question—intelligible, coherent, and so on.

Even assuming a divine or perfect Intellect, it could know only what is intelligible. To aver that it can know All amounts to gratuitously affirming that All is intelligible, that Being is intelligible—in other words, that Being is Consciousness.

In this scheme, to know is to become the known. In the process of a real understanding, the identity between the subject and the object is total. Vedantic and Christian Scholastic philosophies, for instance, defend the ontological significance of the epistemological act. Ultimately, Being is reduced to Consciousness. The epistemological principle of noncontradiction becomes here the ontic principle of identity. Only a noncontradictory thing is identical to itself. *It is* itself (identity) because it is noncontradictory. Thinking, governed by the principle of noncontradiction, amounts ultimately to Being, which is governed by the principle of identity. Thinking and Being form the ultimate paradigm.

The application to our case is easy to detect. There can be a universal theory of religion, or of anything only under the assumption that Theory covers Reality, that Thinking can—theoretically, in principle—exhaust Being—can know Being without any (unknown) remnant. In a word, Being is intelligible (*quoad se*). This is the ultimate presupposition of any universal theory. But it is this ultimate presupposition that is here called into question. To affirm that Consciousness is Being is a postulate of intelligibility, but not of Being. Truth is the result of some equation between Consciousness and Being. But Being may transcend its equation with Consciousness.

Furthermore, de facto, the actual pole for all our truth utterances is not a divine or perfect intellect but human consciousness, individual or collective, situated in space, time, matter, culture, and so forth. We have to take our own contingency very seriously, and our grandeur lies precisely in the awareness of our limitations. Anything we touch, think, speak—including all our ideas about any Supreme Deity—is permeated by the contingency of our being. I am not excluding the possible existence of the supreme consciousness of a realized soul, a *jivanmukta*. I am saying that even *that* language is a relative language and suffused in polysemy. The moment that we come into the picture, all is tinged by our creatureliness, humanness, or whatever we may call it.

To sum up, the pluralistic character of truth does not mean that there are many truths. "Many truths" is either a contradiction in terms if we admit the possibility of many true and mutually incompatible answers to a particular judgment, or it is a displacement of the problem to a meta-truth that would be the conceptual truth of the many truths, as our single concept of sardine allows us to recognize many sardines. Truths would then be many exemplars of the meta-truth, and the problem would begin with the meta-truth all over again.

The pluralism of truth means fundamentally two things. First, that truth cannot be abstracted from its relationship with a particular mind inserted in a particular context. "There is bread on this table" cannot be criticized outside the perspective of the author of the sentence, although "the city of Madras is on this table" cannot be literally true, for lack of internal coherence. We cannot abstract from every context and proclaim the oneness of truth. We have to recognize perspectivism and contextualization. Truth is relationship, and quantification does not occur.

Second, and more importantly, the pluralistic character of truth shows that the notion of truth is not identical, say, with that of goodness. Ultimately truth and goodness may coalesce, but even then they are not the same. History shows us what an amount of evil (nongoodness) has been perpetrated in the name of truth. Truth *alone* in this sense is not enough, that is, it does not fulfill the function that truth is supposed to perform. It also explicitly requires goodness. Truth is pluralistic; hence, truth, truth alone, disincarnated truth, cannot be an absolute and ultimately it is not true. It needs other elements, at the same level of truth, as it were. Goodness is a case in point. Truth is not goodness, and yet truth without goodness is maimed, is not truth. I shall not discuss whether one of the weaknesses of the dominant Western philosophy is that it desired to be merely *sophia*—convened into *epistēmē*—and reduced *philia* to desire (of wisdom), forgetting that it has equally to be (wisdom of) love.

Be this as it may, the pluralistic character of truth denounces the monism of thought and reveals the existential aspect of truth. Each truth is one certainly, but a universal truth in general is just an extrapolation of our mind.

This does not mean that within one particular period in history or within one given culture—I should prefer to say within one living myth—there are no unanimously accepted standards and, in that sense, relatively universal truths. There are such truths, because they are seen as such by that particular group of humans. Slavery as an institution, to give just one example, may today elicit a general consensus as being something to be abolished, so that even those who still practice it do so with bad conscience. God was for a long time and in a great part of the world such a myth or recognized truth. It now no longer is. Anticapitalism and democracy could be adduced as examples of absolute political truths for some and yet contested by others.

My thesis is clear: a universal theory of whatever kind denies pluralism. Any alleged universal theory is one particular theory besides many others that claims universal validity, thus trespassing the limits of its own legitimacy. Further, no theory can be absolutely universal, because theory, the contemplation of truth, is neither a universal contemplation, nor is theoretical "truth" all that there is to Reality.

The Inner Limits of the Logos

We have indicated, so far, the impotency of the *logos* to unify (identify) itself completely with itself, thus showing a dimension of Reality "incommensurable" with the *logos*, or rather, "incommensured" by it. We have implicitly mentioned the Unspeakable and also the Unspoken, as well as the Unthinkable and the Unthought. We have obliquely realized that there is a place for the Unthought and the Unspoken. The Unspeakable and the Unthinkable are, in a way, within the realm of speech and thought inasmuch as we are still aware of them. With the Unthought it is different. We are not aware of it. We recall only later that something remained unthought for a while, and from there we assume that there still may be more, and that perhaps something always remains unthought, but we can neither speak of it nor prove it. We speak about the Unspeakable as that *x* about which nothing *else* can be said. If we were to speak about the Unspoken, we would destroy it; it would be a contradiction in terms.

I want to deal here with the inner boundaries of the word. Language is neither singular nor plural. Like the notion of the personal person, it defies number. A person is not just a single individual. An I entails a thou, and both imply he/she/it/they/we. An isolated I is a contradiction in terms. It is an I only because of a thou, and vice versa.

Similarly, language entails not only more than one speaker—a single individual would not speak: there would be neither the need to speak, nor any meaning in it—it also entails more than language. Language in the singular makes no sense. There is no private language, nor is there a single language. First, de facto, there is not just a single language. There are languages in the world. Second, de jure, no language could exist alone. A single language—and this implies a single speaker—would coincide with the things it speaks about, and words would be the things. The distance between word and thing would be zero. There would be no need to express the thing other than by itself if there were a single language.

By language I do not mean now, say, English. English inasmuch as it is spoken by a number of persons, each one of them having a different perspective in the use of each word, is already a polyphonic and even polysemic language.

English is a set of speeches with certain common sounds and structures. What we now call language, or a language, is the homogeneous integral of a group of speeches. I made reference to a single language in the sense of a single speech by a single speaker—or a plurality of speakers using the identically same speech. Words are not things: things can be worded differently. Otherwise the words would be the thing or no-thing. No word exhausts the thing; no word expresses the thing completely; no name is the real name, the name that could totally cover the thing. Language is language because it speaks, it says, it unfolds things and reveals them, it unveils them, to the persons for whom they are precisely things. This fundamental reflection on language seems all too often overlooked, and it is relevant for our topic.

The phrase "In the beginning was the Word" means in so many traditions from Asia and Africa that in the beginning there was a Speaker, a Spoken To, a Spoken With, and a Spoken About. Without this *quaternitas perfecta* there is no Word. Now, if "the Word was in the beginning," after the beginning there are word, languages, and a plurality of those *quaternitates*. The temptation to make sense of it all by returning to the beginning is comprehensible, but it is also understandable that to "want to be *like* God" was condemned by God as a *hybris* that led to human alienation. Let me close this reference by saying that what that tradition tells us is to become Christ *himself—ipse Christus* not *alter Christus*.

In a simpler manner, we do not speak language. We speak a language, a language that has relationships with other languages and each of which represents a new perspective on the world, a new window, and often a new panorama. We cannot understand all the languages of the world. We can cross the boundaries of, say, a dozen languages and become aware of the multidimensionality of the things we word so differently. Other persons can also cross some other boundaries, and so the net can spread all over the world, but with a center nowhere. This is what happens in predominantly oral cultures.

Illiterates in many countries of the so-called Middle East and India, and I suppose Africa as well, are not persons who do not know how to read and write—this is a Western fixation—but individuals who know only a single language, who understand only the dialect of their own village. As a matter of fact, what we call languages are certain dialects that have gained some power and been endorsed by Royal Academies and Learned Societies, and been printed as the official or correct way of saying things. This is a phenomenon unheard of a few centuries ago in Europe, and still today in most of the world. The real languages are the dialects.

Illiterates are those persons who cannot distinguish a particular locution from what it means, because they know only that locution and are not aware that the "same" thing can be said in different ways, so that nothing is absolute. In point of fact, each village develops its own language, but the villagers know perfectly well that some miles away the "same" thing is given another name, which they also know. In this way they do not confuse the name with the thing. (The importance of this is not to know how to name utensils—so we can buy and sell in the neighboring bazaar—but how to understand living words like beauty, justice, propriety, politeness.) They know that no one word, no one language, can exhaust the immense variety of the human experience. So it is only together, in colloquium, that we touch the universality of human life.

A universal theory claims to be a universal language, a language in which all languages find themselves reproduced, reflected, or into which they can be translated. Yet a universal language does not exist. And if it did, it would represent an impoverishment of the riches of the many languages.

Certainly we can and should stretch the meaning of words as much as we can, so as to make them say things they did not mean before. I have cited the example of "grace" elsewhere, which for a long period of Christian theology was almost by definition the exclusive property of Christianity. Today we have rescued that word from meaning only the saving grace as a share in the divine nature, as the Apostle Peter understood it. There are also Indian religions of grace and Christian theology does not deny it, although it will have to find theological explanations for this fact. But words, in spite of their elasticity, have their limits.

Theology is a case in point. We can say that by *theos* we understand the Christian concept, but can we include in the meaning of this word what a Buddhist means with no proper word and a Marxist by denying the existence of such a being? If we mean just transcendence, let us say it and not speak about the Transcendent.

In order to properly approach cross-cultural problems I have developed a theory of *homeomorphic equivalents* as analogies of a third degree. "Brahman" is not the translation of "God," for instance, but both perform the equivalent functions required in their respective systems. We may perhaps find the homeomorphic equivalents of the word "theology," but we cannot assume that this word encompasses all those equivalents, just as *God* does not cover what *Brahman* stands for. It may even be that on the doctrinal level they are incompatible notions. Either there is a creator God, or an inactive noncreator Brahman, but not both, in spite of the fact that in the respective systems both are not only legitimate but necessary. Or we need to modify the meaning of the two words so as to make them compatible within one single system. It is very proper to have our language and to want to express all that we can in our own language, but it will remain only one possible language, which should not expect to supplant the others.

As I have argued elsewhere, terms, as signs for scientific information—as labels in a nominalistic world—can certainly be all translated more or less artificially into any language. We can say entropy or weight in any language. They all have a measurable point of reference. Not so with words whose points of reference are the historical and cultural crystallizations of human experiences, which can be verified only by sharing in those experiences. How do we translate the French *esprit*, the Catalan *seny*, the Navajo *hosho*, the Sanskrit *rayi*, the English *countenance*, the German *Stimmung*? Poets know something about this. A universal theology of religion would not want to deal only with the equivalent of mathematical infrastructures common to most religions.

There have been in our days efforts at highly formalized theories of religion. They are useful attempts at finding some common structures and formal gestalts of religion. I myself define religion as something fulfilling the equation $y = f(x)$, where x is the human condition as seen by any culture or religion at any given moment; y is the goal, aim, end, solution, meaning, result, or whatever of x, the human condition of life; and f is the function that transforms x into y.

All religions, I submit, claim to fulfill this condition and satisfy this structure. This is a formalized language that helps us to understand religious phenomena by finding an ultimate common structure, so that if something fulfills that equation, like a certain type of humanism, for instance, it should—or could—be called religion although the label "religion" may not be customary. But all this is far from providing us a universal theory by which to understand religion. It provides us, certainly, a kind of algebra about which I have elsewhere also commented on its limitations.

A truly universal theory of religions should be a sort of theory of theories, for every religion has its thinkers and systematizers spinning out theories of their respective religions, calling them theologies, philosophies, or whatever. A theory of theories amounts to a language of languages, a meta-language, a meta-theory. By now we should know the dialectic of such attempts. Either the theory of theories is another theory, and then it falls into the class of which it claims to be the set—which is a contradiction—or it is a meta-theory, that is, not a theory at all but something else. What can that "else" be if not another, more sophisticated theory of a second degree, as it were? But then we may need another theory of a third degree to explain the other possible meta-theories that may emerge, *et sic ad infinitum*. If the "else" is of another order, we can no longer call it "theory"; it ceases to be of the order of the *logos*. This insight will open a door for us (see "The Alternative," below). But there is still another point to consider.

The Outer Boundaries of Any Theory

We have seen the inner limits of a universal theory. But there is still more. There is no need to be a Marxist or to follow any particular sociology of knowledge in order to subscribe to the philosophical insight that any theory stems from a praxis and is nurtured by it, even if often standing in dialectical opposition to it. Any theory not only attempts to explain the status quo—of the physical sciences, for instance; it also springs from that very status quo—of post-Einsteinian physics, in our example. It would suffice to change the praxis—in our case it would be the appearance of an unaccounted-for physical fact—to upset all the existing theories. What would become of a universal theory of religion if suddenly—or less abruptly—a new religion appeared or even a new notion of religion? The universal theory would either have to be given up or it would have to deny a priori the character of religion to the newcomer. Let us not forget that for a long time Confucianism and Buddhism were not considered religions, because they did not fit into a neat theory of religion. I am afraid that something similar happens with regard to Marxism and humanism, to which many would deny the name—and not just the label—religion.

I have already made allusion to the—colonialistic—cultural monoformism from which most of the universal theories come. They assume that we are today in a better position than ever to know the essence of religion. In that we are free from any desire to dominate; all we need to do is to evaluate and understand the present (religious) situation—without being aware that this very attitude both consecrates, as it were, the status quo, and transforms it in one very particular direction. In other words, a universal theory of religion is loaded with political overtones. A telling example today is the so-called theology of liberation within the Catholic Church. It raises waves within the institution because it does not tally with a "universal theory of Christian religions" sponsored by the Supreme Pontifex of that church.

Any theory is only an intellectual explanation of a given datum, but it is all too often blind to the fact that the datum appears first as such when seen under the light of a particular theory. The relationship between theory and praxis is that of a vital circle—not a vicious circle. Any human praxis entails a theory and any human theory entails a praxis, not because the one is *based* on the other and presupposes it, and vice versa—which would constitute a vicious circle—but because the two are intrinsic components of one and the same human factor. Both are interdependent, though not through a causal link, and probably not even by means of a logical dialectic. It is rather a yin/yang dialogical relationship. There is no synthesis possible, but only a constituent and mutually dependent polarity.

The problem has been sufficiently studied so as to spare us the task of spelling it out. It suffices to have mentioned it. In a word: Any alleged universal theory is dependent upon a praxis that is far from being universal. It is an iron colossus with earthen feet!

The Alternative

What, then, is to be done if we reject any grandiose universal theory and even detect in this intent a latent will to dominate and a fear that if we do not make sense of everything we will lose our bearings and become vulnerable? I repeat that I do not minimize the importance of the noble desire to overcome exclusivistic doctrines and to open up ways of communication between compartmentalized and often frozen traditions. Yet, I discover a change in a fundamental human attitude that may have begun very early in human history. It is a shifting from a natural confidence in Reality to a cultural mistrust, even of ourselves. We may recall Descartes's existential doubt: even our mind may cheat us, were it not for a veracious and trustworthy God. It begins with a culture of mistrust—which is different from critique—and it ends with a civilization of (in)security—which has to do with the obsession for certainty. But then, should we give up any critical stance or, on the other hand, any hope at understanding each other? Should we resign ourselves to provincial explanations and eventually to more rivalries and further wars of "theologies" and religions? Far from it. I need not repeat that my life is directed toward mutual understanding and cooperation among religious traditions.

After having criticized a universal theory, I obviously cannot fall into the trap of proposing one of my own. What I espouse could be summarized in the three headings of this third part. First, we must put our house in order, as it were. Second, we must open ourselves to the others; and third, we both—or if need be, we alone—must rely on the overall thrust of the human experience.

I should add here that these three moments are intertwined and require each other. They are three moments of one and the same fundamental religious attitude. This fundamental religious attitude, I submit, is a basic human attitude. It is an attitude of trust in Reality. *Apistia* is a cause of ignorance, said Heraclitus (*Fragm.* 86). Without a certain confidence somewhere, the human being cannot live. I have to trust my parents, my friends, the grocer, language, the world, God, my own evidence, my consciousness, or whatever.

The fundamental error of Descartes, as the father of modernity, along with the founders of the "new science," which since then has dominated Western civilization, is that once the method of doubting of everything is consciously started, there is no end to it, and yet it has a beginning, a foundation that is taken for granted. God, for Descartes, is the "object" that will put an end to the *regressus ad infinitum*, but what he does not see is his taking for granted the *ego* of his doubt as well as of his *cogito*. Even if he doubts that he doubts or thinks, it is always his *ego* that is presupposed.

This is the birth of modern individualism. And once we identify ourselves with our singularity we have to look frantically for a foundation. Singularity needs support, a foundation. I am no longer a constitutive element in the universe. I am no longer in communion with the whole, no longer whole. I no longer am, for I could *not* be. *Angst* is the companion of an isolated singularity. I have to justify my existence and conquer my being; I have become a stranger to Reality, a mere spectator who suddenly discovers I have no ticket (no reason) to see (share) the spectacle of the real. The estrangement begins. We may say this is what the loss of innocence means. It *may* be. We discover ourselves naked, that is, alone, alienated from the rest of the universe.

Whatever this may be, the fact is that the old innocence cannot be recovered. A second innocence is a contradiction in terms. The moment that I become aware that it is second, it ceases to be a real innocence. It is not for nothing there was an angel at the gate of paradise with a sword of fire to prevent return. There is no point in going back. But there can be a new innocence, so new that it does not even remember the previous one or rather that it does not believe in the first innocence. The essence of paradise is to be lost, always and ever lost. It is the necessary mental hypothesis for the myth of the fall, be it of Eve or of Galileo/Descartes and company. The resurrection myth looms on the horizon.

Having discovered the precariousness of the individual—that is, having practically exhausted all the arguments of reason for a better world, or a good life, for total security, or a real foundation of thinking, of behavior, and whatnot—having discovered in the entire explanation of ourselves and of the universe at least one weak spot that makes the whole thing foundationless, we may as well make a jump to *metanoia*, a conversion, and discover that in spite of all our efforts, we were all the time assuming an unconscious trust in Reality, a confidence perhaps in life, certainly in "that" which makes the entire human enterprise an adventure either with sense or meaningless. We discover, in short, that it all may be a game, even a bad game at that, an illusory one, or whatever, but ultimately it is our game, our entertainment, our adventure. In a word, we recognize, we believe that we are created, born, thrown out, existing, dreaming, living, or even imagining it all, but nevertheless doing it. It is to that fundamental human trust that I appeal—and personally confess that I do not find the human adventure so dull, uninteresting, or negative.

The Harmony from Within

If we speak of religious traditions or of religion in general, we should not remain at the surface of the human religious experience. We should begin by living, knowing, and experiencing our own tradition, or particular subtradition, as intensively and deeply as possible. Religion has been probably the place where the worst human passions and the most dangerous human attitudes have occurred. At the same time, religion is the locus where the highest peaks of the human experience have been reached and where the most sublime quality of human life has been unfolded.

I shall not linger here at defining religion as the quest for the ultimate, as the set of symbols and practices of the human being when confronted with the most definitive questions, as the meaning of life and the universe, not just on an intellectual plane, but on an existential and vital level. Religion is, in the last instance, a dimension of human life.

My first point is this: When trying to understand the religious phenomena of the human race, we cannot neglect our own personal religious dimension developed with more or less force in one particular tradition. Otherwise, we distort the entire enterprise. Only those who knew "number" were allowed to enter Plato's Academia, only those endowed with "faith" could duly practice Christian theological reflection. Only those with a medical title are allowed to practice medicine. Only those who know how to rule themselves are the true rulers of others, declared Lao Tzu, Plato, and sages from practically all traditions. Only those who cultivate the religious dimension in their own lives can really dare to enter upon the excruciating task of trying to understand what religion is all about. The study of religion is not the classification of "religious" data, but the study of the religious dimension of the human being. I am not saying that scholars should belong to any particular religious persuasion or that they should be outwardly "religious" in the almost hypocritical sense that the word is used in many circles today. I am affirming that without both an intellectual and an experiential knowledge—which implies love, involvement, and a certain pathos—there is little hope of succeeding in this enterprise. All too often, individuals who seem to pose as exponents of some other religion know fairly little about the riches of their own tradition.

But I am saying still more, and it is a delicate matter to formulate it without being misunderstood. I am not preaching that one has to belong to any religious institution. I am propounding that one has to have reached a certain religious insight, poise, maturity, wisdom, and even inner peace and harmony within one's own being, without which intellectual discourse about religion will be marred at the very outset. I am saying that knowledge requires connaturality and even implies a certain identification with the thing known.

The classic Western word for this gnosis is wisdom (*sapientia: sapida scientia*). Religion is not like geology, which may be cultivated provided we have enough information of the objective facts and the scientific theories. But the study of religion demands a special kind of empathy with the subject matter that cannot be dissociated from one's own life. We can write about the symbolic meaning and extraordinary beauty of dance as an expression of the sacred, and compare Greek with Amerindian rituals, for instance. But if we have not had at least a glimpse both of the transforming effects of the dance and of the inner relationship between dance and the rest of life, we shall not be able to make much headway in the interpretation of the religious phenomenon of the dance. Religion is a certain wholeness. A good oboe player is not automatically a good conductor of a symphony orchestra. One needs something more than the sum total of the skills of the individual instruments. Religion, I submit, is the symphony, not the solo player or singer.

The inner harmony I am referring to is manifested in the spontaneous and creative way in which we may be able to deal with one particular religion because we are really at home there and able to simplify, to relate disparate things, or put practices together. I am speaking about a certain identification with that tradition, which does not preclude, of course, critical opinions and even harsh judgments, but which are always somewhat from within. When dealing with a religion at that level we should speak *ex abundantia cordis et mentis* more than from a catalogue of propositions. The existential reason is obvious. Any authentic religious dialogue dispels misunderstandings from both sides and calls for rectifications and new interpretations. If one of the partners is not at home in the process, because of not knowing almost spontaneously and by an instinctive sense (what the Scholastics, following Plato and Aristotle, called *per connaturalitatem*) the living sources of his or her tradition, discussion will stick to mere formulations and become rigid. No encounter, no dialogue, will take place.

If scholars gain this insight into their own tradition, they will be able to become aware of what I call the *pars pro toto* effect. In order to be brief I may exemplify it with the attitude we find in so many truly spiritual masters. I am aware that I see reality, although through the perspective of my own window. I may believe that I see the entire panorama of the world and the meaning of human life, although through the color, shape, and glass of my particular window. I may further believe that it is the best window, at least for me, and that the vision it allows is not distorted. I may at this moment withhold judgment regarding the validity of the vision through other windows, but I cannot hide the fact that I believe that through my window I see the entire panorama, the *totum*.

Nobody is ultimately satisfied with partialities. A Christian, for instance, will say that Christ represents the totality or is the Universal Savior or the center of the universe, to utilize different metaphors, the interpretation of which does not enter now into the picture. We may well demythicize them. Nevertheless the Christian will not be satisfied with a partial view, that Christ is just one *avatāra* among many, and be content with it as the Christian's lot—or *karma*? In short, Christians will have to say that in Christ they find the truth, and with qualifications, the whole truth.

But there is a third experience still to pass through. We should, further, be aware that we see the *totum per partem*, the whole through a part. We will have to concede that the other, the non-Christian, for instance, may have a similar experience and that the non-Christian will have to say that the Christian takes the *pars pro toto*, for from the outside one only sees the *pars*, not the *totum*—the window, not the panorama. How to combine these apparently contradictory statements? We will have to say that the other is right in discovering that we take the *pars pro toto* (because the outsider sees the window), but that we are also right in seeing the *totum per partem* (because we see the panorama). It is a *totum* for us, but *per partem*, limited to our vision through the one window. We see the *totum*, but not *totaliter*, one may say (because we do not see through other windows). We see all that we can see. The other may see equally the *totum* through another window, and thus describe it differently, but both see the *totum* although not *in toto*, but *per partem*. *Rota in rotae* (*trochos en trochō*), said Christian mystics commenting on Ezekiel 1:16.

This means that we do not need a universal theory as if we could enjoy a global perspective—which is a contradiction in terms. It means that each one of us may be aware of the whole under one particular aspect, and not just that we see only a part of it. Both the subjective and objective models break down. There is neither subjective nor objective universality. We see all that we can see—one may grant—but only *all* that *we* can see, our *totum*. The whole is what is wholesome for us—and healthy, following the wisdom of the words. Something is complete when it has an inner harmony, as we shall still emphasize. Let us recall that the root *kail* (*koil*), from which the word "whole" derives, suggests both beauty and goodness.

Dialogical Openness

Once internal dialogue has begun, once we are engaged in a genuine intrareligious scrutiny, we are ready for what I call the *imparative* method, that is, the effort at learning from the other and the attitude of allowing our own convictions to be fecundated by the insights of the other. I argue that, strictly speaking, comparative religion, on its ultimate level, is not possible, because we do not have any neutral platform outside every tradition whence comparisons may be drawn. How can there be a no-man's-land in the land of Man? In particular fields this is indeed possible, but not when what is at stake is the ultimate foundations of human life. We cannot compare (*comparare*, that is, to treat on an equal—par—basis), for there is no fulcrum outside. We can only *imparare*, that is, learn from the other, opening ourselves from our standpoint to a dialogical dialogue that does not seek to win or to convince, but to search together from our different vantage points. It is in this dialogue, which cannot be multitudinous, but only between a few traditions in each case, where we forge the appropriate language to deal with the questions that emerge in encounter. Each encounter creates a new language.

In these dialogues we do not come up with great universal theories, but with a deepened mutual understanding among, say, Catholic Christianity and *śaivasiddhānta*, or between Lutheranism and Shia Islam, or between modern Western philosophical categories and traditional Bantu religiousness. Once a net of relationships has been developed, it is relatively easy to establish new and more general links and even venture common categories. The great religions of Africa should be mentioned here, for they offer a peculiar difficulty to dialogue on the one hand and a grand facility on the other. It is difficult because often dialogue becomes doctrinal, abstract, metaphysical, and the genius of many an African religion lies elsewhere. We have difficulty in finding common categories. It is easy, on the other hand, because of the charge of humanity and concreteness of such exchanges. The common language is the simplest one.

These mutual studies, relationships, and dialogues change both the opinion of the one partner and the interpretation of the other. Religions change through these contacts; they borrow from each other and also reinforce their respective standpoints; it is a genuine *locus theologicus*, to speak in Christian Scholastic parlance, a source in itself of religious—theological—understanding. A theory of a particular religion today has also to deal with other religions. We can no longer ignore the other. The religions of others—our neighbors—become a religious question for us, for our religion.

In a way, there is many a theory of religion claiming to be a universal theory of religion. But then we are, although on a second and much more fruitful, higher spiral, at the same initial point, namely, having to confront a series of universal theories of religion. We will have to deal with, say, how Islam sees itself in the religious mosaic of our times, or how Marxism confronts the Hindu interpretation of reality.

This process of mutual learning has no end. *Imparative* religion is an open process. A universal theory attempts to clarify everything as neatly as possible in one single place, and eventually ends up stifling any ultimate dialogue. In my alternative the polarities remain, and the ideal is not seen in a universal theory, but in an ever emerging and ever elusive myth that makes communication, and thus mutual fecundation, possible without reducing everything to a single source of intelligibility or to mere intelligibility. The very theory is dialogical. In a word, the dialogical character of being is a constitutive trait of reality. Agreement means convergence of hearts, not just coalescence of minds. There is always place for diversity of opinions and multiplicity of mental schemes of intelligibility.

Human Cosmic Trust

What I am trying to put forward is not a countertheory but a new innocence. We should beware of so many reform systems that began with a greater universalistic impulse than the original systems and became new philosophies, new sects, or new religions. Often they do not subsume or even enhance the others but simply multiply their number. This may not be bad, except they do not achieve what they started to do. Any universal theory will soon become another theory.

We should beware of claiming to understand religions better than they have understood themselves. I do not deny this possibility, but it should carry along some contemporary representatives of such a religion, and at least partially transform that religion, lest our interpretation become a new religion. Religious traditions have more existential than doctrinal continuity. There are not many doctrines in common between a Christian of the first century and a present-day one, for instance. The case of Hinduism is even clearer. Hinduism is an existence, not an essence. The decisive factor is the existential confession, not the doctrinal interpretation.

The study of religion, I repeat, is not like the scientific approach to physical phenomena which even in the sciences is becoming obsolete. We are not dealing with objective facts—supposing they existed. Even in the case of allegedly revealed facts we are still dealing with human constructs which house, as it were, a group of human beings giving them the housing of a more or less coherent and protective universe.

In our days we feel perhaps more acutely than at other times that we do not know each other, that we still mistrust one another, that in fact we are at loggerheads in many fundamental insights of immediate importance for the praxis of our lives. We are painfully aware of our differences because we are more conscious of our mutual existence and the need to intermingle, brought about by the techniculture of our times. But we cannot chop off our divergences to remain only with what we have in common: we all want to eat and to be happy. This is fundamental, but hunger has many causes, and the ways to happiness, and even its very concept, differ.

Religions can no longer live in isolation, let alone in animosity and war. Traditional religions nowadays are not, by and large, very powerful and thus do not present a major threat, except of course in some countries. More secular religious ideologies today have greater virulence and fight each other. They cannot be left out of the picture in a discourse about the encounter of religions. The last two world wars were not strictly religious, and yet they were "theological." Where do we turn for harmony and understanding?

The political and economic situation of the world today compels us to radical changes in our conception of humanity and the place of humanity in the cosmos. The present system seems to be running toward major catastrophes of all kinds. This situation brings near the thought that if the change has to be radical and lasting, it also has to transform our ways of thinking about and experiencing reality. The point in the case of the religious traditions could not be more pertinent. I am prepared to argue that if there is any solution to the present predicament, it cannot come out of one single religion or tradition, but has to be brought about by collaboration among the different traditions of the world. No single human or religious tradition is today self-sufficient and capable of rescuing humanity from its present predicament. We can no longer say, "That's your problem!" Hinduism will not survive if it does not face modernity. Christianity will disappear if it does not meet Marxism. Technocratic religion will destroy itself if it does not pay heed to, say, the Amerindian tradition, and so on. Humanity will collapse if we do not gather together all the fragments of the scattered cultures and religions. But togetherness does not necessarily mean unity, nor is understanding absolutely required.

What is needed is trust, a certain trust that sustains a common struggle for an ever better shaping of reality. I mean something like this: As the very word suggests (especially in Latin: *fiducia*), this "trust" entails a certain "fidelity" to oneself, "confidence" in the world as cosmos, "loyalty" in the struggle itself, and even (as perhaps etymologically hinted at) an attitude rooted in the soil of Reality like a "tree," a basic "belief" in the human project, or rather in the worthwhile collaboration of humans in the overall adventure of being. It excludes only the suicidal and negative desire of self-destruction and annihilation of everything. It does not eliminate the passionate thrust toward the victory of one's own ideals, reprehensible as this may appear to many of us if this is striven for as an absolute.

Elsewhere I have proposed the distinction between the basic and constitutive human *aspiration* by which the human being is constituted precisely as a human being, and the *desires* that plague concrete human existence when not walking on the path toward realization. This, I would submit, takes into account the Buddhist criticism of *taṇhā*, *tṛṣṇā* (thirst, desire), the one-pointedly Hindu concern for realization, and the Christian preoccupation with dynamism and creativity. There is a primordial human aspiration, but there are equally hasty desires. The trust I am speaking of is related to the human aspiration by which humans believe that life is worth living, because reality can, and must, be trusted.

The danger in this aspiration—in our case, we may say toward truth—is that it can become a desire for our own understanding. In other words, the danger lies in the possible confusion between our *desire* to understand everything, because we assume (a priori) that reality is (should be) intelligible, and the *aspiration* of making sense of our life and all reality. This latter is the trust that there is some sense—direction, "meaningful" dynamism—in the universe.

This assumption is not a universal theory, not even a universal praxis. It is only, so far, a relative cultural invariant inasmuch as exceptions are seen precisely as aberrant deviations by the vast majority of mortals. This trust is an impulse simply not to give up in the task of being what we are—or should be—which some may say is that of being human, others divine.

Half a century ago I called this cosmic trust the cosmological principle, and millennia before, it was called *ṛta*, *tao*, *ordo*. Even when we formulate the ultimate metaphysical question—"Why is there something rather than nothing?"—we are assuming that the question is meaningful—that it is a real question—even if we do not find an answer or only a nihilistic one. It may be said of this ultimate ground that there is something somewhere asking whether it all makes sense at all, or that it is all the dream of a dreamer and has never existed outside that dream, or that it is a very weak ground indeed for the unfolding of the universe and our participation in it. Yet it may be enough, for in one way or another, we have to stop somewhere. Traditionally this ultimate ground has been called God, Man, or World. We have further interpreted those words as meaning consciousness, goodness, power, intelligence, nothingness, absurdity, matter, energy, and the like. We may change words and interpretations, but some fundamental trust indeed persists.

The ultimate ground for this cosmic confidence lies in the almost universal conviction that reality is ordered—in other words is good, beautiful, and true. It is a divine reality, say most of the human traditions. There is no need to blow up a wretched universe, because reality is not evil ultimately. We may have to bring it to completion, to achieve it, as the fundamental principle of alchemy puts it, and eventually correct it, but not create an artificial-mechanical universe that we must have under control because we cannot trust reality. Underlying this felt need for control there is a certain Protestant climate that "creation" is a fiasco, combined with some "humanistic" interpretation that the redeemer is Man. But Christian theology will tell us that redemption entails an inner dynamism that ultimately belongs to the "economic Trinity."

Cultural Excursus

To hen [. . .] diapheromenon autō xympheresthai,
hōsper harmonian toxou te kai lyras.
The one [. . .] is brought together by opposition with itself,
like the harmony of the bow and the lyre.

Heraclitus, in Plato, *Symposium* 187a

What I am trying to demythicize is the deeply anchored belief that the true
and the one are convertible: *Verum et unum convertuntur* was the traditional
formulation.[3] It reaches even as far as the curious etymology of Theodoricus of
Chartres: *unitas quasi* ontitas *ab* on *graeco, id est entitas* (un-ity amounts to *on-ity*
[be-ingness] from *on* [be-ing] in Greek, that is, en-tity [be-ingness]),[4] to understand, then, is to reduce everything to unity and this unity is the oneness of Being.
This almost universal insight begins to go astray when interpreted quantitatively.
The One is not the counterpart of the Many. *To metron* is the first endowment
of reality, according to Socrates.[5] The Bible states that God arranged everything
according to measure, number, and weight—but not according to meters, quantities, and gravitation.[6]

In attempting to criticize a utopian single theology of religions, or theology
of religion, and at the same time trying to awaken a new awareness, I would ally
myself here with one of the most incisive leitmotifs of one branch of the Western
tradition[7]—and obviously, predominant in the East.[8] I would even suggest that

---

[3] See Aristotle, *Met.* 2.1 (993b30) as the *locus classicus* from which the Scholastic
principle derived—although Aristotle's dictum is somewhat more subtle: "ekaston hōs echei
tou einai outō kai tēs alētheias." Cf. the traditional Latin version: "Unumquodque sicut se
habet ad hoc quod sit, ita etiam se habet ad hoc quod habeat veritatem," or, more literally,
"Quare unumquodque sicut se habet ut sit, ita et ad veritatem." Cf. Thomas Aquinas, *Sum
theol.*, I, q.2, a.3: "Quae sunt maxime vera sunt maxime entia."

[4] *Commentarium in Boethia De Trinitate*, in P. Gaia, ed., *Opere religiose di Nicolò
Cusano* (Classici delle religioni) (Turin: UTET, 1971), 636.

[5] Cf. the astounding text of Plato, *Philebus* 66a, where, after measure as the first value,
comes proportion, and only third, reason, followed by *technē*, and fifth, pleasure

[6] Ws 11:20: "Omnia in mensura (*metrō*), et numero (*arihtmō*), et pondere (*stathmō*)
disposuisti" (You, however, ordered all things by measure, number, and weight).

[7] The two modern symbols could be the two seventeenth-century figures of Descartes
(*cogito ergo sum*) and Pascal ("le coeur a ses raisons que la raison ne connaît point").

[8] Suffice it to quote the famous *Brahma-sūtra* text I.1.4: *Tat tu samanvayāt* ("But
that [because of] the harmony") of all texts of all the Sacred Scriptures—in spite of the
fact that they write, teach, and even command different and prima facie diverging things.
Harmony is not uniformity. Even today in India religious understanding is rendered as
dharma samanvaya. See *Prabuddha Bharata or Awakened India* 90 (April 1985; Uttara-

this has been the prevalent human vision of reality and that the belief in a possible exhaustive rational explanation of everything is the exception. The alternative is neither anarchy nor irrationalism—even under the cloak of *Gefühlsphilosophien*. The alternative is a dynamic notion of freedom, of Being, and the radical relativity of everything with everything, so that all our explanations are not only for the time being, because ours is a being in time, but also because no Absolute can encompass the complexity of the real, which is radically free. The Absolute is only absolutely incarnated in the relative.

It is not enough to say *multa et unum convertuntur*,[9] or to introduce a *coincidentia oppositorum*. It is not convincing to revert to a new individualistic monadology either.[10] These attempts do not assume a dialogical relationship between the One and the Many (*hen kai polla*).[11] With the concepts of quantity and individuation we fail to do justice to the problem. We should introduce other symbols. The one I would choose here is the widespread symbol of *concord*, which as such defies quantification.[12] Neither multiplicity as such, nor sheer unity brings about, or even allows, harmony.[13] Harmony implies a constitutive polarity, which cannot be superseded dialectically. It would be destroyed.

Concord is neither oneness nor plurality. It is the dynamism of the many toward the One without ceasing to be different and without becoming one, and without reaching a higher synthesis. Music is here the paradigm. There is no harmonical accord if there is no plurality of sounds, or if those sounds coalesce in one single note. Neither many nor one, but concord, harmony.

---

khand, Advaita Ahrama): 190.

[9] As P. Gaia, *Opere*, interprets the *unum* of Nicholas of Cusa as *complicatio multorum*.

[10] See the insightful study of Maurice Boutin, "L'Un dispersive," *Neoplatonismo e religion: Archivio di filosofia* 51, no. 1–3 (Padova: CEDAM, 1983), 253–79, commenting on Francois Laruelle, *Le principe de minorité* (Paris: Aubier, 1981). There are "des monades absolument disperses et dépourvues de monadologie, de raison ou d'universel," says Laruelle, for individuals are the "constituants ultimes de la réalité" (261).

[11] Plato, *Phileb.* 15d, as *locus classicus*.

[12] This is the rich concept of *homonoia*, concord, unanimity, sameness of mind (just as *homonomos* means of the same order, law) in the Hellenic tradition since Demosthenes. This concord is defined as "epistēmē koinōn agathōn" in the *Stoicorum Veterum Fragmenta*, ed. H. von Arnim (Leipzig: Teubneri, 1903), 3:160, as the science of the common goods. See the bibliographical references in Liddell-Scott, *A Greek-English Lexicon* (Oxford: Oxford University Press, 1973), and in Hammond and Scullard, *The Oxford Classical Dictionary* (Oxford: Oxford University Press, 1913).

[13] "Sameness (*ta homoia*) and the similar (*homophila*) do not need harmony; but the different (*anomoia*), the not-similar, and that which is not ordered need to be brought together through harmony," wrote the Pythagorean Philolaus of Kroton, *Fragm.* 6, in H. Diels and W. Kranz, eds., *Die Fragmente der Vorsokratiker*, 9th ed. (Berlin: Weidmann, 1969). The entire text is fundamental.

We find this root metaphor almost everywhere from the last *mantra* of the Ṛg-veda[14] to Chuang-Tzu.[15] It is the thought repeated differently by Heraclitus and taken up by Filolaus,[16] commented upon by Ramon Lull,[17] Pico della Mirandola,[18] Cusanus,[19] and so many others,[20]

[14] "Samānī va ākūtiḥ /samānā hṛdayāni vaḥ / samānam astu vo mano / yathḥ vaḥ susāhāsati" (Harmonious be your intention, / harmonious your hearts, / may your spirit be in harmony, / that you may be together in concord!), *RV* X.191.4. I give here a different translation from that in my anthology *The Vedic Experience* (Berkeley: University of California Press, 1977), 863.

[15] *Passim.* See, for example, *Inner Chapters* 2, trans. G. F. Feng (New York: Vintage Books, 1974), 46.

[16] *Fragm.* 10. See Diels and Kranz, *Fragmente*, 1:410.

[17] "Per ço que enans nos puscam concordar" are practically the last words of one of the three sages—Jewish, Christian, Muslim—after they left the Gentile who would choose the right *lig* [religion] without the knowledge of the three: Ramon Lull, *Libre del gentil e los tres savis*, in *Obres essencials* (Barcelona: Selecta, 1957), 1:1138. However, Lull is perhaps too much in favor of unity. See the dissertation by F. Medeiros, *Judaïsme, Islam et Gentilité dans l'oeuvre de Raymond Lulle* (Munich: Evangelisch-theologische Fakultät, 1976).

[18] "Dopo [Dio] comincia la bellezza, perché comincia la contrarietà, senza la quale non può essere cosa alcuna creata, ma sarebbe solo essa Dio: né basta questa contrarietà e discordia di diverse nature a constituire la creatura, se per debito temperamento non diventa *e la contrarietà unita e la discordia concorde*, il che si può per vera deffinizione assignare di essa bellezza, cioè che non sia altro che *una amica inimicizia e una concorde discordia*. Per questo diceva Eraclito la guerra e la contenzione essere padre e generatrice delle cose; e, appresso Omero, chi maladisce la contenzione è detto avere bestemmiato la natura. Ma più perfettamente parlò Empedocle, ponendo, no la discordia per sé, ma insieme con la concordia essere principio de le cose, intendendo per la discordia la varietà delle nature di che si compongono, e per la concordia l'uione di quelle; è però disse solo in Dio non essere discordia perché in lui no è unione di diverse nature, anzi è essa unità semplice senza composizione alcuna" (*Commento* 2.9.495–96, in H. de Lubac, *Pic de la Mirandole* [Paris: Aubier Montaigne, 1974], 296, emphases added). In *Heptaplus* (*aliud proemium*) he again writes about a discordant concord: Quoniam sc. Astricti vinculis concordiae uti naturas ita etiam appellationes hi omnes mundi mutua sibi liberalitate condonant: [. . .] occultas, ut ita dixerim, totius naturae et amicitas et affinitates edocti [. . .] Accedit quod, qua ratione haec sunt distincta, quia tamen nulla est multitudo quae non sit una *discordi quadam concordia ligantur* et multiformibus nexuum quasi catenis devinciuntur (297, emphases added).

[19] See his work *De concordantia Catholica* of 1433 and his *De pace fidei* of 1453, a few months after the defeat of Constantinople, although Cusanus falls into a dialectical *coincidentia*. Consider his revealing text: Omnia enim in tantum sunt in quantum unum sunt. Complectitur autem tam ea quae sunt actu, quam ea quae possunt fieri. Capacius est igitur unum quam ens, quod non est nisi actu est, licet Aristoteles dicat ens et unum converti (*De venatione sapientiae*, 21).

[20] For example, Postel, *Concordia mundi*; *De orbis terrae concordia*; etc. Erasmus: *Querela pacis*; *Oratio de pace et discordia*; *Precatio pro pace Ecclesiae concordia* (1532); Juan Luís Vives: *De concordia et discordia in humano genere* (1529); *De pacificatione* (1529); etc.

up to St. Francis de Sales,[21] and lately taken as title for a book by R. C. Zaehner.[22] This leitmotif has been often submerged by the predominant trend of victory and unity.[23] The Christian symbol is the Trinity.

"Yield and overcome," says Lao Tzu.[24] Fight and overcome, echoes the predominant spirit of Western culture: *Veni, vidi, vici*, said Caesar.[25] Make everything *inclusive*, India would say.[26] Make everything *universal*, responds the West. Strive to make everything complete by realizing harmony is what this third tradition is saying.

My motto would then be "concordia discors" (discordant concord), and it could have as underplay the opposite, "concordant discord," for as the always paradoxical Heraclitus liked to put it: "The mysterious harmony is stronger than the evident one," or again, "The unspoken harmony is superior to the verbalized one."[27]

See also Augusto Gentili, *Problemi del simbolismo armonico nella cultura post-elisabettiana*, in E. Castelli, ed., *Il simbolismo del Tempo* (Rome: Istituto di studi filosofici, 1973), 65.

[21] "Introduce unity into diversity, and you create order, order yields harmony, proportion; harmony, where you have perfect integrity, begets beauty. There is beauty in an army when it has order in the ranks, when all the divisions combine to form a single armed force. There is beauty in music when voices, which are true, clear, distinct, blend to produce perfect consonance, perfect harmony, to achieve unity in diversity or diversity in unity—a good description might be *discordant concord*; better still, *concordant discord*" (Francis de Sales, *Traité de l'amour de Dieu* 1.1 [1616]).

[22] *Concordant Discord: The Interdependence of Faiths* (Oxford: Clarendon Press, 1970; the Gifford Lectures, 1967/1969).

[23] One quotation may suffice: "So wird also die Universalgeschichte, die Geschichtsphilosophie und die Zukunftsgestaltung in Warheit zu einem möglichst einheitlichen Selbstverständnis des eigenen Gewordenseins und der eigene Entwicklung. Für uns gibt es nur die Universalgeschichte der europäischen Kultur, die natürlich der vergleichenden Blicke auf fremde Kulturen praktisch und theoretisch bedarf, um sich selbst und ihr Verhältnis zu den anderen zu verstehen, die aber mit den anderen dadurch nicht etwas in eine allgemeine Menschheitgeschichte und Menschheitsentwicklung zusammenfliessen kann. Unsere Universalgeschichte ist um so mehr ein europäisches Selbstverständnis, als nur der Europäer bei seiner Häufung verschiedenster Kulturelemente, seinem niemals ruhenden Intellekt und seiner unausgesetzt strebenden Selbstbildung eines solchen universalhistorischen Bewusstseins auf kritischer Forschungsgrundlage für seine Seele bedarf." E. Troeltsch, *Der Historismus und seine Probleme* [1922; repr. [Aalen, 1961], in *Gesammelte Schriften*, 3:71. I feel that most of the efforts at universalizing are still under this post-Hegelian spell. *Der Europäismus* is, significantly enough, the title of Troeltsch's chap. 4, part 2.

[24] *Tao-te Ching* 22; see also 40, 51, 62, etc.

[25] Plutarch, *Caes.* 50.3 (*ēlton, eizon, enikēsa*) and also *Moralia* 206e; quoted also in other sources: Lucius Annaeus Florus (second century), 2.13.63; Cassius Dio (second century), 42, 48; up to the twelfth-century Byzantine historian Johannes Zonaras, 10.10; etc.

[26] See G. Oberhammer, ed., *Inklusivismus: Eine indische Denkform* (Vienna: Institut für Indologie, 1983).

[27] I have now translated my motto differently. *Aphanēs* means literally "without being *phaneros*" (visible, apparent), from the verb *phainō*, "to shine, illumine," and thus "let know, appear manifest." The root *pha* (*phn, phan* . . .) means "to shine" (cf. fantasy),

But we may still quote:
Kai ek tōn diapherontōn
kallistēn harmonian
kai panta ket'erin ginesthai.[28]

(And from divergences
The most beautiful harmony [arises],
and all happens through struggle.)[29]

It is the same Heraclitus who praises harmony as the result of polarity.[30] He formulates it in the most general way: "Nature aspires to the opposite. It is from there and not from the equal that harmony is produced."[31]

This is the insight into the agonic character of reality.[32] In point of fact this

---

but immediately relates to *phēm*: "to say"; *phasis*, "the word"; *phōnē* (cf. prophet). Cf. also voice, symphony, phenomenology, epiphany, telephone, etc.

[28] Heraclitus, *Fragm.* 8 (see also Empedocles 124.2). The text probably refers first to music and from there to the wider reality. See a standard translation: "Das Wilderstrebende vereinigte sich, aus den entgegengesetzen (Tönen) entstehe die schönste Harmonie, und alles Geschehen erfolge auf dem Wege des Streites" (W. Capelle, trans. and Introductions, *Die Vorsokratiker: Die Fragmente und Quellenberichte* [Stuttgart: Kroner, 1968], 134). W. D. Ross's standard translation of Aristotle, *Nicomachean Ethics* (8.1555b4) reads, "and Heraclitus [saying] that 'it is what opposes that helps' and 'from different tones come the fairest tune' and 'all things are produced through stile.'" See the book with which Romano Guardini practically began his intellectual career, *Der Gegensatz und Gegensätze: Entwurf eines Systems der Typenlehre* (Freiburg: Herder, 1917), which had substantial revisions until the second edition of 1955 with the title *Der Gegensatz: Versuche zu einer Philosophie des Lebendig-Konkreten.*

[29] The word *eris*, from *erei* or *er* (cf. German *errege, reize*) means "strife, quarrel, struggle, discord, disputation." Eris is also the goddess of discord in the marriage of Peleus and Thetis. In the *Eumenides* (975) of Aeschylus, *eris agathōn* appears with a positive meaning. For *eris*, see also Heraclitus, *Fragm.* 80: "polemon eonta xynon kai dikēn erin kai ginomena panta kat'erin kai chreōn" ([One should know that] strife is the common thing, along with the right to struggle, and that all things happen by struggle and necessity).

[30] See Heraclitus, *Fragm.* 51, in Diels and Kranz, *Vorsokratiker*, 1:162, and its Platonic commentary in *Symposium* 187, with the famous metaphor of the arc and the lyre, quoted in the epigraph of this excursus. We could also translate: "The one conflicting with itself is brought into harmony with itself like the harmony of the bow and the lyre."

[31] "Isōs de tōn enantiōn he physis glichetai kai ek toutōn apotelei to symphōnon, ouk ek tōn homoiōn" (Heraclitus, *Fragm.* 10; see also Aristotle, *De mundo* 5.39b.7).

[32] "Agonic" contains almost all the elements: it means *assembly, agora*, gathering. This *gathering*, being a human one, is a *place of speech*, where the *word* is paramount. But persons speak in order to *contest* each others' opinions. *Agōn* is the *struggle*, either in battle or the mental agony (as we still say). It is this *vehemence* that elicits *power*, although, of course, sometimes *anxiety, agony*. A *trial, legal action*, can be an *agonizing activity*. All the English words in italics are meanings of this word, whose root means precisely "to lead,

experience is not as uncommon as one might assume.[33] It lasted until our times.[34] It was with Descartes that divergence of opinions created philosophical anguish. It was the beginning of the modern age. I should like to insist on this. Diversity of opinions becomes disturbing once we direct our attention to mere orthodoxy severed from orthopraxis, and the former is thought to express the essence of being human. Once we take individualism for granted, we find it scandalous that there is diversity of opinions—forgetting the beautiful metaphor of Fernando de Rojas.[35] It is the estrangement of the human mind from nature that leads to the assumption that univocity is the ideal. Thinking begins to be understood as measuring, calculating.

I have quoted these texts in order to suggest the spirit and the method in which I should like to situate the entire enterprise. I have on purpose quoted mainly from the Western tradition, because I have been criticizing mainly a Western theory and attempting to enter into dialogue with it. I am far from wanting to reduce all to any unity.

We hear of a friendly enmity, of a polarity between concord and discord, and a link between the two; we hear of a discordant concord, of the fundamental thrust of nature toward diversity, and we try to understand that true concord is not unity

---

to carry, to fetch, bring, take," etc. Cf. *agos*, the leader. The root *ago* means to "lead." Cf. Sanskrit *ajah*, to "drive, push."

[33] As a single and yet multivalent example I may quote the first lines of the Preface of the Spanish classic *La Celestina* of Fernando de Rojas (first edition, Burgos, 1499): "Todas las cosas ser criadas a manera de contienda o batalla, dice aquel gran sabio Heráclito en este modo: *Omnia secundum litem fiunt*. Sentencia a mi ver digna de perpetua y recordable memoria. . . . Hallé esta sentencia corroborada por aquel gran orador y poeta laureado Petrarca, diciendo: *Sine lite atque offensione nihil genuit natura parens*. Sin lid y ofensión [*combate*, in modern Spanish] ninguna cosa engendró la natura, madre de todo. [I note parenthetically that *parens* is here translated as *madre*. In the Roman religion the Earth is called *sacra parens*; see J. Ries, *Le sacré comme approche de Dieu et comme resource de l'homme* (Louvaine la Neuve: Coll. Conferences et Travaux 1, 1983.)] Dice más adelante: *Sic est enim, et sic propemodum universa testantur: rapido stellae obviant firmamento; contraria invicem elementa confligunt; terrae tremunt; maria fluctuant; aer quatitur; crepant flammae; bellum immortale venti gerunt; tempora temporibus concertant; secum singula nobiscum omnia.* Que quiere decir: 'En verdad así es, y así todas las cosas de esto dan testimonio: Las estrellas se encuentran en el arrebatado firmamento del cielo, los adversos elementos unos con otros rompen pelea, tremen [in modern Spanish, *tiemblan*] las tierras, ondean los lares, el aire se sacude, suenan las llamas, los vientos entre sí traen perpetua guerra, los tiempos con tiempos contienden y litigan entre sí, uno a uno, y todas contra nosotros." . . . Mayormente pues ella con todas las otras cosas que al mundo son, van debajo de la bandera de una notable sentencia: "Que aun la misma vida de los hombres si bien lo miramos, desde la primerae dad hasta que blanquean las canas, es batalla" (Bruno M. Damiani, ed., *La Celestina*, 11th ed. [Madrid: Ediciones Cátedra, 1983], 45–47).

[34] See the well-known book by Miguel de Unamuno, *La agonia del cristianismo* (Madrid: Renacimiento, 1931); the French edition dates from 1925 (Paris: F. Rieder).

[35] "No es menor la disensión de los filósofos en las escuelas, que la de las ondas del mar" (F. de Rojas, in Damiani, *La Celestina*, 48).

of opinion or equality of intellectual views, but of an order higher than the intellect, for it entails precisely struggle, strife, antagonic dynamisms—*agon*, the Greeks would say, as already indicated.

Discordia is disagreement—literally, setting our hearts at variance, and yet not asunder. Why? Obviously because we do not absolutize our opinions, or identify our being with our "thoughts," because we realize that, by my pushing in one direction and your pushing in the opposite, world order is maintained and given the impulse of its proper dynamism.

The very words by which we often express what we are striving for—"unanimity," "consensus," "agreement," "concord"—all have a cordial or an existential core. One *animus* does not mean one single theory, one single opinion, but one aspiration (in the literal sense of one breath) and one inspiration (as one spirit).[36] Consensus ultimately means to walk in the same direction, not to have just one rational view.[37] And again, to reach agreement suggests to be agreeable, to be pleasant, to find pleasure in being together.[38] Concord is to put our hearts together.

Another word for harmony may be *sympathy*, which does not primarily mean individual, sentimental compassion, but the common *pathos* among all the constituents of reality. Universal sympathy is another way of overcoming the split between individual and collective interests, the one and the many. And the word here suggests not only a more "feminine" receptivity for a predominantly "masculine" culture, but also a greater awareness of the mystery of suffering (pathos, *duḥkha*) in a civilization that shuns facing this most elemental factor, which awakens us to transcendence and interiority.

This is the discordant concord: a kind of human harmony perceived in and through the many discordant voices of human traditions. We do not want to reduce them to one voice. We may yet want to eliminate cacophonies. But this again depends very much on the education and generosity of our ears.

All this should not be taken as a mere metaphor. If we live only or even mainly on the values of the eye, the intellect, truth, and we neglect—on that ultimate level—the other senses, the heart, beauty—in a word, the concrete over against the general—we shall live a crippled life. Academia, scholarship, and modern education in general, let alone *techniculture*, seem to have almost forgotten all those other values that we find still so prominent and effective in other cultures. No need for me to understand what the animist or the Hindu or the Christian ultimately means

---

[36] *Animus* translates not only the Greek *psychē* but also *thymos* and *pneuma*, although it has its exact Greek counterpart in *anemos*—in Sanskrit, *anita* (*anilah*), meaning "to breathe."

[37] The Latin *sentire* (whence "sense" derives) means to feel (cf. sentiment) and thus also to discern by the senses (sensible, sensibility, etc.); it also means *sentis*, a path (cf. Spanish, *sendero*) and thus direction. Cf. Old High German, *sinnen*—to go and also to think (to feel one's way).

[38] The etymology of Latin, *gratum*; Sanskrit, *gurtas*, pleasure, and also joy, is related to *charis*, meaning gracious, grace, joy, gratuitousness, agreeable, favor, charity. Cf. Spanish, *agradar*, to please.

when voicing their respective worldviews. We may somewhat enjoy the beauty of the symphony, the inexplicable concord out of so many dissenting voices. Pluralism tells us here that one should not assume for oneself—person or culture—the role of being the conductor of the human and much less of the cosmic orchestra. It is enough with the music (the divine), the musicians (the human), and their instruments (the cosmos). Let us play by ear!

Conclusion

I have tried to spell out some of the implications of that attitude. I may sum it up with the word "confidence." I mean by this a certain fundamental trust in reality that impels us to trust even what we do not understand or approve of—unless there are positive and concrete reasons to fight what we discover to be evil or error. To understand that we do not understand is the beginning of transcending knowledge, as most of the spiritual traditions of the world will tell us.[39] Further, to understand that the other is an equal source of understanding, and not only an object of it, is again what many a school has called the beginning of enlightenment.[40]

It all boils down to the experience of our personal and collective limitations, including the very limits of the intellect, not only in us, but in itself. The last function of the intellect is to transcend itself. And this is possible only by becoming aware of its own limitations—and this, I submit, not only in every one of us, but in itself. If we want to reduce everything to consciousness, we are forced to admit that pure consciousness is not conscious of itself. It would then not be pure. Brahman does not know that it is Brahman, says vedānta coherently. Īśvara knows that "he" is Brahman. The knowledge of the Father is the Son, the Logos, says the Christian Trinity. This is not irrationalism. It is the highest and intransferable mission of the intellect, to become aware of its own boundaries. In becoming conscious(ness) of itself, consciousness becomes conscious(ness) of its own limits, and by this very fact transcends them. If pure consciousness is aware of its limits, this amounts to conceding that not all can be reduced to consciousness.

Humankind is held together not because we have the same opinions, a common language, the same religion, or even the same respect for others, but for the same reason that the entire universe is held together. We mortals strive not only among ourselves, but we also struggle with the gods for the order of the universe. And yet

---

[39] See KenU II.3, and also RV I.164.32, etc.

[40] "Knowing others is wisdom. Knowing the self is enlightenment" (Tao-te Ching 33). The reason is apparent. I can know others by shedding the light of my knowledge on them. But I cannot know myself in this way. It needs another light falling upon me from outside me. I need to be illumined in order to be enlightened—that is, I need to be known by somebody else, I need to be loved. Cf. "epignōsomai kathōs kai epegnōsthen" (I shall know as I am known); cognoscam sicut et cognitus sum, in the Vulgate (1 Co 13:12). Here is the locus of grace, again an openness and movement.

this *eris* (*kama* and *tapas* the Vedas would say)[41] is also our responsibility, our answer to the very challenge. To maintain the world together, the *lokasamgrahā* of the Gītā,[42] is precisely the function of primordial *dharma*, of which humans are active factors.[43]

At Pentecost the peoples did not all speak the same language, nor did they have simultaneous translation, nor did they understand the mutual refinements of the respective liturgies. Yet, they were convinced, they felt, they sensed, that all were *hearing* the great deeds of God, the *megaleia tou Theou*.[44]

This cosmic confidence certainly has an intellectual dimension; I have been speaking about it on the intellectual level. Yet, it does not need to be put into words. And it is this cosmic confidence that stands at the very basis of dialogical dialogue and makes it possible. The dialogue—we all agree on this—is not a trick, a stratagem to get to the other, to defeat the partner. There is a basic confidence that, although we neither understand nor often approve of what others think and do, we still have not given up all hope—which is a virtue of the tempiternal present and not of the temporal future—that human conviviality makes sense, that we belong together, and that together we must strive. Some thinkers may be tempted to say that this is an option. I would prefer to suggest that this is an instinct, the work of the Spirit.[45]

---

[41] *RV* X.129.4, 190.1, etc.

[42] *BG* III.20, 25.

[43] *RV* X.90.16: *dharmani prathamani*. Cf. *BG* VII.11.

[44] Ac 2:11.

[45] This ending is not just a phrase. The core of Western culture is based on the ultimate binomial Being/Thinking, or in theological vocabulary, Father/Son (*Logos*). This basic dyad has often obscured the Trinitarian paradigm, which alone overcomes the strictures of science ("the laws of nature are immutable") and makes room for freedom—as I have indicated elsewhere.

11

THE RELIGION OF THE FUTURE,
OR THE CRISIS OF THE CONCEPT OF RELIGION

1. The problem of the "future of religions" is not that of the religion of the future.

The first problem deals with the future of what we usually call *religion* in the Western languages, which monotheisms tend to identify with an organization— since they believe that God is Legislator, something which is outright scandalous for many Eastern religions. It presupposes that religion is a known and more or less accepted notion, and it deals with the forms and characteristics that *this* "religion" will have in the future. This is primarily a sociological question, one that is based on an intense—and Western—reading of the "signs of the times." This would justify the necessary extrapolation that would allow us to predict what this religion would be in the future. The future is not a logical consequence of the present; that would entail falling into the worst dialectical materialism. Besides extrapolating our particular present, we must listen to other traditions, and even bear in mind that new situations can be created since the "future" is also the fruit of freedom. Ultimately, the answers that they tend to give are still monocultural. They predict what "religion" will be like in the future. "Le prévisible n'est pas libre," Simone Weil used to say, and if religion is not free, then we are speaking about a sociological fact, but not about religion, which is a dimension of Man, who is a free being.[1]

But not everything is fully contained in the present, so that, besides extrapolating, it is also necessary to build and even create new situations. Ultimately, the answer to this question belongs to prophecy. It predicts what religion will be like in the future.

The second problem refers to the nature of the concept of religion itself, asking if it might expand so as to nurture in its bosom possible mutations of the notion itself. In this case the very concept must be subjected to a radical critique—so radical that we do not even presume that religion should even continue in the future. This is preeminently an intercultural philosophical question, which requires a different

---

[1] I am unwilling to follow the trend established by U.S. English that does not distinguish between gender and sex. We do not give men the monopoly of the human. Man is a generic and asexual term—just as "God" is of the male gender, but not of the male sex.

methodology from that used to reflect on the first question. It will be based on an analysis of the human situation in the light of an anthropology that cannot be derived from a single religion, but rather from the interpretation that Man gives of itself from within the vast horizon of its diverse cultures. In other words, what *constitutes* Man cannot be disengaged completely from the interpretation Man gives of itself. Indeed, what separates Man from all other living entities is not only that it is an object of study but that it is also the subject studying itself. Its self-understanding is part of its very being. Therefore, mere observation or reflection is insufficient in order to know who and what Man is. We must integrate also what Man thinks it is. And in the present intercultural situation, such an anthropology cannot be based on the experience of only one culture, for this would be only a partial understanding of what it means to be a human being. To be sure, the problems here are enormous, since such an integral anthropology does not exist. But if we want to reflect on the religion of the future in today's global context, we cannot sidestep the issue.

To give an example, let us look at the meaning of this double expression in an orthodox Tibetan-Buddhist context. To ask about the future of *dharma* hardly makes sense in that context. To ask whether the *dharma* will have a more or less attractive future presumes that one lives in the myth of history and accepts the reality of linear time. Moreover, to concern oneself with the vicissitudes of the future indicates that one does not understand what the *dharma* is all about. Strictly speaking such a problem does not arise. The *dharma* will have in the future as in the past its highs and lows; including an increase or decrease in the number of people who genuinely live it, but none of this touches the *dharma* at all. Likewise, to ask about the *dharma* of the future is almost blasphemous since, strictly speaking, *dharma* is not a temporal concept; thence, has nothing to do with the past or the future.

Indeed, if the *dharma* of the future were a slave to the conditions imposed upon it by temporality (either the future or the past) it would not really be *dharma*, but a betrayal of it, a new but different *dharma*, if you like. This second question is fundamentally religious. Even within a Tibetan-Buddhist context, a contemporary philosophical reflection cannot escape the bite of modernity and deny there is a problem to solve. Something is thus imposed *ab ovo*: the problem about the relation between *dharma* and temporality. How does "futurity" affect, if in some way it does, the very essence of *dharma*? Our question does not concern so much the future of religions, of *Vajrayana* Buddhism, Roman Catholicism, or any religion in particular—nor even the future of religion in general. It refers, rather, to the more critical question about the destiny of what has come to be called either appropriately or inappropriately by the name of religion.

It should be very clear that a functional way of thinking, as opposed to a substantial one, justifies that we call *religion* not only those religions that define themselves as such, but also everything that Man believes performs the function of giving his life an ultimate meaning. Therefore, our question is not about the future of religions or of one religion in particular, nor about the future of religion, but rather about the very destiny of that which, one way or another, functions as religion. That is the problem we are referring to when we propose to meditate on the *religion of the future* as distinct from the investigation on the *future of "religion."*

What is the temporal structure of the human being that allows us to say something about the future of that which in the past has been called *religion*? The first difficulty appears when we note that the "that" to which we refer is not a thing in itself, independent of the names it carries and the interpretations given to it. The second difficulty arises when we realize we do not—yet?—possess the universal categories to even a tackle the problem. We can partly obviate the first difficulty by consciously using symbolic rather than conceptual language. We can compromise with the second by imposing a double coefficient of *limitation* and *provisionality*, even to the point of renouncing the very attempt to sketch out thematically the intercultural anthropology to which we previously alluded.

First, we expound our objections to the application of the concept of religion outside its own boundaries; thereafter, we will show how the symbol of religion can illuminate our subject, and we will conclude with some provisional considerations about the religiousness of our time.

2.   *Our ordinary concept of "religion" does not apply to a large part of contemporary systems of belief that, nevertheless, are legitimate religious forms.*

In these postcolonial times, religious studies has begun to realize that the methodology it has employed to study the "religious" aspect of our human traditions must be fundamentally revised. Indeed, we can only appropriately apply the concept of religion to Abrahamic religions, with more or less accidental variations. But to call Hinduism a religion—which, at most, is rather a bouquet of religions—or even worse, to represent Buddhism or Taoism with this unjustified extrapolation would have grave consequences, unless, as we shall do hereafter, we first explain that the word *religion* is a simple symbol that does not lay claim to any content in the conceptual order. Let us not forget that the symbol is essentially functional. A symbol that is not believed in—that does not fulfill the function of a symbol—is not a symbol. This approach would remedy many of the errors caused by the older methodology.

To give an example, it may be helpful to recall the studies of the not so distant past that told us that Confucianism was not a religion but a philosophy; that Buddhism was not a religion either, because it does not accept a supreme God; nor was Christianity, because it was a revelation that judges all other religions as mere yearnings of the human spirit; that Hinduism could not be called religion either because it was better understood as a "Way of Life." Whatever their value, these judgments resulted from having applied a preconceived concept of *religion* to human realities incommensurate with such a conception.

The fundamental methodological error was not realizing that in order to under-stand a phenomenon, one must first apply appropriate categories. In the case of Buddhism, for example, to apply a concept of religion that is totally alien to it will not describe the Buddhist phenomenon, but rather a hybrid in which the Buddhist will not recognize himself. Our difficulties increase when we deal with the herme-neutics of religious traditions, because the religious phenomenon is not a *noēma*, but a *pisteuma*. In other words, it does not belong to the order of what is *thought*, but of what is believed. If there is no communication at this ultimate level, we are no longer speaking of the same thing. The *pisteuma*, contrary to the *noēma*, is not objectifiable—not even phenomenologically. I doubt that there could be a—clas-sical—phenomenology of faith. There can certainly be a phenomenology of beliefs, but not of faith. We conclude, therefore, that extrapolations such as these have not kept in mind the fundamental anthropological axiom we have already mentioned: that self-understanding belongs to the very nature of Man. What Man says or believes about itself belongs to the very nature of what Man is. This is why anthropology, as opposed to chemistry, cannot be a purely objective science: for Man is not a mere object. Moreover, even though many of the non-Abrahamic traditions do not satisfy the concept of religion, they are nevertheless within the ambit of the religious. They are religions, but in another sense. Hence, if we are to speak about the "religion of the future" we must first analyze what religion is and means in the intercultural context of our times. What is this thing we have in mind when we inquire about the "religion of the future"? As we will see, the methodological imprecision outlined above does not refer only to the religions of the past.

3.   *The concept of religion cannot be applied to the majority of ideologies and "religious" concepts in the contemporary world; nevertheless these are also different ways of being religious.*

Ever since Christianity lost its ability to inspire much of the dynamism of Western history, the majority of the cultural movements of the West, such as Marxism, humanism, and the scientific worldview, do not willingly accept that the concept *religion* be applied to them. As a matter of fact, they have often been born out of a reaction against so-called religions, even though the function they attempt to exercise comes to be equivalent to the function that religion tires to carry out: give meaning to life—even if by affirming that it makes no sense. If religion, then, is a symbol characterized by its function, we will have to study its *homeomorphic equivalents*—third-order analogies, as I have explained elsewhere. Goethe's well-known saying about the need for religion for those who have neither science nor art and who thus make of religion a provisional and imperfect substitute for science implies also that science and art are the authentic religions. Obviously, both wish to exercise the same function, although one may do it better than the other. And if we continue Goethe's train of thought, we see the same eminently religious function performed by science, art, and religion, in spite of the inadequacy of the concept.

However, before further describing the crisis of the concept of religion, we must introduce yet a third element of discord as a preliminary step toward a meditation on the religion of the future.

4.   *The concept of "religion" becomes problematic for the contemporary mentality, even at the heart of many traditional religions themselves.*

Due to many complex reasons, which vary according to the diverse cultures of the world, but which have in common the impact of modernity, contemporary consciousness often finds that a large part of the dogmas and ethical precepts of the traditional religions do not seem to correspond to what was originally intended to be the function of these religions: that is, the salvation and liberation of Man, its happiness, plenitude, or realization, or whatever we may call it. Perhaps a few examples might spare us the need of having to elaborate more on this.

Undoubtedly, both the sacred character of the cow and the caste system are essential elements within the orbit of a certain orthodox Hinduism. Nevertheless, we cannot deny that modern Hindus have ceased to see the connection between such doctrines and the very meaning of life as Hinduism understands it. And yet they consider themselves Hindu, even if they no longer fully perceive the religious content of such institutions. Likewise, for many Christians, priestly celibacy and the injunction not to interfere in the act of procreation are not considered to belong to the heart of the Christian tradition. The modern Christian refuses to see an essential link between these practices, which to him can best be explained as manifestations of a certain cultural orientation, and the very essence of Christianity. The contemporary Muslim intellectual may also wish to reinterpret many of the practices sanctioned by the Qur'an without, because of this, ceasing to consider himself a Muslim.

There are many other examples that make us aware today that a profound inadequacy exists between what traditional concepts of religion theoretically affirm and what religious institutions practically realize. It would seem that religiousness has been displaced from the temple to the street, from sacred rite to secular practice, from institutional obedience to the initiative of the conscience, and others. Sentences like, "I have ceased being Catholic in order to be able to be Christian," "I have left the church in order to be able to be religious," "The scientific spirit represents true Buddhism," "Precisely because I am a Hindu, I do not believe in such superstitions," and so on, all indicate this displacement, however easily they might be rebutted from another point of view.

In fact, the gap is widening today between the kind of religious praxis that has been crystallizing in history and the teachings derived from the fundamental intuition that gave rise to the concrete religion in the first place. The average Christian, for example, must exercise his imagination greatly to see in the set of practices and beliefs of most Christian denominations an authentic expression of what is written in the Sermon on the Mount, for example, on the Spirit of its initiator—a term that I prefer to *founder*. To be sure, the ordinary contemporary consciousness sees and suffers such contradictions, however they might be legitimated or even justified as authentic religious developments or as products of cultural evolution. Moreover, for a growing number of followers of traditional religion, the real religious problems have been displaced from the orbit of the sacred, classically understood, to the terrain of the secular without excluding political and technical activities.

This religious consciousness perceives the great *religious* problems of humanity to be hunger, injustice, the exploitation of Man and of the Earth, intolerance, totalitarian movements, war, the denial of human rights and even colonialism and neocolonialism, to mention only a few. Obviously these terms are not just technical representations; they refer, rather, to authentic religious problems that touch the ultimate structure of Man, society, and reality. Moreover, differences of opinion about how to resolve such questions are very different from those that divide the traditional religious confessions. A large part of the Christian people, for example, find it strange, not to say scandalous, that the Roman Church maintains a—prudent?—silence on these issues and yet it still concentrates on problems of individual morality.

Today, as many Confucians, Buddhists, Christians, humanists, Jews, and Muslims are on the right as on the left of such issues. Religious loyalties have been displaced, and the chasm between religiousness and religion has deepened in the mind and heart of many people. If for some the religious has been displaced to the social and humanitarian, for others it has been reinforced in the cultic and the "supernatural."

5.   *In a pluralistic society, the traditional concept of religion is unable to supply meaning to the totality of human life, and becomes either a private reality or a religion of the state.*

In "monoreligious" societies certain tensions exist, but not to the point of divorcing the different facets of human life—between the political and the sacred, the temporal and the suprahuman, the destiny of the individual and the goal of the state, and so on. However, religion supplies the all-encompassing myth about life and the horizon against which different human activities unfold. There may be differences, even conflicts about the means to the end, but Man's ultimate destiny is determined by religion. Ample evidence of the reality of this fact can be supplied in Hindu society, Islamic history, and the Christian medieval world. In a pluralistic society, however, where many religions coexist and claim an equality of rights, it is no longer religion that offers the all-encompassing myth, but the security of the state. The state must exercise a meta-religious function, which ultimately will be incompatible with any of the religious traditions. Religion no longer offers the all-encompassing myth, but rather the state's own self-understanding. This not only provokes debates on the means but also makes room for different conceptions on the actual ends and the ultimate meaning of human life.

Within this framework, coexisting religions automatically become sectarian, embracing only a certain sector of human life—each one addressing only a segment of the population or directing only one part of the life of its own members. Moreover, once its religious teaching is not accepted by all citizens it becomes relegated to confessional institutions, and the state as representative of all citizens, cannot do its promotion. Thus ensues the famous separation between church and state with the consequent danger of dichotomizing religion and life—which are not the same. A pluralistic society automatically recognizes that there is something superior to institutionalized "religions," and thus emerges the super-religion of secularity, which coordinates the interplay between the distinct "religions," with often a greater tolerance and religiousness than the "religions" themselves.

Religions that theoretically want to be instruments of union and cohesion frequently become factors of discord and division. India is a typical case in point, although not the only one. In brief, there seems to be a discrepancy between the concept of religion and its lived reality. In our day the religion of secularity has finally inherited the function of being the judge. Historically, we find at least three models.

- *The Liberal Solution*

The so-called liberal solution: the state does not interfere in the religions of its subjects as long as they comply by the rules of liberal society. Religion then is viewed as a private right of the individual as long as it does not constrain the equal rights of others or the common ends considered as genuine ones by the state. In cases of conflict, the state is the final arbiter whose decision is binding on all. The weakness of this solution is twofold. First, the full development inherent to almost all religions is not permitted. Second, the ultimate religious function of integrating all of human activity is not realized, thereby creating a vacuum that leads to one of the other two solutions. The liberal solution is basically a-religious.

- *The Totalitarian Solution*

The so-called totalitarian solution could be of communal or communist vintage, individual or fascist. In this schema, the state assumes the ultimate function of religion—and of religions—thereby becoming the true and superior religion that determines the ultimate ends of human life. Religions become something like political or religious parties, dependent on the whole that is represented by the state. The weakness of this solution is also twofold. On the one hand, it robs other religions of their status as religions by converting them into mere techniques or cultic activities to be more or less tolerated. Moreover, by establishing itself as the unique and supreme religion, the state creates a profound resentment among adherents of other religions, which ultimately points toward a third solution in as much as this is tolerated by the state religion.

- *The Meta-Religious Solution*

The solution we might call meta-religious is that the state is transformed into the accepted myth of the immense majority of citizens and their religious leaders, by representing a kind of common denominator of the religions themselves. Two examples suffice to illustrate this model.

The sacred meta-religiosity of traditional Hindu society prior to the entrance of Islam in India is an obvious example; the meta-religiosity of contemporary North American society is yet another. The first example is inherent to the character of a large part of Southeast Asian religions. Although very different and never lacking in disputes among themselves, they nevertheless all recognize a common and superior sacred element that belongs to the order of myth, and that the state can embody very well without diminishing the particularity of other religions. This has permitted the sacred pluralism of the Hindu states, concretely illustrated by the rite of enthroning the rajas and maharajas. The second example—called by some the American civil religion—emerges likewise from the peculiar formation of the North American continent. The common denominator in the American civil religion is a revalorized myth of biblical origin, seemingly recognized by the predominantly Christian denominations in the United States and illustrated by the inauguration rite of the president of the United States. However, the moment a mythic heterogeneity exists between the different religions in a pluralistic society, the unifying function of the American civil religion is no longer valid. In all cases, we are talking here of a meta-religious solution.

All this brings us immediately to considering the importance and the urgency of finding a notion of religion that is neither disconnected from nor identified with any particular religion. The unresolved discussions on the natural right or the natural religion follow this trend of thought—which we can only point to here.

6.   *The traditional concepts of religion are in crisis.*

Religion today has two concrete meanings. On the one hand, it refers to the conjunction of symbols, beliefs, and practices that are crystallized in a visible social institution, such as the Calvinist church, Iranian Shiism, the Sioux Confederation, and so on; on the other hand, it is distilled from living praxis of institutions in order to acquire a kind of conceptual quintessence that is formulated in doctrines about the meaning and end of reality in general and of the human in particular. Religion is then what joins us to a superhuman or mysteric reality that some would call *God* or the *Absolute*, which makes us be who we are, gives peaceful balance to our lives, shatters our limited horizons, liberates us from every obstacle, unites us with our ancestors, and so forth. But this concept of religion is an abstract religiosity, and Man does not live off of abstractions. We have already enumerated above the four factors that delineate the rift between the concept of religion in its twofold meaning and the lived human reality among an ever growing number of persons. Of course, there exist many theological refinements and positive reforms that can justify the status quo and give hope to some. But for the great majority of members from the most varied traditions of mankind, the crisis persists through it all. For Man is a religious being, ever thirsty for a something more. But it seems that traditional religions have abandoned this something more. The concepts of *dharma, din, dao,* and others are also in crisis. To be sure, enclaves of orthodoxy exist that do not experience this crisis, but, generally speaking, such orthodoxies are preserved by shielding themselves from contact with the outside world, or simply by ignoring it. Nevertheless, the orthodox enclaves that shelter themselves from the impact of other ideologies and visions of the world are diminishing in number.

7.   *The crisis of the concept of religion cannot be overcome by the negation of religion.*

We know by historical and personal experience that, in general, revolutionary and negative attitudes do not escape the confinements they wish to overturn or negate. Revolutions against religion simply become other religious ways of life. Religious substitutes may be better or worse but remain "religious" nonetheless. In the life of a people, or even in the case of individual persons, we cannot expunge everything and start all over again. The past cannot be erased. Indeed, zero does not exist in history or in human life; even in mathematics it is not a number. To combat religion is already a religious act. To declare oneself an unbeliever is another form of belief. To believe in nothing except the exclusively empirical, for example, constitutes another religious doctrine.

It is possible that a salient characteristic of the contemporary religious spirit is a conscious awareness of the constitutive crisis of religious institutions—and perhaps of all institutions as well—because life is movement and change, and thus everything that comes to us from tradition must pass through the sieve. But this does not mean that rupture and alienation from our heritage is the solution to the present cultural crisis. This author's conviction is that, in the present moment of convergence, none of the cultural and religious traditions of mankind, by themselves or in isolation from each other, can offer a satisfactory solution to the problems of the human condition or to the destiny of Man. Let us call this *karma*, Mystic Body, *puruṣa*, microcosms, or any other name; humanity is unified.

In the contemporary pluralistic and intercultural situation, we need mutual fecundation among the different human traditions of the world, including the secular and the modern traditions, but without falling into a simplistic eclecticism or a loose syncretism, and even less into believing that "progress" will have the last word. The present religious crisis cannot be solved by simple reforms, no matter how necessary these may be. To simply adapt to the actual situation is insufficient because old wineskins cannot hold new wine. Returning to the sources of the various traditions with the intention of purifying the originating impulse from its time-conditioned and time-worn elements, important as it may be, is no solution either. Such an attitude presupposes, on the one hand, that the solution to the future lies in the purity of the first creative act. It assumes that the original intuition of the Vedas, the Buddha, Christ, or Muhammad, for example, offers the key for solving the problems of mankind today. This is nothing but a repetition, under a different form, of the claim of absoluteness of any given religion, with all its nefarious results for the history of human life on Earth. Not even the living God of the Old Testament is an immutable Being.

Even if the Buddha, for example, had intuited the solution to all our problems, we would still have to clarify how to interpret his vision, and in order to explain how this vision could offer solutions to problems that were not even raised in his own time, at least not in their current form; for this, we need *our own* interpretation. On the other hand, the very criteria that one utilizes to extract the purity of the original intuition already contain within themselves elements and influences from other traditions. One might try, for example to find the model of the secular, humanist, scientific, and other attitudes in Christ, while others might see in him the paradigm of a pure spirit, a Trinitarian being, a universal judge, or something along these lines. One may see in the Vedas a dynamic, evolutionary, and materialistic attitude, and another the model of world renunciation, ritualism, and spiritualism. "Truth *lies* in the interpretation" is an old play on words of mine. This means that we approach reality when we overcome its lies, recognizing the relativity of our interpretations.

This crisis cannot be resolved by negating the problem and rejecting everything "religious." Such a negation presupposes, first, that "a-religion" is the authentic human stance when facing reality; that is to say, that it is the true religion. Such a rejection is not a negation of the "religious," but a negation of those aspects that appear to be negative when seen in the light of criteria provided by other cultures and traditions, like the scientific or the humanistic, for example. That is to say, it is already a religious response and reaction.

8.   *The word "religion" denotes a symbol and not a concept.*

The road to the solution of the crisis of the concept of religion begins with the acceptance of a radical mutation of the "concept" of religion that opens us up to its value as symbol.

A lot of discussion in contemporary religious studies has focused on the two types of definitions of *religion*: definitions that describe religion in terms of *content* and definitions that stress religion as a *container*. The first define religion in terms of objective beliefs, supernatural powers, divine entities, and so on. The second define religion in terms of the function it purports to fulfill: to save Man, liberate him, give him peace, lead him to fullness of life, and so forth. While the first type fundamentally rest on the distinct cosmologies, metaphysics, and theologies of the many human traditions, the second are based on the various anthropologies at the basis of the religious attitude.

In many Asian religions, the problem presents itself differently because, generally, the functional is not divorced from the ontic. For example, the Vedas that are not recited are not the Vedas; the *dharma* that does not give cohesion to my being or to the universe (the root dh-, "to hold it all together") is not the *dharma*, just as fire that does not burn is not fire. In a word, a religion that is not believed in is not religion.

Too often we forget that in dialogal dialogue we are not speaking of the same thing if one believes and the other does not. The *noēma* is not the *pisteuma*, as we have pointed out. Dialogue is alive between symbols, not between concepts. Dialectics has a role, but it is a purely conceptual one. Both container and content, function and substance have to correspond in order to define something. The problem cannot be solved, however, with a simple semantic decision in favor of a given conception or definition of religion. While the functional aspect is essential to understanding what a religion *is*, especially in an intercultural context, it must also be said that this aspect itself cannot be expressed, even abstractly, without employing concepts and words that belong to the first type of definition—that is, that describe a definitive content within a given conception of the universe. Something more than a simple academic discussion about the nature of religion is at play in these disputes. They open up a fundamental reflection into contemporary Man's self-understanding.

What is going on here is a particular example of the interdependency between *mythos* and *logos*. The human *logos* can only function within a concrete *mythos*, but this *mythos* in turn is conditioned by the interpretation the *logos* gives to it. In our day, definitions of religion, most of them of Western mint, cannot avoid presenting the content as well as the function of religion from within a given perspective basically conditioned by history. Therefore, if today the myth is undergoing a mutation, our fundamental understanding of religion must also undergo modification. This is not so much a matter of "new religions" of the future as of a new experience of the religious dimension of existence. This is the locus of the aforementioned mutation.

It is well-known today that the majority of religions, including that of the New Testament, do not even have a word for the concept of *religion*. The concept of religion, like all concepts, is only valid within the cultural arena in which it has been conceived (*conceptus*). If the discussion concerning religion is to have validity for the future, that is, if the expression "religion of the future" is to have any meaning within an intercultural horizon, the word must be taken as a symbol and not as the concept that Western tradition has been elaborating ever since the term first started being used with this meaning. It is not enough to defend that we are dealing with a set of analogous conceptions grouped together under a single word, because in this instance the difficulty is rooted in the *primum analogatum* and not in the myriad similarities that can be found between rites, customs, or ideas.

There is no essence of religion because religion is not a concept but a symbol. There are two channels that open us up to the symbol. The first is via polysemism; the second, via relativity. Let me explain: if there are various *concepts* of religion that do not coincide among themselves, we take away the very common ground of debate from under our feet: we have eliminated the *religion* we wanted to speak about, since each concept conceives "it" differently and we have no other organ, in the conceptual order, that can indicate to us what we intend to speak about. Here lies the root of the belief that only *one* religion—our own—is the true one. A super-concept or a common conceptual denominator would not resolve the problem either, because it would eliminate precisely the richest and perhaps most fertile divergences.

We need not defend one concept over another, or accept one definition as better than another; rather we must recognize religion as a symbol. And it is not necessary to state that polysemism, which is a weakness of the concept, is the strength of symbol. Concepts claim not only objectivity, but also—and for this very reason—universality, even if only within the sphere in which they are conceived. This explains why we cannot arrive at any unanimity concerning what religion is when we are dealing with different religions that, in part, are different precisely because their very conception of religion is different. The symbol, on the contrary, does not suffer from the concept's transcultural inadequacy.

At variance from concepts, which claim—at least intentionally—to have only one meaning, symbols are multivalent in meaning. If a concept shows an ambivalence of meaning, a distinction and consequent division into two subconcepts will be necessary in order to avoid misunderstanding and inexactness. But this is not the case with the symbol. While the concept claims to be univocal, the symbol does not. Nor is the symbol simply a concept in gestation that has not yet reached its necessary precision. The symbol exists precisely because it denotes a richer or cruder (if you wish) and multifaceted reality than the analytical is able to grasp. The symbol is polysemic precisely because it is not merely subjective nor exclusively objective either, nor can it be objectifiable. The symbol is eminently relative, not in the sense of relativism but of relativity. The symbol is such only to the one for whom it is a symbol: it implies the relationship between a subject and an object. The symbol is dialogal and not dialectic; it does not claim to be universal nor objective. It seeks rather to be concrete and immediate—that is, to speak without intermediaries between subject and object. The symbol is at once objective-subjective; it is constitutively a relationship. Thus the symbol does not identify with the object symbolized. The symbol is precisely what appears in the relationship between the symbol and the symbolized. It is not a "thing-in-itself."

A symbol that does not speak immediately to the person who comes in contact with it ceases to be a symbol. The symbol includes one part of subjectivity as well as one of objectivity. This is why there are no eternal or universal symbols, because they are only so to the extent that humans hold them to be such. The concept of religion, whatever the three possible etymologies (*religare, religere, relegere*) as well as its sociological development in those cultures where the word *religion* is valid, implies a series of presuppositions that, in fact, are not accepted by a good number of human—religious—traditions. To apply, for example, the concept of religion to Marxism, Hinduism, or Buddhism implies a series of misunderstandings that stem from the illegitimacy of such an application. What, for example, would the metaphysical transcendence of Marxism be, or the fundamental doctrine of Hinduism? What would the notion of Supreme Being or Principle be in Buddhism? These questions are irrelevant because of the aforementioned problem of illegitimate extrapolation.

The problem would be practically irresolvable if the word *religion* did not shelter more a symbol than a concept. Now, dealing with symbols requires a special methodology. It is part of the methodology necessary to approach intercultural problems. These cannot be treated as simple conceptual questions. There must be something extraconceptual to relate the different conceptual systems. The symbol does not stand in opposition to the concept, but it cannot be treated as a kind of potential concept. If reason is the human organ of the concept, the symbol requires a global sense that includes reason, but that cannot be reduced to it. The symbol is not exclusively logical: it is also cordial. The symbol requires *dialogal dialogue*, as I have so often stated.[2]

9. *The symbol of "religion" designates first and foremost a human transcendental and then a sociological category.*

A cross-cultural study of human reality presents the following trilogy:

1. Every culture conceives what we might call the *human predicament*—the consciousness that every person in a given culture has of his situation in the world. We could call it x—that is to say, the enigma of Man as he sees himself and believes himself to be, collectively or individually, in isolation or as part of a larger reality.

2. An ideal end of this same human reality also exists, that we might designate as y; this refers to what Man believes he really is, should, or will be.

3. In the third place, all human cultures believe that x is different from y, and that a path or a relation exists between both. We might express this relation by saying that y is a function of x:

$$f(x) = y$$

What we might appropriately call *religion*, therefore, is the way that leads from x to y.

It is obvious that both variables mutually condition each other: however x is conceived, the conception of y will follow, and vice versa; however y is conceived, the reality of x will be understood. We have already said that the symbol is fundamentally relational. *Revealed religions* highlight the importance of y, even for the intelligibility of x. In other types of more immanent, including more rationalist, religions, dependence of y on the reality of x will be underscored. We might also arrive at a certain typology of the human tradition and classification in developing this formula, but that is not the topic right now.

To continue then, religion is that thing people *believe* will exercise this function; that is, what they believe will take them from x, their human condition as they perceive it, to y, the end of human life itself, whether this is called *liberation, salvation, the perfect society, justice, absurd, void, death, heaven,* or, in other words, *sōteria, mokṣa, nirvāṇa, wu,* and so on. Neither the nihilist nor the more extreme monist position would be found outside this definition. For the function to be real, the only thing necessary is for x to be different from y, and this applies even when it is said that y is the void, or that x in the last instance is identical to y. In the latter case, the proclaimed ontological identity notwithstanding, the fact remains: I do

---

[2] Cf. R. Panikkar, "*Símbol i simbolització*," in *Myth, Symbol, Cult* (*Opera Omnia*, IX.1).

not "know" that x is equal to y. The distinction would then be epistemological. Religion is then the discovery that $f = 1$ because the x that appears to be different from y is equal to it.

Obviously, so-called traditional religions aspire to carry out this function, but another series of ideologies, bodies of ideas, and movements intend to fulfill this function as well. They are not normally called religions, however, because of a kind of monopoly exercised on the word *religion* in the West. But theologians like Tillich, for example, have ventured for some time now to call these movements "quasi-religions." I believe the moment has arrived to suppress the *quasi* and properly call them *religions*, with the same right as traditional religions. It may be true that the name does not make the thing, and it has even been written in a nominalist context that *de nominibus non est disputandum*; it is also true that the thing obviously depends on the name adopted. Therefore, even though we must not minimize the difference between traditional religions and these other movements, it is also certain that people in fact dedicate themselves to such religions because they *believe* they will realize the function they promise: to give the greatest possible meaning to human life—even if it is something senseless that they have to accept unquestioningly.

In other words, religion in this wider sense is a human transcendental, an existential, if you wish—that is, a form of *being* inherent to the human being and, therefore, concomitant to all the activities of human life, not a separate category or class of beings or of human actions. In this sense, religion can be defined as the dimension of ultimacy of the human being. The distinct forms of understanding and interpreting this dimension constitute the different religions in their anthropological aspect, and the historical embodiments of these forms, the sociological meaning of religion.

10. *The crisis of mankind's religious consciousness is both effect and cause of our actual cultural crisis.*

The famous relation between religion and culture is another of the age-old themes concerning the crisis of human religious consciousness. Without attempting to express a total consensus among scholars in this field, we might easily accept the three following affirmations, keeping in mind all the necessary nuances.

•   *Religion is a cultural fact.*
We are not saying here that it is necessarily a monocultural or exclusively cultural fact as if to bring to an end the belief of many religions that consider themselves extra- or supracultural. But even in the latter, it does not deny the fact that religion can be a cultural fact, not only in its institutions and concrete incarnations, but also in its doctrine and ultimate intuitions. Even in the purest of orthodoxy of a directly revealed religion, the latter would make no sense unless its divine language itself were equally an intelligible one to the people of its time. Religion is hence a cultural act.

- *Culture is a religious fact.*

If, from the notion of culture, we exclude the religious factor—that is, that dimension of ultimacy that offers Man the ground from which it can develop all its potentialities—culture ceases to be culture and becomes a configuration of technical means in order to reach predetermined ends. Each culture claims to be something more than such a system of techniques to reach other purposes. It seeks to offer Man possibilities of integral development along a more or less explicit vision of what Man is. The means are not only means to an end. Not only is this same Man the subject of both culture and religion, but both pursue the same purpose that consists in making possible the perfection of the human being, its realization—happiness, peace, passing through life, or whatever we may call it.

- *Culture gives religion its language, and religion gives culture its ultimate content.*

The religious act could not express itself were it not to find an adequate language, which is precisely the one that the culture of a given time and place gives it. Religious doctrines are one and all dependent on the cultural situation in which they were formulated. At the same time, however, human culture is nothing else than the crystallization of Man's achieved efforts to reach its ultimate and intermediate goals. The example of the West, in this last century, is instructive as regards the intrinsic relationship between the crisis of culture and the crisis of religion. After Romanticism, traditional Christianity has taken pleasure in criticizing and condemning the spirit of modern culture in its multiple manifestations: science, technology, rationalism, modernity, and so on. But at the same time, those who most influenced modern culture and contributed to modern progress did so by critiquing traditional religion, making it almost impossible for an educated person to be its follower. Culture and religion mutually attacked each other, leaving both wounded in the fray. Contemporary modern Man finds himself unable, in a way, to believe, using old frameworks. But at the same time, the present cultural situation of Mankind is clearly incapable of resolving its own problems. Thinkers from the most varied persuasions are in concordance regarding the diagnosis; we are witnessing, they say, the demise of a particular cultural period of humanity. Contemporary culture is in the grips of a mutation. The religion of modern Man must also undergo a corresponding radical change.

And the first step, it seems to us, consists in a mutation of the word *religion* itself. It is not that the concept needs to be demythicized and secularized, but the new situation of mankind has made us more sensitive to the inevitable religious and cultural pluralism, and consequently has invalidated any concept of religion that would have a single context. This new situation, however, has not yet come into the light; it is still in a period of gestation. The experts in the matter say that we are in a chaotic situation. Hence it is not at all strange that the symbol of religion manifests similar characteristics.

The situation in non-Western cultures and religions is somewhat different, but the crisis has also arrived at its gates. The crisis here is provoked not so much by an internal fight between culture and religion as by the extrinsic challenge from other cultures and religions—especially from the West.

In the first place, the Western distinction between culture and religion generally does not exist, unless we artificially limit the religious to the official cult—Chinese or Japanese, for example—and reduce culture to a system of means—that lose their meaning if the ends are not specified. Culture has a religious nucleus, and religion follows the same movements as culture. The representatives of culture (*paṇḍts* and *achaya*, in India, for example) continue to be the same representatives of religion. It is they who determine the religious calendar, for example.

Second, as soon as the Western model of education penetrates into these cultures, the "treason of the clerks" and the abuse of power of religious institutions that provokes the opposite reaction, the division between *paṇḍts* and intellectuals, between men of God and laymen, for example, begins to appear. Religion and culture then begin to speak two languages between each other, and the crisis accelerates which rapidly wreaks havoc on both.

Third, the influence is at once cultural and religious in virtue of the aforementioned traditional connection between the two. Science, education, and even technology become not only cultural contributions—whether positive or negative—but so many other religious messages as well. When the symbiosis can be effectuated, the religion that is sufficiently hospitable becomes scientific. This is what has occurred in a large part of the so-called educated classes in India: their Hinduism is a scientific hybrid. Where the symbiosis does not appear feasible, the same external influences become religions: science itself becomes a religion, for example.

But complete substitution cannot be made so easily; hence the crisis.

11.   *The religion of the future is, above all, a personal religiousness (not necessarily individual), and not a single, unique religious confession.*

For religion to be faithful to its function, it cannot be a foreign body within the cultural complex in which it lives. But this does not mean that religion must renounce its prophetic work of acting, often at least, as a challenge to society and to its status quo. Cultural and religious pluralism of humanity both impede our finding common traits applicable to a situation that is global—except in the abstract world of concepts. We all desire Goodness, by definition, but there is diversity of opinion as to what constitutes this Goodness.

Precisely because the crisis of our time can be reduced to the more or less total loss of the basic *mythoi* underpinning the diverse cultures of the world and to the lack of a unifying *mythos* of global proportions that is called for by the technological, scientific, and in a way political unification of the planet—precisely because there does not exist today a cultural harmony that could permit the emergence of this unifying *mythos*—the religion of the future is still far from becoming visible. But precisely because of the radical provisionality that must affect our considerations, we can at least say this much. This religion cannot consist of a monolithic, doctrinal, or cultural block. Neither will it be one of the existing religions that will have conquered or converted all the rest. But of course, it is inevitable for people to dream of a universal religion if they believe to be on the way to a global human consciousness. But a living religion is not an abstraction, and in this yearning we already see the essence of the fundamental mutation in the concept of religion.

A universal religion cannot be any of the existing institutional religions. To put it more concretely, the six present missionary religions (Buddhism, Christianity, Islam, capitalism, democracy, and Marxism—the latter dying out in its political form) can aspire theoretically to convert the whole world, but they will have to take a few facts into consideration, one intrinsic and the other extrinsic. The intrinsic fact is that, supposing that one of the religions were completely successful in doing just that, it would have had to undergo a deep opening and mutation of itself in order to harbor in its bosom the immense diversity and variety of the human family. And supposing that this were done in all sincere conscience, this could not take place unless the same religious faith was expressed in a great divergence of beliefs, myths, and manifestations. The history of these religions demonstrates that when they reach a certain cultural diversity, they splinter into groups, both more human and more appropriate to their concrete realities; these used to be called *heresies*. Even the most recent and perhaps the most monolithic of these religions has already subdivided into various different confessions—communism, Maoism, nonaligned socialism, eurocommunism, neo-Marxism, and others—after the Soviet collapse. A lovely Buddhist parable says it all: a noble gentleman wished to marry the most beautiful girl in the land. His couriers asked him if she should be dark or fair, tall or short, round or almond eyes, and so forth. But he could only answer that she must be the loveliest. . . . And he never married!

We all aspire to the truest religiousness, but like the noble gentleman we do not know how to answer if it has to be young or old, dark or fair-haired, from the country or from the city. . . . Perhaps our problem is that we are trying to objectify something that is constitutively relational. This problem is sufficiently important to merit a new paragraph, if only parenthetical. The extrinsic factor is equally conspicuous. There is something undeniably grand, beautiful, and even true in the claim to universality of the six above-mentioned religions. If I am convinced of the truth, utility, and goodness of something, it makes sense that I want my fellow man to participate in it, too. But there is something equally disturbing when this universality is interpreted as exclusivity, and when the relativistic character of the world is lost from view. To say that beauty is universal does not exclude multiple interpretations of the same reality, or that something might be beautiful only in relation to someone. Personally I believe the universalistic spirit of such religions can be conserved without diluting their greatness and their message; at the same time, this universality can be interpreted in a sense not only of tolerance, but more profoundly, as though each one represented one dimension of the human being—

but without falling into "perspectivism," which would be falling into subjectivism or into the objectification of points of view. We have already stated that pluralism has not yet found its proper language—perhaps because we have not yet overcome conceptual thinking.

As the unity of humankind tends toward conciliation, it cannot help but tend also toward a religious unity. This unity, however, does not signify uniformity but *harmony*; it does not imply a single dogma or ideology, but rather one *mythos*—that is, a common horizon. This unifying *mythos* cannot be the conscious creation of any individual. Nor can it be a matter of organization. It seems to me that the first characteristic of this religion of the future will be its personal aspect, what could be called *religiousness*. By personal, we do not understand individual or individualistic. We only wish thereby to underline the relational aspect of religion with all the other facets of reality.

In thus emphasizing the personal aspect of religion—let us remember that for the Christian scholastic, religion was a virtue—we want also to indicate the essentially liberating character of the religion of the future: the harmony, intellectual as well, between persons and between peoples. All too frequently, individuals as well as peoples are victims of the "system"—that is, of a state of things that is more or less rigid and fossilized—be it called *capitalism, Buddhism, Christianity, socialism, dictatorship, orthodoxy, democracy*, or whatever. As a personal dimension, religion makes Man conscious of its undeniable dignity and of its place in the cosmos and in society. Religion is converted then by antonomasia into the reality that liberates Man from its alienation. This kind of religion can be an organism, but not an organization. This is because the soul of an organism is Life itself, the spirit, whereas the cohesive force of the organization is an ideal extrinsic to the system. God, as a symbol of the Infinite, would be that which, by "re-bonding" us with Him, and in Him in all things, allows us to be free—because He has no limits.

Another consequence of the personal character of religion is that it eliminates not merely the possibility but even the ideal itself of a universal religion. Just as there cannot be a *lingua universalis*, there can never be a universal religion. Lived and spoken human languages are of necessity vernacular because they emerge from the concrete and specific reality of a human community that lives, sees—and speaks—their world in a particular way. And so it is analogously with religion, if it is understood to mean the conjunction of symbols that represent for a human community their ultimate convictions.

From a historical perspective, the idea of a universal religion—as distinct from religiousness as a personal dimension of Man—is a sequel from the colonialist period that, theoretically at least, is at an end, even if its *mythos* lives on. A single universal and uniform religion would represent an impoverishment of the rich religious experience of humanity. Human beings do not think, feel, express, speak, or believe in the same way. Indeed, the *mythos* of the tower of Babel shatters the dreams of every great monocratic, uniformistic, and totalitarian scheme of Mankind. Neither human nor religious unity belongs to the order of discourse or to the order of thought; they do not pertain to the order of *logos* but to the reality of the spirit that knows not whence it comes nor where it goes. They pertain, if you wish, to the reality of *mythos*, not to the order of mythemes. It is not a matter of speaking the same language or of practicing the same religion, but of remaining with an awakened consciousness, aware that we are intoning different notes in the same symphony, and that we are walking on different paths toward the same peak—even if, in the meantime, we are attentive to the instrument we use and trying not to stumble on the way. Religion "religa" just as the *dharma* maintains the cohesion with the vertical or transcendent, with the horizontal or human, and with the base: the earthly and material. This relation is fundamentally personal and only secondarily collective and objectifiable in doctrines and behaviors. At Pentecost everyone spoke different languages, but they understood each other—better yet, they *knew* what it was about.

Religion appears then as personal religiousness with as many different manifestations as there are different persons. Religious institutions will continue, but this institutionalization will not attempt to smother the margin of freedom and personal interpretation. Likewise, religious loyalty will not center as much on discipline within the institution itself as in obedience to personal conscience. The institutions themselves will not be exclusive or totalitarian. The interpretation of the "Word of God" grows with he who interprets it, as St. Gregory the Great said. One will rightly affirm that authentic religion has always been considered as a personal virtue. The novelty of the religion of the future will consist, more than anything else, in the recognition of the legitimate plurality of interpretation that extends the margin of such freedom to the very level of the person. I repeat that by *personal* I do not mean that it is reduced to the whims of the individual. Dialogue is a necessity, and error, a possibility.

Religion is personal in the sense that it is not necessarily tied to a cosmology, nor to a metaphysics, nor therefore to a monolithic doctrinal interpretation. Religion is a characteristic of the person, and even if its characteristics, advantages, beauty, can be disputed, one never doubts that these are the characteristics of the person. Religion thus transforms itself into religiousness; that is, it is united to the person as its idiosyncratic way of being and living in order to realize its being and fulfill its life. This does not mean that there are not any human groups that are more or less homogeneous that do not allow classifications between religions, but the demarcations between these groups will not be conditioned so much by archaic doctrines about the nature of the world, human destiny, or the existence of God, but rather by personal interpretation of life and of its meaning for each individual. Obviously, the glue, so to speak, that holds them together will be other anthropological *mythoi* in the process of gestation; it is obvious that the analysis of these *mythoi* will uncover their cosmological and ontological assumptions, so as to constitute a challenge for philosophers and intellectuals. But there will have been a displacement from the cosmological and metaphysical myths to anthropological ones.

Thus, the religion of the future is not really in the future of "religion" but rather in the future of Man in its constitutive religiousness. There is a fundamental difference between the personal religion that we are defending here and individual or individualistic religion that I consider insufficient. An individual religion is a little less than a contradiction *in terminis*, because religion is an aspect of Man in society and thus an elementary societal factor. A personal religion, on the contrary, underlines the unique role of each individual in the whole of personal and other religions that constitute religion.

An individual religion supports an individualistic interpretation of the practices and symbols of a given religious confession. A personal religiousness, on the contrary, underlines a global interpretation of which my viewpoint is also an integral part. It requires a dialogical method in discussions about reality, and therefore cannot be content with a dialectical method.

12.   *The religion of the future is not a subjective devotion.*

We insist on this point because we must overcome the misunderstanding of religion reduced to an individualistic interpretation. This is a delicate topic, especially in the West, because we live within the anthropological *mythos* of individualism. It is not about a "custom-made religion" but rather a personal one, that is, in relation to the whole human context. And for this, it is necessary to obey reality, which means, as etymology reminds us, the attentive auscultation (*ob-audire*) of all the voices of reality, among which tradition offers us the most important words.

The art of knowing how to listen is a fundamental religious activity. The Veda already say that they are living Word when they are listened to, *Śruti*; and St. Paul corroborates this when he affirms that faith comes from listening. However, in order to listen we must pay attention, make an effort to understand, and—above all—be silent—that is, be empty of prejudices and judgments. Discernment, *viveka*, comes at a second stage. Listening is not only an ascetic act—to empty oneself of oneself—but also an eminently communitary one. One does not listen to oneself. You listen to others—in others and *ātman* (if I may be allowed, without now carrying out exegesis).

Man is not the origin of his ideas or of himself. When this silence—primary condition to be able to listen—is profound, not even the chatter of banal voices is heard. In other places I have described the theology—that is, the *logos* of the *theos*— as the art and science of knowing how to discern the word of God (*theo-logia*) in the voices and cries of our brothers. So-called liberation theology is nothing but the opportune memory that God speaks through the voice of the humble and the oppressed.

Perhaps we could bring all this together in our last section.

13.   *The religion of the future is a cosmotheandric religiousness.*

A study of the human experience of the last six thousand years, however necessarily risky, provisional, and imperfect this endeavor might be, can shed a certain light on the religion of the future—as I have tried to describe in many of my previous studies on what I have called the *cosmotheandric intuition.*

Man is not the only reality, but rather an irreducible pole of reality itself, and as such, a center of all reality also. If traditional religions have displaced the center toward the divine and modern ones toward the human, we may yet arrive at a more mature conception of the entire universe, even after all these vicissitudes of history.

The word that suggests itself is *theanthropocosmic,* or for euphonic reasons, a *cosmotheandric* spirituality. This expression signifies that the religion of the future cannot be exclusively theocentric nor anthropocentric, but must harmoniously join together the three ultimate dimensions of reality: (1) the material and corporeal aspect with (2) the diverse facets of Man and his activities, and both of these equally with (3) the recognition of the mysteric, divine, or immanent/transcendent principle, which guarantees a freedom that is completely unmanipulable.

Man is not one more being among things, but neither is he the Lord and Master of the Universe. God is not an absolute being disconnected from the rest of reality, considered nothing more than mere appearance. Nor is the material world a mere projection of consciousness, be it finite or infinite, but it has its own consistency. The religion of the future can no longer be a simple cry toward transcendence nor a merely immanent spirituality. Rather, it will have to recognize the irreducibility of these three poles of reality, thereby changing forever the unilateral sense of the concept of religion. Religion will still "religare" certainly, but not exclusively the human person with God but also with the whole universe, and thus discovering it in its cohesion and meaning.[3]

If our hypothesis is correct that the era of specialization has come to an end, and that mankind is searching again for a holistic conception of reality that goes beyond rigid compartmentalizations, without succumbing to an embittered primitivism; if it is true that cultural enclaves and religions are condemned to sterility, the religion of the future can no longer be the specialization of a few, nor take refuge in the so-called numinous or sacred sphere, but it must permeate all of reality. Religion is again becoming central in human life, but without dominating anything, for its limited function is to secure linkage (*religio*) and the cohesion (*dharma*) between every sphere of reality. Thus, it is not tied essentially to any one specialized institution. The *logos* is then not exiled, but the *mythos* recovers its place. And the bond is the Spirit that fills the face of the Earth—and makes all things new.

---

[3] Cf. R. Panikkar, *Trinitary and Cosmotheandric Vision: God, Man, Cosmos* (*Opera Omnia*, VIII).

12

EVERY AUTHENTIC RELIGION IS A WAY TO SALVATION

The subject we are going to discuss is extremely important both in itself and from the point of view of its general meaning. We must bear in mind, however, that in the context of Christianity in which most Westerners live, it is a subject of vital significance, especially from a sociological perspective, if Christianity is to survive in a world that no longer allows existence in watertight compartments. It is also vital from a theological point of view, if Christianity is to overcome its current particularistic phase and "convert" to the Good News offered to all men in the universe.

We will give a brief outline of the problem, therefore, in the light of this universal consciousness, pointing out certain historical elements of particular importance, before dwelling on the theological elements of the problem in greater detail. Considering the informative nature of this study, we obviously will not be able to dwell on erudite questions or polemic elements.

The Basic Problem: "Faith" and "Religion"

When a vital dialogue is established with the other religions, one of the first emerging results is the dual meaning of the very concept of "Christianity." It may, in fact, be considered in two ways, different but not totally separable from each other. Christianity may be regarded as a socioreligious matter and, therefore, having a set structure, with precise doctrines formulated in a given language within the context of an established culture. In this sense, Christianity appears as a religious and social phenomenon; this is the outward and phenomenological view of Christianity.

Another way of considering Christianity is to begin from within Christianity itself as a belief in Christ and in the truth that Christianity incarnates. In this sense, Christianity is no longer viewed as a phenomenon, but as the noumenon (the actual reality of a thing) that produces the sociological phenomenon. On the basis of this noumenic aspect a religious dialogue is established, as a coming together of religions on the common ground of religion itself and, therefore, within the sphere of faith.

In the context of a sincere interreligious dialogue another clear factor appears: the distinction between a phenomenological vision and a theological vision must also be applied to the other person in the dialogue. He also will judge his own religion based on an experience of faith or on a higher form of mysticism that allows him to be free of all the negative aspects for which the Christian, relying solely on phenomenology, may conceivably have held his own religion accountable. We would see clearly what I am saying here if we were to discuss, for example, the Crusades with a Catholic or the caste system with a Hindu.

Without venturing for the moment into further discussions, let us simply call "religion" the global sociological factor and "faith" the inner experience, that element that allows a man to regard his religion as true.

This immediately brings us to an initial consequence of fundamental importance, both from a methodological-scientific standpoint and a practical and pastoral perspective: we cannot compare the "faith" of one religion with the "religion" of another faith without being perfectly aware of the fact that such a comparison is not homogeneous.

The same problem applies from the point of view of history, which must also be taken into account.

The relationship between Christianity and the other religions of the world becomes the object of historico-religious studies when the various sociological factors are considered within the context of the complex human condition. The conversion of populations, the crusades of the Christian Latin period, the Western colonization, the religious wars and the martyrs, but also the civilizing function of the church, works of goodwill and charity of the missions and the defense of autochthonic religious values—these are just a few examples and elements of the complex encounter between Christianity and the religions of the world.

Yet the situation appears quite different when the elements of the comparison are not historical events or doctrinal disputes but the Christian faith and the faith of other religions. There are many possible reactions, ranging from total rejection to conversion, from mutual tolerance and co-existence to acceptance of the other faith. The history of theology shows us that through the centuries each of these attitudes has been basically defended.

Up to the present day, the religious factor has been almost indiscriminately bound to the historical destiny of the respective populations; political events, consequently, almost invariably led also to a socioreligious confrontation that did not necessarily encourage religious dialogue. Today, the separation between religion and public life offers the advantage that the religious dialogue is more easily kept apart from the complications of political life. The religious relationship takes place more in the sphere of faith than in that of the complex socioreligious phenomenon.

This type of dialogue is, however, still new, since up until today the sociological conditions that make it possible were practically nonexistent. In the past, one left to conquer and convert a given land, or to convert it without taking it over, with the almost certain consequence of martyrdom; likewise, one went to teach without learning anything, or to learn without teaching. For the most part it involved monologues and abundant dialectics, but dialogue was, in actual fact, almost impossible. Like friendship, dialogue in turn presumes and creates a certain parity and equality that no religion is able to accept. Religions, in fact, are not equal; only faith can in some way bridge the gaps.

The Oneness of Faith and the Diversity of Religion

Christianity does not have to assimilate or, in some way, absorb the other religions; the Christian "faith," however, is a (human-divine) theandrical light capable of illuminating all other faiths. First of all, we declare that faith, by definition, is one. Gone are the days when each clan, each people, each religion worshipped and possessed its "own" God, naturally excluding all others from such possession. But if there is a God, he can only be one and, known or unknown, professed or denied, he must necessarily be the God of all. Men and concepts may be different, and theologies much more so; but the true and real God, despite all the different men and ideas, is one and only. We must acknowledge, nevertheless, that the days when Man still believed he possessed an exclusive faith are not completely over.

Similar to the problem of God is that of faith. If faith is not distinguished from its nominal or conceptual expression, the various beliefs of the people appear to be very different from each other; if by faith, however, we mean not a collection of crystallized dogmas but the act by which Man opens up to transcendence—to use a given terminology—or a suprarational and supraconceptual adherence to the truth—to use a different conception; if by faith we mean the fundamental attitude of Man by which he recognizes himself as "relative" to the Absolute and, therefore, dependent, contingent, then faith is one by definition, in the same way that God is one. The expressions of faith may be different, divergent, and they may even become contradictory; there are also different degrees of depth and knowledge of the same faith, but if there is something fundamental that can place us in relationship with the Absolute, this something cannot be multiple. Summing up this explanation as much as possible, we may say that if God is one, then that by which Man recognizes himself as referring and relating to God must have one ultimate and sole foundation: this foundation is faith.

The Christian faith is simply this one faith freed of its ambiguity and vagueness and completed in its constitutive anticipation by the revelation of God in Christ; this, in fact, is the self-revelation of that "something" that is found at the beginning and the end of the very act of faith. The Christian faith fills with a relatively adequate "content" the human act by which Man is *capax Dei*. Christian faith is human faith made fertile by the revelation of "the mystery hidden for generations and centuries," as Paul says—and this mystery is called "Christ." The Christian does not believe in another "thing," different from what any other believer believes; what actually happens through his faith is that the Christian is conscious of the crucial revelation and manifestation, the final historical realization and the salvific mission of that "thing" that the non-Christian names in his own way and interprets differently than the Christian.

We arrive at this conclusion through a simple philosophical reflection and on the basis of the very need of the Christian faith. Philosophically speaking, we might express this as follows: if the human being is "relative" he must be so with regard to another who is not; this relation to the Absolute, consequently, is the constitutive and basic characteristic of Man. If the ultimate dimension of this relationship is called "faith," this is precisely what any faith requires. Such faith, in fact, can only be one, and this oneness will remain while the elements of knowledge, of degrees of clarity and depth, of volitive adaptation or suchlike may differ greatly from one faith to another.

From the point of view of Christian theology we may say that the only ontological link by which we are joined to the Absolute is Christ; therefore, every man who goes to the Father does so only through Christ and in the Spirit, whatever may be the form and type of his faith. With Christianity, however, an essential truth is that faith is the salvific element: without faith Man cannot be acceptable to God and be saved. The immediate consequence of this is that either only those with an "orthodox" faith can be saved or else faith is not merely "orthodoxy" but, rather, an existential "ortho-*praxis*" through which Man may believe in Christ without even having the slightest idea of his name or existence.

Based on this point of view, therefore, the relationship between the Christian faith and any other faith is not a relationship of substitution or negation, but rather of assumption, integration, and sublimation. The constitutive singleness of faith does not prevent us from claiming that the grace of God and free human co-operation are necessary for recognizing in Christ the beginning and the culmination of faith; on the contrary, it makes such a claim easier. Faith in Christ is, precisely, faith in Christ, in a Christ who is not identified with Jesus, as we have already said and yet now reiterate.

Every Authentic Religion Is a Way to Salvation

It is not necessary to refer to the Scriptures in order to prove that God wants all men to be saved; we have only to consider the end they must reach and for which they were created. This becomes evident once we have accepted the two basic assumptions of the existence of God and of Man.

Likewise, it should not be difficult to acknowledge that this salvation offered by God to men has been made possible through the various religions of mankind; this, in fact, is the purpose of religion, and in the life of the different populations there is no other aspiration where means of salvation might be discerned; religion is the element to which Man refers when he must deal with the ultimate problems of his real, tangible existence.

Granted, religions may contain errors from a doctrinal point of view and may be criticized from a moral point of view; aberrations and degenerations may occur in any religion, not excluding Christianity. Without venturing into more detailed disquisitions on how divine providence cannot leave men without guidance and without light, however, we may say that every authentic religion is a way to salvation for those who put their faith in it.

We explained earlier why we believe this statement to be true. There must, in fact, be an instrument of salvation if Man is to fulfill his purpose, and this instrument is, precisely, the religion of each people, in every age and in every culture. To accuse religions of being false, from a Christian point of view, means refusing to see reality. We cannot be so blind as to not see the transcendent truth that is emerging in every religion; in failing to acknowledge this we would condemn ourselves, since the arguments against other religions also apply to Christianity itself, as the post-Christian West is clearly capable of demonstrating.

At the same time, however, it would be a negation of divine justice and goodness to denounce as a lie the only hope that Man has of fulfilling his purpose, however this purpose may be called or conceived. This does not mean that the human mind cannot reveal erroneous doctrines or condemnable practices regarded as such from another, and perhaps superior, context.

A Hidden but Real and Effective Presence

If God wishes all men to be saved, it goes without saying that He also provides them with the means to do so. These means are offered through the various religions of mankind; or, more accurately, it is these means themselves that religions in their concrete form are made of. Another essential truth of Christianity is that there can exist no other means of salvation outside of Christ, since He is the only mediator and, in other words, the only bridge that can unite the "relative" with the "Absolute."

All this brings us to underline the second point in our theory through a third statement regarding the action of Christ within every authentic religion.

Salvation is the work of God, but God acts in time and historical order through the Spirit and the work of Christ. Christ is the light that enlightens every man who comes into this world. He is the invisible light—as all light is invisible—enlightening the various religious images that express human religious intentionality. Let me make an example: either a man's sincere prayer does not reach God in any way, or else, if it reaches Him, it does so through the mediation of Christ, and this means that Christ is truly present at the beginning and the end of the prayer, even though He may be completely unknown to the supplicant.

The Christian idea of revelation brings us to the point of view expressed above. The "Mystery" is not declared as being inexistent or ineffective, in fact, but only hidden and, therefore, unknown. Revelation—as the term *re-veal*, or "unveil," indicates—removes the veil that conceals the true face of divinity, but it neither creates not makes effective that same divinity. Revelation belongs to the gnoseological order, though it nevertheless has profound ontological repercussions on Man as an intelligent being. In spite of this, however, it does not represent anything new in relation to the original, that is, it does not introduce a new reality of its own creation, but simply reveals to us that which already exists *of itself*.

Christians do not have a monopoly on Christ; not only did He exist "before Abraham" but He is also both the Only Begotten of the Father and the Firstborn of all creatures, the *Pantokratōr* (Lord and Ruler) for whom all was made and all exists, and the end toward which everything leans. He is not only the *alpha* but also the *ōmega* of all extra-Trinitarian action. Christ is not merely a "Jew" or a "Christian"; the Son of Man is the head of all mankind, the lord of the angels and the prime cause of the cosmos.

The Christian faith consists precisely in *recognizing* that Christ, that is, the Messiah of Israel, the *Īśvara* of Hinduism, the *Tathāgata* of Buddhism, the Lord, the Light, the Mediator, the Prime Cause, the temporal God, the visible Face of the Most High, and the Redeemer, according to how he is called by different religions, is Jesus of Nazareth, the son of Mary and the Bridegroom of the Church. This means that there is a distinct correspondence between the *Icon* (substantial image) that is in the bosom of the Father, the bosom of Mary and the bosom of the Church: there is an unbroken line between the mysteries of the Trinity, the incarnation, and the Eucharist. The Christian message has meaning only if it proclaims, "That which you hope for, believe in and love—this is Jesus Christ." The evangelical message consists in proclaiming that Jesus Christ is He who reveals the ultimate subject of every unfinished matter.

From this perspective—which is the only one that allows Christian faith the universality it claims to possess—Christ appears as present and active in all religions; it is He who inspires and saves in every religion; it is He who stimulates religions from within through a dynamism that the theology of the history of religions is today clearly beginning to discover, arriving at a convergence that transcends them all, without excluding current historical Christianity itself. Religions are instruments of salvation because Christ as Savior is present in them.

The Ultimate Wholeness of Every Religion

Strictly speaking, Christ did not found any religion; he founded his church, which basically means that He gave human continuity to His theandrical presence among men, following the climax of the mystery of His death and resurrection. The Christian faith does not mean faithfulness to a new religion that made its appearance only in the last twenty centuries, that is, in the last phase of Man's time on Earth, and has so far extended to no more than a quarter of mankind. The Christian is not a sectarian and his faith is not something that sets him apart and separates him from other men; on the contrary, it is through his faith that he is able to recognize and establish bonds of brotherhood and friendship with all the children and creatures of the Father who is common to all. Christ came at the end of time to complete and carry out the work of the Father and to gather together into the Trinitarian unity all the sons of men lost through creation itself and the fall. Christ did not come to destroy but to complete and perfect; he came not to abolish but to fulfill the Law and the Prophets, to bring together in himself and seal in a liberating embrace the different pacts or alliances, all the most varied alliances that Man and God have succeeded in making in the course of history. In Christ, not only is the Old Testament completed but God's alliance with Noah is also fulfilled, His priesthood is continued, and the line of the cosmic priesthood of Melchizedek is fully realized, His Blood flows through all creation, and His arms stretch out to embrace the boundaries of the universe. Christ did not die for the Jews or the "believers," but for all men and all beings. Only a certain individualistic conception has lessened the historical sense of this truth that Christianity has always held and upheld intensely. Christ, in fact, did not die solely for individual men chosen individually; He died and rose from the dead to give life to Man and all his human-historical condition, and thus, his vital environment, the culture in which he lives and the religion through which he seeks salvation. Christ, therefore, is not the *plēroma*, the fullness and completeness of Hebraism alone but of all religions. The mystery of the Christian Easter is the fulfillment not only of the Jewish Passover but also of the Vedic oblations, Buddhist asceticism, the sacrifices of African religions, the Chinese rites, and the Muslim personal mystic fasting. We must acknowledge that the bond by which Christ is united with Man is not of an atomic-individual but a historical-personal nature. It is the populations, with their history, their culture and religion, that desire and honor Him. Christ did not come to judge the world, but to save it; judgment supervenes on the world when it is measured against the sign of contradiction represented by the cross of Christ; the *krisis* of Christ implies a true differentiation in pre-Christian religion in order that it might reach its fullness.

Judgment at the hand of Christ does not mean the condemnation of all religions, but a special discrimination attained through the specific Christian dialectics of death and resurrection. For the very fact that Christ did not come to replace the old religions with a new religion but, rather, to complete, to perfect, to bring to fullness all that God has caused to germinate in this world—for this we say that the relationship of the religions of the world with Christ is similar to that which history shows us has already existed in the case of Judaism. Christ appeared as a Savior, as a liberator from the yoke of rigid tradition and suffocating formalism, as the bringer of the "good news" (*euanggelion*) that from then on God must be worshipped "in spirit and in truth," that the "Sabbath" is made for Man, and not Man for the "Sabbath."

The fullness that Christ brings to all religions is bought at the price of death and resurrection, yet this does not mean there can no longer be true continuity with the old religion, albeit in its new form. Just as Christ and, with him, the baptized man, possesses a new life yet remains the same being as before, so likewise, when a religion meets Christ it "converts" to another, which is precisely all that is most genuine and authentic in the same religion.

The Sense of "Conversion"

We mentioned earlier the ambiguity of the concept of Christianity understood as the sociologico-historical "phenomenon" of a given religion or as the underlying "noumenon" of the same religion, which, for the time being, is the only one to have made the "conversion" we referred to above. The identification of the Christian faith with a given doctrinal and sociological formulation has been the cause of a great many fatal misunderstandings throughout Christian history.

That which today we call Christianity, and rightly so, is no other than the Judaic-Hellenic-Roman-Celtic-Gothic-modern religion "converted" to Christ. In short, today's Christianity is actually converted "paganism"; it is the collection of Mediterranean religions that have found their completeness in Christ. This is the basic theological explanation for the "pagan" origins of most of the forms of Christian life, from the religious festivals to liturgy and theology itself. Christianity, in fact, is not a meteorite fallen from the sky, an erratic mass: it is rooted in the pagan soil of Europe, and to this it owes its strength and its weakness. A "chemically pure" Christianity would quickly disappear; not only would it fail to take root in the concrete human reality, in fact, but it would not even have the possibility to exist. The dimension of incarnation is essential to its survival. A pure *gnosis*, if it could exist, would not be Christian. To explain this in more tangible terms, we could say that Mediterranean religiosity met Christ and, with positive and less positive results, converted to Christianity.

Consequently, that which many identify with Christianity as a single religion and as the Christian faith is only one possible form of Christianity. To give an example, Christianity in India is not the sociological religion of the West that today we call Christianity, but is Hinduism itself "converted" to Christ. The faith would evidently be the same Christian faith, but the religious forms could not coincide with those of today's "Mediterranean" Christianity. In the church, which, as the Gospel says, is "the great tree upon which all the birds of the sky come to rest," there is room not only for theological pluralism, but also for religious pluralism.

The idea of the plurality of religions should not be regarded as scandalous, because if Christianity-religion were the only *true* religion we would have to acknowledge that creation was a disaster and redemption a failure. Plurality should be seen, rather, as a historical dynamism that urges us to a constant overcoming. And if we speak of "conversion" in the sense specified, we must admit that it applies also to Christianity-religion, especially in this age of historical change in which we are living today.

The very concept of "mission," in the sense of the knowledge of Christianity introduced into other environments and other cultures, does not, as a result, lose its meaning but takes on the full significance of its true greatness. It is no longer, obviously, a question of "saving the poor negroes" from being cast into hell without fault or punishment, going to the extent of baptizing them furtively at the last moment. It is a matter of imitating fully the Master in his task of redeeming the world, extending to the utmost in time and space the effectiveness of his eternal-temporal and theandrical (human-divine) act. It is a question of continuing the mystery of the cross through every Christian's calling to "martyrdom" (= testimony), since in order to be "reborn" we must obviously die.

Christ went to the cross not because he preached another religion, but because he strove to liberate it and purify it and lead it to fulfillment.

However, this liberation, this purification, and this fulfillment do not destroy and suffocate the true and great values that animate all authentic religions.

13

NINE WAYS NOT TO TALK ABOUT GOD

The following nine points are intended as a contribution to resolving a conflict that tears many of our contemporaries apart. It would seem, in fact, that many people do not succeed in resolving the dilemma of whether to believe in a caricature of God that is nothing but a projection of our unsatisfied desires or to believe in absolutely nothing at all, and consequently, not even in themselves.

At least since Parmenides, a major part of Western culture has been centered on the limit-experience of being and plenitude. A large part of Eastern culture, on the other hand, at least since the *Upaniṣad*, is centered on the consciousness-limit of nothing and emptiness. The former is attracted by the world of things as they reveal to us the transcendence of reality. The latter is attracted by the world of the subject, which reveals to us the impermanence of that very reality. Both are preoccupied with the problem of "ultimacy," which many traditions have called God.

The nine brief reflections I am presenting say nothing about God. Instead, they would simply hope to indicate the circumstances in which discourse about God might be adequate and show itself to be fruitful—if only to help us live our lives more fully and freely. This is not an excuse but perhaps the most profound intuition: we cannot speak about God as we do of other things. It is important that we take into account the fact that the majority of human traditions speak of God only in the vocative. God is an invocation.

My nine-faceted reflection is an effort to formulate nine points that, it seems to me, should be accepted as the basis for a dialogue that human conversation can no longer repress, unless we accept a reduction to being nothing but completely programmed "robots." On each point I have added only few sentences—concluding with a Christian citation that serves as an illustration.

1.   We cannot speak of God without having first achieved interior silence.

Just as it is necessary to use a Geiger chamber and mathematical matrices in order to speak knowledgeably about electrons, we need the purity of heart that allows us to listen to reality without any self-seeking interference to speak responsibly of God. Without this silence of mental processes, we cannot elaborate any discourse on God that is not reducible to simple mental extrapolations.

This purity of heart is equivalent to what other traditions call emptiness, that is to say, maintaining oneself open to reality with neither pragmatic concerns nor expectations, on the one hand, nor resentments or preconceived ideas, on the other. Without such a condition, we would only be projecting our own preoccupations, good or bad. If we seek God in order to make use of the divine for something, we are overturning the order of reality. "When you wish to pray," the Gospel says, "go into the deepest and most silent part of your house."

2. It is a sui generis discourse.

It is radically different from discourse about anything else, because God is not a thing. To make God a thing would be to make God an idol, even if it were only an idol of the mind.

If God were simply a thing, hidden or superior, an object—a projection—of our thought, it would not be necessary to use such a name. It would be more precise to speak about a superman, a supercause, a meta-energy or thought, or I don't know what. It would not be necessary, in order to imagine a very intelligent architect or an extremely powerful engineer, to use the term *God*; it would be enough to speak of a super-unknown behind those things we have not come to know completely. This is the God of the gaps, whose "strategic retreats" have been revealed to us during the last few centuries. "You will not take the name of God in vain," the Bible says.

3. It is a discourse of our entire being.

It is not just a matter of feeling, reason, the body, science, or academic philosophy and/or theology. Discourse about God is not the elitist specialty of any class.

Human experience in all ages has always tried to express a "something" of another order, which is as much at the basis as at the end of all that we are, without excluding anything. God, if God "exists," is neither at the left nor the right, neither above nor below, in every sense of these words. To want to place God on our side like other things is simply a blasphemy. "God is not a respecter of persons," St. Peter says.

4. It is not a discourse about any church, religion, or belief.

God is not the monopoly of any human tradition, not even of those that call themselves theistic, nor of those that consider themselves religious; any discourse that attempts to imprison God in any ideology whatsoever would simply be sectarian.

It is completely legitimate to define the semantic field of words, but to limit the field of God to the idea that a given human group makes of the divine ends up defending a sectarian conception of God. If there exists "something" that corresponds to the word God, we cannot confine it through any kind of apartheid. "God is the all (*to pan*)," says the Hebrew Bible, and the Christian Scriptures repeat it.

5.   *It is a discourse that always takes place by means of a belief.*

It is impossible to speak without language. Similarly, there is no language that does not convey one or another belief. Nevertheless, we should never confuse the God we speak of with the language of the belief that gives expression to God. There exists a "transcendental relationship" between the God that language symbolizes and what we actually say about God. Western traditions have often called this *mysterion*—which does not mean enigma or the unknown.

Every language is conditioned and linked to a culture. Every language depends on the concrete context that provides its meaning, as well as its boundaries. We need a finger, eyes, and a telescope in order to localize the moon, but we cannot identify the latter with the means we make use of. It is necessary to take into account the intrinsic inadequacy of every form of expression. For example, the proofs of the existence of God that were developed during the period of Christian scholasticism can only demonstrate the nonirrationality of divine existence to those who already believe in God. Otherwise, how would they be able to know that the proof demonstrates what they are looking for? Jesus called Him *'Abbā*, Father, in his language, though with a certain tension within the Judaic tradition of his times.

6.   *It is a discourse about a symbol and not about a concept.*

God cannot be made the object of any knowledge or any belief; God is a symbol that is both revealed and hidden in the very symbol of which we are speaking. The symbol is a symbol because it symbolizes, not because it is interpreted as such. There is no possible hermeneutic for a symbol because it itself is the hermeneutic. What we make use of in order to interpret a so-called symbol is the true symbol.

If language were only an instrument to designate objects, there could be no possible discourse about God. But human beings do not speak simply in order to transmit information, but because they feel the intrinsic necessity to speak, that is, to live fully by participating linguistically in a given universe. "No one has ever seen God," St. John says.

7.   *It is necessarily a polysemic discourse.*

It cannot be limited to a strictly analogical discourse. It cannot have a *primum analogum* since there cannot be a meta-culture out of which discourse is constituted. That would already be a culture. There exist many concepts about God, but none of them "conceive" God.

This means that to try to limit, define, or conceive of God is a contradictory enterprise, since what is produced by this would only be a creation of the mind, a creature. "God is larger than our heart," St. John says in one of his epistles.

8.   *It is not even the only symbol to indicate what the word wishes to transmit.*

Pluralism is inherent, at the very least, in the human condition. We cannot "understand" or signify what the word "God" means in terms of a single perspective or even by starting with a single principle of intelligibility. The very word "God" is not necessary.

Every attempt to absolutize the symbol "God" destroys links not only with the divine mystery—which would then no longer be *ab-solutus*—but also with men and women of those cultures who do not feel the necessity of this symbol. The recognition of God always proceeds in tandem with the experience of human contingency, and of our own contingency in the knowledge of God. Christian catechism sums this up by saying that God is infinite and immense.

9.   *It is a discourse that inevitably completes itself again in a new silence.*

A completely transcendent God—in addition to the fact that it would be contradictory to hope to speak about such a God—would be a superfluous, if not perverse hypothesis. A completely transcendent God would deny divine immanence at the same time that it would destroy human transcendence. The divine mystery is ineffable, and no discourse can describe it.

It is characteristic of human experience to recognize that it is limited, not only in a linear sense by the future, but also intrinsically by its very foundation, which is given to it. Unless wisdom and love, corporeality and temporality, are united, there is no experience. "God" is the word, pleasing to some and displeasing to others, that by breaking the silence of Being permits us to rediscover it once more. We are the *ex-sistence* of a *sistence* that permits us to be *stretched out* in time, *extended* in space, *consistent* with the rest of the universe when we *insist* on living, *persisting* on our search while *resisting* cowardice and frivolity, and *subsisting* precisely in that mystery that many call God and others prefer not to name.

"Be silent and know that I am God," declares one of the psalms.

Some will complain that, despite everything I have just said, I have a very precise idea of God. I would answer that I have, rather, a very precise idea of what God is not, and even that idea falls under the attack of this nine-pointed critique. This does not constitute a vicious circle, but rather a new example of the vital circle of reality. We cannot speak of reality while remaining "outside" of it, nor can we think "outside" of thought, any more than we can love "outside" of love. Perhaps the divine mystery is what gives a meaning to all these words. The simplest experience of the divine consists in becoming conscious of that which shatters our isolation (solipsism) at the same time that it respects our solitude (identity).

14

ARE THERE ANONYMOUS RELIGIONS?
The Name and the Thing

The thesis of this chapter affirms that religion in the singular is neither a thing, an entity, nor a concept, a notion, but a name, a word. It further affirms that this affirmation becomes the most plausible one due to the cross-cultural approach of the "phenomenon religion." And it finally suggests that the centuries-old problem of universals plays here a fundamental role.[1]

Significantly enough, as far as I can gather, contemporary philosophers (Carnap, Wittgenstein, Maritain, Husserl, Frege, Church, Russell, . . .) as well as classical ones (Mill, Locke, Berkeley, Hobbes, Spinoza, Hegel, . . .) when discussing the question of universals do not analyze a complex word like "religion." Prior philosophers could not do it, because *religio* at that time had another meaning.

We shall preface our considerations by a reference to (1) sociology of knowledge and (2) methodology, before entering into our topic.

Why Do We Compare? (Sociology of Knowledge)

This first question is not without relevance. Three features of our times explain the proliferation of "comparative studies": (1) the easy mobility of people, (2) the internal crisis of the predominant techno-scientific civilization, and (3) the mainly Western syndrome of wanting to understand everything under one single pattern of intelligibility that is considered universal.

Every comparison, in fact presupposes (1) a certain exposure to the things to be compared, (2) certain relativization of the validity of one's own conviction, and (3c) a certain belief that we possess a universal or at least an independent norm to effect the comparison—elements that correspond to the three above-mentioned features.

Almost every human group wants to learn from other traditions, be it to be enriched by, to overcome, or to refute them. But to compare is more than to learn or

---

[1] From Heraclitus, as represented by Hermogenes in Plato's *Cratylus*, to W. van Quine, almost every philosopher has touched upon this problem, which ultimately refers to the relationship between thought, expressed in names, and reality. Indian philosophy is equally concerned with the similar question. Cf. (because less known) Raja Ram Dravid, *The Problem of Universals in Indian Philosophy* (Delhi: Motilal Banarsidass, 1972).

to criticize. We dare to "compare" because we claim that we can put the *comparanda* on a neutral scale. To be sure, we shun "apologetics" and abhor conquests, but we seem to believe that we have got the tools for fair comparisons, because we are so objective and impartial so as to be able to cultivate a universal science—of religions in our case.

Without developing the pertinent reflections of sociology of knowledge, I only signal the *Sitz im Leben* of the general theme and mention the context of this paper.

How Do We Compare? (Methodological Remarks)

I submit that there are two implicit presuppositions in this type of research. We allegedly try to better understand the very notion of religion by comparing religions. It is fair enough. How else could we do it, if we want to avoid prejudices and overcome the blunders of times past?

Yet neither can we jump over our own shadow, nor can we step totally outside our own culture. We may assimilate another culture and reject some explicit tenets or customs of our prior culture, but by doing all this we contribute to create a new culture whose origins we cannot annihilate.

The two underlying presuppositions are: a *crypto-kantianism* and a *diffuse platonism*. We seem to assume, in fact, that there is a *Ding an sich* (thing-in-itself) called religion, in spite of the many qualifications we may introduce into the crude Kantian idea. To speak about religion makes sense; it is no idle talk, it refers to "something," which is not a chimera.

We seem to assume, further, that this underlying "thing" not only somehow exists, makes sense, but that it is also important. It is the essence of what we are looking for, even if this essence is called *noēma*, notion, concept, or a pragmatic sign.

There is nothing wrong with this method, provided we are conscious of it, and affect it with the pertinent coefficients.

We compare, of course, doctrines, sometimes attitudes, aims, and often enough myths. This study would like to clarify one single point of this complex problematic.

What Do We Compare? (Philosophical Consideration)

We compare, of course, religions. But what is religion? An increasing number of people today are uncomfortable with that name and in general with labels. Many a person would not like to be pinpointed as being Christian or Hindu, for instance, or atheist or Marxist. Many would reject the notion of religion altogether and declare themselves a-religious. But saying this they may very likely adopt for their lives the same basic attitude as many who call themselves religious.

What is to be *religious*? To belong to a tradition known as *religion*, or to a self-appointed religious institution? To believe in God(s), spirits, values, transcendence, immanence, or just in something more than ourselves? Where do we draw the line, and first of all, who draws the line?

In sum, what is the "thing" we compare? Why is humanism not a religion? Or is Confucianism a religion? If *kami* is a sacred reality, is not a car also a sacred entity for many? Is the so-called community of scholars the supreme—and self-appointed—authority to decide what is and what is not a religion? Are we even sure that our translations are not co-optations into a single worldview? *Dharma, shinto, den, daena,* and the innumerable sometimes artificial African names for *religion*: Do they all mean the same state of affairs?

What is then *religion*? What is the "thing" we compare?

Drawing from an almost universal scheme that divides all that there is in *realia, mentalia,* and *verbalia,* that is, in things by themselves, in concepts in our minds and in words in our mouths, I maintain that religion is neither a thing, an entity, an existence, nor an essence, a notion, a concept, but a name, a word. And I open here the Pandora's box of the problematic on the universals. Let us proceed by discarding the first two hypotheses and in order to defend the third.

1. That religion is not a thing, a particular existence, a substance, should be accepted almost by everyone. A thing, an entity called religion, does not exist.

2. But religion, I submit, is not a concept either. It is certainly not an essence. But it is not even a notion.

There are disparate notions of religion, some of them also mutually contradictory. And unless we define more or less arbitrarily who enters into our club and who does not, we cannot dictate legitimately what a religious attitude is. If a Marxist or a humanist tells us that all what a religious person considers paramount is subsumed and even enhanced by the values of the habitually called nonreligious person, what right or reason do we have to exclude those human movements from the field of our study? We know well that each epoch has a prevalent myth that describes the contours of any given concept. What is a Catholic and a good Roman Catholic today is almost unrecognizable if seen with the eyes of equally "good Catholics" of another time or space. For millennia Hinduism has functioned without this name, and even today the word is somewhat suspect to many.

The notion of *religion* reduced to *pure belief* in God has been debunked long ago. We may enlarge it to awareness of any dealing with the *sacred*. But then the very extension and meaning of the last word remains open to the most variegated and even contradictory interpretations. Nobody has the monopoly on words. The official name of East Germany was "The German Democratic Republic." There was no power on Earth to forbid the use—or abuse—of that peculiar concept of "democracy." Now, that power, for good or for ill, has dwindled. Has the notion of "democracy" changed?

I adduce this example to bring to light the political relevance of any genuine intellectual discussion. Who has the power to determine what *religion* means? Even today the very word *religion* in the United States and in the United Kingdom has different connotations, let alone the word *religione* in Italy—without trespassing the linguistic-etymological constituency of the Latin word *religio*.

"Un croyant qui s'ignore," "anonyme Christen," "un buen pagano," "infideles in bona fide" are so many historical phrases of the not so distant past that in spite of the allegedly good intentions are today unacceptable, not to say injurious to the ears of many.

Even accepting that under the most divergent concepts of religion—I have collected over a hundred definitions of it—there was a common denominator, like "dealing with the sacred," no living religion would identify itself with such an abstract formula, and no follower of any religion would owe allegiance to a merely formal concept.

In sum, not even scholars, let alone people, are agreed upon a concept of religion, and unless we impose our concept as normative we cannot duly compare religions on a neutral scale. There are many concepts of religion, there are many notions of religions, but religion is not a concept. And this should be the first fruit yielded by a "comparative study."

3. My hypothesis is now clear: religion is neither a thing nor a concept. It is a name. Now, a name is neither a thing, nor a mere concept, nor a simple *flatus vocis*—as Anselm wrote (PL 158, 265A) attributing the meaning to Roselin, who never used that expression. But a name is a powerful and even dangerous reality.

From the very presentation of the problem it becomes clear that I am defending the *ontonomy* of words in respect to things, on the one hand, and to concepts, on the other. The experimental proof would precisely be the power that words show, although they are neither things nor clear-cut concepts and thus with no precise intellectual content.

We can reserve the word *religion* for *de vera religione*, as a certain Christian theology did, so that the others are not even authentic religions, because they do not deliver the goods, although this was not Augustine's original meaning of his work with that name. Or we can enlarge the meaning of the word to certain historical constructs, or open it up to a functional interpretation. The politics of words is known, at least since Confucius, to be of paramount importance in human life.

Habeni sua lata nomina: I could paraphrase the Latin writer and change his first words saying, *pro captu temporis:* according to the understanding of the times words have their own fate.

But there is more. Whatever the destiny of this word may be, the reality of religion is in fact enshrined in the word. It is the word which from meaning a virtue or a particular cultic activity came to mean, against the message of the Gospels, the quintessence of Christianity and, by extension, was applied to those cultural constructs that were akin to the Christian religion, the Abrahamic traditions first, the African later, and by further extrapolations was used to refer to all those "similar" movements in the East, not without confusions and misunderstandings. Many words, like the Japanese *shukyō*, were artificially formed to suit Western scholarship: the "teaching" (*kyō*) of the "original or essential component" (*shu*).

Now, a word means both what we instill into it and what the word itself allows to be instilled upon. Confucianism, Buddhism, and Jainism were for a time forbidden to be included in the clan. Later on they were admitted. Marxism and humanism are generally not admitted—besides the fact that these latter groups, unlike the Buddhists, Jainas, and Confucianists of olden times, do read what "religionists" write and generally are not keen in being co-opted under the name *religion*—unless, of course, the use of the word opens up to new connotations. Anybody teaching "religion" in secular schools and universities will remember the jokes and smiles of "scientific" colleagues who link the name religion with a pietistic, narrow, and unscientific spirit. In many countries, in fact, the teaching of religion is still considered a peculiar case in the educational curriculum of a "modern" citizen. The word *religion* sounds sectarian and unacademic to many, or at best a private affair. Once again, the power of the name.

This hypothesis does not empty the name of content. It simply does not freeze the meaning of the word. At any given time and place the predominant myth delimits the contents of each word. Our myths are changing. Our use of words follows more or less reluctantly the dynamism of myths.

In this sense there are not anonymous religions because a *religion* without its name is not a religion. We cannot stick words at pleasure like labels on the pots of a supermarket or posters on a wall. The very activity of giving names to things—the very *etymo* means human assembly—is, since Adam, a human action charged with responsibility. When Confucianism was not included under the name of religion, the study of religion did not and could not include Confucianism, and if a Confucianist was discovered to be a religious person this was in spite of and against the fact of being a follower of K'ung Fu-Tzu. No wonder that Christian missionaries would aspire to convert the "a-religious" person to their own religion. When an atheist collaborates with a Muslim in a common project, say for peace, that activity is a religious one for the Muslim, not so for the atheist. No wonder that they may eventually part ways if the meaning of the word *religion* is not clarified and perhaps deepened or changed. Human relations are mainly linguistic relations; the interactions are dialogical. The academic study of religion is also a political factor influencing the very meaning of the word.

The difficulty of this hypothesis for our times, and at the same time its importance, lies in this threefold fact.

1. It overcomes the nominalistic ideology, which, being reasonably justified in the field of modern science, does not apply to the area of the humanities or sciences of the spirit. We cannot treat human realities as abstract mathematizable constructs—in spite of the glaring success of technology.

2. It allows for a more open, tolerant, and truly scientific (or philosophical) approach to the study of the problem. We eliminate unnecessary a prioris, and do not artificially force religion into rigid, and often obsolete schematisms.

3. It allows the possibility of overcoming the epidemic of fragmented and partial cognitions that obliterate and cannot reach the whole by compartmentalizing fields of knowledge as if they were spheres of reality, when in fact all is intrinsically interconnected.

Religion is as much a question of socioeconomics, politics, and cosmology, as it is of cultic actions, moral doctrines, and metaphysical beliefs.

In sum, religions are not *things-in-themselves*, they are not separate essences, they are not nominalistic labels. They are words; and words have life of their own, they are incarnated in history, they have power. *Religion* is one of those words.

15

GOD IN RELIGIONS

I shall begin with an important methodological consideration that is all too often ignored, which consists in detecting the methodological error implicit in the actual question that is put forward. The claim "God in religions" contains itself a double methodological error: it aspires to solve extrinsic issues with one's own categories. The error is double: of *form* and of *content*. Of form insofar as the claim takes for granted that every culture has its "God." Of content in that it also assumes that we know the object we want to speak about, that we know what "God" means.

In other words: one cannot a priori suppose that all cultures share the same discursive universe. God is the main and ultimate point of reference of all Abrahamic traditions, but not of all other religious traditions. To begin by inquiring after God in Buddhism, for example, constitutes a methodological error. Just because something is important to me does not mean it is so for everyone else. Furthermore, it does not take into account that the question of God is sui generis because it entails asking oneself about something that is unique and peculiar: ultimately, we do not really know what we are asking about.

Thus, I will not speak of other notions of God, but rather I will let other traditions do so themselves, trying to make my language understandable in the sphere of our own tradition. I will summarize my reflection in the following points:

There Is No Such Thing as
Valid Human Discourse about God

Only God may speak of Himself; this is why theology must always be intratrinitary (cosmotheandric). We all agree in regard to apophaticism; but because we do not relinquish discourse, we immediately add that we can only babble about God, the unknowable and ineffable. However, the formulation of my first thesis has not been insisted upon enough: only God can speak of Himself. We cannot speak of God, but God can certainly speak. He is the Word itself. God is He who speaks, or more exactly, the Word itself—when the word is authentic.

Must we be quiet, then? No! But not because we speak improperly of God, rather because God Himself speaks, is word, as so many of humanity's traditions assert: "In the beginning was the Lord of the universe. His Word was with him. This Word was his second," says a Vedic text. Within the more strictly Christian tradition we can speak in second person and say: "You *are* the Son of the living God." "Tat tvam asi"

(You are that). You are this, in the Upaniṣadic tradition. To discover yourself is to discover God, and this means loving your neighbor, which in almost all traditions is equivalent to loving God. Your neighbor is not an object, it is *you*. This discovery is a revelation: God is discovered in the form of *you*.

It is also possible to speak of God in the third person, affirming that it is He who *is* divine. We may also, in this case, say that to discover what is, to find reality, is to discover and find God. But in each case the ontological status is different.

The first person is the very affirmation of God: the subject, the lover, the knower from our epistemological angle. The second person is the progression of God. The third person is the procession in the very dynamism of reality—knowledge and love. *I am* God, you are—insofar as generated by—God, that is—from—God. Only if we can listen to God's saying Himself will we be able to say something, if we can listen to the echo of His Word. This perfect echo needs the complete resonance of the word that God engenders, it is the Spirit from which it proceeds. Our words about God pick up this resonance. The word is prayer. Prayer is the resonance of the Spirit in which we participate.

The Trinitarian vision of reality is almost a cultural constant. It is found in practically all of humanity's traditions. A certain elitist and self-sufficient conception of the Christian trinity has propagated the idea of a Christian monopoly on the trinity.

True discourse about God—and this is theology—is God's discourse about Himself, which implies neither relegating God to pure transcendence nor suffocating Him as mere immanence. It implies a notion of God that I would like to outline with the help of other religious traditions.

The Nature of God and the Experience of Life

Considering what is important—the nature of God and of reality—must not distract us from the praxis of what is urgent—the destruction of idols. But the praxis of what is urgent—the fulfillment of justice-justification—cannot be effective if it does not integrate the theory of what is important—the experience of life.

The dichotomy between urgency and importance is fatal. We find an example of this in the religious schizophrenia that has led to the sacrifice of the most important: the justification (eternal life), for the benefit of the most urgent: justice (human life); or vice versa, the most urgent (social justice) is sacrificed for the benefit of the most important (Man's justification) in spite of their being, as they are, inseparable. We challenge the most scrupulous scholars to see if they are able to split *dikaiosynē*, and separate justice from justification anywhere in the New Testament. There is neither justice without justification, nor justification without justice. Human, political, economic, social, temporal injustice is a sin, and it is incompatible with justification; and vice versa, sin, which includes Man's inner action against the right order, is an injustice in the sphere of temporal things. "On Earth as in heaven!" The relationship is not dialectical but rather a-dual; if we do not overcome this dichotomy we will not genuinely understand liberation theology. This theology does not consist in making the celestial paradise descend to the Earth, or in catapulting the earthly paradise toward heaven, but rather in recognizing that there are not two paradises. The trail of dust this has provoked—regardless of the threat it entails to the levers of power—comes from Western culture's incapacity to confront anything that cannot be harmonized either with dualism—temporal-eternal—or with monism—materialism or spiritualism.

Ultimately, in liberation theology we feel a contemplative breath, which is what has transformed it into praxis. As I have often said, thinking leads to intelligibility, while contemplation leads to action. An ancient philosopher is satisfied with understanding one thing, the true monk does not stop until he transforms it.

We must overcome the "urgency-importance" dualism without falling into the monism inherent in its nondifferentiation. In the end, it is about the tension between theory and praxis. If what is urgent is not important, we throw ourselves into a false praxis, and if what is important is not urgent, we enter into in mere abstraction.

The Theoretical-Practical Recognition (Adoration) of a Living God, without Idols, Is Important and Urgent

But "God" can become another idol. A God who is spoken about is already an idol: He does not speak. The essential verity does not lie in our speech about God, but rather on the God who is Himself Word.

The method here is not speaking, but rather *listening*. Speech is the *logos*, listening is the Spirit. We have lost the ability to listen—we merely learn or converse. We have become estranged from our very own source: Silence, Non-Being, God. God speaks in the stones, in the mountains, but also in the poor, in the people, in men's cries of pain and of joy. God *is* this speech. God is only silent in reflection. Then, it is we speaking, it is our turn. We can do science, but not theology; the *logos tou Theou* of theology is not our *logos* in regard to him, but rather His (subjective genitive). For this task we must keep a pure heart—said the Church Fathers—we must believe—conceded the Scholastics—we must commit—insists contemporary liberation theology.

Some call God's speech revelation, but revelation is not a book—God is not author, but Creator—nor is He a doctrine—God is not an idea, but life—nor a people—God is not racist, but Father, in the sense of origin, source. God is nothing without us, we are nothing without Him. God is not *He* who speaks, rather He is speech, or—more exactly—speech, *logos*, is God. Every authentic word is divine. Every real word, that is, that which truly *says*—something, to someone, about someone, with someone—is a sacrament. It is obvious that we are speaking about living *words*—symbols—and not about scientific *terms*—signs. The nominalist disposition that characterizes science cannot be applied to what we are saying. We can easily agree on the fact that God is not an object, but after that, if we do not change how we act, we will keep treating him as such. A God as concept, a God as object, a God who does not speak, is a God who is the product of thinking; ultimately, He is a thing, an idol.

From what we have said, we can deduce that God cannot be the product of thought. All our thinking is a failure. It is written that we must not plan what we are going to say before giving testimony (Mt 10:19–20; Lk 12:12, etc.); that one's own testimony is not true (Jn 5:31; 8:14); that Mary did not understand what she pondered in her heart (Lk 2:19, etc.); that neither those on the left nor those on the right *knew* that it was Christ: "Lord, when did we see you hungry and feed you, or thirsty and gave you drink?" (Mt 25:37). Doing things for, or by means of, Jesus is of no use. We must do things for their own sake. Christ is not an intermediary but a mediator. "It is for your own good that I am going," otherwise you will make me king, that is, an idol (cf. Jn 16:7). An action is valid when the left hand does not know what the right hand is doing (Mt 6:3). The religious act, therefore, is salvific, it is the free act par excellence. It is about conquering a *new innocence*.

Theism and Deism

The God of religions is only that of the religions of God—theisms and deisms. But God is not the basic category of all religions. This is where the critique of the notion of God from the point of view of other religions comes from.

We are barely coming out of theological colonialism. God is not a universal category. What is God? What do I, what do we, understand by God? We are readily willing to admit other attributes, but all are attributes of a mysterious *x* we refer to as God. This is Kantism: there is a "thing-in-itself," unknowable, that afterwards we name in a different and indifferent form. This God only exists for a certain number of cultures; the living God has never wanted to be a universal God; this is the great abstraction of the philosophers, or at least of many of them. We have to accept the existence of mutually immeasurable religious traditions, and a hypothetical common denominator would not be the God of any real tradition. The living God that speaks by means of a people who suffer, who cry, or who sing and dance does not constitute any kind of common denominator. The experience of "God" that the Christian has through Christ is not that of the follower of Viṣṇu through Kṛṣṇa. God is unique and therefore incomparable; and the same can be said of every experience of that which we agree to call God. Every God is unique, is what the evil called polytheism teaches us. It does not allow for any common base that would permit comparisons. The intention of finding something broader, with a range that makes it possible to compare the different notions of divinity, constitutes a deformation of thought. Only a deified reason would dare to do so, and consequently, it would fall in the vicious circle of supposing for itself—its own divinity—that which it denies others—the divinity of the Gods.

In more academic language: the concept of religion as the ultimate path to salvation is broader than the notion of God. There are religions that have no need for the notion of God, and there are those that have a very different concept of Him from that of monotheistic religions.

A Necessary New Path

I will limit myself to considering the Christian West. The crisis in the consciousness of God in Europe is sociological—God is superfluous; in the United States it is pragmatic—God is understood as a luxury; and in Latin America it is existential—God seems to have fallen asleep. In spite of so many endogenous efforts, only a mutual interreligious fertilization can help us escape this impasse. We need a new path (method).

On the one hand, the God of history—unless we remain determined to justify holocausts *eschatologically*—has failed, has lost credibility. In order to defend Him, we must perform all kinds of somersaults, which are ultimately reduced to two: the first affirms that, in the long run, in the end of time, God will triumph; the second is based on only considering, in the short run, the historical God of the conquerors. We then assist, as in remote times, to a battle of the Gods.

On the other hand, the a-historical God, transcendent, selfless, indifferent, and cruel—unless we justify the need of human monsters to become celestial angels—has lost His divinity: He is not good if He is omnipotent; He is not almighty if He is merciful. To affirm that He possesses a different kind of logic means to *condemn ourselves* to irrationality. The a-historical God can affirm that the phenomenological world is mere appearance, that pain is not real, and that injustice is only passing: we are immersed in a nightmare. But here, people's growing consciousness also revolts against the banalization of the human condition and the fact that we are reducing it to a "bad night spent in a bad inn."

We need a God who is neither our creature nor our creator. He cannot be our puppet nor we his. We are mutually conditioned. God generates us—He is Father—he does not create us. Our relationship is Trinitarian. The purification of the notion of God can only take place by listening to the voice of all men, without excluding anyone—the theological West should be thankful for so-called atheist thinking. The *locus theologicus* of God are the voices of all men, including, naturally, the ones of those who do not believe. The method is a common study in which that which is researched constitutes the problem itself. This is why it can be called Mystery, provided it is turned into an object or a function, that is, if both the metaphysical and the epistemological meanings remain empty. From this it follows that the research itself is constitutive. Moses did not enter the Promised Land, and he did not reach the top of Mount Sinai, either. There is no room for two people on any peak.

The Trinitarian Overcoming of Monotheism

The great Christian theological question consists in the Trinitarian overcoming of monotheism, that is, of any monarchic system: theological (there is not only *theos*), human (Man is not the only one who counts), historical (there is not only history), religious (there is no Christian monopoly), masculine (most religions are scandalously male chauvinistic), economical (monetization of culture), political (one sole project of human coexistence), racial. . . .

Most Oriental traditions have understood that that which the West calls God cannot be the being, the whole, the only reality, the only thing which is real, nor a Supreme Being, the omnipotent Lord—a deified pharaoh—nor a no-thing, a *flatus vocis* or a psychological projection of Man's unsatisfied desires. Is there a way of overcoming this "trilemma": either the whole (being), or the Maximum (Supreme), or the No-Thing?

A sociology of knowledge would invite us to reflect upon the fact that the God of thinking or of a certain philosophy tends to be Truth, Being, the Whole. The God of feeling, which the biblical image approaches, tends to be the Lord and the Lord who loves, the God of the armies (*Sabaoth*), the leader of history or the imam of the hearts. The God of action "has set the world in their heart"[1] and does not let himself be seen either in the battle fields or in the cities of men. The tendency is toward atheism.

The culture of India speaks of the Lord of *jñāna*, of the *bhakti*, and the *karman*: knowledge, love, and action. In the current world, all three images are problematic; thus the crisis of God. What a great part of Asian wisdom offers the West—in short—is the *a-dualist* vision of reality. And this is the vision that stimulates a more complete image of the Trinity. God is neither the *same* (monism) nor the *other* (dualism). God is one pole of reality, a constitutive pole, ineffable in-Himself but speaking through us, transcendent but immanent in the world, infinite but limited in things. This pole is nothing in itself. It only exists in polarity, in its relations.

In the West, God has been the supreme paradigm of reality. The predominant image has been that of monotheism: there exists an Absolute Being or a Supreme Being; or a supreme principle exists, be it called Truth, or Good, or Justice.

This is the monolithic scheme that many non-Abrahamic religions want to overcome. I say overcome: atheism is not an overcoming, but rather its material denial within the same formal scheme: the principle of noncontradiction.

Overcoming monotheism does not mean that Christianity has to break with its tradition, but rather that it must develop the potential of its Trinitarian intuition. The Trinitarian intuition overcomes any monarchic vision, that is, any reduction of reality to one single principle: temporality to eternity, matter to spirit, the human to consciousness, the real to the divine, and so on. The task is immense and the *metanoia* that it requires, radical; the alternative is death in self-destruction.

---

[1] Cf. Qo 3:10–11, in the Latin Vulgate: "vidi adflictionem quam dedit Deus filiis hominum ut distendantur in ea cuncta fecit bona in tempore suo *et mundum tradidit disputationi eorum*" (I contemplate the task that God gives humanity to labor at. All that he does is apt for its time).

SECTION II

16

APORIAS IN THE COMPARATIVE PHILOSOPHY OF RELIGION

How can there be a no-man's land in the land of Man?

Comparative Philosophy (of Religion)

The thesis of this chapter is that there is no such thing, strictly speaking, as comparative philosophy, and consequently comparative philosophy of religion. The concept is inherently self-contradictory since philosophy claims to be ultimate by nature, yet for philosophy to be comparative there must be a neutral basis outside the philosophies compared. Comparative philosophy would then mean robbing philosophy of its ultimate nature and accepting a metaphilosophy as the real and authentic philosophy. This allegedly neutral basis can only be a prephilosophical conception of reality, which ceases to be neutral when critically examined by any one given philosophy. In other words, this prephilosophical conception then becomes an evaluation of the neutral basis within the evaluating philosophical system itself. In fact, philosophies always grow out of critical reflections on and from prephilosophical positions. This is what philosophy has always claimed to be.

Something similar also happens with religion. Comparative religion is not a mere juxtaposition of religions, nor just an evaluation of one religion from the point of view of another; rather it purports to be the *comparative study* of religion(s). Thus the problem of comparative religion entails a critical reflection on the nature of comparative studies and therefore becomes a question of philosophy: philosophy of comparative religion. It presents the same *aporetic* as comparative philosophy, which means that the relation between comparative philosophy and comparative religion is very close. However, I shall not deal here with comparative religion at large, but will confine myself to the problem of comparative philosophy of religion.[1]

---

[1] The number of books on this subject is growing rapidly. For an extensive bibliography of authors who died before 1967, see J. Waardenburg, *Classical Approaches to the Study of Religion*, vol. 2 (Paris: Mouton, 1974). For a more exhaustive list, see *International Bibliography of the History of Religions* (Leiden: Brill), and the corresponding section of *Bibliography of Philosophy* (UNESCO; Paris: Vrin). The latter has the advantage of including a small abstract on each work. See also *Repertoire bibliographique de la Philosophie* (Louvain: Editions de l'Institut Superieur de Philosophie). Useful, though not exclusively

Comparative religion may want to compare particular aspects of several religions under one definite perspective. We may, for instance, undertake a comparative study of the use of dance in the cultural acts of several religions under the perspective of the participation of bodily rhythmic movements in worship. This is the comparative study of one religious problem and not the comparative religion I am submitting to critique. I have in mind the more fundamental question of an ultimately philosophical analysis of the self-understanding of different religions.[2]

The objective of philosophy of religion is to examine the nature of religion.[3] This would not present more difficulties than any other philosophical investigation were it not for the fact that we are here dealing with at least two entities that claim to be ultimate, each one of which provides different tools to approach the problem. The very concept of religion, for instance, is not univocal.[4] The various "religions" of the world have a different understanding of what is meant by the term *religion*.[5] Not only its nature, but even its very existence is called into question.[6] This has

---

for problems of philosophy of religion, is *Bibliographie zur Symbolik: Ikonographie und Mythologie*, ed. M. Lurker and H. Schneider (Baden-Baden: Verlag Koerner).

[2] Cf. G. Lanczkowski, *Begegnung und Wandel der Religion* (Düsseldorf-Köln: Diederichs, 1971); "Erscheinungsformen des religiösen Pluralismus," *Numen* 21, no. 3 (December 1974): 161–62.

[3] For example, W. B. Kristensen, *The Meaning of Religion* (The Hague: M. Nijhoff, 1960); J. Callins, *The Emergence of Philosophy of Religion* (New Haven, CT: Yale University Press, 1967); H. Dumery, *Phenomenology of Religion* (Berkeley: University of California Press, 1958); M. J. Charlesworth, *Philosophy of Religion: The Historic Approaches* (New York: Herder, 1972); M. Dhavamony, *Phenomenology of Religion* (Rome: Gregorian University Press, 1973); G. Widengren, *Religionsphänomenologie* (Berlin: Walter de Gruyter, 1969); G. van der Leeuw, *Phänomenologie der Religion* (Tubingen: J. C. B. Mohr [Paul Siebeck], 1956); P. Heiler, *Erscheinungsformen und Wesen der Religion* (Stuttgart: W. Kohlhammer Verlag, 1961); U. Mann, *Einführung in die Religionsphilosophie* (Darmstadt: Wissenschaftliche Buchgesellschaft, 1970); J. D. Bettis, ed., *Phenomenology of Religion* (New York: Harper and Row, 1969); A. Guzzo, *La Religione* (Torino: Accademia delle Scienze, 1963–1964); J. E. Smith, *Philosophy of Religion* (New York: Macmillan, 1965); M. M. Olivetti, *Filosofia della religione come problema storico* (Padova: CEDAM, 1974); Louis Dupré, *The Other Dimension* (New York: Doubleday, 1972).

[4] On the theological question concerning "other religions," cf. H. R. Schlette, *Die Religionen als Thema der Theologie* (Freiburg: Herder, 1963); see also his *Die Konfrontation mit den Religionen* (Köln: Bachen, 1964), and his more recent work *Einführung in das Studium der Religionen* (Freiburg: Rombach, 1971). U. Mann, ed., *Theologie und Religionswissenschaft* (Darmstadt: Wissenschaftliche Buchgesellschaft, 1973). Also World Council of Churches, ed., *Dialogue with People of Living Faiths and Ideologies*, Minutes of the Third Meeting of the Working Group, Trinidad, May 1978 (Geneva: WCC, 1978).

[5] Cf. R. Panikkar, "La philosophie de la religion devant le pluralisme philosophique et la pluralité des religions," in E. Castelli, ed., *La Philosophie de la religion: L'herméneutique de la philosophie de la religion* (Paris: Aubier, 1977), 193–201.

[6] Cf. W. C. Smith, *The Meaning and End of Religion* (New York: Harper and Row,

led many scholars to affirm that the scientific study of religion today is "essentially a comparative discipline,"[7] overlooking the fact that we are not a priori certain of what we are trying to compare.

Now, the very method and problem of comparative philosophy of religion entails a critical reflection on the nature of the different religions.[8] Only then can we compare them. In other words, is there a thing—religion(s)—that we are able to compare? Moreover, assuming that such entities exist, do we have a *metron*, a measure, to compare them?

The prima facie meaning of comparative philosophy of religion seems to imply that there is a neutral ground outside any religion from which we can compare, weigh, critically scrutinize the different religions, and arrive either at a new understanding of religions or at a new corrective of existing ones.[9] This article raises some critical and methodological remarks on the very nature of this enterprise.

The *sūtra* in which I sum up this reflection is expressed in the subtitle of this chapter: *How can there be a no-man's land in the land of Man?* How can there be a *neutral* ground in the human arena? The very notion is self-contradictory because such a ground would not be human.[10] If anything, it would have to be a *common* ground.

1963 [1978 ed.]).

[7] Cf. R. Pummer, "Recent Publications on the Methodology of the Science of Religion," *Numen* 22, no. 3 (December 1975): 170. A number of important scholars are quoted.

[8] Cf. G. Lanczkowski, ed., *Selbstverständnis und Wesen der Religionswissenschaft* (Darmstadt: Wissenschaftliche Buchgesellschaft, 1974); K. Goldammer, *Die Formenwelt des Religiösen* (Stuttgart: Alfred Kröner Verlag, 1960); Th. P. van Baaren, "Science of Religion as a Systematic Discipline: Some Introductory Remarks," in van Baaren, ed., *Religion, Culture, and Methodology* (The Hague: Mouton, 1973), 35–56; U. Bianchi, *Probleme der Religionsgeschichte* (Göttingen: Vandenhoeck and Ruprecht, 1964); Bianchi, *La storia delle religione* (Torino: Tipografia Sociale Torinese, 1970); Bianchi, "The Definition of Religion: On the Methodology of Historical-Comparative Research," in Bianchi, C. J. Bleeker, A. Bausani, eds., *Problems and Methods of the History of Religions* (Leiden: Brill, 1972), 15–26 (discussion, 26–34); A. Brelich, "Prolégomènes à une histoire des religions," in H. C. Puech, ed., *Histoire des Religions*, vol. 1 (Paris: Gallimard, 1970), 1–59; R. O. Bird, *Category Formations and the History of Religions* (The Hague: Mouton, 1971); H. Desroche and J. Séguy, eds., *Introduction aux sciences humaines des religions* (Paris: Cujas, 1970); M. Pye, *Comparative Religion: An Introduction through Source Materials* (Newton Abbot: David and Charles, 1972). For the phenomenological approach, cf. G. Widengren, "La méthode comparative: Entre philologie et phénoménologie," in Bianchi, Bleeker, and Bausani, *Problems and Methods of the History of Religions*, 5–14; also Widengren, "Some Remarks on the Methods of the Phenomenology of Religion," *Acta Universitatis Upsaliensis* 17 (Uppsala, 1968), 250–60; M. Meslin, *Pour une science des Religions* (Paris: Seuil, 1973).

[9] This is what sociology of religion is trying to do in the contemporary scholarly scene. Cf. the rich bibliography of over sixteen thousand entries compiled by the Instituto Fe y Secularidad, *Sociologia de la religion y teología: Estudio bibliográfico* (Madrid: Cuadernos para el diálogo, 1975).

[10] Neutral = *ne utrum*, none of both (either).

My overall impression is that many a conception of comparative religion still comes from a precritical philosophical position that assumes there is an unmistakably recognizable divine or transcendent point of view, even if it is often called objectivity. Religionists might do well to recall that the passion for objectivity, the so-called scientific spirit, is the secularized heir of the *furor theologicus*. For many today, objectivity stands sovereign, aloof, and nonnegotiable, as the fundamentalist interpretation of the word or the will of God stood in ancient times—and even holds today.

That I may not be altogether wrong in this is substantiated by the historico-cultural origin of comparative disciplines, which proliferate at particular historical moments.[11] This is an interesting chapter in the sociology of knowledge.[12] The problem of comparative studies arises when we become aware of the insufficiency of any given discipline to handle its own subject matter exhaustively, and we suspect that the corresponding subject matter is dealt with meaningfully in other disciplines.

Critical philosophy was once upon a time the ideal of any philosophical enterprise worthy of the name. Comparative philosophy of religion seems to be the heir of such an attitude and aspires to being the proper way of studying religion in our time. Having discovered that "we" (as Christians, Indians, Westerners, Buddhists, humanists, Americans, etc.) were provincial in our philosophizing about religion, we now want to philosophize in a world context.[13] Thus, the philosophical study of religion turns to comparative philosophy of religion.[14] Now, if there are no funda-

---

[11] The boom in comparative studies is not yet over. Societies for comparative civilizations; journals for comparative politics; books on comparative aesthetics, comparative history, etc., are appearing all over the world.

[12] The classic work in the sociology of knowledge is still Max Scheler, *Versuche zu einer Soziologie des Wissens* (Munich: Dunker und Humblot, 1924). Cf. also the article by Lewis A. Coser, "Sociology of Knowledge," *International Encyclopedia of the Social Sciences*, vol. 3 (New York: Macmillan, 1968). Long before Scheler and the modern writers on sociology of knowledge, Schelling had already emphasized that truth is not something static, and that the truth of a statement cannot be severed from the movement that it entails and of which it forms a part. Otherwise, he says, it would dry up like a fruit cut from the living tree. See the influence of this insight on Ferdinand Ebner as reported in a letter he wrote to Luise Karpischeck, August 25, 1913 (F. Ebner, *Schriften*, vol. 3 [Munich: Kösel, 1965], 40).

[13] Cf. the enormous leap between P. Ortegat, *Philosophie de la Religion* (Bruxelles: L'Édition Universelle, 1937), and the work by J. G. Caffarena and J. M. Velasco, *Filosofía de la Religión* (Madrid: Revista de Occidente, 1973), both within the same orthodox Roman Catholic milieu. While the former distinguishes three different sciences—"philosophy, theology, and apologetic"—the latter distinguishes a phenomenology that must "assume the historical and current reality of the religious phenomenon" and a philosophy that must "deal with the fact studied like in this manner, judging it critically." The author finishes with the assertion, "Between the *Scylla* of a-critical and depersonalizing dogmatism and the *Charybdis* of rationalizing reduction, navigation will be difficult for the hermeneutist."

[14] Cf. A. J. Bahm's sincere and moving attempt in *Comparative Philosophy* (Albuquerque: World Books, 1977). Also the more classical works of Jan de Vries, *Perspectives*

mental changes in our methods, this new style of philosophy may turn out to be a euphemism for a more comprehensive, but perhaps also more shallow, philosophy of religion. It might even be a misnomer, or worse, an inveterate remnant of intellectual colonialism.

Sociology of knowledge discloses yet another reason for the academic popularity of comparative philosophy of religion: the intellectual and sociological impact of the natural sciences on the conception of philosophy, religion, and theology.[15] We may recall that the distinctive feature of the natural sciences consists in finding mathematical paradigms capable of expressing the behavior of natural phenomena: the famous *sōzein ta fainomena* (saving appearances) of the ancient Greeks.[16] Human phenomena may require a more complex method than the mathematical but there can hardly be a comparison without recurrence to mathematics. In other words, the quantitative method has become an alluring model for comparative studies. In fact, only if we succeed in bringing the data of philosophy and religion to quantitative parameters can we properly compare them.

Quantities, in effect, are the only strictly comparable entities. Comparison demands a scale of comparison, and all scales are quantitative. Comparative philosophy of religion then becomes a "science" in the sense of the natural sciences. It becomes the science of formalized religious paradigms. It acquires "scientific" status.[17] It can claim to be taught like any other "objective" and respectable scholarly science. It has become comparative, but can it still be called philosophy?

At this point I present some philosophical reflections in the form of aporias we must face in the comparative study of religion.

I am, of course, assuming here that the comparative study of religion(s) is a critical enterprise that tries to be conscious of its own methods and wants to be fair to the self-understanding of each of the religions compared. We should, as I hinted at the very beginning, carefully distinguish between comparative religion(s) and a critical evaluation of religion(s) from the point of view of one particular religion or philosophy. In the latter case, we are also comparing, but from a scale of values

---

in the History of Religions (Berkeley: University of California Press, 1967); E. O. James, *Comparative Religion* (London: Methuen, 1938 [1961 ed.]); J. Wach, *The Comparative Study of Religions* (New York: Columbia University Press, 1958).

[15] Cf. R. Pummel, "Religionswissenschaft or Religiology?" *Numen* 19, nos. 2–3 (1972): 99 and following, which shows the tendency of modern "religionists" to distance themselves from pure philosophy and particularly from the bête noire of theology.

[16] Cf. P. Duhem's monumental work, *Le Système du Monde: Histoire des doctrines cosmologiques de Platon à Copernic* (Paris: A. Hermann et fils, 1913). Also his *An Essay on the Idea of Physical Theory from Plato to Galileo* (1908, trans. from the French; Chicago: University of Chicago Press, 1969). O. Barfield, *Saving the Appearances. A Study in Idolatry* (New York: Harcourt, Brace & World, 1957); R. Panikkar, *Ontonomía de la Ciencia* (Madrid: Gredos, 1961).

[17] Cf. G. J. Larson, "Prolegomenon to a Theory of Religion," *Journal of the American Academy of Religion* 46, no. 4 (1978): 443–63.

that may not be shared since it belongs to only one of the parties being compared. For proper comparison we need, I repeat, a common scale. This scale can only be found if both sides, comparer and compared, stand on a common ground where they agree in applying a particular criterion as the *comparans*. Only then we shall have a proper *comparandum*.[18]

Exploring the Nature of a Common Ground

Comparative philosophy of religion claims to distinguish itself from any other form of philosophy of religion by the fact that it takes into account the compared religions from the point of view of their own self-comprehension. It does not want to impose one particular philosophy—or religion—as the indisputable standard against which to evaluate the other worldviews, philosophies, or religions. This does not exclude possible criticism and even rejection of a particular system, but the reasons adduced in the comparisons must also be cogent for the criticized system. Comparative philosophy of religion therefore needs a common ground, a mutually accepted norm, an agreed point of reference—ultimately, a common language.

However, the very nature of this common ground presents difficulties, for it can be

- Taken for granted
- Mutually accepted
- Converted into a common structure
- Reduced to a common tool
- Seen from a common perspective
- Minimized to internal autonomous coherence
- Finally agreed upon that it is only found in a common language

Taken for Granted

If the common ground needed for comparison is uncritically taken for granted, we find ourselves philosophizing from a base that evanesces the moment anyone asks for a justification of the premises. In the final analysis we revert to a single basic philosophy that we assume is shared by the different traditions. We can undertake proper comparisons because we do not question the common ground. But this comparative philosophy of religion is no longer sufficient when the compared religions—with their underlying philosophies—do not share the assumptions of the comparing philosophy. We then have a critical philosophy of religion from the standpoint of one particular philosophy, but it is not, properly speaking, comparative philosophy of religion.

---

[18] Cf., as an example, Kalidas Bhattacharyya, "Comparative Indian Philosophy. A Sample Study," *Philosophica: International Philosophical Quarterly* 7, no. 2 (June 1978): 1–15.

For example, if we take for granted that the human being is an individual, any religious tradition based on the tribal—or ethnic—nature of Man will be disfavorably compared regarding a concept of salvation that does not consider individual salvation as Man's ultimate aim; in short, we can no longer validly compare if the compared religion does not admit the scale of comparison. Moreover, this is bound to happen the moment that the compared religion finds the comparison to be "unfair." We must then recoil to examine and justify the alleged basis of the comparison. In other words, comparative religion is only truly comparing if it is based on a common myth which the religions compared accept as an indisputable starting point. We can, for instance, compare Semitic religions from the common ground of the Abrahamic "faith"—monotheism, reality of this world, obedience due to the Will of God, and so forth. But this is not an adequate basis for including in the comparison, say, Hinduism, Buddhism, or modern humanism, since they stand on other grounds.

Mutually Accepted

If the common ground is mutually recognized by the philosophies or religions concerned, we have a proper, basic, philosophical comparison that serves as a point of reference as long as it is not contested; that is, we can have comparative religion of those religions that have joined one particular philosophical club. Comparisons made from this philosophical point of view may convince those who hold said point of view, but cannot be applied to adherents of other philosophies without previous justification. Such comparisons constitute comparative philosophy only *secundum quid*: they are critical studies of religious systems from a particular philosophical position. What we have here is philosophical comparison of religions from a particular philosophy, but not comparative philosophy of religion. There can be, for instance, a psychology of worldview, if we agree on what is meant by *psychology*.[19] But there cannot be a worldview about worldviews—that is, a meta-philosophy. Any worldview is a view of the world and not of worldviews. We can, of course, consider human worldviews as part of the world and, thus, of our conception of world today; that is, our worldview about "worldviews" is simply another worldview that in no way can claim an a priori superiority. If this were not the case, we would be thrown into a *regressus ad infinitum*—another worldview about the worldviews of worldviews *et via dicendo*.

If we happen to defend a realistic philosophical position we may compare and criticize all those religious systems that accept a realistic view of the universe, but "idealistic" philosophies cannot be properly compared within the parameters of a realistic philosophy. They can, at best, only be described from an alien perspective. Comparative religion is something more than a mere classification of doctrines; classification is an aid to understanding, but not synonymous with it.

---

[19] Cf. the unfortunately little known work by Karl Jaspers, *Psychologie der Welstanschauungen* (Berlin: Springer, 1960).

In sum, if as in (a), a common ground is taken for granted, we will only have a comparison of religion from its own perspective, which is not "universal"; that is, we will have evaluative religion, but not comparative religion properly speaking. If, as in (b), the common ground is only postulated as a pragmatic starting point, we shall have valid comparative religion among the "signatories" of the treatise, as it were; that is, for all those religions that have adopted the axiom of the agreed common ground. Thus, if pragmatism, for instance, is our postulated assumption, those religions that, under this criterion, yield better results will get better scores. Yet, in order to agree on what a better result is, we need a previous agreement as to those values. Therefore, we have done nothing more than shift the problem. In other words, if philosophy has any claim to ultimacy, at least in its own sphere, there is no place for the meta-philosophy needed for a true comparison. We can only philosophize on and from a given situation.[20]

Converted into a Common Structure

It can be argued, as has often been the case, that any compared study must recur to the analysis of common structures or to detecting common formalities.[21] Now, if the comparative principle of comparative philosophy is merely formal comparison, we shall have to find the corresponding comparable entities by reducing philosophical or religious facts to *quantifiable* formalities. This is, indeed, an indispensable method and a very fruitful one despite the fact that it reduces the religious phenomenon to a mere formality. It helps us find affinities and common patterns among different world religions. It is scientific comparison of certain data extracted from the complexity of the religious traditions. Yet it can be argued that the complete nature of the religious *symbol* is neither contained nor expressed in the formal *sign* that has been ascribed to it.[22] I would call this relatively new science of religious signs *religiography*, but

---

[20] The now fashionable sociology of knowledge has been present in the German scene since the beginning of the century. Cf. the following triple quote, which already places us in the line of an important "apostolic" succession: "Was im Menschen denkt, das ist gar nicht er, sondern seine soziale Umwelt," says Ludwig Gumplowicz in the second edition of *Grundriss der Soziologie*, 1905, as quoted by Wilhelm Jerusalem in his posthumous essay "Die soziologische Bedingtheit des Denkens und der Denkformen," published in the volume edited by Max Scheler, *Versuche zu einer Soziologie des Wissens*. Wilhelm refines the psychological overtones of Gumplowicz, and Scheler situates the sociological parameters of Jerusalem.

[21] Cf. "tout comparatisme débouche sur une recherche des structures," M. Meslin, *Pour une science des religions* (Paris: Seuil, 1913), 156.

[22] I am making a basic distinction between *signs*, which are epistemic by nature, and *symbols*, which are of ontological character. Cf. my *Worship and Secular Man* (New York: Orbis Books, 1973), 20ff.

would add that this is neither religiology[23] nor what is understood as comparative religion or as comparative philosophy of religion.

We may, moreover, uncover some of the assumptions of this formalizing method. In fact this method assumes the following:

1. All relevant philosophical and religious insights—facts or phenomena—can be properly translated into algebraic or formal signs.[24] Otherwise, we would not have a working correspondence between the sign and the thing, and mental operations with the signs would not reveal the behavior, let alone the nature, of things. For example, we assume we can have appropriate signs for love, guilt, sin, righteousness, grace, and so on. By appropriate, I mean a semiotic system that allows us to operate with those signs, so that if, for instance, "grace" is what destroys "sin" and "guilt" is consciousness of "sin," then consciousness of "grace" and "guilt" are mutually exclusive. Thus if you have a sense of guilt, you cannot believe you are *simul iustus et peccator* (at once justified and sinner), as was Luther's intuition.

2. Heterogeneous philosophical and religious systems can be adequately translated into a homogeneous set of signs. If this were not so, operation within one system would be incommensurable with another. For instance, it is assumed that (a) *prema*, (b) *bhakti*, (c) *agapē*, (d) *eros*, (e) *amor*, (m) *bhagavan*, (n) *deus*, (o) *nirvāṇa*, (p) *hypsistos* can be rendered by simply adding some distinctive coefficients to the same basic sign. One could write the signs for the different forms of as "love" as ax, bx, cx, dx, ex, and my, ny, oy, and py for the various forms of the "ultimate." The x and y are assumed to be univocal and are only distinguished by an equally univocal corresponding coefficient for each tradition or subtradition. According to this method, the spirituality of Mīrābaī and of Catherine of Genoa, for instance, could be formulated as $ax + my$ versus $ex + ny$.

3. The internal laws of the chosen algebra correspond to the external concatenation of the philosophical or religious data. Otherwise the results of algebraic speculation would not reflect the real behavior of the original. For example, if g stand for the infinite God and c for the finite creature, it follows that $g/c = ¥$ and $c/g = 0$, although for further qualifications it may be necessary to accept that $g = ¥c$ and $c = 0g$, from whence it follows that $c = 0$. Which translates as: if God is infinite reality, the creature cannot be real; or, if I = total surrender to the will of God (W) and this Will is enshrined in a Book (Q)—that is, if $I = W$ and $W = Q$—it follows that total confidence in Q is surrender to God: $I = Q$. This point translates as: the only authentic Muslim is the man who totally surrenders to what is written in the Qur'an. Any hermeneutics diverging from the accepted ones will be, at the least,

[23] Cf. the above quoted article by R. Pummer, "Religionswissenschaft or Religiology?" for the problematic surrounding the word "religiology." The article also includes a useful bibliography.

[24] For the ontological shift from philosophy to science due to the birth of modern epistemology, see the chapter "Conocimiento científico y conocimiento filosófico," in my *Ontonomía de la Ciencia*, 86–132.

an infidelity. Now the question as to who interprets the "accepted" view cannot be raised without blasphemy, if the formula holds. In these two cases we have a typical example of reductionism.

4. The quantitative clarification of the problems amounts to the philosophical understanding of the facts. If this were not the case, we would not have comparative philosophy—of religion—but only analysis of basic structures extracted from a particular point of view. For example, religious wars would have to be explained by factors like the economy of the country, the desire for fulfillment or happiness, along with the difficulty of attaining it by observing the prescribed rules of a particular religion, and so forth. We might, in this way, understand the Christian Crusades, the Islamic *jihād*, the Hindu conquest of Greater India, the Jewish-Arab war, the Irish situation, and the Iranian Revolution. Scholars would underscore a number of other determining factors, of course, but they would have to basically agree that the method explains the comparisons between different facts.

We could study religious festivals, to give a second example, according to their calendar, that is, considering time, seasons, and so on as the proper pattern to understand them. But we could equally study festivals under the perspective of gender or dividing them into festivals with or without gods, and so on. This method assumes that operating with variables will also help us predict the appearance of similar phenomena. However, prediction does not require understanding of the fact, but only knowledge of its dynamics.

In sum, the originality of the possible religious dimension of Man does not lie in the substructure that we may eventually find analyzing religious behaviors or phenomena. Eating, dancing, chanting, uttering words, celebrating, defending one's convictions, formulating schemes of opinions, giving moneys or goods away, and so forth are all structures to be found in economic, commercial, intellectual, and simply human dealings. The possible specificity of religion lies in the contents and meanings given to such patterns: this eating, dancing, praying, theologizing, confessing, almsgiving, and so on may be filled with something that distinguishes it from formally similar behaviors. In a word, the formalizing method is methodologically blind to detecting the very nature of the phenomenon under discussion.

I wish to stress, however, that this method, if properly followed, may yield paradigms and patterns of understanding hitherto unknown. If the formalizations of the primarily mechanical transformations of nature have given birth to the modern conception of the natural sciences, there is no reason why the religious dimension of the human being should prove refractory to its corresponding mathematization.

Yet the quantitative paradigm should not forget (a) the possibility that the religious dimension as such be sui generis and thus incommensurable with quantitative parameters, (b) the possible existence of a plus irreducible to any type of formalization, and (c) the fundamental distinction between mathematical comprehension and human understanding.

• In order to investigate whether the religious dimension represents something irreducible to any other category, we cannot apply a method based on the opposite assumption, nor can we postulate a priori that religion is an inexpugnable bulwark. This is a central methodological problem of philosophy of religion today.

• Assuming that there are mathematizable aspects of religious facts, we cannot assume a priori a total and exhaustive mathematization of the world, nor can we assume that a religious fact may not contain factors impermeable to mathematical analysis.

• Even if we had a mathematical explanation of religious facts, this could not be equated with an understanding of these facts. Accepting Newton's and Einstein's formulae, for instance, allows us to calculate and to predict, but from there to understanding the nature of gravity, mass, force, and energy is a big leap.

Reduced to a Common Tool

There may be a middle way between the reductionist view of pure quantification of reality and the atomistic conception of incommunicability and impossibility of mutual understanding between human cultures. This fourth search for a common ground underscores the unity of human nature. Man is one, a single species, homogeneous in itself and different from all other beings on Earth. So far, so good. But the moment that we formulate this unity, we are bound to give it concrete intellectual contents, and this conceptualization is already far from being universal. We cannot identify "common human nature" with our concept of "it."

One word has had special fortune in the West to characterize the *humanum*. This word, in fact, has been considered the common basis on which to build a comparative science of religions and even a world order.[25] The word is *rationality*.[26] Man is *animal rationale*.[27] Rationality is the human condition.[28] Now, to come directly to the point, if rationality is considered to be the primal method and the ultimate judge in the field of comparative philosophy, many philosophical and religious systems not subscribing to this view will be excluded from the comparison or reduced to a rational structure that does not represent their own nature as they understand it. Even in the case of formal agreement, the interpretations of "rationality" may differ fundamentally so as to invalidate the method until the meaning of "rationality" has been agreed upon. But this is obviously a *petitio principii*, since comparative philosophy is here relying on a basis that should first be the outcome of comparative

---

[25] Cf. G. and P. Mische, *Toward a Human World Order* (New York: Paulist Press, 1977).

[26] Cf. the Plenary Session of the last World Congress of Philosophy, Düsseldorf, 1978, on *Scientific and Non-Scientific Forms of Rationality*, which attempted to offer a universal spectrum for a philosophical dialogue on a world scale, and my critical remarks in the Proceedings on the question "Neun Sūtras über die Ratio."

[27] Cf. the shift in meaning from the Aristotelian formula of Man as "ton logon echōon zōon" (a living being pervaded by speech, word, *logos*) to the medieval translation (a spiritual being), and then to the modern interpretation (a reasoning, i.e., calculating being: *ratio* as *rechnen*).

[28] Cf., by way of example, B. R. Wilson, ed., *Rationality* (New York: Harper and Row, 1970).

philosophy, namely the philosophical understanding of the nature of "rationality" from a "compared" perspective. In other words, "rationality" itself must be studied comparatively before being used as a comparative tool.

It should be added that rationality may be envisaged as a common *necessary condition* in most cases. Anything contradictory can hardly be accepted and it certainly cannot be intelligibly and coherently formulated: a contradiction is such because it cannot be said; it negates itself. Yet rationality does not cover the whole of reality or of human existence.[29] Rationality is not yet a *sufficient condition*. Many religions deal with the fields of the prerational, a-rational, and suprarational. To eliminate those fields because the method does not allow us to deal with them is a methodological error. In sum, reason as a common tool will not be sufficient to do the job.

Seen from a Common Perspective

One way to obviate the difficulty consists in shifting the problem from systems and traditions to concrete human issues. This may, for a short time, be a successful, pragmatic position. We might then consider comparative philosophy as the study of philosophical issues in light of more than one philosophical or religious tradition. So that in the case of comparative religion one would not compare one tradition with another, but would study various fundamental issues—for example, evil, God, suffering, peace of mind, the destiny of human beings, and so on—in light of, say, the Hindu and Christian traditions.

Personally, I am convinced of the fecundity of this method.[30] But there is, at this point, a major obstacle because we must first critically prove that there are, in fact, certain philosophical and religious problems that can be considered independently of the tradition in light of which they are seen. If I claim that God is a problem, that original sin is a fact or a fruitful myth, that peace is a supreme value, I am already speaking from the vantage point of certain particular systems. The truth of the matter is, rather, that there is no such thing as naked "texts" that we can study from a remote position and from different angles. There are no pure facts or pure data in philosophy, in religion, or in any type of human awareness. The *factum* or the *datum* is already a philosophical construct from the moment that reflection steps in. Facts are only such for an intellect, and this intellect is already active at the time of their elaboration. What is given (*datum*) is only such if it is received, that is, if it is conceived as such

---

[29]   Cf. the intriguing *conclusio* of one of the theses of Pico della Mirandola, "Contradictoria in natura actuali [var. Intellectuali] se compatiuntur," *apud* H. de Lubac, *Pic de la Mirandole* (Paris: Aubier, 1974), 257; also H. Seuse, "Büchlein der Wahrheit," in *Deutsche mystische Schriften* (Dusseldorf: Patmos, 1966), 346. "Sofern sich der Mensch nicht zweier widersprüchlicher Dinge als eines bewusst sei, so ist zweifellos nicht leicht von solchen Dingen mit ihm zu sprechen."

[30]   More and more works are appearing in this direction. Cf., for example, J. Bowker, *The Problem of Suffering in the Religions of the World* (Cambridge: Cambridge University Press, 1975).

by an intellect (*conceptum*). Even if we were to grant the reality of *noēmata* as pure data in a transcendental consciousness, there could not be *pisteumata* independent of the particular beliefs of the adherents.[31] The relation between spectacle and spectator is constitutive: there is only spectacle for a spectator. And the spectator is inscribed in a space and time from which he acquires his actual spectacles.

An instructive, because extreme, example is the case of Buddhism. The Enlightened One introduced a fact that could hardly be more universal: "*sarvam duḥkham*" (everything is *duḥkha*). And immediately the problem begins: What is *duḥkha*? Suffering, uneasiness, evil, discomfort, ailment, dissatisfaction, discrepancy . . . ? Even if the word meant physical suffering alone (which is not the case), the experience of corporeal pain is inextricably connected not only with our physiology but also with our psychology and cosmology.[32] And even physiological facts are not independent of psychological factors and cosmological coefficients. At any rate, the word means different things to a yogi, a Tibetan, a Christian of the European Middle Ages, a modern Japanese, and a Bantu. To say "suffering" in modern English or *duḥkha* in Sanskrit is not to say the same thing, and to start off from one particular understanding is already to abandon the comparative perspective.

Minimized to Internal Autonomous Coherence

The next step may be that of delimiting the scope of the comparison. If grand comparisons are not fruitful, let's see if they can become so by applying a comparative approach on a more modest scale. Let us, then, do comparative studies using the criterion of *internal coherence* according to the inner logic of each philosophy. But then this exercise ceases to be philosophy—and by the same token ceases to be comparative philosophy—and becomes instead a criticism of the coherence of the respective formal languages that claim to express philosophical statements. Moreover, we are left without criteria for comparing the different sets of systems because the various rules of internal coherence are not necessarily the same. This may be a sound classificatory analysis, but again, is it comparative philosophy? Does it help us understand the issues at stake?

The forceful example of *mādhyamika*, which claims to destroy all philosophies using their own conceptual tools to show their internal inconsistency, comes immediately to mind. The first comment to be made is that such a criticism of all philosophy, if successful, then becomes a true philosophy of its own, with the consequent danger of self-destruction through the application of its own methods on itself.[33] However, more important to our case is the fact that we would then have a powerful philosophy

---

[31] "The religious phenomenon appears only as *pisteuma* and not as mere *noēma*" (R. Panikkar, *The Intrareligious Dialogue* [New York: Paulist Press, 1978], 52).

[32] Cf. the different contributions in *Le Myth de la Peine*, ed. E. Castelli (Paris: Aubier-Montaigne, 1967).

[33] Cf. R. Panikkar, "The Crisis of Mādhyamika and Indian Philosophy Today," *Philosophy, East and West* 16, nos. 3/4 (July/October 1966): 117–31.

and perhaps also a philosophy of religion, but certainly not comparative philosophy of religion, comparative religion, or comparative philosophy.

This short review of several attempts at a foundation for comparative philosophy shows that the discipline might well have been thought out differently with a brief reflection on its alleged nature. Comparative studies deal with human realities, human constructs which are neither dumb nor inanimate; therefore, if we compare speaking beings, we must learn to listen to them. Consequently, we will now direct the question of comparative studies to the problem of communication.

Finally Agreed That It Is Only Found in a Common Language

To come to an agreement or disagreement about a possible ground, or about any common issue, we require a common language. The problem of comparative philosophy then becomes the issue of a common human language. And, in fact, comparative linguistics, since Max Müller, is at the very basis of most comparative studies. Now linguistics may denote either comparison of the linguistic structures of different languages or philology—that is, a fundamental reflection on the nature of language itself.[34] Comparative studies have often used the paradigm of *comparative linguistics*. My suggestion here is that we also apply the paradigm of *philosophy of language* to the reflection on the nature of comparative philosophy.[35] I shall limit myself to some very elementary considerations, leaving a study of the relation between comparative philosophy of religion and philosophy of language for another occasion.[36]

In order to have a proper comparative religion or comparative philosophy we need

- To believe in the translatability of the different philosophical and religious languages
- Actual and proper translations

Now, translations are possible only if there is a flexible language capable of expressing the insights of the different parties. To put it more existentially: We need proper translators who can be such only if they are philosophers in their own right, since translation is merely an expression of the synthesis of the translator. Comparative philosophy depends, then, on the problematic of "translational philosophy."

It should be stressed here that, in spite of individual coefficients proper to the actual translators, translation is not only an individual activity. In fact, the translator can only exist within a common frame of reference that he does not create but finds already existing as a result of historical osmoses and societal intercourse. A single

---

[34] Cf. the classical meaning of philology parallel to that of philosophy, which is still alive in seminal thinkers like Ferdinand Ebner.

[35] I have in mind the work of M. Heidegger, H. G. Gadamer, P. Ricoeur, and many others, as well as the above-mentioned F. Ebner.

[36] The author has been working along these lines for many years and hopes to publish some of the results of his investigations soon.

earthling returning to our planet from another world would find it much more difficult to translate what he has "heard" than, for example, an Indian translating a Sanskrit text for a young Californian audience already influenced by Oriental spiritualities. A modern Roman Catholic would find it much easier today than a few decades ago to use the word "grace" to express an at least analogous conception found in some Asian religions. There is a peculiar dynamism, due to the intermingling of cultures, in the movement from "proper" to common nouns.

Syncretism and eclecticism are often cultural forms that create the foundations for particular comparative philosophies.[37] Here comparative philosophy is an expression of the factual praxis of the human situation, and this seems to be precisely the case today, when a new philosophical *theoreia* is emerging from the praxis of our pluralistic situation.[38] We feel the need for comparative philosophy of religion to the same degree that actual religions have already made contact, been mutually influenced, attracted, rejected, and so on. What I am saying is that comparative studies have to be historically situated and temporally understood.

Now, a translation by its very nature entails evaluation and implies a certain comparison in the mind and heart of the translator, and not only because he is conditioned by what he understands, but because the words he chooses to express his understanding imply an evaluation. However, this cannot be properly called comparative philosophy or comparative religion because it does not offer explicit comparison but tries to integrate an expression of a more or less partial view of the world with another, as represented by the language into which the translation is made.[39] The last section of this chapter develops the idea that the cross-cultural language needed for comparative philosophy of religion is a *dialogal* one.

Dialogal Philosophy

Having briefly outlined some problems in the form of the above aporias, I would now like to suggest a possible way to overcome these antinomies by recovering the original sense of philosophy and overcoming the modern Western—post-Cartesian—conception of philosophy as an exclusively rational effort at avoiding error in the autonomous functioning of reason.[40]

Philosophy has, since the beginning of the use of this name, operated by comparisons. Originally it was not an isolated reflection around a *poêle*, as with Descartes,

---

[37] Cf. R. Panikkar, "Some Notes on Syncretism and Eclecticism Related to the Growth of Human Consciousness," in B. A. Pearson, ed., *Religious Syncretism in Antiquity: Essays in Conversation with Geo Widengren* (Missoula, MT: Scholars Press, 1975), 47–62.

[38] "Tantum scit homo, quantum operator," often quoted in the Renaissance and attributed to St. Francis of Assisi. Was not in fact St. Francis's message that we can understand the gospel only in as much as we put it into practice?

[39] Unfortunately, it is not within the scope of this chapter to pursue this point further.

[40] Cf. my chapter "Necesidad de una nueva orientación de la filosofía India," in *Misterio y Revelación* (Madrid: Marova, 1971), 51–82.

but, as with Socrates, a lively exchange in an agora. It was not about the segregation of an "I" over against a "non-I" but the result of an exchange between many "I's," and many "thous." When the individual reflects in contemplative solitude upon Man's total situation in the universe, he finds that others have also tried to do the same. Thus Man becomes aware that "his" ideas do not come to him out of nowhere, but are shaped by the environment in which he lives. This awareness of surrounding ideas is the basis of his stance and contribution.

Thus, Aristotle's classical works can be called the first history of philosophy in the Western world. Aristotle tried to weigh and judge what went before him, and on that basis offered his own views. But his work cannot be called comparative philosophy in the modern sense of the term that we are developing here. Before him, Plato offered us an initial attempt at a more polycentric philosophizing—in spite of the towering figure of Socrates—in which each philosophical view has its own representatives: one philosophizes by means of dialogue.

The dialogues of the Upaniṣad would be another example of an incipient dialogal philosophy. In fact, each thinker confronts what he assumes are generally held views with his own convictions. The philosopher weighs his insights over against the context that makes them comprehensible and, in this way, compares his own worldview with those of others. In order to demonstrate the convincing power of his insights, he needs to make himself understood. This he achieves explicitly or implicitly by situating his discourse in a framework given by the opinions of others. Every philosophy entails an explicit or implicit dialogue with the world of Man.

However, in the present-day situation there is another factor. The two disciplines, comparative philosophy and especially comparative philosophy of religion, are not only born from the old universal desire to understand; they also have a complementary, even a contrary, origin. In fact, they begin by suspecting that it might not be possible to understand foreign cultures and religions without deforming, or at least compromising, them, and they question whether one can understand without reducing the "phenomenon to be understood" to our own patterns of understanding. This is the sincere query of a postcolonialist era, which, inasmuch as it has overcome colonialism, consequently stands against the deleterious results of monistic ideologies: one God, one church, one empire, one economic order, one economic world government, one reason—in brief, exclusivism.

The desire to understand foreign cultural constructs, whether philosophical or religious, in their own terms is very much alive today, and there is a widely felt need for a justification of pluralism that aims to overcome unconnected plurality without, however, falling into undifferentiated unity.[41]

To be sure, the old approaches, when they were genuine, always tried to be fair to the "adversary," the *pūrvapakṣin*, the "opponent." But, by and large, it was a double monologue in which each party sincerely attempted to work out what the other

[41] Cf. R. Panikkar, "The Myth of Pluralism: The Tower of Babel—A Meditation on Non-Violence," *Cross Currents* 29, no. 2 (*Panikkar in Santa Barbara*; Summer 1979): 197–230; now in *Pluralism and Interculturality* (*Opera Omnia*, VI.1).

meant. Ultimately, however, the process was aimed at convincing, that is defeating, the other who was usually judged in absentia. It was a deadly game of domination by comparison. In present-day dynamism, behind so-called comparative philosophy, there is, I suspect, not so much a desire for comparison as the need for dialogue. In other words, it is not so much a desire to understand *what* the other says (*aliud*) as *who* the other is (*alius*): it is not a new idea to be incorporated or rejected but a new ideal, a new perspective to consider. What is at stake is not what I think about the other, but whether I can also grasp what the other thinks about himself. It is obvious that this task cannot be performed in isolation, for we need the other not as other (*aliud*), but as self (even as another self: *alius*). *Brahmavidyā* becomes *ātmavidyā*.

This is a constitutively dialogal philosophy since the comparison is not from one side only, that is, from the point of view of one philosophy or philosopher, but is a multivoiced philosophy in which the different problems are allowed to express themselves according to their own categories, contexts, and self-understanding.[42]

From the foregoing it should be clear that I am not referring to the multiperspectivism of a democratic situation in which we have several perspectives favoring several options of *one* and *the same* question. Rather, I am referring to dialogue among the perspectives themselves that already diversify the very problem. "Democracy" works when we all accept the same myth, which presents the same goals as evident, and we only diverge in regard to the means to reach them.

This leads me to suggest a hypothesis derived from an analysis of the situation from the viewpoint of the sociology of knowledge. That attitude that renounces the total comprehension of a foreign element—philosophy or religion—is brought about by a predominantly *functional* thinking as opposed to a *substantial* thinking.[43] In other words, it is born of a predominantly scientific mentality that aims to discover the functioning of the elements under study rather than their nature. The impact of the natural sciences here is evident: we can operate with matter, force, energy, acceleration, and the like, without needing to know exactly what they are. Similarly we may want to functionally "comprehend" the inner dynamism of *vedānta*

---

[42] I recall how my friendship with the late Benjamin Nelson, founder of the Society for the Study of Comparative Civilizations, reached a deeper level than mere academic collegiality. He sent me list of twenty-five Latin words supposed to be the most fundamental basic notions of classical Latinity and wanted the Sanskrit equivalents. His idea was to have some tangible and solid basis for comparative civilizations. I replied that I would never do this, since it appeared to me to be an unconscious remnant of intellectual colonialism. I was prepared, however, to send him what I thought were the twenty-five most important Sanskrit words. Then when we had other similar lists we could begin to analyze the basic symbols of different civilizations. Nelson was delighted with the idea and said that this was what he had ultimately meant.

[43] Cf. my chapter "Pensar substantivo y pensar funcional," in *Ontonomía de la Ciencia*, 101–7. Also the two volumes of H. Rombach, *Substanz, System, Struktur* (Munich; Alber, 1965), followed by his more recent work, *Strukturontologie: Eine Phänomenologie der Freiheit* (Munich: Alber, 1971).

philosophy without really understanding *what* its followers say.[44] It is enough to apprehend *how* and *why* they say it.

Yet, from the moment that there are two philosophical or religious·systems side by side, and assuming that I have a relatively complete, although independent, understanding of both, I must move beyond the functional. System A is convincing under option *a*. System B is also coherent under a set of principles *b*. I may also concede that there is no logical compulsion, or one of any other sort, to choose the set of principles *a* over *b*. Assuming that being is formed by the incidence of existence upon essence, and that act and potency are the constitutive elements of being, I may "understand" the "truth" and coherence of Thomism. Assuming that being is univocal and that existence is real being, I may discover the "truth" and coherence of Scotism. But I will probably feel more sympathy for one system than for the other, and I cannot remain content with a double view in my own vision of the world. I may suspend my judgment until more light is shed on the question, as in the case of the corpuscular and wavelength theories of physics, but ultimately I will not be able to compare the two systems, nor understand them fully.

Now, philosophy has an inbuilt claim to understand the nature of things to the deepest possible level; it is not satisfied with exclusively scientific, behavioral explanations. This claim distinguishes it from the natural sciences and is, at once, its strength and its weakness. This means that philosophy can never cease investigating ever further. In other words, we cannot renounce or ignore the ultimate urge that calls comparative philosophy and comparative religion into existence.

This is the reason why we cannot be satisfied with a mere description of philosophies. Philosophy's intrinsic urge to know transcends comparative philosophy. In other words we do not compare "philosophies" (or religions, for that matter). What we try to do is to grow together, to interact, to understand each other, and above all, to learn from one another. This is why I prefer to speak of dialogal philosophy, or *imparative philosophy*, if I may. This neologism suggests that:

1. We should first and foremost be aware that all religions or philosophies regard themselves as unique and often as ultimate. Thus we cannot justifiably compare— that is, being together (*com*) on an equal (*par*) footing—that which purports to be unique and incomparable.[45]

2. We may instead *imparare*, that is, learn by being ready to undergo the different experiences of other peoples, philosophies, and religions.[46]

---

[44] Cf. R. Panikkar, "Verstehen als Überzeugtsein," in H. G. Gadamer and P. Vogler, eds., *Neue Anthropologie*, vol. 7. *Philosophische Anthropologie* (Stuttgart: Georg Thieme, 1975), 132–67.

[45] From the Latin *comparare* (*comparo*), to match, pair (*par* = equal), to couple together. Cf. also the Latin word *compar*, from *com-par*—that is, reciprocally alike. To compare implies to correspond, to restore. Cf. the opposite disparity, to disparage and parity (*paritas*) in the sense of distributive justice (*suum quique*).

[46] *Imparare* is a nonclassical Latin verb *in-parare*. *Parare* (*paro*) = to prepare, furnish, provide. *Comparare* has the same sense of making things ready, thus to arrange. *Paratus*

3. This learning is reflective and critical because it takes into account the cumulative human experience up to the present time, thus maintaining an openness and provisionality for the time being, namely, our being in time.

Imparative philosophy would thus be that philosophical attitude that is, first of all, convinced that we cannot avoid taking a stand when we philosophize; that this stance is not only relative to the time and space from where we start, but that such subjection also makes it relative to similar enterprises undertaken from different diachronical and diatopical vantage points.

Put another way, imparative philosophy does not pretend to possess a fulcrum outside time and space that acts as support from which to scrutinize (compare) different human philosophical constructs, but rather, the fact of starting from the particular standpoint of any one given philosophy takes the following into account:

• It is critically aware of the contingency of its own assumptions and the unavoidable necessity of resting on both limited and still unexamined presuppositions. We are not the only source of (self)-understanding.

At this point I should make a fundamental distinction between "supposition" and "presupposition." Suppositions are the conscious axioms that I set in order to study any one given subject. I assume them—that is, I place them at the basis of my thinking. The presupposition, on the other hand, is unconscious. I presuppose them, that is, they are underneath my constructions, at their basis (supposition-*subponere*); they are formed "before" my examination, as it were, and before my eyes, so that they allow me to examine and see where I stand (*prae-suppositio*). Indeed, once I have become aware of a presupposition, I can choose either to accept it, in which case it becomes a supposition, or to reject it, in which case I will have to change my earlier standpoint. In other words: reflection transforms presuppositions into suppositions. In this sense imparative philosophy is critically aware of the plausible pluralism of suppositions and the necessity of always resting on as yet unexamined presuppositions.

By definition, therefore, I am not aware of my presuppositions and take them so much for granted that I neither see them nor detect that they could possibly be

---

sum (I am ready, available). We may note that there is the *par* (*paris*) = equal, from which comes the *comparare* of comparative religion; and the *paro* (*parare*) = to set, to put, from which the *imparare* of imparative religion is derived. The verb is alive in modern Italian with the meaning of learning, i.e., to prepare oneself with study or praxis. The neologism also hints at the Greek *peirō* = to pierce, penetrate, break through, drive right through or across, traverse. *Peirō*, to pierce, run through, and *peiraō* = to attempt, endeavor, try to do, test, experience. Imparative religion would be a sort of coupling together of the different experiences of humankind by learning, i.e., passing through equivalent processes in order to come to a certain integrative wisdom. The *imparare* of imparative religion suggests the opposite of the *disantepare* of medieval Latin, from which the Spanish *desamparo*, dereliction, despair, comes. Imparative religion does not formally compare, but brings together, in order to deeply penetrate appearances and overcome the dispersion and despair of the prima facie antagonistic tendencies and tenets.

problematic. It is the other who, although unaware of his own presuppositions, causes me to see mine by questioning a presupposition he cannot accept, and vice versa. Thus, the presupposition belongs to the order of myth. As I discover the other's myth he may feel as uncomfortable as I do when my myth is uncovered.

• It is constitutively ready to question its most basic foundations, if this is requested by any other philosophical school. Nothing is nonnegotiable.

• It makes the search for the primordial ground of philosophizing (understanding) its first thematic concern.

• It tries, furthermore, to form its philosophical view of reality by systematically taking into account the universal range of Man's experience inasmuch as this is possible in any concrete situation.

• It is open to a dialogal dialogue with other philosophical or religious views, and not only to dialectical confrontation or rational dialogue.

This last point offers a passage from imparative philosophy to what I call *dialogal philosophy*.[47] Philosophy has largely been the work of single individuals or, at best, differentiated schools. Imparative philosophy has three basic rules:

1. To have the internal disposition to listen and learn, with all that this entails.
2. To try to speak a language that has prospects of being understandable outside its own formal enclosure. This might necessitate the use of metaphor, different symbolic forms, algebra, myth, and so on.
3. Language must be capable of revealing the *truth* of the respective philosophies and not only of expressing their formal *correctness*. And again, this last point leads us above and beyond imparative philosophy toward the above-mentioned dialogal philosophy.

Dialogal philosophy is constitutively open and processual. It is in dialogue itself that the way is paved for eliminating misunderstandings and where criticism and, eventually, mutual fecundation may take place. It is within the same dialogue that its own rules and criteria are elaborated. Philosophy, not only de facto but also de jure, is pluralistic. Philosophical pluralism does not undermine the truth-content of any philosophy, but only acknowledges the itinerant and finite condition of Man and his philosophy.

Dialogal philosophy considers dialogue not only a method but also an essential part of the subject matter, that is, of the object under investigation. Dialogal philosophy does not only study being, or whatever it is in each case, but is well aware that being, or whatever it is in each case, also includes your perspectives on the matter, even if they do not coincide with mine.

---

[47] Cf. M. Buber, *Das dialogische Prinzip* (Heidelberg: Lambert Schneider, 1962); and F. Ebner, *Fragmente, Aufsätze, Aphorismen* (Munich: Kosel, 1963), vol. 1, along with the study by B. Casper, *Das dialogische Denken* (Freiburg: Herder, 1967). Cf. also D. K. Swearer, *Dialogue: The Key to Understanding Other Religions* (Philadelphia: Westminster Press, 1977).

Now, in order to encompass not only my vision, say, of the *Uccedāvada* or of the *Vedānta*, but their vision, I must understand them as they understand themselves. This will not prevent me from criticizing those views, at a second moment, if need be. But the first moment is paramount. In scholastic vocabulary the first moment is constituted by studying not only the material-object of the other philosophy—or religion—but also its formal-object thematically, that is, the very angle or perspective under which the other philosophy—or religion—views the very problem. Only then, after a profound union from within has been reached, can we, at a second moment, find inadequacy or fault with that particular perspective.

When philosophical speculation moves within one cultural area, even if it has wide differences, like the interpretations and commentaries within—for example, the Mediterranean or the Indian worlds—it generally takes the first moment for granted and stresses the critique of the second moment. At most, the gap to bridge here is a diachronic one. History of philosophy becomes philosophy.

But comparative philosophy on a global scale cannot be reduced to diachronical hermeneutics. Philosophy here implies a new hermeneutics that I have called *diatopical*, and it becomes a collective and dialogal enterprise. It does not deal exclusively with our own problems and our perspectives, but also attempts to integrate the ways in which others are dealing with their corresponding issues, starting from a *topos*, a locus that does not need to have connection with our own.[48]

Two considerations are appropriate at this point. The first is by way of example, and the second is a methodological commentary.

Worship is certainly a religious concept. It is an English word, and so any philosophical analysis will have to begin by the study of those phenomena which are, more or less, referred to by this word. Early in the investigation it is easy to see that the English word is much too broad to express the diversity of Christian concepts: in Greek, *latreia*, *eusebeia*, and so on; or in Latin, *cultus*, *adoratio*, *sacrificium*, *oratio*, and so on. Each of these words has different connotations. But if we now go on to *li*, *pūjā*, *yajña*, *bhajana*, we find a whole world of differences and associations.

The question arises: Must we expand the concept of worship to convey all the other meanings, or do we introduce new words? Are we sure that we share the same or even analogous meanings when using these words? Because the real issue is not so much to know what a Christian, a Buddhist, a humanist, or an atheist understands by "worship" but to integrate these very understandings, so that we may use words in a meaningful way.

This leads us to the methodological comment. The content of dialogal philosophy is twofold. On the one hand there are the things themselves, the problems, the facts, in all their complexity—in short, the object, the spectacle, as I see it. On the other hand, however, the content also includes the other thinker, his view, seeing, understanding—in short, the subject, the spectator, as he sees himself. Indeed, there is

---

[48] Cf. R. Panikkar, *Myth, Faith, and Hermeneutics* (New York: Paulist Press, 1979), where this concept is further discussed.

nothing new in trying to become aware of my own relativity and my limited perspective as a particular spectator. The novelty lies in the fact that dialogal philosophy wants to understand the *other* understander, the other fellow being qua source of understanding, of self-understanding and independent understanding.

Until we became aware of the diatopical situation of humankind, the other's independent understanding was hardly visible. The other was an illiterate, a primitive, someone underdeveloped (or developing). The other was a *mleccha*, a *goim*, a *kafir*, a *barbarian*, a *gentile*, a *pagan*, a *nonbeliever*. His only salvation was conversion to "our" way of living, thinking, behaving, believing. It is only when, without falling into agnostic relativism, the radical relativity of all human perspective dawns upon us, that the problem of the other appears as another problem and not just another's problem or another aspect of our problem.

To sum up, the present-day interest in comparative studies has only been possible because of the impact of the natural sciences on other fields of knowledge. This impact is not only sociological and pragmatic but also epistemological: we must be content with knowing *how* systems behave, even if they are not scientific systems, but rather facts of nature or of human culture.

Unlike sciences, which have an objective criterion of measurability, comparative philosophy in general and comparative philosophy of religion in particular discover that one cannot assume a universally accepted *metron* or criterion for comparison.

We then have the dilemma of either accepting an unrelated plurality of philosophies of religion, renouncing a really philosophical understanding of the ultimate human problem, or envisaging the possibility of a dialogal philosophy that was probably already surmised by the master of Alexandria when he described the philosophical enterprise as wisdom that constitutively searches itself.

The hope of our times lies in the fact that, theoretically, nobody is excluded in this search, because in this "kingdom" there is no discrimination between theists and atheists, Hindus and Christians, animists and Marxists, Buddhists and Bantus.

17

THE AMBIGUITY OF THE SCIENCE OF COMPARATIVE RELIGIONS

Noēma and Pisteuma

The Science of Comparative Religions

Is "comparative religion" at all possible? The question is pregnant with practical and ethical consequences. If we answer negatively, the temptation of religious apartheid is tremendous. Each one of us should then stick to our own religion with the danger of leaving the way open to the victory of the strongest or the most unscrupulous. In a word, we would again open the door to another war of religions. History is full of religious conflicts that are partly responsible for the low prestige of religion in a great part of the modern world.

If the answer is positive, we will have to struggle again to find an impartial platform from which to compare religions. Can we find such a neutral stance outside religions, when these claim to offer precisely the right standpoint from which to see reality? Would a dogmatic and fundamentalist *laicism* be the only neutral judge, then? We are reminded of Solomon's famous judgment. Is that the only solution?

I should immediately add that my remarks in no way intend to denigrate this new science of religions, which I myself have cultivated, and which has played an invaluable role in helping to further the knowledge of religions and in dispelling misinformation and fanaticism. My critique is not criticism. On the contrary I would like to improve the importance of comparative religions by preventing one possible pitfall.

The topic I intend to address is prompted by the self-description of *Vidyajyoti: Journal of Theological Reflection* from Delhi.[1] It is a reflection on the mystery of our human approach to that ever-elusive symbol that we call *theos*.

Science Is More Than Rational Discourse

As is well known, modern phenomenology began with the noble *intention* of solving such issues by helping us overcome a biased approach to *vital* problems,

---

[1] *Vidya-jyoti* ("knowledge of the luminaries, heavenly bodies, stars; astrology, astronomy"), see Ò. Pujol, ed., *Diccionari Sànscrit-Català* (Barcelona: Enciclopèdia Catalana, 2005), 358.

making us aware of our underlying prejudices and overcoming, for instance, assumptions such as: the external world is real, our knowledge objective, our perspective sufficient, our religion the best, and the like.

Indeed, the phenomenon of phenomenology is not the Greek *phainomenon* as mere appearance, but the pure "essence" that appears to our consciousness after the purification of the "eidetical reduction." The assumption here is the *belief* that pure consciousness reveals to us the *essence* (of beings), whereby the essence is the *real* appearance in the field of our consciousness—as Husserl explicitly states in the introduction to the first part of his *Ideen*. Phenomenology of religion would then be that science that describes the pure essence of religion disregarding other concomitant factors (useful, objective, good, etc.). We can certainly compare essences according to universally accepted rational methods, although this acceptance already implies the more or less conscious acceptance of a common *mythos*. But religions are more than pure essences—leaving aside the idealistic background of all our phenomenological analyses, for now.

Furthermore, is there not a qualitative leap from essence to being—and to existence? Of course, our ultimate referent is our consciousness, and any effort to reach pure transcendence has to fall back on *our* consciousness—on the consciousness we have of it. In academic language, it is the *intentionality* of consciousness. That is to say, even our consciousness of transcendence is only immanent to our consciousness. I affirm that we can be aware of transcendence in an analogous way as we can be conscious of what we cannot understand. We cannot understand what for us is incomprehensible, but we can be aware that we do not understand it. And here lies the challenge to rationality. Our consciousness is our last resort. Even if we speak of the unconscious and the transcendent we need to be aware of these phenomena, and this awareness does not imply rational understanding. It would be uncritical reductionism to limit reality, as well as truth, to rational evidence. Not even certainty is reducible to rational certainty—as even Descartes could not brush away the possible existence of a *daimon* that could entice him into error were it not for the existence of a just God who would not allow such a fraud.

I will not pursue this basic problem further, but I felt the need to insert this paragraph in order to elaborate on the still widely spread *belief* that pure science—in our case, the phenomenology of religions—is neutral and unbiased.

Coming to our point, if by religion we understand a rational system of more or less doctrinal problems, I could be inclined to answer positively to the question of whether the "science of comparative religions" is at all possible. In that case, rationality is the ultimate criterion. Doctrines should be rational, otherwise they are not doctrines. We should nevertheless not forget the hidden vicious circle of the very question, namely that of using our mind to inquire into the *possibility* of any such thought—of our own mind—as if the possibility of thinking were identical to the possibility of being—Parmenides. Rejecting such a postulate does not amount to falling into irrationality. Only dialectical thinking identifies what is nonrational with irrationality. But our field of awareness is wider than that of rationality. We are aware of many things and events that we cannot comprehend. A certain type of "monotheistic rationalism" (still very widespread) entails a trick that needs to be revealed: it displaces the rational comprehension of everything to an infinite mind: we cannot understand everything, but we postulate an infinite, rational mind that can, because everything that really is must be understandable—Parmenides again! But this is already a nonrational extrapolation prompted by an underlying rationalism that dares to impose the same postulate even on the ultimate mystery. God does not always need to be the transcendent recipient of all our shortcomings. We are undoubtedly rational, but not only rational, and to define Man as a "rational animal" (besides being a biased translation of a sentence by Aristotle [sic]) is again a vicious circle, defined by our own rational mind. Aristotle textually says that Man is that living being (zōon) in which the logos transits, which is not exactly the same as the usually accepted definition.

We can surely compare ideas, but religion is more than ideology. Śaṅkara in the third book of his commentary to the Brahma-sūtra already said that in order to compare two ideas we need to find a common point of view first. Yet religions claim to offer us a proper and ultimate worldview. Who decides in case of conflict? It all depends on what we understand by "reason" and, in the last instance, by "philosophy," which undergirds all our reflections. Yet reason cannot enthrone itself as the ultimate criterion precisely because this same reason does not accept anything superior to itself. Even traditionally, science (jñāna, gnōsis, knowledge) is more than rational discourse, and philosophy more—not less—than "love of wisdom"; it is also the "wisdom of love." The divorce between knowledge and love is a fundamental weakness—a capital sin—of modern civilization: "amor ipse intellectus est," wrote William of St. Thierry in the twelfth century, expressing an idea of Gregory the Great's († 604) already suggested by Gregory of Nyssa († 395). This was a common opinion up to the Renaissance, even in the West. Love without knowledge is blind, when not mere sentimentalism; knowledge without love is unaware of reality, when not sheer calculation. The consequences are far reaching, but I propose to unfold only one single issue of this complex question.

Religion Transcends Reason

The word "ambiguity" in the title of this chapter does not merely refer to a theoretical indecision about the meaning of a word—which we call ambiguous. The Latin ambigere also implies a practical perplexity (from agere, "to act"). Our question is an existential one, and it is pregnant with the practical problems of peace and human conviviality. The modern world cannot ignore the most important anthropological question about what the term "religion" implies, as if it were a secondary issue concerning a discipline called "religion" identified with a particular "confession" of a more or less compact organization—or even confuse religion with (religious) doctrines.

I should insert an a priori methodological query here. What does it mean to say that "the science of comparative religion is not possible"? That it is not logically possible? Then we would be comparing logical (rational) doctrines, not religions. Do we mean the possibility of *thinking* with our mind or the possibility of *being* in reality? Are we not—again—uncritical followers of Parmenides, as the West tends to be? Does logical possibility cover the entire field of philosophy? Is reality obliged to obey our ways of thinking? Is reason our only guide? Are we not at least equally led by our love, ideals, ambitions, pleasures ... ? This does not displace reason from its legitimate power of veto, nor exonerate us from our responsibility of cultivating a pure heart. On the contrary, it increases our responsibility because being free we should not allow hate, envy, and other negative urges to dominate us. Let us recall that the word *dharma*, which is rightly translated as *religion*, implies primarily holding things in harmony and union (*dharayati iti dharma*) as much as right, duty, and ethics. It is highly significant that the word *religion*, which has at least a similar etymology (*religare*), has almost lost its original meaning: that which *links* us with all of reality, and has been reduced to mean only a special link with transcendence.

I have already said that rationality is not the only criterion for truth. May not reality surpass all our understanding? We are not the masters of reality. If we apply an exclusively dialectical pattern of thinking in our approach to reality, the dilemma stands. Either the theoretical possibility of thinking implies that of being, or the impossibility of thinking does not carry with it that of being. Yet, if we opt for the second horn of the dilemma we do not necessarily fall into an irrational notion of religion, but rather recognize that religion is above reason—not contrary to it—because we are more—not less—than exclusively rational beings. We have already said that the nonrational is not the same as the irrational. The dilemma is not between the rational and the irrational, but between truth—the real—and the unreal. A square circle is not a true concept; it cannot and does not exist because it cannot be thought, but reality is not reducible to concepts.

Coming to our case, asserting that the field of religion transcends reason does not mean that it is irrational. The irrational is not a logically possible concept, but the logically possible does not cover the entire field of reality—as a symbol of *that* of which we are aware in one way or another. In other words, onto-*logy* is not coextensive with the ontic, assuming *being* (ōn) to be synonymous with reality—a formidable question that I just mention, but leave untouched.

To those theologians who would retort that "In the beginning (*archē, agre*, as the Vedas say), was the *logos* [*vāc*]," and that the word is word if it has an intelligible meaning, I would point out that the sentence affirms that the *logos* was *in* the beginning, but it does not assert that the *logos* was *the* beginning. Furthermore, *logos, vāc*, means *word* and not exclusively reason.

In brief, to affirm that something is not logically possible is not the same as to affirm that it is not real. To recognize something as nonrational does not mean that it is irrational. The principle of noncontradiction covers our rational "dictions," but to identify rationality with reality is a gratuitous postulate. It would even be a logically unwarranted extrapolation to extend rational intelligibility to reality, as I have tried to explain elsewhere.

This example proves that we require a new method of cross-cultural studies, which have generally fallen into another methodological error: that of approaching a problem exclusively with the *tools* from only one side (of a single culture)—or, what is worse, of absolutizing our ways of thinking by assuming that they are truly universal; this is often the assumption of colonialism.

Pisteuma Is Deeper Than *Noēma*

Our problem reveals a still more elementary confusion. As I have said time and again, it is the confusion between the *noēma* (that which we understand) and the *pisteuma* (that in which we believe), the uncritical acceptance that we could apply or use reason outside its proper field. Here phenomenology helps. The "phenomenon" (of) religion appears very differently to the believer—in that religion—than to the outsider. The two do not "intend" the same phenomenon; it is not the same *pisteuma*. As I have profusely written elsewhere, we have three ontonomically interconnected doors that open us to reality: *senses, reason,* and *faith,* the latter understood as that peculiar awareness of the unknown—of our ignorance, of the infinite, of the mystery. We should not confuse *faith,* which is a human dimension, with *belief,* which is our interpretation of faith according to our categories.

Religions *have* doctrines, but they *are* not identical to doctrinal systems. Real religions are such because Man believes in them. Religion *is not* just a rational concept. Religion is primordially an existential concern and implies a personal belief, a *pisteuma.* The real "religion" of my neighbor is not the concept I have of it if I do not believe in it. Religion is a faith-construct and not just a system of beliefs. If I believe in one religion and my neighbor believes in another, then when we imagine we speak about religion, we do not speak about the same *thing.* The "phenomenology of religion" makes us realize that if the beliefs are different, we do not have the same phenomenon. Or more academically: the *noēma* is not the *pisteuma.*

We have all witnessed the tragic confusion between religion and ideology. The concept of religion does not disclose the essence of religion to us, unless we *reduce* religion to ideology. I do not need to stress the capital importance of this distinction, even for our times. Only the mystical experience of religion can free us from this confusion, and from fanaticism. Mysticism is neither just an accident nor the crown of religion; mysticism forms the very core of religion.

If "comparative religion" is loyal to its name, it must deal with "religion"—and religion is such if we believe in it; otherwise it is not authentic religion. No wonder, then, that we don't understand each other. We mean a thing in which the other does not believe, while belief belongs essentially to religion. We may converse about doctrines as conceptual constructs or even—under certain conditions—about symbolic systems, but not about two different issues without first clarifying the subject of our disagreement—and the etymology of this word (from *gratus*) is revealing. It reveals that our whole being is involved, including our feelings. I do not minimize the paramount importance of doctrinal discussions; I do not defend relativism, let alone irrationality. I only stress that because cultures and religions are intrinsically related, the proper method to study religions implies the knowledge of the different cultures that offer the patterns of intelligibility—and empathy—for the study of any particular religion—or groups of religions.

Here lies, in my opinion, the importance of the distinction between the *noēma*—which belongs to the rational field of consciousness—and the *pisteuma*—which appertains to the third degree of consciousness, the "third eye" of many traditions. As I have already said, reality becomes visible to us through the door of our senses, the door of our reason, and the door of our faith, as it is stated, under different names, by the wisdom of most human traditions. The rest is reductionism.

At this point I should stress that when I say that a religion is such when we believe in it, I do not imply a kind of blind and absolute belief in all the doctrinal tenets of that religion. Authentic belief is never apodictic; it is open to dialogue, improvement, correction, and even conversion. This is what makes dialogue important and delicate. In philosophical language, there is a transcendental relation between faith and belief. Faith expresses itself in beliefs. The mystical experience is aware of such a distinction. But this, again, is not my topic.

I may now revert to a cross-cultural commentary. The essence of a being—what a being really *is*—does not need to be identified by the "specific difference" that characterizes that particular entity—this is generally a feature of Western thinking.

This identification—between essence and specific difference—has had momentous consequences, and it is all the more important because the logical mistake is done unconsciously in *bona fide*.

It belongs to Western *mythos*. "God," for instance, as supreme Reality, is considered to be different from all the rest: the Transcendent, "das ganz Andere," the Pure, Unmixed . . . Brahman; on the other hand, as symbol of the same mystery, He is seen as the Immanent, the Indistinguishable, the Inseparable from anything, the indwelling *ātman*. Comparative religion cannot ignore different ways of thinking.

The problem is more profound than it may appear at first sight, because the question of truth is involved. If I believe in something it is because I believe it to be true—even if we do not need to absolutize our convictions. Faith is not rational evidence.

As I have elaborated elsewhere, if we reduce truth to a concept we expose ourselves to the danger of either falling into relativism—then there are different concepts of truth and one concept may sometimes be as legitimate as the other—or into absolutism if we recognize only one single concept. I maintain that truth is a symbol and not just a concept. A symbol is not a rationally intelligible object. Truth is not an object. A symbol is not objectifiable. Truth is not merely subjective either. A symbol is essentially relationship. It is the symbol that stands for an arguable connection between ourselves and what we hold to be real—whereby the word "arguable" stands for the Indo-European root *arg-* (clear, brilliant, white).[2] If something is not a symbol

---

[2] *Arjuna* (the white, pearly, brilliant, silvery [argentums]), as something that illumines by itself the human spirit (*svayamprakāśa*); see Pujol, *Diccionari Sànscrit-Català*, 89.

for me, I cannot call it a symbol. We do not refer to the same "thing" if we do not see that "symbol" as a symbol. The problem is paramount, and laden with consequences, and all too often ends up in the tragedy of historical misunderstandings about different religions. With the best of intentions we caricaturize each other and become prone to believe that we combat error, unaware that we are actually fighting against the truth—of the other. In other words, the "dialogue of religions" is not an appendix of human conviviality or something that only demands tolerance. It is a truly religious act and an art that demands the practice of all virtues. It would be a total misunderstanding of what I am trying to convey if dialogue were interpreted as sheer subjectivism. As Thomas Aquinas states, we do not possess truth, but we are possessed by it, and therefore we are not only respectful and intellectually humble, we are also aware of the other—who is also a source of understanding. Dialogue becomes, then, indispensable. A solipsistic truth is a contradiction in terms, since truth is relationship—"cum fundamento in re" (grounding ourselves in existing things) as Thomas would say. But this foundation is *in re*, not in us.

But the problem of tolerance is not only moral. "The truth shall make us free"—and freedom is not constrained by extrinsic rules. In the Trinity, to offer an extreme example, nobody commands. The equality is total, and the harmony, not imposed. A long time ago I timidly introduced the notion of "*imparative* religion" . . . we *learn* from each other.

There is no need to stress the importance and urgency of this problem for our times. Religious dialogue is about living religions that we believe give at least a certain meaning to our lives. Obviously, many names may be used to describe religion and, as I have written elsewhere, "religions" do not have the monopoly on religion.

We should not be rigid about our convictions. This leaves room for dialogue. But this dialogue is not dialectical—based on the principle of noncontradiction— but dialogical, or rather *dia-logal*, piercing the *logos* without denying it—as I have described several times.

18

PHILOSOPHY OF RELIGION IN THE CONTEMPORARY ENCOUNTER OF CULTURES

The rise of secularism at the expense of traditional religions is undoubtedly one of the most striking features of the second half of the twentieth century. Leaving aside the fact that secularism as well as many other movements of thought and life may also be considered religion another fact seems incontrovertible—namely, the new and increasing interest not only in religion but also in philosophy of religion or, as some would prefer to put it, in the scientific study of religion. The publications, new university departments, and even learned societies dedicated to this question are innumerable. All these facts seem to indicate the importance and the vitality of the problem. To sum it up with an overstatement: Philosophy today is afraid of being barren—nothing comes from philosophy; religion is equally afraid of being impotent—of losing its traditional hold on the peoples of the world more and more. It seems as if the symbiosis between them might raise hope of a new fecundity. This is our problem here.

To put a very complex problem in a nutshell: In one way or another, for good or bad, the religions of the world have been among the most important factors in shaping particular cultures. Now, for the first time in history, these cultures may no longer be determining and organizing human life for a particular group, but there arises a really worldwide way of life with room, indeed, for subcultures. The religious core of every culture stands for its most specific and intimate values. Only when the meeting of cultures reaches this religious core shall we have reached that depth where understanding will be lasting and where a mutual fertilization may take place. Intermarriage is not only the solution for problems of individuals of different races but also for different cultures and religions.

In this perspective, philosophy of religion is becoming something more than a discipline for specialists or a purely speculative branch of knowledge. As with theoretical physics and pure mathematics, which are undoubtedly theoretical sciences and yet the most relevant research fields for practical purposes, philosophy of religion can be considered of great practical importance. It can provide some clues, if not the main clue, for dispelling misunderstanding among men of different cultures and contribute effectively to the harmony between peoples. What is happening in Asia and Africa today is ultimately not a political or an economic problem, but a theological issue, and concerns the philosophy of religion.

The problem in itself is beset with difficulties, which explains the enormous growth of other related disciplines tackling the question from the outside. In order to offer a brief survey of the question, let us postpone for a few paragraphs the philosophical *aporia* and simply recall some of the other approaches.[1]

The Sociological Approach

Every religion is a bulwark zealously defended from within by its adherents. You will be told again and again that you cannot understand a religion from without. Sociology of religion tries to avoid this charge by considering the social aspect, studying either the social laws of a particular religion or the possible patterns of the dynamism and transformation of religions in our times.

The merits of the sociology of religion are great and obvious. The more or less splendid isolation in which religions and cultures used to live is no longer possible today. No Chinese Wall, Iron Curtain, or customs barrier can isolate or curtail ideas, even if personal freedom can, only too often, still be restrained. Contact teaches tolerance, if not for other reasons, from the sheer necessity of survival. Dialogue is unavoidable. Communication is bound to take place, and the sociology of religion shows the common pattern of those exchanges, as it shows the universality of sociological laws in the realm of religion.

It is a significant fact that until recently most works on sociology of religion were looked down upon with suspicion by orthodox believers, who were afraid of losing their self-identity the moment they discovered that very similar phenomena were also to be found in other religious traditions. Only Christians go to heaven, only Muslims adore the true God, only Hindus are tolerant, only Buddhists are humanist, only the so-called primitive religions are pure, only modern secularists

---

[1] Modern scholarship has begun to be aware of these problems. E. Benz, "Ideen zu einer Theologie der Religionsgeschichte," in *Akademie der Wissenschaften und der Literatur* (Wiesbaden-Mainz, 1960): 3–75; W. C. Smith, "Comparative Religion: Whither and Why?" in M. Eliade and J. M. Kitagawa, eds., *The History of Religions: Essays in Methodology* (Chicago: University of Chicago Press, 1959), 31–58; M. Eliade, "Methodological Remarks on the Study of Religious Symbolism," in Eliade and Kitagawa, *History of Religions*, 86–107; F. Heiler, "The History of Religions as a Preparation for the Co-operation of Religions," in Eliade and Kitagawa, *History of Religions*, 132–60; H. R. Schlette, *Die Religionen als Thema der Theologie*, Quæstiones disputatæ 22 (Freiburg i. Br.: Herder, 1964); J. H. Randall Jr., *The Meaning of Religion for Man* (New York: Harper & Row, 1968); J. Collins, *The Emergence of Philosophy of Religion* (New Haven, CT: Yale University Press, 1967), among others have been thinking along these lines. Our main purpose is not to give a survey of philosophy of religion in the last decade, but to formulate as briefly and clearly as possible one of the important problems facing this discipline today. The selective and very limited list offered throughout the chapter has to be understood as introductory information on the problem of the philosophy of religion. This said, everyone should be able to discover subsequent contributions and find their own way within the existing literature. With very few exceptions, the authors mentioned are all contemporary, and the publications belong to the last decade.

are honest and sincere, and so on and so on. For a long time, exclusiveness has been mistaken for uniqueness, and openness for syncretism.

It is the merit of sociology of religion to have given us a working pattern for the understanding of a fundamental aspect of religion. But even so, sociology of religion needs a guiding line that it has to receive from somewhere else. The most fruitful, but at the same time problematic, approach—if used as a general framework—is the evolutionist hypothesis, be it of a historical or an idealist type. Two issues arise immediately. One is the question of how to justify such a hypothesis; the second is the problem that, though this hypothesis may help us to understand better our own religious situation, it may not necessarily enable us to understand the particular religion we want to study.[2]

The Historical Integration

Another important contribution to the understanding of the role played by religion in the lives of the various peoples is history. We are beginning today to write a world history worthy of the name, in which the "others" are not merely mentioned in an appendix, and the particular national, racial, religious, or cultural bias is being overcome, at least in principle.

Concepts like "right or wrong, my country," "white supremacy," "racial superiority," "spirit of crusade," "the good and the bad cause," "the only true religion," and the like are no longer possible in our times. There are indeed still many authors showing blind spots and deep-rooted prejudices, but even these try to justify themselves by claiming to conform with universally valid principles or at least generally accepted views.

Not only is this trend spreading in the political and economic realm, but it is also evident in other manifestations of human culture, like history of philosophy or of religion and so on. Cross-cultural studies are found more and more often today in all realms of thought.

History of religion has become today an accepted term, but an ambiguity is present that is still the cause of tension among different schools. The ambiguity

---

[2] Names like E. Durkheim, *Les Formes élémentaires de la vie religieuse* (1912; Paris: 1937); E. Troeltsch, *Aufsätze zur Geistesgeschichte und Religionssoziologie* (Tübingen: J. C. B. Mohr, 1925); M. Weber, *Gesammelte Aufsätze zur Religionssoziologie*, 3 vols. (1920–1921; Tübingen: J. C. B. Mohr, 1974); and more recently G. Le Bras, *Études de sociologie religieuse*, 2 vols. (Paris: P. U. F., 1955–1956); J. Wach, *Sociology of Religion* (Chicago: University of Chicago Press, 1944); G. Mensching, *Soziologie der Religion* (Bonn: Ludwig Rohrscheid, 1947); R. Bellah, *The Sociological Study of Religion* (Boston: Beacon Press, 1966); T. Parsons, *Sociological Theory and Modern Society* (New York: Free Press, 1967), and others are to be mentioned here. A great number of specialized studies have appeared in recent times, like those of W. Stark, *The Sociology of Religion*, 2 vols. (London: Routledge & Kegan Paul, 1966–1967). Any survey concerning the sociology of religion will provide a bibliographical introduction. L. Schneider, *Religion, Culture and Society. A Reader in the Sociology of Religion* (New York: J. Wiley & Sons, 1964), has edited a reader in the sociology of religion, which, with many other similar works, gives an idea of this discipline.

consists in the fact that, on the one hand, it denotes the knowledge of the historical development of that peculiar cultural phenomenon that we call religion, and on the other hand, it stands for what in German is rendered as *Religionswissenschaft*, a discipline that embraces not only history but also an effort at comprehension, transcending mere historical explanation.

Nevertheless, history of religion is considered as one of the fundamental factors in shaping a new[3] or integral humanism,[4] and thus as a central discipline for the understanding of our present-day cultural situation.[5]

The Phenomenological Attempt

The sacred word today for a scientific and universal study of religion is phenomenology. It aims at giving an unbiased description of the phenomenon, thus overcoming all partisanship. All over the world the religious phenomenon—so the representatives of this trend say—shows the same structure and thus enables us to obtain a truly universal view of religion and its function in human life.

Perhaps the most important contributions in the field of science of religion today come from this way of thinking, which is a methodology rather than a school.

The phenomenological survey of the religions of the world today is far from being complete, but, broadly speaking, the map has been drawn and the terra incognita carefully circumscribed.

The greatest difficulty with this attempt lies in the fact that the so-called presuppositionless approach has proved impossible not only in practice but in theory. Further,

---

[3] Cf. M. Eliade, "History of Religions and a New Humanism," *History of Religions* 1, no. 1 (Summer 1961): 1–8 (introductory note in the new publication *History of Religions*, subtitled *An International Journal for Comparative Historical Studies*).

[4] Cf. A. Brelich, *Introduzione alla storia delle religioni* (Rome: Edizioni dell'Ateneo, 1966).

[5] A. J. Toynbee, writing either as a historian, as in *An Historian's Approach to Religion* (London: Oxford University Press, 1956), or as a student of the problem of Christianity, as in *Christianity among the Religions of the World* (New York: Scribner, 1957), as well as several journals, such as *History of Religions: An International Journal for Comparative Historical Studies* (University of Chicago, since 1961); *Numen: International Review for the History of Religions* (International Association for the History of Religion of Leiden, since 1954); *Studi e materiali di storia delle religioni* (Scuola di Studi storico-religiosi, University of Rome, since 1925); *Revue de l'histoire des religions* (Paris, since 1880); *Zeitschrift für Religions-und Geistesgeschichte*, Leiden, since 1948); *Journal of Religious Studies*, Japanese Association for Religious Studies, since 1955, which since 1995 also publishes *Religions East and West*, in English with extracts of Japanese studies); *Journal for the Scientific Study of Religions* (Philadelphia, since 1962); *Religion and Society* (Bengaluru, India, since 1953); and many others, that offer an introduction to the historical approach. There are today fairly good and detailed histories of religion, either in general or of particular aspects. The bibliography is almost interminable. H. Boas, *International Bibliography of the History of Religions* (Leiden: Brill, 1954–), has done useful work compiling a yearly bibliography for the history of religion.

how can the description of a phenomenon be sufficient for a thing that claims first of all to be a *noumen*? A chemical reagent only reacts in a chemical process, and even the latter has to be conveniently prepared. Is the phenomenological test fit to detect the core of the religious "fact"?

Students of the phenomenology of religion today are well aware of this situation and, recognizing its importance, do not claim that they have the tools for the total understanding of religion. Yet they do say that without phenomenology we would still either be using the a priori approaches to religion—which may foster one particular religion, but do not do justice to the whole of religion—or the more or less superficial descriptions of external features.[6]

The Psychological Study

In spite of its ancient roots, the psychological study of religion is a relatively new topic in our times. We have already mentioned William James. Neither an almost frozen and objectified psychology nor a mainly behaviorist and experimental psychology are the best basis for understanding the religious soul. While we have nowadays important contributions to the psychology of religion, the comprehension of the psychological structures of other cultures and religions is just beginning. Depth psychology and related studies are to be mentioned here. Carl Gustav Jung[7] offers an important starting point.[8]

---

[6] R. Panikkar, "The Internal Dialogue: The Insufficiency of the So-Called Phenomenological 'Epoché' in the Religious Encounter," *Religion and Society* (Bengaluru) 15, no. 3 (1968): 55–66. See also the second and revised edition of G. Van der Leeuw's famous book *Phänomenologie der Religion* (1933; Tübingen: J. C. B. Mohr, 1956). The posthumous English version of W. B. Kristensen's *The Meaning of Religion* (1953; The Hague: Martinus Nijhoff, 1960) appeared the same year as K. Goldammer, *Die Formenwelt des Religiösen* (Stuttgart: Alfred Kröner, 1960). F. Heiler's magnum opus, *Erscheinungsformen und Wesen der Religion* (Stuttgart: Kohlhammer) appeared in 1961, while the original French edition of M. Eliade's *Traité d'histoire des religions* (Paris: Payot) appeared in 1949. In 1969 there appeared a third and fully revised edition of G. Widengren's *Religionsphänomenologie* (Berlin: de Gruyter), first published in 1946. We may keep in mind that W. James's classic *The Varieties of Religious Experience: A Study in Human Nature* was published in 1902. These very brief references may help us to center the phenomenological problem. We should also mention J. A. Cuttat, "Phänomenologie und Begegnung der religionen," *Studia philosophica* 18 (Basel: Schwabe, 1958), 45–89, in this respect.

[7] See C. G. Jung, *Aion: Researches into the Phenomenology of the Self* (1969), in *Collected Works*, vol. 9, ed. R. F. C. Hull, Bollingen Series (Princeton, NJ: Princeton University Press, 1959), and also his *Psychology and Religion* (1938–1940), in *Collected Works*, vol. 11, 1970.

[8] From the point of view of psychoanalysis in a critical and modern context, see A. Vergote, *Psychologie religieuse*, C. Dessart, *Psychologie et sciences humaines* 13 (Bruxelles: 1966), offers a general introduction to religious psychology. From a more general psychological starting point, W. Pöll, *Religionspsychologie: Formen der religiösen Kenntnisnahme* (Munich: Kösel, 1965), among many others, has studied the growth and assimilation of

One of the most important factors for the growth of this discipline is the gradual appearance of religious texts, based on sources and starting from presuppositions other than those of the Western world. Those works not only serve the purpose they aim at but also are themselves firsthand material for the psychological understanding of religion. Nothing helps us more to understand another person than to experience how he focuses on a problem in which we, too, are vitally interested.[9]

The boundaries between psychology and anthropology, at least in one of the meanings of this term, are not fixed. The efforts to understand the religious soul by means of anthropological patterns disclosed in dreams, symbolisms, and so on prove very fruitful for the understanding of the primordial religious dimension of Man and thus help to form a better and more comprehensive idea of the human being.

One's anthropology largely depends on the type of man one is, or rather on the cultural pattern in which one lives.[10] In other words, in order to become critical of its own presuppositions, anthropology has to become philosophical anthropology. Thus, we land in the field of philosophy.

---

religious ideas. The German *Archiv für Religionspsychologie* (Göttingen: Vandenhoeck & Ruprecht) is a good source of information. H. Sunden, *Die Religionen und die Rollen* (Berlin: Töpelmann, 1966), enters new fields of research, etc.

[9] [Translator's note: In this sense, it is worth mentioning that the same year that Panikkar published this article (1969), transpersonal psychology had just seen the light with the publication of the *Journal of Transpersonal Psychology*. Abraham Maslow referred to it as the fourth power of psychology, since it aspires to go further than behaviorism, psychoanalysis, and humanist psychology itself, in the study of the highest human and spiritual potentials, as a science of the spirit that links its theories to diverse religious traditions and wisdoms—Hinduism, Buddhism, Zen, Sufism, Taoism, shamanism, Christian mysticism, Jewish kabbalah.... Its representatives, among many, include Roberto Assa-glioli, Viktor Frankl, Charles T. Tart, Stanislav Grof, Ken Wilber, Daniel Goleman, John Welwood.... See the collective works compiled by two of its originators, which may be considered founding documents: R. Walsh and F. Vaugan, eds., *Beyond Ego: Transpersonal Dimension in Psychology* (Los Angeles: Jeremy P. Tarcher, 1980); and *Paths beyond Ego: The Transpersonal Vision* (Los Angeles: Jeremy P. Tarcher, 1993).

[10] Important stages in the growth of mutual appreciation of religious values included the UNESCO General Assembly in New Delhi in 1956. At that assembly that the UNESCO Major Project on Mutual Appreciation of Cultural Values of the East and the West was launched. It was my privilege to have helped to make the project an exchange, on equal terms, of the spiritual and intellectual contributions of East and West, and thus to have prevented the predominance of Western contributions. Also, at the Pax Romana–UNESCO Conference in Manila in 1960, experts, who at the same time were believers belonging to the various traditions of the world, discussed their different perspectives. Many discovered to their amazement that almost everybody saw in his or her own religion the embodiment and the expression of the same religious and human values. See UNESCO, "Les grandes religions face au monde d'aujourd'hui," *Proceedings of the Manila Conference, Paris, 1960, Recherches et débats du Centre catholique des intellectuels français* 37 (Paris: Fayard, 1961), and the leaflet distributed at the Conference of Manila, 1960.

The Philosophical Problem

All the aforementioned approaches are valuable and important. They are all necessary for a comprehensive study of the subject and have their justification, but they do not fill the need for a strict philosophy of religion. And in fact, there are today many attempts at a philosophy of religion, plainly differentiated from all other disciplines. But philosophy in the second half of our century can no longer consist simply in reflecting on some supposedly given data. In other words, it cannot be a noncritical philosophy. Yet it seems to be the case that in this particular field philosophy has not yet overcome its crisis. No wonder, then, that many religious believers have turned their backs on philosophy and devoted themselves to phenomenology, history, sociology, and other branches of the science of religion.

Until very recently, with noteworthy exceptions, what was commonly circulating under the name of philosophy of religion were certain types of philosophical studies, which by their very nature could only be fitted into the concept of philosophy of religion with great difficulty. I find two reasons for this: a philosophical one and a religious one—or, in other words, one based on a reflection on fundamental principles, and one based on a methodological consideration.

Philosophical Reflection

What was generally called philosophy of religion was in fact *a* philosophy of *one* religion, that is, a philosophical reflection on a particular religion, considered as a model religion, from which one would extract, as it were, some categories, which were in turn postulated as universally valid and applied to other religions or to a hypothetical universal religion. In scientific language this is called an *extrapolation*. What has been considered valid and true in a particular cultural context is applied to other cultural situations, all too often without asking if those categories are also applicable in different fields. I am not saying that generalization and extrapolation should not be used. I am pointing out that such procedures need to be critically analyzed and the conditions for the validity of such extrapolations properly studied.

To be sure, the problem of finding a universally recognized basis is not new, and the approaches previously mentioned try to overcome the difficulty by finding a supracultural criterion. But the difficulty in the field of philosophy is much more basic. There is, at least theoretically, the possibility of finding a universal viewpoint in sociology, history, and so on that may allow us to have a guiding principle in the study of multicultural phenomena. But with philosophy it is somehow different, since by its very nature philosophy will not allow anything beyond or previous to or more fundamental and universal than philosophical principles. Here lies the problem.

As long as cultures lived in isolation, as long as the adherents of one religion were thinking that theirs was the only true religion, and were at most prepared to tolerate the others, as long as the typical mentality of the believer was a conviction of the absolute truth of his or her religion, a certain type of philosophy of religion was possible. It was a philosophical analysis of that particular religion, put forward as the paradigm of truth and of religion. The philosophy of one religion became philosophy of religion. The study of comparative religion was then the effort to find in other religious traditions structures analogous to those of one's own religion.

But this procedure is hardly possible today, even among simple believers. The intermingling is too widespread; the personal acquaintance with people of other religious traditions is a sociological fact almost all over the world. The average believer discovers, to his amazement at first and reassurance afterward, that other believers or nonbelievers are also good and sincere people and by no means worse than his own coreligionists. In a word, "the absolute character of religious data"[11] that the phenomenological thinker hoped to discover as a feature of the true believer does not hold any longer. Even the believer, and not only the historian or the scholar, is confronted with the pluralism of religions.

We need, then, a philosophy of religion that is the fruit of a philosophical reflection that emerges out of a philosophical knowledge of practically all religions.

How can we have a philosophy of religion valid for every religion without knowing the religions of the world or religion as such—if such a thing is possible? But how can we know religion or the religions of the world if this knowledge is dependent on the philosophy of religion we are looking for?

The long-standing attempt to avoid this difficulty is well known: there is a common human nature, there are universal values, there is a unique human reason and a fundamental law of thought, there is a Natural Law, and the like. Building on this basis one would want to construct a perennial philosophy or discover the essence of religion with universal validity. How precarious these attempts are becomes evident each time they have to go out of the boundaries in which they were forged. However this may be, two remarks have to be made here at the very outset: first, how do we know that there is a universal and common human nature? If we know a priori—that is, if we are able to have such a knowledge of the universality of human thought previous to any checking—such a knowledge implies a whole set of epistemological principles that are far from being universal, much less universally accepted. If we know a posteriori that there is such a common nature, experience should confirm in an almost unequivocal way that this nature is the basis of a truly human philosophical or religious unanimity, which cannot be said to be the case. Indeed there are strong arguments in favor of a common human nature: our sense experience, human language, certain basic logical laws, some fundamental anthropological characteristics, and so on. But these features hardly admit being the basis of a philosophy of religion, because the moment we begin to reflect upon those primordial features we begin to differ. We may agree that there is a human *nature*, precisely because it

---

[11] Cf. Kristensen, *Meaning of Religion*, 7.

is a raw datum, which cannot be said of a human *culture*. Philosophy, on the other hand, belongs to the cultural and not to the natural realm. From a common human nature to a common human philosophy, there is a big step indeed.

Having said this, the second remark is already in sight: taking for granted that there is such a thing as a common nature, how do we proceed further to a philosophy of religion valid for every religion? For, undoubtedly, only in the abstract is there such a thing as "religion" or "Man." How do we sift, as it were, the essentials from the accidents, or that which belongs to "religion" from that which constitutes only a particular embodiment? The problem here is rather subtle. How does this hypothetical human nature yield its "natural" religion? If we were to use the metaphor of the sieve, we would have to say that no purely religious residue will remain in our hands when trying to sort out religion in general from the several religions of the world. It is not as if religions were crystallizations, examples, or species of something finer and more fundamental than would be religion itself. In fact *religion in itself* does not exist. Nor does *natural religion* make any sense in this context because, whereas "nature" can be abstracted or postulated as a common principle, "religion" cannot. "Religion" cannot be abstracted or severed from the faith of its believer. It cannot be objectified. What the religious man believes of himself also belongs to religion. I may discover or postulate the notion of human nature—which is there independently of whether Man knows it or not—whereas I cannot do the same with the notion of religion, because the latter involves my conception and apprehension of it. My "religion" cannot be severed from my idea of it. The latter belongs essentially to my religion—whereas my idea of nature does not belong to the notion of nature.

This explains the inadequacy of those types of philosophy of religion which for the sake of universality and an impartial attitude separate out the genuine and specific religious contents of religions and deal with them as mere outward manifestations of the so-called religious soul. This may be a beginning of a good phenomenological study, but it is not the proper way to an authentic philosophy of religion. Since philosophy is also a hermeneutical process, it cannot bypass the golden rule of any hermeneutics: the interpretation of a datum must be such that it is at least acceptable to those who are involved in such a datum. Any interpretation of Christianity, for instance, must be such that those who profess themselves as Christians recognize themselves in the interpretation. A philosophy of religion cannot leave aside the faith of the religious people, which constitutes a fundamental element of religion. Unless science becomes another religion, the scientific study of religion cannot overlook what the several religious traditions—through their representatives—think of themselves. Having said this, we have already arrived at our second consideration of the present-day problems of a philosophy of religion.

Methodological Consideration

A philosophy of religion undoubtedly has to be authentic philosophy and not simply apologetics. It has to take into account the special subject matter of the philosophical investigation: religion, understood as the set of practices and beliefs that Man considers conducive to his ultimate goal.

I have been saying that the philosophical interpretation of religions has to integrate what religions think of themselves. This has to be done, not only out of human and scientific honesty, but also because the self-understanding of religious consciousness belongs essentially to the religious phenomenon.

This confronts modern philosophy of religion with an almost insurmountable difficulty. Reduced to its basic terms it comes to this: Any philosophy about religion will most probably be rejected by religion itself and thus will not be able to fulfill the condition of philosophy as hermeneutics.

This difficulty is present on two levels: (1) the level of philosophy of religion as a philosophical interpretation of a particular religion, and (2) the level of philosophy of religion in general. Let us consider this double aspect before trying to suggest in the next section a possible way out.

Philosophy and Religions

History of philosophy proves—though there may be some rare exceptions: we may suggest some types of Buddhism—that there have frequently been deep conflicts between philosophy and the religions of the world. Whatever the concrete cause might have been, the reason, in the last analysis, lies in the fact that philosophy and religion both seem to raise the same claim to ultimacy as constitutive of their very nature: philosophy is wisdom or science in the ultimate sense, or it is not philosophy at all. Religion contains its own justification or it ceases to be the path of salvation it claims to be. If philosophy of religion submits religion to the tribunal of philosophy and passes a judgment on it according to philosophical criteria, religion becomes automatically subservient to philosophy; a substitute of philosophy for the unphilosophical masses, it ceases to be ultimate and disappears as religion. If religion resists the philosophical analysis, on the other hand, the outcome is even worse, for in this case religion becomes simply the bulwark of obscurantism and the very symbol for fanaticism, justifying by this very refusal the attacks directed against it from outsiders. It collapses as a way of salvation for the thinking man.

How can there be a philosophy of religion accepted by religion itself and genuine philosophy at the same time? If philosophy is at the service of religion it ceases to be philosophy. If religion has to obey philosophy it is no longer religion.

Philosophy and Religion

If a particular religion shuns the philosophical approach—unless the independence of philosophy is tamed and converted into mere apologetics, which no genuine philosophy will ever agree to—the repugnance will a fortiori be greater toward a general conception of a truly universal philosophy of religion. Let us grant that we succeed in having such a philosophy. It may in this case be true philosophy, but will it be of religion as religion understands itself? First of all, religion in general, which would be the subject matter of such a philosophy of religion, is nowhere practiced as a living religion and consequently is not a living and concrete religion at all. There may well be a philosophical study of some patterns underlying religious life, but it will hardly be a real philosophy of religion so as to serve as an intelligible structure for religion as a living experience.

*

Is there any possible way to overcome such difficulties? Before an attempt to suggest some guidelines for the philosophy of religion in the second half of this century, let us sum up the demands of a philosophy of religion from the point of view of philosophy, relegating to the next section the exigencies of religion.

Philosophy today has to be a critical philosophy, as we have said, that is, a philosophy aware of its proper limits, of its assumptions—insofar as this is possible—and which considers both the subject as well as the object of the philosophizing. Further, it has to be ultimate in a sense that was not necessary until now, namely in a geographical or rather multicultural way. Until now the limits of the validity of a philosophy lay within a certain cultural area; now, if philosophy has to accept the challenge of our times, it cannot shun the exacting claim to a universality of global dimensions.

At the same time, precisely because of its critical awareness, philosophy seeks to be universal but not absolute. It is well aware that there are fundamental options, several possible perspectives, and perhaps even different patterns of intelligibility. All this amounts to saying that pluralism is also the fate of philosophy.

A philosophy of religion, in order really to be philosophy, has to enjoy the freedom of a free and ultimate inquiry, and it has to be limited by nothing else than by its own, self-acknowledged limitations; it cannot tolerate the imposition of any religious condition and cannot accept any guidance coming from without its own investigation.

All these requirements are not easy to fulfill, but there is no use in minimizing them. Better to confess that philosophy of religion is not possible at all than to make it cheap by explaining away real difficulties.[12]

---

[12] Among the recent works on philosophy of religion we may mention H. Dumery, *Philosophie de la religion*, 2 vols. (Paris: P.U.F., 1957), and Dumery, *Critique et religion: Problèmes de méthode en philosophie de la religion* (Paris: Societé d'Éditions d'Enseignement Supérieur, 1957); H. Lang, *Wesen und Wahrheit der Religion: Einführung in die Religionsphilosophie* (Munich: Max Hueber, 1957); and A. K. Reischauer, *The Nature and Truth of the Great Religions: Toward a Philosophy of Religion* (Tokyo: Tuttle 1966), just to cite different sources. A reader, like that of W. E. Arnett, *A Modern Reader in the Philosophy of Religion* (New York: Appleton Century Crofts, 1966), may be useful. Indeed a collective work like M. Jung, S. Nikhilananda, and H. W. Schneider, eds., *Relations among Religions*

The Religious Challenge

The only possible way I see for a true philosophy of religion, which both is really philosophy and does not destroy the very nature of religion, is to revert to the most basic and genuine meaning of philosophy *of* religion—not philosophy about religion (objective genitive), but philosophy of religion (subjective genitive), that is, that philosophy that is also religion, or in other words, the philosophical dimension of religion itself. If religion is more than a set of unreasoning practices and blind beliefs, if it is something embracing the existential human being in his confrontation with his final destiny—however this may be interpreted—it must also contain an intelligible element; it has to make room within itself for the reflective and truly philosophical awareness of the human condition as such. Philosophy in this sense would be the intellectual dimension of religion. Philosophy of religion would be the religion of philosophy.

On the other hand, if philosophy is to be more than just a dry and lifeless speculation about what a privileged individual's mind can discover, and if it is to be connected with human life, as it really is, it cannot be severed from religion, nor can it go its way simply ignoring or despising what religions have said through the prophets and substantiated through their believers. If philosophy is to be more than simple logical or analytical talk about given data it cannot bypass religious language, nor can it uncritically accept what religions say, but has to involve itself in a noble pursuit of clarifying the issues and opening new vistas.

The true tension between the two is not to be seen as that between two rivals: either philosophy or religion being ultimate, but as two elements of one and the same human endeavor: that of facing the ultimate concern of the human being.[13]

But this relation can no longer be an uncritical one; it can neither be taken for granted nor adopted as a compromise. It has to follow from the very analysis of religion and philosophy. It is here that the concept of ontonomy may prove again to be useful.[14]

The relationship between philosophy and religion can be envisaged in a threefold way.

Heteronomy would be the word for a dominion of one over the other on the ground that one is superior in such a way that it provides the laws according to which

---

Today: A Handbook of Policies and Principles (Leiden: E. J. Brill, 1963), offers an invaluable mine of information for understanding the other's point of view. Bibliographical references such as that of E. Benz and M. Nambara, eds., *Das Christentum und die nicht Christlichen Hochreligionen—Begegnung und Auseinandersetzung: Eine internationale Bibliographie* (Leiden: E. J. Brill, 1960), are also very valuable.

[13] Cf. Raimon Panikkar, "Necesidad de una nueva orientación de la filosofía India," in Panikkar, *Misterio y revelación* (Madrid: Marova, 1970), 51–83.

[14] Cf. R. Panikkar, "Le concept d'ontonomie," *Actes du XIe Congrès International de Philosophie: Bruxelles, 20–26 August 1953*, vol. 3 (Louvain: Nauwelaerts, 1953), 182–88; also in Panikkar, *Misterio y revelación*, 83–90.

the lower one has to behave. The history of religion as well as that of philosophy furnishes us with numerous examples of this attitude: philosophy as the servant of religion or religion as a type of popular and cheap philosophy for those who have not yet awakened to philosophical enlightenment. Needless to say, we cannot accept this position. To submit philosophy to religion amounts to destroying philosophy, to degrading it into a mercenary ideology at the service of some other power—even if it is called God. To submit religion to philosophy, on the other hand, means the death of true religion and its reduction to a mere translation into popular beliefs of philosophical speculation.

Autonomy is the second attitude, the comprehensible reaction to any imposition from outside, and the affirmation of their total independence and disconnection, ignoring that they, willy-nilly, have a common and equal concern. Ultimately, it would amount to a starvation of both: religion without philosophy is blind fanaticism, and philosophy without religion is sheer analysis of a corpse and not of a living man. The relation between the two is not merely a question of peace at the frontiers because there is only one territory.

Ontonomy is the concept expressing this peculiar relationship, which is neither one of dominance nor one of a rebellious independence. Both disciplines are inwardly connected, and their relation is an internal one, constitutive of their own natures; both are interrelated in such a way that the laws of the one have a repercussion on the other. Philosophy is neither a substitute for religion nor religion an excuse not to have a philosophy. Philosophy itself is a religious problem, and religion is also a philosophical inquiry.

This has been the most traditional and the deepest conception of philosophy at all times. In fact, philosophy did not grow under the protecting wing of religion, but as an integral part of it. The rupture took place at a much later stage, and specifically in the Western world it was due, on the one hand, to religion's having become fossilized and tied to a particular brand of philosophy, and on the other hand, to philosophy's claiming to be independent and equal when it had outgrown its subservient position. But both have always preserved this constitutive mutual reference: a religion without a more or less explicit philosophy would hardly be a religion, and a philosophy without concern with the religious problem of Man—whatever name may be given to it—would not be philosophy at all.

Now, whereas this attitude was originally spontaneous and natural it was also uncritical. The process of tension and mutual distrust between philosophy and religion has served to purify both, and this is one of the most important achievements of Man and of Western civilization in particular. The concept of philosophy of religion I am propounding suggests a new avenue of research reconciling once more these two pillars of every culture.

Now, this conception of philosophy and religion as two aspects of one and the same human quest for the ultimate meaning of life may solve the problem regarding the relationship between one particular philosophy and one particular religion. It may also justify philosophical pluralism insofar as it makes room for several philosophical interpretations of the religious dimension of Man as viewed by a particular religion. Or vice versa, we may be able to see how a particular philosophy can become the intellectual vehicle of more than one religion.

We may somehow be able to discover the religious core of a philosophy or the philosophical one of a religion, but in doing this we have not yet tackled the problem concerning the more universal philosophy of religion we are looking for as an expression of the human situation of our times.

Let us try to state the problem as briefly as possible (a) from a *philosophical* point of view, and (b) from a *religious* perspective.

The Philosophical Point of View

In order to have a philosophy of religion valid for a religious world other than that which has more or less inspired that particular philosophy, I shall have to understand the religion of the other believer. Now, how can I understand the other as he understands himself? To understand the other as other already represents a step in the right direction, but it is not enough. The other in fact does not understand himself as other but as self. This amounts to saying that unless I can understand the other as I understand myself there is going to be not only a gap but also a misunderstanding between us. But the other will have to do the same. That is, we shall have to meet in a self larger than our previous selves were before the encounter. All this implies a theory of understanding regarded as a growth in consciousness rather than as an assimilation of an object by a subject.

In other words, how can I, with my particular philosophy—that comes out of a particular philosophical experience and that is linked up with a particular religious tradition in the broadest sense—how can I, out of an experience that is at home in a particular context, interpret another religious and philosophical experience that emerges from a different insight? Am I not bound to always be biased, always considering my own religion or philosophy from within and the other religion or philosophy from without?

We are assuming that a philosophy of religion worth the name is a philosophy that has experienced that particular religion so as to be a genuine expression of the philosophical contents of that religion. Now, the problem amounts to this: Can I have an equally valid and authentic philosophical or religious experience within another religious tradition?

We consider this an inescapable question. Indeed, I can try to understand the second religion through a philosophy created by a follower of that religion. We shall have in this case a type of comparative philosophies. Somebody, out of the internal experience of a religious tradition, draws a certain philosophical picture, and somebody else is doing the same from a second religion. This is indeed a necessary and important step, but this cannot be said to be the philosophy of religion we are looking for as an authentic philosophy, giving expression to the philosophical core of more than one religion. Is this possible? Here I see the great challenge, to philosophy as well as to religion.

It comes to this: I can only have a real insight into a particular religion if I share the fundamental convictions of that religion, if I, in one word, have a faith that allows me to draw from it the philosophical insights of that religion. Now, can I have a faith that is at home in more than one religion? Can I be at the same time a Christian and a Muslim, to put it on a concrete level?

Fundamental distinctions may be necessary here, such as that between the primacy of the personal faith—and good faith—of the person engaged in such a venture and a more or less static idea of orthodoxy, or that between the supraconceptuality of almost all religions and the necessary conceptualization of a philosophical expression, and so forth. But one thing remains incontrovertible: If such an experience is not possible, philosophy of religion in this full sense of the word is simply an illusion and a dream.

Let us take an example at random of what I am intending to say. I am a Parsi trying to understand African so-called idolatry. Having passed the first stages of repulsion and bewilderment and having tried to enter into the mentality of a particular tribe, I shall come to a further understanding of the idolatrous cult in two more steps. First I shall discover the motivations, the underlying myths, and the conceptual framework under which such a tribe operates. Then, taking those things for granted I shall discover that those representations that are at the basis of the cult are ways of saying something that I also find in my religion under different structures. I shall then be able to share in the beliefs of the tribe because I shall have discovered their motives and their archetypes—for lack of a better word. I shall discover, second, that the idolatry itself is most probably not what I surmised at the beginning when I was projecting my own conceptions, but something much more simple—or primitive, perhaps—and also deeper and richer in symbolism. I shall discover most probably that the idol is not substance, and that the worship pierces the fetish as it were and goes into the limitless, and so on. I may also discover that some people, though perhaps subjectively in good faith, hold true something that I find to be an aberration. I shall be able to integrate, though negatively, those parts also into my general picture. I may be able to accept that worship, and I shall consider it as true, though not appropriate for me, for I believe I have in my personal faith everything they have. I believe, in a word, that I take up the faith of the others into my personal faith, and only in this way can I understand the others. The following step is going to be a confrontation with the explicit beliefs of the tribe itself. I may not share everything the tribe believes, but I shall be able to share, and even to get their sanction for my interpretation. To be completely sincere, I may still believe that the religion of that tribe is elementary and primitive because they stop at a very low and preliminary point, but insofar as I understand them, I share their beliefs and I integrate them into what I consider to be a wider and deeper framework. This must serve as an example, since I do not now wish to develop a whole theory.

The Religious Perspective

The challenge is even more acute seen from a strictly religious perspective. If religions do not want to disappear from the world today and remain only as monuments of the past, they have to face the future, looking first of all with open and realistic eyes at the present. And the present says that religious life cannot be a mere repetition of the past, that the religions of our time are confronted with an entirely new problem: the encounter between religions has ceased to be a peripheral or a scholarly or a purely theological affair and has become a central religious issue. Religious people, not only experts, have to face one another, and the religious traditions have to come to grips with one another. Dialogue becomes not only a means of mutual understanding but one of the forms of authentic religious life.

In other words, religions have to be ready for change and open to progress or evolution. The interpretation of religion, as I said at the beginning, belongs to religion itself, but this applies also to the new interpretations that may emerge out of the encounter at the level I am describing. When a religion finds a more comprehensive or a deeper interpretation of its message, this philosophy or theology becomes part and parcel of that religion that is enriched in this way. If I can give an interpretation of Hinduism, for instance, that satisfies adherents of other religions and even permits them to share in the main tradition of Hinduism, this religion is enriched, and my interpretation becomes part of its very nature. If an increasing number of Buddhists and Hindus consider themselves as belonging to both these religions, official representatives of these religions and scholars simply cannot ignore this fact. One should not force reality into a more or less artificial schema. If, to give another example, owing to a Christian need, Christ is found to be present in Hinduism in a peculiar way, and this allows believing Christians to declare themselves Hindus, or vice versa, these are all living religious facts that no theoretician of religion is allowed to overlook. Philosophy after all is there in order to understand reality, and religion is there in order to serve Man, and not the contrary.[15]

---

[15] Some of the philosophical and theological reflection of our times is already going in this direction. Names like K. Rahner, *Schriften zur Theologie*, 16 vols. (Einsiedeln-Zürich-Köln Benziger, 1954–1984); R. Guardini, *Religion und Offenbarung* (Würzburg: Werkbund, 1958); W. C. Smith, "Comparative Religion: Whither and Why?" in M. Eliade and J. M. Kitagawa, eds., *The History of Religions: Essays in Methodology* (Chicago: University of Chicago Press, 1959), 31–58; J. A. Cuttat, *La rencontre des religions* (Paris: Aubier, 1957); and W. E. Hocking, *The Coming World Civilization* (New York: Harper & Brothers, 1956), come to mind. In spite of very different presuppositions, S. Radhakrishnan, *Recovery of Faith* (London: G. Allen & Unwin, 1956); K. Nishitani, *Shūkyō to wa nani ka* (Tokyo: Sobunsha, 1961; published in English as *What Is Religion?* in four chapters in *Philosophical Studies of Japan*, vol. 2 [Tokyo: Japanese National Commission for UNESCO, 1960; in 1982 it appeared revised and extended in German and in English]); and others are also pointing toward the same goal. The elaboration of a theology of religion is still a task of the future. Works like those of H. Heislbetz, *Theologische Gründe der nicht Christlichen Religionen* (Freiburg i. B.: Herder, 1967); G. Thils, *Propos et problèmes de la théologie des*

The New Perspective

I am not advocating syncretism as an amorphous amalgam of religions, but isolation and rigid compartmentalization are no longer possible. What I am aiming at is that religions should stimulate each other to be loyal to their respective traditions and to draw from them all that they can yield. Furthermore, they should mutually inspire each other so that new insights and ways to lead Man toward his goal may be found. For this mutual fertilization real love is obviously required. It may bring forth not a new child which may grow and disown its parents, but a renewed and rejuvenated religion with a direct message for the peoples of our times.

It is obvious that in this dialogue not only the traditional denominations should have their say, but also all those forms of religion that have hitherto not been officially recognized as such.

Summing up, philosophy of religion in our contemporary situation cannot be a simple continuation of the efforts that have been made until now, because the situation has changed radically. It has to take into account not only one but several religions. And if philosophy has to transcend the sphere of mere phenomenology, it has to take into account the internal religious experience of more than one religion, not believing blindly but philosophizing authentically.

Unless we quarrel over names, we are not going toward an a-religious Christianity or Buddhism, or humanism, but first of all toward a less rigid and narrow idea of religion and second toward new religious forms, which may leave behind the classical forms of religious expression. In a word, the philosophy of religion in the contemporary encounter of cultures demands of modern Man a radical examination of conscience in the face of the new situation in which he finds himself, in which perhaps for the first time in world history every man becomes his neighbor, and every neighbor his brother. God is that which makes it possible to discover my brother in my neighbor.

---

religions non chrétiennes (Tournai: Casterman, 1966); R. L. Slater, *Can Christians Learn from Other Religions?* (New York: Seabury Press, 1963); R.C. Zaehner, *The Convergent Spirit: Toward Dialectics of Religion* (London: Routledge & Kegan Paul, 1963); and others give some valuable hints for an integration and understanding of religions.

19

THE SCANDAL OF RELIGIONS

If religions are so good, why is the world in the state it is in? I am aware that this is a delicate problem and that we cannot blame religion exclusively, but I also believe that assigning all responsibility to human evil and consoling ourselves with eschatological messianisms is not enough. Let us be realistic!

In our contemporary world, religion is a scandal. I would like to perform an exercise of self-examination from three points of view: first, praxis; second, theory; third, the interpellation of Spirit—conversion.

Praxis

Historical evidence shows us two things: first, there is no such thing as a chemically pure religion, just as there is no such thing as a chemically pure element. A religion not incarnated among men and in history is nothing more than an ideology. On the other hand, it is easy to ascertain that the fruits of these incarnations are not too flattering. In this sense, historical testimony is cruel: religions that preach peace, make war, religions that preach the importance of the human family are divided into sects, casts, and a diversity of organizations that do not communicate among themselves—when they are not fighting, that is. This is why I believe that this new initiative is such a positive factor, and I am pleased to have been able to make a contribution in its initial stages.

Nonetheless, we cannot take refuge in that which we read in a very profound and well-intentioned book by Nicolas Berdyaev, a great philosopher whom I love and admire—even if I am critical of the title of his book, written more than half a century ago: *The Dignity of Christianity and the Indignation of Christians*. It is very easy to excuse oneself with good theories and blame it all on the existence of human evil.

If this were true, responsibility would not lie in Christianity, which is perfect; or on Buddhism, which is marvelous; or on the Beatitudes, which delight one and all. Religions are theoretically pure and fantastic, but when one has lived in countries where the population of Christians is less than one in a thousand, the only way to explain Christianity is by pointing out what Christians do. In the beginning, when they were first persecuted, people said, "Look at how they love each other." I am not so sure the same could be said now.

"You will know them by their fruits." But from a historical point of view, the fruits of all religions, without exception, do not appear either very mature or very appetizing. It is easy to comprehend why a considerable portion of those whom we call our brothers—the six thousand million people who constitute the totality of humanity—frown when they hear the word *religion*. An exercise in self-recognition is much needed: we cannot simply hand over responsibility to praxis and order the "secular arm" to execute the verdicts coming from the inquisitions, while we go and pray to God. This is no longer convincing. I have no need to entertain myself by making a detailed description of historical testimonies. I will limit myself to saying that persecution, violence, and injustice have characterized all religions without exception during thousands of years of history, and that to assign sole responsibility to Man's weakness is a much too unilateral explanation. The problem is complex. Human nature is not innocent. It is possible that we would be even worse off without religion to hold us back. But this does not absolve us from carrying out an exercise in self-examination. I can criticize multinational companies and the stock exchange, for example. But these institutions do not lie to us: they clearly state that what they want is to make money. Religions aspire to transform Man, make him better. There is a difference.

I repeat, "By their fruits you will recognize them." And when something produces such disconcerting results, it means that the self-examination must go deeper, not be merely moral. We must all love each other, we must be better: all religions say so. But this is not enough. If we still lack grace, courage, and force, perhaps we must delve into something deeper. And I would venture to say that this is the responsibility of pretty much all of us who are superprivileged, who have leisure time to think, to reflect, to meditate, and thus even to pray, and I say *superprivileged* because so many people have no leisure time at all.

Yes, it is true that religions are the best side of Man: they put him in contact with the mystery that has no name and all names, they inspire him and lead him to the most heroic and sublime actions; but at the same time, let us be honest, they are also his worst side: the cruelest of crimes have been committed in the name of religion, the bloodiest wars have been waged under the banner of God. This is why the self-examination must go a bit deeper still.

And this leads to my second point, the theoretical one.

Theory

The danger is real: It is the danger of degeneration or the danger of the demonic when it meets the divine, using these two words as symbols. Life is risk; life itself is dangerous. Religion is at once divine and demonic, and if we do not perform a discernment of spirits we may fall into the same traps as the millenary history I just mentioned.

Today we realize the need for dialogue among religions. We are not the first. When someone speaks to me of interreligious dialogue as if it were a novel idea, I cannot help thinking about India, where dialogue has been practiced, theoretically and practically, at least for the past twenty-five centuries. We should not believe that we are the ones who have invented dialogue and discovered the other. This would suggest categorical historical ignorance.

Life is dangerous: What has happened to religions? Allow me a brief theoretical reflection. Religions, in one way or another, deal with the Absolute—I do not like this word, but it is useful—and when one faces the Absolute and accepts it as symbol, everything else becomes so intranscendent, superficial, indifferent, and of little importance that we believe we can leave it aside. As the bishop who wiped out the Cathars said, "They will go to heaven, if they are good," which also means that, if they are bad, then "they deserve it." When we deal with the Absolute, we are invaded by a feeling of holy indifference that is precisely what allows us to condemn each other to death, as so many religions accept. This is now beginning to change, because of what I mention later. When we face the Absolute, the eternal, the definitive, that which does not pass, which is much more profound than anything else, it seems corollary to deduce that everything else is trifle, futile, and of no great concern; and it is because of this that we feel like we can treat secular affairs without paying much attention: "Life is but a fleeting moment." In other words, when one becomes obsessed by the Absolute, one becomes convinced that the truly important things take place on a different level and that there is not much point in bothering with the affairs of this Earth.

This sort of fascination for the Absolute has led to a certain disdain for historical facts. We have committed the sin of self-sufficiency and also another sin, fruit of the past few centuries—both in the West and in the East. I am referring to our obsession for objectivizing. We have turned religion into an object, even an object of study, which explains how we can teach a class on religion the same way we can teach one on engineering. We have objectified religion and left the subject behind—the believer, as we can call him, the person, the human being; this is the reason why, ultimately, what we do is discuss ideologies, ideas, and beliefs, while eliminating or leaving aside the true faith that heals, the faith that is lived and makes us vibrate. We have identified religion with a doctrine, with an institution, and religion is much more than that, not less. Religion is much more than a doctrine or an institution. We have reduced the richness of religion to a mere concept: there are so many books that speak about this! But religion is not a concept. If it were a concept, it would be something abstract, which would neither heal, nor move. We have identified religion with an objective truth and with something impersonal, which does not look to the other, and which is absolutized the moment we believe we possess it. Objectifying anything leads, in the long run, to its dehumanization.

From another point of view, the scandal of Western culture—and this is not only true as of the French Revolution, even though it has grown in intensity since then— is demonstrated by the fact that religion becomes a sectarian phenomenon in the most exact definition of the word, as if it were a private practice. This constitutes the degradation of the religious core. Perhaps we should meditate a bit on what religion is.

The Evangelical text, "Heaven and Earth shall pass away, but my words will never pass away" (Mt 24:35), should make us think. Words must be felt in order to be truly words. It does not say, "My writings will never pass." It does not say, "Writing will never pass"—the letter kills, as the same Christian Scripture also says. However, in order for words to be words, they must be heard, and in order to listen to them I have to have silence within myself, and in order to become conscious of the meaning of silence I need a discipline that will allow me to listen to the word. The Vedas say, "If a thousand sacred texts say that fire does not burn, I will not believe them." If our religion, whichever it may be, is not a lived experience, then we are creating the perfect conditions for it to become a mere concept. The word must be listened to, which is why living religions cannot be reduced to "religions of the book," but should rather be religions of the word: "The devil can quote Scripture to suit his purpose," says an English proverb, because interpretations of a book can be diverse. But in order to listen to the word, one must have a clean, pure heart and inner silence, something which is often in tension with the turmoil of the modern world. We have objectified things, beginning with truth, forgetting the most traditional thing: that truth is a relationship, and this is why it can make us free.

The dangers of objectifying can be even more subtle than falling into the trap of the selfish, who believe they possess the truth. And this trap is a danger that lies very close to a certain spirit that is called religious: "Woe is me, as an individual I have not [yet] been able to grasp the truth, but we, as a religion, do possess this objective truth, over and above any and every subject." "The Church has its doctors. . . ." "Our religion is the Truth." I remember a significant change of meaning given to a book by St. Augustine; the title was *De Vera Religione*, which means, "Of Veritable (Authentic) Religiosity," and it was interpreted as, "Of True Religion."

But I do not wish to extend myself on this point, so I move on to the third section, which represents a special challenge for all of us who consider ourselves more or less intellectuals.

The Interpellation of Spirit

If things have gone as we have said, should we not rethink what religion is more profoundly, and overcome this dichotomy between a theory we believe to be perfect and a praxis that is anything but perfect?

First, we need the conversion of religions. It is easy enough to see that we have not been faithful to their messages: what has happened, for example, to the Sūtra of the Lotus? Perhaps religions, as sociological strata, have betrayed their messages to a greater or lesser degree, and it is a sign of hope to see that they are becoming increasingly aware of this. But becoming aware also implies regret; it also implies change.

Religions have not been faithful, but we are still missing another step. Perhaps religion itself, that which we understand by religion, is in need of radical change in the dawn of the so-called twenty-first century: otherwise we will not get very far. More than three thousand years of experience are proof that it is not enough to do things by goodwill alone; we need something else. And here we (though we are not alone) have a positive, active, and creative function. Many people do not wish to be puppets, little marionettes dancing to the beat of trends set by multinational companies, by the mass media, or by the inertia of history itself. In order for the "rebellions of slaves" to not be crushed from the start, we must first free ourselves from the feeling that we are slaves; for this inner freedom of religions we need personal freedom from all fear first; to sincerely believe in the liberating, that is, the saving force of the Spirit.

What does a deeper notion of religion mean?

Simplifying, we could perhaps agree that there have been three kairologic moments in the understanding of human beings and of religious events—I call them *kairologic* and not *chronologic* because I do not think of time like a highway that leads to heaven, to hell, to no-thing, or anywhere, for that matter; I believe time to be something completely different. The words I use to refer to these three kairologic moments may seem rather abrasive, but they certainly carry no bad intentions. I simply wish to allude to a series of things that I can merely suggest here.

The three moments are as follows:

1. Religion's totalitarian moment. Religion comprises the totality of Man's actions, with all its consequent perils as well as all its enormous advantages. Religion is lived like a cultural and anthropological event with its own cultural constructions, its institutions, its persons, its cathedrals, and so on. Religion occupies everything; it is the circle that impregnates the entire circumference of human life.

2. Due to exceedingly complex historical reactions, religions—not only in the West—have been gradually displaced toward the periphery, marginalized, until becoming consigned to the sphere of personal freedom or of particular groups, tolerated as something almost strictly private. We have reacted against this sort of heteronomic dominion of religion from the start, that is to say, of the religion that wants it all, that wants to permeate everything, and we have marginalized it; we have turned it into a specialization. Religion has been banished to the extremes of the circumference, toward the "afterlife," toward another world, as this respects the autonomy of other human activities.

3. In keeping with the spatial metaphor, I believe the moment has come to consider religion neither as the whole, nor as a marginal phenomenon, but rather as the center of all reality, of all human life, of all activity. The center is neither the circle nor the circumference; the center has practically no dimension; the center has no influence and no power, but it makes the circle and the circumference possible. It makes it possible for things to fully be. I believe the image of the circle overcomes, on the one hand, marginalization and, on the other, totalitarianism. This would be the ontonomy of the religious dimension with the rest of Man's activities.

Religion is not a specialty. It is not only an institution or a doctrine. It is the central aspect—that is to say, it is the center of all reality. And this brings me, to put it briefly, to what I believe is the novum of this coming century: the recognition of the sacredness of secularity.

I spoke before of the appeal and of the message of the Absolute. Strictly speaking, the Absolute contains an internal contradiction: it can only stand as a concept of the limit. We can only think of the Absolute in relation to ourselves, so that it is not in fact the so-called ab-solutus, but rather the other pole of the "relative," and in this sense it is also present in all that which is relative, so that if God is absolute reality, then He cannot be left out of daily life nor of technocracy. Understanding this is very difficult for us because we have to modify our idea of God and of the world and, obviously, also of religion.

I believe the conversion I have referred to is necessary for the survival of humanity; it is much more radical than a simply moral conversion. We must discover the central nucleus that is here, that is in things, and that is in people, in animals, in the heavenly bodies, and everywhere, that is the center. But the center does not move; it is things that move. In more controversial terms: religions—in plural—do not have the monopoly of religion. Religion is a human dimension that specifically differentiates us from all other beings that we know of in the sublunary world, and which opens us up to the infinite, to the unknown, to the hereafter, to that which, ultimately, moves us. To be clear, I call this dimension Man's *religiosity*. Religion is not the totality of life, but it is, following the metaphors we have established, an indispensable color of all things. If we eliminate color from things, they disappear. Color is not the entire thing, but a thing without color could not exist in itself.

Secularity is not secularism—which is an ideology—or secularization—which is a historical phenomenon; rather it entails recognizing the sacred meaning, the religious meaning of human existence, of matter, and of temporality. In Christian terms I would say that this is precisely what incarnation is: in skin, bone, meat, tiredness, etc. . . .

The novum that I have mentioned is the consciousness that religions are constitutively secular, that the saeculum is not only profane (*pro-fanum*) but also sacred. That God is the soul of the World, which is His body, as so many traditions announce, does not mean either pantheism or monism. The soul and the body are not the same thing, but their separation equals death.

If I believe, for example, that Christ resuscitated, but that this event is unrelated to me and does not mean that I too resuscitate, then it is all in vain. The great challenge is to begin to eliminate all labels, even religious ones, and reach the depths of the religious dimension in human beings—a dimension that is afterward expressed in a great variety of forms, languages, manifestations, and cults. Obviously, we could discuss which is the more adequate, the best, and so on, but this would be on a second level.

From a philosophical standpoint, I draw the cardinal distinction between faith—which is a constitutive dimension of Man—and belief—which is the cultural and historical (and so forth) articulation of the dimension we call faith. Beliefs are quite diverse, and they can be debated—but not faith, because if faith had an object, it would be idolatry. Faith is not objectifiable; rather, it is Man's consciousness of being constitutively open, of being infinite. Many religions would say that this is precisely the divine dimension of reality. In a commentary on the Delphic Sibyl, Plato already said that "know thyself" is equivalent to "know God"; Meister Eckhart writes that "he who knows himself knows all things," and there is a *ḥadīṯ* by the Prophet that says, "He who knows himself knows his Lord."

I believe this self-examination should be the starting point of any initiative put forth to bring a ray of hope. But I insist that we must begin by admitting that we are not doing this well, and not because we are bad, but because we have not been prepared for the task of the free man, which consists precisely in cooperating in the creation of the world. And this is our responsibility. We are still ashamed to be told we are religious because it seems as if religion is equal to a sect and not to the consciousness that we actively participate in the cosmic adventure of all of reality. How do we combine this sacred secularity with the purely sacred? In order to answer this question we must recall what I said at the beginning: that the purely sacred does not exist. God is the God of Man, in the same way that Man is the man of God.

An act of self-examination must not discourage us, but make us much more realistic.

All the work is ahead of us! Because Man is not only a historical being, fruit of the past, he is co-creator—co-operator as St. Paul would say—of the force that creates all of reality. And I believe this is the profound nucleus of these movements, which realize that we are getting nowhere with small remedies here and there. When the world is burning, when our historical moment finds itself at a crossroads between life and death, I think it is time for us to discover the nucleus that has led us to this place together, and that at the same time makes us more human and unifies us more with everyone and everything. Religion is that which binds us, unites my soul to my body, links me to others, to the Earth and to the mystery that we call the divine or any other name. Religion, in a word, is that which binds us to all reality in an interdependent link.

Religion is not archaeology; it is new each day. The Spirit makes all things constantly new. But this novelty, if it is the result of creation, has no model, no paradigm, no guideline: We are given freedom and therefore the responsibility of actively participating in the dynamism of history and of reality.

SECTION III

20

THE STUDY OF RELIGIONS

The Crisis: An Inadequate Perception of the Situation

My thesis here is a simple one. The crisis today undermining the identity of religious studies in the university setting comes from the high demands placed upon this emerging discipline. We ask religious studies not only to direct its efforts toward solving ancient riddles but also to come to grips with the real challenges today confronting human and planetary life. Not so very long ago, programs and departments in religious studies sprang up all over the academic world in Europe and North America, raising high expectations on many fronts. Today this very discipline seems to be in danger of becoming an accepted but minor academic sideline for those few universities that can still afford the "luxury" of truly humanistic studies. This much said, let me briefly outline what I take to be the principal challenges today facing the study of religion.

The proper "field" of "religious studies," as I see it, is *the religious dimension of Man*. To be sure, this religious dimension transcends the enclosures of the academic world and of institutionalized religions, though it is often expressed in these institutions. Yet living institutions do not thrive by severing their connections and interactions with human life at large. We have before us instances from the natural sciences, which operate in close symbiosis with industry, defense, politics, economics, and many other perceived social needs. Religious studies has no need to legitimize itself by appealing to examples from other disciplines, but by the same token it must be conceded that this discipline runs a considerable risk of losing touch with reality altogether unless it strengthens some similar connection with the genuine human concerns of our time. The study of religion is neither mere scholasticism nor archaeology. Religious studies should feel neither so secure nor so insecure that it neglects interaction with the world at large. Nor, obviously, should it still be clinging to remnants of the aloof superiority sometimes implied by the words "holy," "sacred," and the like, segregating its *ultimate* concerns from *immediate* human and secular crises.

In a secular setting I would describe the religious dimension as the *human face* implicit in any human venture. Mathematics, physics, politics, music, and so on are all activities of the human spirit dealing with particular aspects of reality under determinate perspectives. When they touch, and insofar as they touch what I call the "human face," they touch the religious dimension. How these disciplines enhance, help, or transform human life—positively or negatively—is precisely the religious dimension of the phenomenon.

In a more traditional setting, I could describe the religious dimension as the *reference to transcendence* implicit in any human venture. Geometry, chemistry, sociology, architecture, and so forth are all human activities that focus on particular objects. When they encounter an elusive element, a *plus* or a *more* irreducible to the proper parameters of their disciplines and yet inextricably connected to them, they meet what we call transcendence. They meet the religious dimension.

I submit that here we have two languages that do not say the same thing but do refer to the same problem: the question of the religious dimension of Man. I should simply mention here that the sacred is opposed to the profane, but not necessarily to the secular.

The challenge facing religious studies is to enter the arena of today's life and not shirk its responsibility to criticize and even to inspire actions, people, and issues in the public domain. Don't misunderstand me. I am not proposing to "politicize" religious studies. I am, however, suggesting that we recover for religious studies the traditional meanings of both "religion" and "study." I am also urging that we do not content ourselves with being curators of antiquities or hoarders of ancient treasures. Something is amiss in a society where the ladies keep their diamonds and emeralds in a safe and wear glass baubles in public—for fear of the many robberies in our time, or for fear of envy, like there was in the "ancien régime." Likewise, there is surely "something rotten in Denmark" when scholars of religion are conspicuously silent on many of the most important *religious* issues of our times. There is, undoubtedly, a political facet to religious studies.

I should stress that I am not defending a shallow involvement in discussions à la mode, as if the religious scholar's only task were to offer a set of fixed clichés or even brilliant theories without any viable roots in history or tradition. On the contrary, we must take up a dialogue with the most pressing issues of our times, a task that requires bringing to bear all the precious and indispensable human wisdom accumulated through the generations and throughout the world. Certainly we should not cease poring over the treasures of the past, or developing purely theoretical or "disinterested" investigations. But we should also be carrying out the incessant task of taking these intuitions all the way into the present human world and exhibiting their lessons in their full and proper setting and in the overall enterprise that pertains to religious studies.

The challenge is to go from the past to the present—that is, to undergo the transition from describing what religion has been to understanding what the religious dimension of Man is now. We need to analyze ancient worldviews and diverse mentalities, but it is also necessary to *assimilate* these alternative ways of being, knowing, doing, and becoming. We should indeed, for example, cultivate as much knowledge as possible about the ancestors of the Bantu, about Vedic sacrifice, and about the Eleusinian mysteries, and so on, but we should never forget that all this knowledge is part of our own self-knowledge. This knowledge has to be integrated not only into our understanding of what *Homo sapiens* were like, but also of how *we are*—not only as individuals but also as a collectivity and as cosmic beings. The challenge lies in the fact that our theories about religion and religious issues are not independent from our praxis. Religious studies is not a "normal" academic discipline in the sense that it is specialized and has untouchable, fixed limits. It is a sui generis human activity, due precisely to the nature of its subject matter: religion. We must bear in mind today's world scene in order to see how the arena of our times has suffered radical changes and how these changes now demand a parallel transformation of religion.

The Great Confrontation:
Neither God, nor Nature, nor Man, but a Factitious World

The great confrontation of our day is no longer the old struggle with the Divine or human efforts to tame Nature. Until recently, God and Nature were the great challenges. When confronted by ultimate questions, Man had to wrestle with God, appease the gods, entreat them, obey divine rules, and follow supreme laws. This was the classical domain of religion. Through a kairological shift—which need not follow a strictly chronological order—when confronting ultimate issues, Man found that Nature also had to be known, that her rules had to be discovered, that humans had to be able to predict her behavior and observe her laws—precisely in order to bring Nature into a higher form of harmony with human beings. This is the classical domain of *science*. At the same time, third, people have always been aware of the danger posed by fellow human beings. Men have had to compete with one another: women with men and vice versa, one generation with the next, commoners with their chiefs, and the like. One "tribe" could always be a menace to another, whether such tribes were called families, clans, nations, empires, corporations, or superpowers. This is the classical domain of *politics*. The divine, the cosmic, and the human constituted the natural habitat of Man. Religion, science, and politics were the three main spheres of human life.

Something new is emerging now. Human beings have always threatened each other, but Man was not the foe of humankind, nor was he powerful enough to sweep away the entire human species or alter the gene pools of whole races. When self-understanding ceases to be an authentic understanding of the Self, the old paradox of knowledge as the "science of good and evil" recovers all its diabolical force.

Today, prepared by modern technology—which is more than just "applied science"—and triggered by the split of the unsplittable (the *a-tomos*), the great challenge facing Man is an artificial world that has become independent of its engineer. The great confrontation is no longer that of Man facing God or Nature or other people, but Man facing the historical, technological, and scientific forces that a certain human calculating power has set into motion as a fabricated world. Before this factitious system, the individual feels more lost and forlorn than humans ever did before the divine, the natural, or the human worlds. Nobody seems accountable for today's menacing disasters. The system, unlike God(s) or Nature or human society, resists "anthropomorphization": it cannot be personalized; it is anonymous; nobody seems to have any real control over it. In this "Fourth World" the gods are silent, the cosmos is dead or dying, and people are convinced of their own impotence. It is pathetic to hear the leaders of the world's superpowers saying they would like to have a future free of nuclear weapons, but that they cannot—that it is an idealistic pipe dream. What is this power that is uncontrollable by its controllers? In this regard, we should by no means confine our worries to an atomic holocaust; we should equally bear in mind certain disturbing initiatives undertaken lately in psychology, genetics, and biochemistry that also have their own autonomy and also seem to have escaped human control.

We should, moreover, become increasingly aware of the prisons we have made for ourselves under the guise of protection or security. The very magnitude of modern cities puts up higher walls of segregation than did medieval gates, especially for those—the majority—who cannot afford to "escape" to the suburbs. Working under electric lights and artificial climates, working within the megamachine of the industrial metropolis, submitting to the entire web of routines and regulations regarding each and every human transaction makes us terribly vulnerable to any failure of the system and robs us of our human spontaneity to an almost unimaginable measure. No wonder that, having built such a splendid prison for themselves, people are so easily exasperated when the system of controls breaks down, as has lately occurred in tourism and space travel.

In short, the global destiny of the human being today is no longer mainly subject to the Will of God, the whims of Nature, or the programs of the politicians, but to the sphinx of the dehumanized and artificial technocratic complex. God, Nature, and society may still play important roles for many, but for those who manage the technocratic complex, their predominance has been precluded. Famine, for example, which has never been as widespread as in our own day, is now seen neither as divine punishment nor as a disorder in the seasons of Nature, nor even as a principally political failure, but rather as a technical and economic problem of logistics.

A Basic Religious Issue: Civilization as Human Project

The world today is obviously in dire straits. We live in the midst of a global malaise that cries out for us to investigate its hidden roots. The so-called system of modern civilization—the interlocking complex of economic, political, and technological mechanisms—has today come to the point of actually threatening not only its "enemies" but the majority of the peoples of the Earth and, indeed, the life of the planet itself. We are becoming aware that it is more than just a mistake or computational error that has crept in somewhere along the line and extended over the entire network. The modern predicament alerts us that something is intrinsically wrong at the very basis of our civilization. The nuclear issue is just the tip of the iceberg, the bulk of which is still obscured beneath all the current technical, political, and economic upheavals. I submit that the culprit is the project of civilization that has prevailed for the past six thousand years.

The roots of this problem go all the way back to the Neolithic passage from decentralized agricultural villages to the organization of centralized cities and states, and probably also to the transition from matriarchy to patriarchy. In brief, the roots of the problem are tangled up in the urban revolution we have come to call civilization—where the *civitas* becomes the center of "civilized" life. There are certain fundamental differences between *culture* and *civilization*—that is, between village life and city life. While the *town*, as its etymology indicates, needs fences, the village has none, or at the most has gates. While the city is largely parasitic on the agricultural provinces, the village and its people live in symbiosis with the Earth and her rhythms. While every *polis* requires slaves, under one name or another, the village requires only a certain type of caste system—which, obviously, can also degenerate. While the city is not self-sufficient, the village usually gets by on its own with a natural commerce or exchange of goods. While the modern city demands technology, the village needs only technique; I make a fundamental distinction between *technē* ("technique"), which is a cultural invariant, and modern technology, which is a product of modern civilization. While the city requires political, military, or police *power* to bring it under control, the agricultural tribe or hunter-gatherer cultures make do with hierarchical structures that confer *authority*. Only with the city does the schism between authority and power become acute. Power implies the capacity for physical, psychological, and epistemological control. The very word "authority" suggests a kind of sanction that allows things and people to grow (*ab augendo*) and evolve. One has power, however one is conferred authority. It is true that the village also has its own flaws, and the issue of totally de-urbanizing civilization or of idealizing village life is completely out of the question. What we do need is the *paganization* of civilization, that is, the integration of the *pagi*—the villages, and thus of those who dwell there, the "pagans"—into the human project of life, which today must overcome not only the dichotomies spawned by overspecialization—including the body/soul split—but also the Man-Nature and God-World dualisms. This can be understood and acted upon only if we integrate into our vision of reality perspectives that are different from the predominant modern one.

Let me put forward just one example. We are accustomed to viewing history as a succession of wars followed by more or less stable truces. We are told that wars have occasioned great discoveries, given opportunities for the exercise of heroic virtues, and provided outlets by which the accumulated aggressive energies of a people were discharged. We are able to live with such rationalization only because they are partial truths. Down through the ages, the military castes in various cultures have had the sacred duty of keeping the world from falling apart, of saving the *cosmos* from disintegrating into *chaos*. We are told, or rather, we choose to believe, that wars are natural phenomena, without facing up to the fact that they are highly institutionalized phenomena of civilization. No other animal species wages war. There are battles, but not wars.

Today we are beginning to see the mutation that has taken place in the very notion of war. Since the splitting of the atom, all of these traditional attitudes have begun to undergo radical change. We are finally surmising that the human project must find a new direction. Most of us may not care to, probably should not, and certainly cannot turn back to a simple agricultural lifestyle, but we are equally aware that simple reforms with minor remedies of the present-day technocratic system will not manage to keep it afloat much longer. What is really emerging here is a mutation in human life altogether, the end of the hegemony of historical consciousness. Unless we undergo this transformation, this *metanoia*, humankind will indeed soon commit *terracide*. The collaborative search for answers to such questions will eventually help us discover the new directions that human beings need to take in order to survive in this nuclear age.

Significantly enough, poets, thinkers, artists, and even religious authorities have for well over a century now been descrying the end of this Western civilization. They have tended to have minimal impact on the world situation, mainly because what they foresaw was not yet conspicuous enough to ordinary people. Today a neo-millennial climate is being felt all over the globe, although it differs in many respects and carries with it fewer eschatological elements than former millennial movements. We should be equally wary of both prophets of doom and messiahs of optimism.

I am suggesting that we are approaching the end of historical *civilization* and at the same time witnessing the discreet dawning of a possible meta-historical or transhistorical *culture*.

I make these rather disturbing overstatements—which I have tried to substantiate and qualify elsewhere—in order to show that the problem is basic. It calls into question the very foundations of human civilization, and it requires a cultural metamorphosis, the *metanoia* alluded to above, to be even adequately perceived. As such, it is a specifically religious question. It cannot be solved technically, politically, or economically. It requires a cultural transformation of the first magnitude. This issue strikes the very basis of human existence, indeed, the heart of life itself. And if such an issue is not a religious incumbency, I am left wondering what religion is all about.

Definition of Religion: Way to Peace

There is perhaps a semantic problem here. Should we confine what we call *religion* exclusively to the first struggle, that of Man with the Divine, and reserve the name of *science* for the second, namely that of Man with nature? Should we call *politics*, the art of the dealings of people with one another, the third main human activity? What about the fourth and present technocratic world? Is this then to be the field of human and physical engineering? Are all four not intermingled? Was religion not always concerned with the vital issues of a particular tradition? Are we to limit ourselves to being priests in the service of the past and shrink from becoming prophets—or even martyrs—in the service of the future? Can we not plant our feet firmly in the soil of tradition, fix our eyes on the horizon of the future, and also begin to raise our voices amid the hue and cry of the present? "Religion and science" and "religion and politics" are classical problems. "Religion and engineering," in the sense just indicated, is an urgent modern issue.

My long-standing definition of religion, which at the very least has the advantage of being the shortest, is this: ultimate way. In Greek, it is a single word: *eschatodos*. If we want to give this definition a specific content, we can translate "ultimate way" by "way to salvation"—a respectable traditional word that stands for liberation, fulfillment, paradise, joy, God, justice, or any of the other *homeomorphic* equivalents from the various religious traditions. The task of religious studies is to critically investigate these ways, with all their concomitant sets of symbols, myths, beliefs, rituals, doctrines, and institutions, which people *believe* convey the ultimate meaning of the human pilgrimage or of existence in general. I am proposing to render the same idea contemporary by putting it as follows: *Religion is the way to peace.* Peace becomes the present-day homeomorphic equivalent for all those earlier interpretations of "salvation." This peace is obviously not an exclusively political peace or only an internal concord. It is a complex and polysemic symbol standing for the cosmic and personal harmony of and within reality. It is something like the Pauline "recapitulation of all things in Christ." In full coherence, the Epistle to the Ephesians speaks of Christ as "Peace."

Peace is the synthesis—in the sense of balanced play, not of system—between *harmony, freedom,* and *justice.* Some cultures stress *freedom,* and often only individual freedom. They are sensitive to the constraints that hamper human blossoming from without. Human life is seen as development. One example is the modern ideology of development, which leads us to speak of developed and underdeveloped countries—or worse, of LDCs, "lesser-developed countries."

Other cultures stress *justice,* often viewed collectively. They are sensitive to the structural obstacles to the construction of a "just" social order. Human life is seen as *well-being,* and this well-being is usually framed only in terms of the material needs of the people.

Other cultures stress *harmony,* most often viewed in connection with nature. They are sensitive to the kind of human happiness that comes from playing one's part in the unfolding drama of the universe. *Life* becomes the main category, and human integration into that life is the main value.

Freedom points to truth. Justice points to goodness. Harmony points to beauty.

A genuine peace would have to blend these three values, visions, and experiences both in a temporal and an eternal—"tempiternal"—manner as well as in a personal and cosmic one. The traditional word for this synthesis is *Love.* Significantly, these are all religious categories.

One of the most urgent tasks for religious studies today is to rethink its proper subject matter. Religious studies simply cannot leave the ultimate queries of humankind to the voluble responses of merely technical "solutions," or to analysis generated solely by sciences working within a single culture, or to the ideologies of politicians, not even to those of institutionalized religious bodies. This does not mean trying to supplant technical, scientific, and political efforts, or abandoning all churches altogether. It does, however, mean that we must become more acutely aware of the present human predicament and its continuity or discontinuity with the world's religious and cultural traditions. The worst service to tradition is to freeze it.

Let me reformulate all this: *The object of religion is not God, it is the destiny of Man*, and of Man not just as individual but also as society, as species and genus, as microcosm, as one constitutive element of reality that mirrors and shapes that same reality. Life on Earth may not be the ultimate destiny of Man according to some traditions, but even eternal life, *nirvāṇa*, and *Brahman* depend, for their very formulation, on the continued existence of this earthly life. If the planet is threatened or obliterated, this may not be an ultimate tragedy for the galaxy at large, but it is without doubt a universal religious concern here on Earth. God, a traditional name for the object of religion, may indeed represent the true destiny of the human being, but surely it is not the only such symbol. The study of religion properly deals not with any one symbol alone but with all symbols standing for the ultimate meaning of life and the means to reach it. In a word, the concern of religion is human destiny. This human destiny is what is at stake today.

External Changes

Any contemporary approach to a truly human problem that is not tackled in a cross-cultural way smacks of cultural ethnocentrism. This ethnocentrism is the intellectual heir of the colonialist attitude of times allegedly past. We need to study the problem of Man, drawing into the study the various self-understandings of the different peoples of the Earth, for the very essence of Man includes precisely this self-understanding. Man is that entity that has self-understanding as its most relevant characteristic. We cannot study Man without integrating the way in which human beings understand themselves. This self-understanding may vary for different times and cultures. Religious studies offers hospitality, as it were, to representatives of the most diverse worldviews. It allows them to have their say in their respective languages, but it must also recognize that inviting them to come together in this way is a risky venture, one that brings into sharp focus all the questions we have alluded to above. Here we concentrate on (1) the challenges religious studies is facing, and (2) the challenges religious studies itself poses to the existing status quo.

Challenges to Religious Studies: New Tasks for Religion

The challenges that religious studies faces as we enter the Aquarian Age are very complex and bewildering. For clarity's sake I group most of them under three headings:

1. *The world at large* obviously confronts religious studies with a set of new and pressing problems. Peace, justice, hunger, war, armament, nationalism, intolerance, mutual

ignorance, and ideologies of all sorts—political, economic, and religious—represent a host of problems that cannot even be approached adequately, let alone understood, unless the religious dimension is included in the problematic. Human problems, unlike purely objective problems, cannot be solved by the Cartesian rule of dividing them into as many minor parts as possible. The whole is a good deal more than the sum of its parts. All of the aforementioned problems challenge religious studies to carry out an analysis that contributes to its clarification, and eventually to take a stance if need be. By and large, religious studies is not yet sufficiently prepared to tackle these issues. I see here a theological remnant seeking to hold itself above merely human disputes because its goal is the supernatural destiny of the people. But those who fear to risk by taking sides might already have taken the wrong one and are probably going to be shoved aside. Religious studies cannot be silent on such worldwide issues.

2. *The world of organized religions* is encountering any number of new situations that forces each one not only to adapt but also to transform its very conception of itself and its role in the world. Present-day Islam, Hinduism, or Catholicism, for instance, cannot be studied merely from books and traditional or canonical documents. The internal dynamism of each religion as it undergoes change demands that the field of religious studies applies new categories of understanding that have to be forged in the study of these new phenomena. I am not so much referring to the so-called new religions as I am to the new religious spirit pervading in all sorts of institutions. These questions are not marginal in religious studies, and merely sociological research into such phenomena, though it is necessary, is not enough.

3. Finally, *the academic world* poses the most embarrassing questions to the study of religions. Within a university, certainly, all departments are fully within their rights to set new challenges. Too often, not even dialogue is attempted because the "experts" in religion are in many cases ignorant even of the languages of the other disciplines, let alone of the worldviews implied in them. Biology, for example, today presents us with a series of crucial questions regarding the ultimate makeup of the biosphere and the meaning of life therein. Such questions originate in a strictly biological approach to what are apparently purely biological issues, and yet in the long run they transcend the realm of those sciences and spill over into every domain of *human* life. Without more real dialogue between disciplines, the study of religion will soon find itself swallowed up into a branch of history, anthropology, or philosophy and lose its raison d'être in the academic world. I am not claiming that religious studies has the answers. I am saying that it ought to be helping frame the proper questions, those that avoid reductionist solutions. It is a great challenge, but it is not the only one. The study of religion cannot ignore the questions that emerge from transdisciplinarity and interculturality.

Challenges from Religious Studies: Upsets in the Status Quo

Insofar as religious studies is not sufficiently prepared to meet the challenges of the outer world, it has to ready itself for this momentous task. But insofar as it has begun to face these issues, religious studies itself presents certain unsettling challenges to the world at large, to established religions in particular, and to the academic world more specifically.

1. The fact that religious studies is a secular activity, albeit an academic one, puts it on much the same level as any other secular affair. It has to deal with human problems in the fields of industry, politics, government, business, the judiciary, and so on, without recourse to any higher external authority. But by the same token, religious studies cannot artificially truncate and enclose itself in a separate compartment exclusively dealing with "its own" problems. The field of religious studies cannot be objectively delimited from the field of *humanity at large*, although it primarily concentrates on a specific aspect of the human enterprise. But this aspect is just that, an aspect, a perspective, that cannot be artificially segregated from anything human. Human beings have a constitutive religious dimension. Every cultural activity contains more or less conspicuous religious elements insofar as it is an activity of the whole human being. Religious studies has something to say regarding atomic research, consumerism, democracy, economic standards of well-being, nationalism, justice, and peace, so this discipline may often appear to challenge predominant ideologies. And if religious studies ceases to do this, it ceases to perform one of its primary tasks. Even if one were to say that religious studies is not directly concerned with what Man "is," but with what humans believe, beliefs qua beliefs—not as mere doctrines—cannot be severed from Man, from the believer.

2. Religious studies similarly challenges *religious institutions*, both in their day-to-day operations and in their key assumptions. In variegated ways and forms, religious organizations are dedicated to the pursuit or practice of a particular religious ideal. In many countries these institutions suffer the intervention of the state, and in many others they have to act within a certain framework erected by the state. Nonetheless, they try to keep their autonomy. But religious studies is in a peculiar position. It is neither a mere outsider nor only an insider. Many of the same problems that occupy the time and attention of the various religious organizations are also taken up by religious studies, but from a different perspective. Religious studies is neither confessional nor normative; it is not apologetic, nor is it even concerned with the apologetics of religion. It is not an assumption of religious studies that religion is necessarily a good thing. It could equally be diabolical or alienating. The thoroughgoing critique of religion belongs essentially to religious studies, which may often be sensed—rightly or wrongly—as a threat to more than one religious organization. I am not saying that organized religions are inherently exclusivist and proselytizing, but there is no doubt that the academic discipline of religious studies, particularly within religious organizations, often comes to the table as a rather embarrassing guest.

3. To the *world of academia* the challenge sometimes appears so great that it may be perceived as an outright threat. Religious studies does in fact challenge a certain liberal and individualistic scheme of things, which has lately become more and more prevalent in the worldwide academic community. Religious studies seems

to impinge on the almost totally independent sovereignty of many a faculty or department—not only by pointing out inescapable ethical dilemmas inherent to the various disciplines, but also by uncovering the cosmological, anthropological, and even religious assumptions of the particular sciences. Religious studies asks questions that are disturbing for many of the sciences, both "natural" and "human," which they prefer not to hear. Asking whether we should perform experiments on living beings may be a recognized ethical question, but asking whether atomic fission alters the natural rhythms of matter may be a cosmological query issuing from another worldview altogether, which is equally legitimate. In this sense, religious studies tends to bring the sciences together, but it also creates problems for them that would not arise were it to continue its investigations in isolation. Should we let the atomic scientists do their jobs without interference, even if they end up exploding the planet? Human abortion is certainly a religious question, but the cosmic abortion represented by fissioning the very womb of the atom is equally a religious inquiry, and probably a greater one. In short, religious studies contributes to the unity of knowledge by confronting the disunity of present-day academic disciplines. Helping to overcome the fragmentation of knowledge is one of the major tasks of our culture. It is common knowledge that the fragmentation of knowledge leads to the fragmentation of the knower.

The Internal Challenge: The Question of Truth

I have already suggested that the understanding of religion can no longer be restricted to phenomena of the past. The very word *religion* must embrace wholly new human reactions to the ultimate questions that face human life today. In my opinion, *history of religions* is already an obsolete term for the contemporary study of religion. Similarly, it may now be incumbent upon religious studies to recall that *studium* once meant, and could mean again, the complete, diligent, and enthusiastic application of our entire being. It is fitting to recall Cicero's memorable words defining *studium* as that "animi assidua et vehemens ad aliquam rem applicata magna cum voluntate occupatio" (the intense and enthusiastic activity of the spirit directed to something with great will), that is, with all the power of our striving and commitment.

In other words, religious studies as a discipline should be able to overcome the deadening trend of our times and dare to be religious studies, that is, the intellectual and existential study of the roots of our being, our place in the cosmos, and our destiny as human beings implicated in the very warp and weft of reality in its entirety.

The final challenge comes from one inescapable feature of religious studies, a question that can often easily be avoided in other disciplines but that is actually formative and constitutive of religious studies altogether. It is the axiological aspect. Religious studies cannot afford to avoid the question of values. In fact, religious studies cannot skirt the axiological component. The venture toward an authentic understanding of religious problems cannot stop short of evaluating whatever hypotheses are studied. To be sure, religious studies is not identical to religion; it is not confessional, and yet it is professional. The study of religion can never be quite like the study of crystallography, for instance.

This is a delicate question. I submit that there is a via media between being normative and being purely descriptive. Religious studies cannot be normative. It has neither the tools nor the power to set the rules. But it is not merely descriptive either. Human genetic manipulation, totalitarian ideologies, social genocide, the defoliation of nature, unjust laws, degradation of human dignity, and many another issue could be adduced in regard to which religious studies simply has to take a stand, a stance that follows directly upon its internal clarification of the problem and analysis of its assumptions. Where other disciplines may remain on the level of description and continue to function, religious studies has to take a stand in order to link particular issues with the overall picture of human fulfillment. Any stand taken is, of course, provisional and open to criticism, dialogue, and refutation, but it is nevertheless a stand. There is no neutral ground. Failing to take a stand amounts to a tacit endorsement of the status quo. This final challenge may seem daunting: nuclear weapons, abortion, state terrorism, apartheid, militarization, but also liberalism, capitalism, socialism, nationalism, and nonviolence, among others, may serve as examples here. It is a risk, and a responsibility.

To put it more pointedly, present-day scientific disciplines are not directly concerned with truth. Their primary concerns are to acquire the most accurate possible descriptions of objectifiable data, to develop pragmatic knowledge of how things work, and eventually to put that knowledge to "good" use. But truth is more than (mathematical) exactitude, (physical) consistency, (historical) coherence, (political) efficacy, or (psychological) plausibility. Human life cannot avoid the question of truth. Religious studies is, in this sense, closer to common sense and to human life as it is lived: the question of truth cannot be brushed aside. And it is precisely because truth is central and unavoidable to its concerns that religious studies soon discovers that truth itself is polyvalent, polysemic, certainly relational, and probably pluralistic at the ultimate level—which does not mean *plural*, as I have tried to explain elsewhere.

The Cross-Cultural and Interdisciplinary Nature of the Study of Religions

I have been uncapping all these highly debated questions only in order to bring home the role of religious studies. Literally hundreds of excellent books are available today that explore alternatives to the present world order. Many of these present workable options and are thus a sign of hope. Such studies have thousands of readers. They wish to reflect the existence of "movements" and of people who are putting the new ideas into practice. These are islands for survival, links to a new and truly human lifestyle. But most are still grafted onto the old system, mainly because it is almost impossible to do otherwise. Too often these new movements do not take the possible contributions of other cultures, religions, and worldviews seriously enough.

Today we need much more than a handful of isolated options, meaningful only to small groups of people reacting to some common frustrating experiences.

Here the contribution of religious studies may well be crucial. Religious studies offers the natural and cultural platform where dialogue and possibly mutual fecundation may take place. The different religious traditions of the world simply do not speak the same language—that is, share the same myths, symbols, context, and so on. How can American Indians, for instance, present a case against the construction of a highway or an atomic power plant because their ancestors were buried on the site and the proposed "development" would render communication and even personal identification with them impossible? Mainstream American civilization may yield in one or two instances out of political necessity, but the Indians are never going to convince the engineers of the reasonableness of such "absurd" and "ridiculous" demands. The retorts are familiar: "Ghosts do not exist," "Land is just a resource, a plot of measurable Newtonian space," "Development means progress," "We will pay you for it." That the ancestors may be real or the Earth a living organism is sheer nonsense and superstition for the engineer. Or again, to claim India could solve her protein deficiency by slaughtering her "sacred" cows amounts, in its context, to suggesting that North America balance its budget by consuming human flesh. These are clashes at the mystic level, involving not just one behavior or another but entire modes of organizing human life. And to suppose that we "respect" the Hindu, the Christian, or the atheist without having even an inkling of their values or ideas comes to no more than political expediency.

I propose, therefore, that the discipline of religious studies take on the role of a sort of *clearinghouse* where contributions from the most divergent disciplines and disparate cultures are brought into dialogue and interaction *on their own terms*, that is, without undue violence to the respective insights and worldviews of those disciplines and cultures. In so many words, the role of religious studies today is to offer a clearinghouse where the ultimate problems of the human world may be sifted, clarified, discussed, perhaps understood, and eventually solved. The "discipline" would then be nothing less than the concerted essay to understand Man's ultimate predicament in a world context by all the possible means at our disposal. If religious studies is concerned with studying ultimate human values and disvalues, without excluding those of contemporary humanity, then its task should be that of trying to understand the traditional and modern contexts that make these values meaningful. Religious studies is thus by its very nature not only cross-cultural but also interdisciplinary. In short, religious studies has links with every discipline inasmuch as it relates to the *humanum*, but while some links have almost eroded and ought to be reinstated, still others are far too overgrown and ought to be trimmed.

Out of such dialogue new problems emerge, new methods may be found, and new hermeneutics invented. This process has already provided religious studies its own specialized group of scholars. But they alone cannot adequately cope with all these fields and subtopics, which require abundant input from the other disciplines. The nuclear issue is a particularly acute example here, but hardly the only one. It is indeed methodologically wrong to try to deal with all these "borderline" issues in isolation, as if religious studies had some sort of special dispensation or revelation that would entitle it to make judgments about such problems, independently of their complex connections with the disciplines concerned.

There is, in this regard, another holdover from former theological methods that should stringently be avoided. It is not adequate to "obtain" results from various sciences and then mix them up in a religious studies cocktail. It is a false assumption to suppose that we can really know the results from a particular field without having participated to a certain degree in the very methodology of that field. If we cannot speak about a religious tradition without at least some empathy and inner knowledge of that tradition, how can we expect to do so for the other branches of human knowledge? The methods are intrinsically connected with the results of the study in question. Many astoundingly inaccurate ideas about modern physics, for instance, would disappear straightaway if those who think of elementary particles and energy quanta as little "material" or "energetical" things would get to know the methods by which modern physicists have come to speak about these "entities." Religious studies is a clearinghouse, I said, not a packing and baling depot. We cannot deal with ready-made ideas. The dialogical character of religious studies is central to its method.

It could be said that I am proposing to replace the old role of philosophy, and that the religious studies faculty member should be a kind of philosopher-in-residence in each department. In a certain way, it could also be said that I am resurrecting the classical idea of the *studium generale*. Here I should have to respond, "Yes and no." "Yes," since the university has to be loyal to its name and not become a "multiversity" or a sheer "diversity." To avoid this, some agency or discipline has to try to bring together the different branches of learning and of reflection upon reality; it has to make the attempt, pluralistic though it may be, to assemble and integrate the dispersive vectors of human consciousness into the most comprehensive intellectual picture possible. "No," on the other hand, since religious studies has neither a higher source of knowledge nor an a priori method, much less the power or the inclination to follow the lead of medieval theology and crown itself "queen" of the other sciences and disciplines.

The challenge posed to religious studies today is to try to reach some form of in-depth understanding and to confront all the implications—sometimes terrifying—of human freedom, to draw the appropriate conclusions, to act on them responsibly, and to abide by the consequences.

21

REFLECTIONS ON RELIGION AND EUROPE

My words will take this title seriously, avoiding any application of soothing poultices. It is increasingly seen to be less diplomatic to speak about basic underlying things. This could be because it is less immediately effective to do so and one is straightaway taken for a utopian dreamer, someone who is not in touch with reality because of the constant remembrance of history, the attempt to determine the perhaps invisible dimension of life, and the refusal to live life on the surface. And banality, I believe, is a widespread epidemic that has proliferated throughout the world, and we in this country are certainly not exempt.

A "new" Europe may seem like a challenge for Christians.

First and foremost I shall quote thinkers who have taken the time to develop this subject.

Reinhold Schneider states, "The realization of freedom is a tragic problem."[1] He tells us that the intention behind his study is "to probe . . . the consciousness of our historic existence in depth, precisely in the knowledge and acceptance of the tragic aspect of our Christian historic existence [and by doing this] to encounter its [possible] renewal."

Instead of explaining what this quote actually means, I would prompt readers to reread it, this time bearing in mind that human (and Christian) freedom does not mean the prolongation of the status quo.

The second quote goes practically in the opposite direction. It is a triumphal hymn. I refer to Daniel Halevy. The quote comes from an article that caused a bit of a stir a few years back, comparing Europe with another model, China. He states,

China presents us with Europe's counterpart. China does not know this new hope. There, new knowledge springs forth but its result is generally aborted, although the Chinese are certainly not lacking in ingenuity. They invented gunpowder, along with the printing press and the magnetic compass [apart from many other discoveries which were first ignored, and then rediscovered at a later date], but they never took advantage of these three inventions, except for making fireworks, printing playing cards, and it never occurred to them to use the compass to travel to Europe. Armed with the same instruments, we

---

[1] Schneider, *Erbe und Freiheit* (Cologne: Hegner, 1945), 9: "Verwirklichung der Freiheit ist ein tragisches Problem."

blow up walls [artillery], carry out the revolution of the spirit [the Guten-
berg press], and sail to China. This is because Europe possesses a collective
mentality of change, absent in China, without which we would have become
culturally sterile.[2]

Translation: Narcissistic, belligerent, and violent Euro-centralism. If only we
had followed the example of Chinese wisdom!

Another quote among many states that in European history everything that
has been accomplished has been thanks to Christianity.[3] In other words, not only
is Christianity considered the bridge, but it is also held that the roots of modernity,
rationalism, freedom, and so on are actually found within Christianity. Here I present
other testimonies that imply that the European problem is central for the history
of humanity.[4] From our present-day viewpoint, everything contains the seeds of
tragedy. It is imperative that we ask ourselves what this is all about and thus accept
the challenge. A recent symposium shows us the diversity of opinions that exist.[5]

It is encouraging to see the new Europe taking a critical look at itself, even if this
intra-European reflection has not integrated extra-European perspectives sufficiently,
in particular non-Western ones.[6] Only when there is violence does Germany inquire
into the fact of having almost 2 million Turks. And "the new Europe"—for instance,
France—closes its borders.

Obviously, we should also reflect upon intercultural aspects. First, the historic
framework is not the only reference point from which to reflect upon religion.
Second, history itself has many different meanings. To put it in schematic order:
history for Judaism, and for a large part of present-day Christianity, is a *promise*;
for Marxism and Liberalism, it is the *future*; for Islam, an *epiphany*; for Buddhism,
a *stimulant*; for Hinduism, a *temptation*; and, at bottom, it is a *mystery* for them all.
But we shall stick to the intra-European reflection alone.

If I were to summarize my thinking, I would say that the religious crisis in
Europe resides in its incapacity to go beyond *monism*—and monotheism. It has
sought to overcome this with *dualism*—creator/creature, man/woman, sacred/
profane, church/state, individual/society, religion/politics, and so forth—and

---

[2] Halevy, *Essai sur l'eccéleration de l'histoire* (Paris: Fayard, 1966), 66, *apud* Nazario
González, *Europa: Posibilidades y dificultades para la solidaridad* (Barcelona: Cristianisme
i Justicia, 1991), 22.

[3] See the collected works edited by S. A. Burrell, *The Role of Religion in Modern
European History* (New York: Macmillan, 1964).

[4] M. Schmaus, *La aportación del Cristianismo a la unidad de Europa* (Salamanca:
Universidad, 1965); H. Scharp, *Abschied von Europa?* (Frankfurt: Knecht, 1953).

[5] D. Théraios, ed., *Quelle religion pour Europe?* (Genena: Georg, 1990).

[6] Cf. J. M. Aubert, J. Comby. and B. van der Maat, eds., *Les actes del colloque: 1492–
1992—Conquête et Evangile en Amerique Latine: Questions pour l'Europe aujourd'hui* (Lyon:
Profac, 1992): see my contribution, "Meditation européenne après un demi- millénnaire
(29–52).

when this has not provided positive results, it has felt the temptation to fall back on anarchism, which has been "dominated" by quantitative democracy. The middle way of *a-dualism*, while at the core of Christianity—Trinity, incarnation, redemption, and so on—seems not to have been contemplated. Neither God nor creature, male nor female, individual nor society . . . these are neither one nor two. Equality makes two and difference subordinates Man to God, female to male, individual to society, and so on. Reality is neither one nor two. It is *advaita*. But I shall limit myself to the more concrete parameters of this problematic issue.

Reflection upon religion and Europe is a never-ending subject. Yet it is up to philosophers to reach its depths—regardless of the outcome. I shall immerse myself in the quest, summing it up with the aid of three questions.

1. Can Europe get by without religion?
2. Is Christianity the religion for Europe?
3. Which religion, then?

Can Europe Get By without Religion?

By *religion* I understand the accepted myth that endows the ultimate meaning to life. This obviously has to do with a phenomenological description that sees in religion the myth that is accepted as conferring ultimate meaning on life, whatever that may be.

What do I understand by *Europe*? Those of you who have been to Finland will have noticed the character of the Finnish people, which is totally different from that of Russians or other Scandinavians, as well as that of people in Latin countries, but is also not found in Australia nor Patagonia, either. And the Finnish are just as European as the Austrian or Swiss, at least in terms of number of inhabitants.

Which Europe? That of the thirteenth century, which built the cathedrals? That of the eighteenth century, which produced the Enlightenment? That of the twentieth century, in which 100 million people were killed in artificial wars? Is there one unit that is not purely geographic? Or is it, perhaps, a vicious circle? We speak about Europe as certain Europeans have seen and interpreted it. We speak about a nucleus that has already made history, so to speak, where all those other countries, from Macedonia to Finland, hardly count, even though they are more or less marginally accepted.

Idealists and Romantics are not the only ones who talk about the European spirit in terms of a colonialism that is the offspring of its times; much more recently we find the description given to the European man is significantly the same as the description of Man in general, as we find in so many tribes in Africa that refer to themselves simply as "men."

Dénis de Rougemeont comments that the West is characterized "by maintaining the two terms [unity and multiplicity] not in a neutral balance, but rather, in a creative tension, and the success of this forever renewed effort, although always threatened, indicates the state of health of European thought."[7] Who could not say this about practically all civilizations?

Europe. Let us be generous by giving it three thousand years of existence, and despite its diversity, let us try to see it as an extremely complex cultural-historical reality that possibly has a reason for being one unit. There is a certain uniformity. Europe's achievements in these past three thousand years cannot be denied, although there is still a narcissism, sometimes unconscious or unspoken, after three and a half centuries of being made to believe that humankind's evolution ranges from *Pithecanthropus erectus* to the man who first set foot on the Moon, evolving in a linear fashion. If this is the case, we have no necessity of the experience of others to know what Man is, or know what Europe is, as Westerners see themselves as the peak of this evolutionary pyramid of *Homo tecnologicus* that has overcome *faber* and *sapiens*. Many still take for granted that a European viewpoint of events is obviously universal.

And notwithstanding, there *could* be something that is specifically European (archetype? myth? symbol?). Europe was a Phoenician princess—from the pre-Arian, mercantile, sea-trading Orient—whom Zeus, the bovine Sun God—aggressive and Indo-European—carried off to make her give birth on the island of Crete—the Mediterranean par excellence. There are telluric forces and ancestral energies that could provide us with an important hermeneutic key, but at this point in time I do not wish to broaden upon this issue, although part of what I will explain later on does take into account the chthonic roots of this ancient civilization.[8]

To be clear I shall relate an anecdote. I recall an event that shocked me when I was studying at the Indian University of Varanasi in 1954. One of my lecturers there, the late professor T. R. V. Murti, undoubtedly one of the most renowned contemporary Indian philosophers of all times, only after long hours of intense discussion—owing to our need to warm up motors—confessed something to me—I, being an Indian (thus obviating the complexity involved in talking to a Westerner) but also a Catholic priest (hence, belonging to the colonists' religion)—that he had never before revealed to a Westerner, but which he felt deep down: that he considered Adolf Hitler to be the prototype of a Christian. After my initial protest—we carried on talking for three more hours—I began to realize that from his point of view, he was not so wrong. When I said to him that I thought that Hitler was a bad Christian, a bad Catholic, a frustrated seminarist, a paranoid monster, he countered by arguing that if he were such, he would have been locked away in an asylum and certainly

---

[7] Rougemeont, *L'Un et le Divers* (Neuchàtel, 1970), 23. See also his book *L'Esprit européen*, 144. "European man is said to be crucified between the opposites of imminence versus individual and collective transcendence, security and risk. . . ." Quoted by Giulia Paola di Nicola, *Reciprocidad hombre/mujer* (Madrid: Narcea, 1991; translation from the Italian *Uguaglianza e diferenza*, 1989), 109, 179.

[8] See, for example, the chapter entitled "Eurofrateria," in Andrés Ortiz-Osés, *Las claves simbólicas de nuestra cultura* (Barcelona: Anthropos, 1993), 23–32.

would not have risen to power. If there had not been fertile ground for his ideas in this world where he succeeded in touching the deepest and most unconscious fibers at the core of so many Christians, he would not have gained such popularity, nor been able to foment anti-Semitism, and much less the war. He dared to unleash the ultimate consequences of Christian absolutism. And, in fact, Christian churches, with very few exceptions, failed to condemn him for his macabre achievement. We have to be a little more aware of the fact that there are other interpretations of the history of European accomplishment. Just ask yourself: Why is it that Christian missionaries find it so difficult to obtain a visa in modern-day India?

Can Europe get by without religion? Which Europe? The New Europe. And I think this means one thing. I think it makes sense to talk about this new Europe, to talk about a mutation in European consciousness, which, without forgetting those three thousand years, makes us realize to a greater or lesser extent that we are entering a new age, precisely because of Europe's most treasured fact: modern science. Even if it is currently present worldwide, this science has deeply engrained European origins, roots, and levels of connaturality. The managing director of a Bangalore tool factory, a man streets ahead of most European engineers, commented to me some years ago about the lack of connaturality of practically all his workers concerning the subject, concerning everything that we call the mechanized (mechanistic) world of machines and the tools they make. For them, matter, time, space, and fifty thousand other things they were doing had other vibrations and were something else. The material world was something very different from a *res extensa* that followed "the laws of physics," without mentioning animism or whatever else. Another cosmology [*sic*]!

This fact of modern science, unique in the history of humankind, does in fact allow us to be able to talk about a new Europe. I do not mean technology or science as an external fact, but rather as a *forma mentis*, that something which has made the West's achievements possible. Traditional Europe was brought about by religion, but it has also been undone by it—by religious wars. Someone said that religious wars prompt states to search for a steady foundation not based on faith in God. This is the beginning of secularization, where God becomes a hypothesis superfluous to the functioning of the world. Everything has a price. These days, we have a new Europe on our hands, but traditional Europe was forged and also practically undone by religion. Here, Christianity has played a leading role. We have a "Christian" Europe dating from the third century up until the twelfth century, one that comes apart from the thirteenth century onward and is regained in the seventeenth and eighteenth centuries, to again become undone in the twentieth century, to simplify the subject considerably.

Now let us now consider this present-day Europe, which is far more historic, sociologic, political, mercantile, and economic than religious; this Europe, whose every sneeze is heard all over the world despite the fact that it is not the leading world power—can this Europe get by without religion? Let us not forget that the initial force that joined us together was coal and steel: merchant Europe. This has been the driving force behind the new Europe. This Europe is the Europe of science and of economy, not of religion. Because of this, the question springs to mind whether religion is needed and consequently, if the religious age has already passed—Auguste Comte, if you wish—if the real, actual, present-day, living Europe could function without religion.

We can entertain the suspicion that the act of Christians questioning themselves about the challenge of a Europe with a new religion or without one at all might not be an anachronism, because this religious fact that was essentially vital from Greek times until the Enlightenment is not present in modern society. Could it be that Christians want to take part in a Europe that they have not assisted in constructing?

The sad, mad, yet not insane, genius prophet Friedrich Nietzsche states in *The Gay Science*, "For a long time now our whole civilization has been driving, with a tortured intensity growing from decade to decade, as if toward a catastrophe: relentlessly, violently, tempestuously, like a mighty river desiring the end of its journey, without pausing to reflect, indeed fearful of reflection. . . ."

And yet, nevertheless, thinkers who get to the crux of the issue of modern Europe tell us that stripped of the ultimate meaning of life, of reality, of human constructions—stripped of religion, as we have defined it—we cannot live, nor can Europe get by.[9]

Can Europe get by without religion? My response is a resounding No! Religions are invented, and new ones will be invented. Even the most diverse ideology may take on an ultimate, definitive meaning, thus converting it into a religion, including more or less secularized religions. But the fact is that without this other factor, which is not included in empirical data, people would do nothing, nor could men live. In the last sentence of a short article we can read, "It is necessary to have the courage of a historic consciousness as the foundation for the ethical options whose reason for being cannot be found in history."[10]

And this precisely is the new religion that in one way or another is resurgent. If we accept the phenomenological definition we have given of religion, all recent wars have been religious. When a nation is prepared to kill, it has to have some kind of definite and ultimate reason, and religious ideology is itself an attitude that is ready to go to war. If someone steals a coin from me, I will certainly not kill that person for it, but if someone tries to take my freedom away from me, anything could happen. War only has one rational foundation—because you fight to kill—if we are talking about something where everything is at stake. If Europe believes in anything, it cannot get by without religion. The fact that the new Catechism from the Vatican justifies

[9] I just wish to mention the indispensable works of the passionate late historian Freidrich Heer, *Europäische Geistesgeschichte* (Stuttgart: Kohlhammer, 1953); *Europa, madre de revoluciones*, 2 vols. (1964; Madrid: Alianza Editorial, 1980); *Das Wagnis der schöpferischen Vernunft* (Stuttgart: Kohlhammer, 1977).

[10] A. Carile, "È necessario avere il corragio della coscienza storica a fondamento di scelte etiche che non trovano la loro ragione nella a storia," *L'Europa dall'Atlantico agli Urali* (Bologna: Centro San Domenico, 1992).

the death penalty and, on some occasions, even war should make us think. I began with a text that reminds us of the tragic sense of historic-Christian consciousness. Our subject is religion and Europe, not morality and Europe.

Is Christianity the Religion for Europe?

We must ask this question from its radical point of view. The *aggiornamento* is certainly extremely necessary, but we already take it for granted that the answer is a "renewed" Christianity as the religion that Europe needs. "New evangelization" means "evangelzed" again, or could it mean transforming the very concept of evangelization—that is, at bottom, transforming religion itself? The *aggiornamento* is imperative for the life of Christianity, yet our problem does not refer to Christianity, but rather to Europe.

The radical question is not *which* Christianity suits the new Europe, but rather we should bravely ask ourselves whether Christianity has already done all it has to do. "Strategic retreats" are not too convincing these days. Redeeming Joans of Arc, Eckharts, and Galileos centuries later, or condemning crusades and conquests after five hundred years or more, is not too convincing. Soon they will tell us that Giordano Bruno's burning at the stake was an oversight, and all other events just mistakes owing to bad cardinals and ill-advised Vatican politics, or what you will. Is a five-hundred-year-late mea culpa really enough? Can one not understand the reaction of many Christians who are hardly enthusiastic about the beatification of José Maria Escrivà or put little store in the reinstallation, a few centuries on, of the Bermejos, Curran, Fox, and Boff alongside Zen meditation and the practice of yoga? Or should we ask *which* Christianity?

It seems that when forging Europe and its colonies, Christianity gave all it could give, and now it is out of steam. Christianity is a historic fact, and just as all those who are not Christians say, we have no other criteria or source of knowledge to know what Christianity truly is, except through what Christians do. "By their fruits they shall be known." From this point of view, the great icon that was Europe before 1914 that allowed Europeans, for the mere fact of being European, to find reserved spaces, to be listened to and respected anytime they entered any place in India, has now come to an end. Missionaries in British India had first-class passes on all trains. This must be paid for, but in those days it was plain: Europe was superior, and Christianity was its power. Before the First World War, 80 percent of the planet's surface belonged to Europe. The myth of Europe in Asia above all, but also in a large part of Africa, began to totter in 1918. The writings of Max Scheler are both a pathetic and a precious documentation of this. The European myth began to totter even more so after 1945. And after the last Gulf war, in which the old Europe denied *its* Christianity and its humanity, the "new Europe" has lost all authority. The West has not lost its power, but it has completely lost its authority. It has lost respect. It is feared, pacts are made with it, which is where the pragmatic Latin obtained the word *pax* (peace), on the contrary to the German, where *Friede* is related to *Freund* (friend) and *Freiheit* (freedom).

The claim of "dignified Christianity and undignified Christians" is no longer valid. In the first place, it can be applied to any other religion or ideology. Second, religion is no longer a sublime doctrine, but rather an embodied, social, and historical reality. Third, because defending it with the argument that the others have done no better (or would not have done it better) would only prove that we wish to make an a priori apology, and that we are avoiding the fundamental question about the kind of religiosity Europe needs.

It is a fact that Christian-based European culture has spread all over the world. But it is also a fact that the balance of events, seen from three-quarters of the world, is not very positive, and lambasting technology and certain "bad people" is not a convincing enough argument.

It is hard, it is lamentable, it is painful to have to say, for instance, that the abolition of slavery cannot be attributed to the Christianity that forged Europe, that it was carried out despite the Church, or that nowadays established religious institutions, with some exceptions, remain passive before the institutionalized injustice of the present-day system, with the excuse that changing the status quo—just as with slavery—would cause disaster, that is, disaster for vested interests, of course. It is significant to observe how they have sought to co-opt so-called liberation theology, for it to only reform the system, not to transform it. It is true that we have not done everything badly. Some extraordinary achievements have taken place. But we shall now take a look at the general balance of events to see what kind of future lies ahead, because the future in store is not based on the same parameters as presented by Greece or India, precisely because of the furor brought about by scientific facts. And the new generations of the present day say this loud and clear, in down-to-earth fashion.

At this point I was going to say that Europe betrayed the message of Christ. Yet I immediately correct myself and say Europe *interpreted* it. In other words, from Constantine, Theodosius, and Charlemagne, to Boniface VIII and John Paul II, Europe has interpreted the message of Christ in a way that perhaps is not mine, that perhaps is not ours, that perhaps we could not defend with the Gospels in our hand . . . but which we must not judge. It is a fact that, rightly or wrongly, Europe has interpreted the message of the Nazarene. We can go on to discuss the criteria applied and whether we accept it or not, but our opinion is only yet another interpretation. Europe has interpreted the message in a way that these days seems to have lost vitality and credibility. The "Mellifluous Doctor," St. Bernard, preaching the action of the Crusades like a good contemplative, says that "whoever kills a Muslim on a crusade, *non est homicida sed malicida*"; it is not homicide, it is malicide, a honorable man killing badness. That is why there were indulgences. This Christianity is historic Christianity, even if there were prophets and saints who have tried to swim against the tide to bring us another message, perhaps a purer one from my point of view, but now is not the time to judge.

Is Christianity the religion for Europe? No it is not, not because there are also atheists, Muslims, Jews, and so many others, but rather because Christians themselves do not seem to take their own religion too seriously. If all Christian churches disappeared from Europe, the cataclysm would be more economic than spiritual. Religion in Europe is a private and secondary affair. We only have to take a look at the Islamic and Hindu worlds to see the difference. In fact, Christianity is not the main religion in Europe. Money or technocracy is more important. Without these, Europe could certainly not live; it already lives without Christianity.

We ask ourselves if a Europe without religion still has the will to live?

I have said (first thesis): Europe cannot get by without religion. I added (second thesis): Christianity is no longer the religion for Europe.

Which Religion, Then?

This situation can be described in the expression of the poet Martial: "Nec tecum possum vivere, nec sine te" (I can live neither with you, nor without you). This is a problem in many marriages: "neither with you nor without you." What religiousness can be foreseen to respond to this challenge of the new Europe? And to recall the Latin poet, Europe, despite our negative response to the second question, cannot be rid of Christianity, it will not free itself. Europe will not let go. It is possessed by the most profound archetypes: from those who "thanks to God, are atheists"— who are usually antitheists, in fact—to those who, thanks to society, "believe" in God. Christian archetypes range from science to debauchery, from disbelief to the conception of practically everything forged by the Christian myth. Neither with nor without Christianity.

Which Religiosity, Then?

The category I wish to employ is precisely the consequence of the Christian archetypes we have been filled with. It is the category dealing with the *resurrection*. Or perhaps we might use a slightly more academic and equally evangelic term, which, from another point of view, causes fewer disputes, *metanoia*. *Metanoia*, not in the sense of doing penance, of being punished, of converting, or of changing your life. It is interesting to observe the changes in the translation of this term over the past hundred years. I would like to interpret *metanoia* not as a change in mentality—as it is generally translated these days—but rather as an overcoming of the mental reduction to which the Enlightenment led us. This does not mean scorning rationalism, but rather taking a leap above and beyond the mental, the rational, the rationally coherent, the intelligible. The Christian resurrection entails a new life and not simply a continuation of the old one. The resurrection of Christ does not mean the prolongation of Jesus of Nazareth's physiological body, although I believe it does have something of this meaning. This implies we are not necessarily the good Christians and those who betrayed Christianity the bad ones. Here and now, it is not about defending or attacking. It consists, rather, in seeing this challenge of the new Europe in an inherently European situation, although having repercussions that extend throughout the world. We cannot isolate ourselves and make a Europe all on its own.

I have talked elsewhere about *Christiania* as the way of living the Christian reality in the third millennium, going beyond the second millennium, which was *Christianity* coupled with *Christianness*.

So as not to be too long-winded, I would like to limit myself to three adjectives that I shall use to sketch out this new religiosity, which, from within, could be named *Christian*, though from the outside this adjective would not be necessary. In reality, to us it means the metamorphosis, the transformation, to the new light we are now capable of seeing.

The religiosity Europe needs is a more *evangelical*, more *ecumenical*, and more *mystical* one.

A More Evangelical Religiosity

A more *evangelical* religiosity, in the most literal meaning of the word, from the Sermon on the Mount, means more humility and less institutionalization, more trust in the spirit and more time spent observing lilies and watching birds instead of shutting them in cages, or taking their lives. Evangelic means annunciation, in the sense of joyful discovery. There is no message until it is discovered. Wisdom is the joy of knowing how to live. To say we have complicated life and complicated Christianity is to go over old ground, as true as the observation may be. There is no question of reverting back to being cave dwellers, or defending illiterate people who live life enveloped in romance; what I argue for does not mean turning the Sermon on the Mount into a bucolic, utopian manifesto. Rather I mean something much more profound. In other words, what is concerned here is a radical change in culture: not the agriculture from the past, or techno-culture of the present, but rather the *cultivation* of one's spirit, the *harvest* of humankind and all cosmotheandric reality. Religion has always been at the core of any new culture, any new change in civilization. We find ourselves at the moment of human mutation. Without new and authentic religiosity, the force of inertia would drag us down into catastrophe. What I mean concerns continuing tradition, not repeating it, but re-creating it once again, in a totally unforeseen fashion, with the process I have named resurrection. Not the resurrection of the old man. Christ is Jesus resurrected and not the physiological continuation of the son of Mary. And so, it is not about returning to the Middle Ages, not even to so-called primitive Christianity. If Christianity does not know how to resurrect, it will remain utterly dead and gone.

A More Ecumenical Religiosity

Ecumenism has many meanings. One does not have a monopoly over words, but I would like to employ this one in the more feminine sense rather than the masculine, in a much more passive way than active. Ecumenism does not so much mean that I reach out to others, take interest in them, and tell them I tolerate them, see that I can learn from them, and that we can converse on neutral grounds—all this is necessary—as much as my welcoming them to my home, whether they are believers or not, opening myself up to the danger of being invaded, being influenced by them, along with the risk of being violated, that is, of changing. Change myself, opening myself up to others. In this sense of allowing oneself to be influenced and fecundated, I renounce myself and go beyond myself. Christianity renounces itself and is resurrected—renouncing, that is, going beyond the repeated universality of Christianity, the specific nature of the Christian message, and the superiority of the Christian religion.

That is what being ecumenical means. If we lose the sense of the quality of things and only take refuge in their quantitative aspect, interpreting universal events quantitatively, then all kinds of theological problems and political disasters arise. If we do not know how to perceive and live the uniqueness of things, if I think a friend is not unique, a religion is not unique, a child of mine is not unique, or my homeland is not unique, I lose the sense of uniqueness in all things that is only acquired when knowledge goes intrinsically hand in hand with love. No one wants to change their child for someone else's even if the other child is more beautiful, a better person, or a richer one, because everyone loves their own offspring. I desire the beauty of one, the goodness of another, the quickness of another . . . , but I want all of this for my own child, not for any other. That would not make sense. But I am not going to enter into philosophic matters at this point.

A much more ecumenical religion. Hence, the problem is not the Muslims or the Orthodox, one or the other. It is the capacity to enjoy the truth in a rainbow, awareness that without green there is no red, without yellow there is no green, that each color is unique, and that there is no outer spectator who sees things without being located somewhere. The Enlightenment instilled the belief that mankind from the rostrum of righteousness can judge all religions. This is how the discipline of comparative religions came about, when it was believed that there was a platform presided over by the Goddess of Reason, who was above all religions, and could judge and classify them. Some things in life cannot be classified. Yet this would demand an extremely extensive digression on the obsession with the classification of things that from Aristotle to the science of today has continued to dominate the West.

Ecumenical means a religiosity that I would not precisely call specifically Christian, yet neither would I denominate it non-Christian. Ecumenism is an inherent characteristic of any mature and critical religiosity, capable of facing up to the problematic human situation in this third millennium. The fact that we are all unique persons, different from each other, does not prevent anyone of us from being just as human as anyone else.

Humanity is not summed up in just one person or in just a single type of person (man, white, from the twentieth century and so on and so forth). Yet, however, I am more of a man when I am more truly myself, with all of my specific characteristics. Religiosity cannot be summed up in one sole religion, and each one will be truer to itself the better it cultivates its "personality." Religion is eminently personal, which does not mean individual, and it cannot be compared to being member of a club, or of a state for that matter. One is not Catholic for being a follower of the current pope or Muslim for being a follower of Khomeini, or Jewish because he or she believes in the state of Israel. This is a complex issue, as humankind also needs institutions, political parties, and religious groups. But when it comes down to religion, to religiosity, it is from my own that I participate in others by deeply accepting diversity, because I realize that diversity is the form of universality itself. It is what Nicholas of Cusa means when he speaks of one single religion with a wide range of rites: "una religio rituum varietate."

A more ecumenical religiosity does not mean more eclectic, but rather more profound. In this sense, its universality is not a quantitative or geographic issue, and neither is it cultural. It is more the expression of uniqueness that each person discovers for oneself. To explain it in a sociological fashion, when people comment, "Those poor Indian people, how do they manage to get through life? I wouldn't put up with their situation for more than five minutes; I would rebel." Obviously, if all Indians converted to the speaker's Western Christianity tomorrow, the day after tomorrow 50 percent would commit suicide; if tomorrow they took on a form of Western consciousness, they would not be able to bear the weight of their own existence the day after tomorrow. But vice versa, if all Europeans were converted to Hinduism tomorrow, the day afterward half of them would also commit suicide. They would realize that they are slaves, that they have no time for anything, that they eat oodles of protein but do not play, that they only make love but without loving, that they live overwhelmed by one moment, only to dive straight into another. Their lives would become impossible, living in concrete jungles which are far worse, far more frightening than any real jungle. They would become aware of this, and they would inevitably fall into the deepest of depressions.

What does all this mean? Is it that one thing is better than the other? Of course not! We criticize Westerners for showing off their new cars, so proud of their machines, and sweetening their lives with one whiskey too many. Yet we also criticize those Orientals who seem to lack any initiative, who resign themselves to injustice, or perhaps are just unaware of it. It is not that we are inferior. It only implies that we have to learn from each other, talk about things, correct ourselves, and be attentive to mutual fertilization. Ecumenism precisely means not closing off any doors. And I apologize for this simplified cliché for an answer.

A More Mystical Religiosity

I do not mean a mythical mysticism, but rather an existing third dimension in things and in humanity. I am talking about the "third eye," as Victorines would say. I am talking about the experience of the loss of fear; because I live life fully at every instant. Symeon the New Theologian stated that those who do not live eternity now would not live it later either. That is the Paschal Experience. This means that I do not have to worry about the future because I have already seen the truth. And, consequently, it is not that I am very brave because I overcome my fear—but that I am not afraid because fear does not exist; there is no fear in me.

A mysticism that discovers that the meaning of life is not found at the end of this one, but rather in life itself. A Hindu friend of mine said this in a beautiful way: "You would say the meaning of a Beethoven symphony is found in the last finale, and everything else just leads to this conclusion?" It is not so; each moment has its own beauty and holds its own meaning. This is the overcoming of time: every moment is unique. The *tempitern* moments, as I would say. A mystical religiosity that lives in real hope because it has realized that hope does not lie in the future; it is invisible. Hope enables us to live in this other dimension and therefore allows us to live at peace with ourselves. It is that "mē merimnate" (do not worry) of Christ: *Do not rush, do not suffer; live with more eudemonic, more joyful, more profound fullness.*

This is no digression. What is the meaning in life? What does Europe mean? If Europe is solely a historical project for conquering the world, to convert it or to improve upon it, we simply fall into the same old trap. Messianism has not been overcome. This is what is asked by all the best European spirits. And if not, go to Britain and talk to people who have little time for those who, for exclusively economic reasons, defend the slogan "the common house." Some things are not said, as no one has ever come up with a good enough way to say them. Many people in Britain are fearful that if they embark upon a plan together with the rest of Europe, they will lose their own identity.

A mystical religiosity that has overcome the mental sees things *sub speciei aeternitatis*, if you will, but also has an immediate, practical consciousness: politics. Not just because it has lost its fear of acting, but also because it is in action where the mystical life is cultivated, is lived, grows, and finds its criteria of authenticity. That is to say, in its political commitment—social, if preferred. It is precisely mystical religiosity that does not recognize institutional boundaries.

The separation between church and state has nothing to do with the separation of religion from life. And if we let ourselves be trapped by a certain scheme, it is obvious that priests should not dabble with the discourse of right- or left-wing political parties, although we would need to go into this in more depth. We have to overcome watertight compartments and cultural schizophrenia, where religion forms one part and politics another, as if they were two separate and separable worlds. Intellectual distinction is not a synonym for existential separation. Mystic religiosity penetrates all human activity, and nothing controls it from the outside. The mystical dimension is within everything. If we lose this sense of mystic religiosity, then politics become falsified. It loses its true sense of the *polis*, the sense of the *ecclesia*—which is the same thing—the sense of the realization of the human person, which is precisely brought about in the complete game of life. And then it is not the action of Christians as such, coming from the right wing or left wing, from democracy or wherever, it is something completely different. And we lack the categories that enable us to think about it.

Fullness of life implies "getting your hands dirty," so to say, which does not mean soiling them, but the total opposite, it means getting them in tune, exercising them, making them work in the activity of the *polis*.

*

So, to close, reflecting upon religion and Europe is a great challenge.

1. *Religion is indispensable* because it is the soul of all the people, of every civilization for better or worse. It always has been.

2. The *restorationist* "project"—returning to Christianity—is not *viable*, either from the historical-European point of view or from the viewpoint of the theological-Christian inner reflection.

3. *What is imperative is a resurrection.* The majority of that which we here classify as Christian is a resurrection of Celtic, Greek, and Mediterranean beliefs: pre-Christian beliefs resurrected in Christian ones. What is needed now is the resurrection of all this into a new life that begins with us and ends at the confines of the world. Humanity has no singular or plural. This resurrection can be called Christian, seen from within, just as a Celt, a Greek, or a Hebrew could think of Christianity as being the resurrection of their respective religions. The game is not played between those who favor progressivism and conservatives. It concerns a transformation. And this is the task of the Spirit. Men of Galilee, why stand ye gazing up into heaven? Fear not!

22

RELIGION AND BODY

Over the course of millennia Man has been attracted, often obsessed, and some-times fascinated by two forces that mystics would call *transcendence* and *immanence*; the poets, *heaven* and *Earth*; and the philosophers, *spirit* and *matter*. Man has been torn between these two poles, either attributing more importance to one or the other, scorning, neglecting or perhaps negating the reality of one of them—matter is evil, the body is slavery, time is illusion—or vice versa—heaven does not exist, the spirit is merely a projection, eternity is a dream.

Religion, interpreted as a human dimension that could be called *religiousness*, faced with the problem of the meaning of life, has fluctuated between these two extremes without being able to completely forget the other. *Carpe diem*: The Earth is too attractive not to enjoy its pleasures. *Fuga mundi*: The world is too transient for us to place our trust in it. However, there is no doubt that many of the principal religions today have decidedly shifted the balance toward the transcendent, the spiritual, and the beyond. "How to go to heaven" is the task of religion; "how the heavens go" is the duty of science: this was the subject of the discussion between a scientist (Galileo Galilei) and a theologian (Roberto Bellarmino).

The dichotomy has been lethal for both. Religion is banned from human affairs, and science has become an abstract specialty detached from human life. Religion becomes an ideology and science an abstraction. In both cases, the body is practi-cally irrelevant.

The task of our generation, if we do not want to contribute to the extinction of *Homo sapiens*, is to resume the celebration of the union between heaven and Earth, that *hieros gamos*, the sacred union of which many traditions, including the Christian one, speak.

The study of humanity's religious traditions demonstrates that "science"—so as not to use other terms—has tried to say something more than the empirical description of "religious" behavior and its "scientific" interpretations, and that religion cannot be reduced to practices or beliefs defined as "religious" from the point of view of rationality, understood as it was interpreted by the so-called Enlightenment. Once we leave monocultural modernity, the traditions themselves that we study make us realize that they have an understanding of themselves by which they become the subject and not just the object of our discipline.

In saying "sciences" we do not wish to exclude any form of consciousness or wisdom. In saying "religions" we do not wish to be part of the monopoly that religious institutions have over this word; what we are referring to is that ultimate nucleus of every culture, and also of every human life, that one *believes* gives a certain meaning to life.

Religion: Truth

It is significant that the polysemous word "religion" has been considered more or less inappropriate in certain circles and has been substituted with "spirituality." This demonstrates that the aversion to the word "religion" is only superficial, seeing that the word "spirit" could easily lead us to fall into another "ghetto," exclusive to "spiritualists." If religion is criticized as a closed oasis that excludes so-called nonbelievers, spirituality in its turn could be understood as the confederation of religions in antithesis to those who deny what is spiritual. Since the times of Confucius it has been common knowledge that a politics of the word has existed. We could eliminate these two words from the dictionary if we just give up and have nothing better to suggest. We could, on the other hand, also retrieve the true sense of the words.

The Religious Fact

If religion claims to lead Man to his ultimate destination, it can also be described as a project for the salvation of mankind, using the words "project" and "salvation" in the widest sense. "Projects" can also fail, just as there can be illusory or evil projects. "Salvation," for its part, is not necessarily a liberation from the human condition nor the epitome of Man's perfection.

So as to stay with our subject we will not go any deeper into definitions of content. Suffice it to say that the field of religion is made up of the symbolic world in which Man ultimately lives. The word does not just originate with the New Testament, and its translation into other languages is in no way univocal (*den / din, dharma,* etc.). Nor will we ponder on its triple etymology: *re-eligere* (Augustine), *re-legere* (Cicero), and *re-ligare* (Lactantius).[1]

Referring to the third term for heuristic reasons, we could describe religion as that project that attempts to *religare* Man to the whole of reality in order to liberate him from all forms of solipsism by establishing liberating bonds that stem from Man himself. Thus we could claim that one of the functions of religion actually consists in healing the wound that the separation between soul and body has caused in human beings. Second, so that the union can be complete, it must be extended to society itself. Peace among men is the unavoidable and essential task of religion, to the point that I would go so far as to describe religion as "the path toward peace."[2] However, religion cannot be limited to a proud human race that, believing in its self-sufficiency, has distanced itself from the world. Religion must also reach out to the

---

[1] See this volume, chap. 3, note 1.
[2] R. Panikkar, *Paz y desarme cultural,* 2nd ed. (Madrid: Espasa Calpe, 2002).

Earth. The Christian message says "peace on Earth" and not only "glory in heaven." In fact, most religions reveal a cosmic aspect. Finally, it is part of religion to unite human beings to the divine, the transcendent, the ultimate, emptiness, nothing, or whatever way each religious system chooses to define this mystery.

It is superfluous to say that this quadruple link is susceptible to the most varied interpretations. Elsewhere I have described the nine aspects of religion: ontical-mystical, dogmatic-doctrinal, ethical-practical, sentimental-emotional, ecclesiastical-sociological, corporeal-cosmological, angelic-diabolical, immanent-transcendent, and eternal-temporal,[3] to which I have added a further three: personal-impersonal, conscious-unconscious, geographical-historical. Religion is a complex matter.

The Triple Meaning of Religion

To introduce some kind of order into the use of this word, it would be useful to make the following distinctions:

Religiousness is the anthropological dimension that allows Man to be aware of his constituting bonds, even if he evaluates them in different ways. Every man, even if only because he is such, is open to the other, to that which he is not—yet—to the transcendent, the unknown, the "more," whether it be understood as the divine, a divinity, or simply the ability to project, or something else altogether. In this way, every man is religious and possesses a characteristic ability that opens him to what he is not—yet?—and allows him to grow, fulfill himself, or fail. This is an anthropological trait that can be defined in many ways.

Religionism is the social aspect of religion. Man is a social being and feels the need to belong to some human group. These social groups are not merely those forms of aggregation that in some places are called churches, congregations, or confessions; they can also be more or less compact or organized groups that offer an identity to their members and confer an ultimate meaning to their lives. Not only Buddhism and Christianity belong to this category but also Marxism, atheism, and agnosticism, as well as scientism, positivism, nationalism, and so on. Not all human groupings are religious, only those that make us feel that we are in communion with that which we believe is the meaning of life. It is a sociological aspect that can have many names.

Religiology is the intellectual structure of religion that may go by the name of theology, philosophy, ideology, cosmovision, and so on. It is a matter of conscious articulation, more or less complete and consistent, of the belief system of a person, a group, or a population. The consciousness of Man's place in reality could be another way of describing this meaning of religion. It is an intellectual place that can take on various aspects.

De nominibus non est disputandum, but I believe that one can agree on the fact that these three characteristics of human beings are those that make up that which one calls religion. This description may seem too wide and generic to those who

---

[3] See this volume, chap. 4.

defend that very particular concept of religion, which is really undergoing a crisis and under discussion at the dawn of the third millennium. We must distinguish these three aspects: Man is a consciously open, unfinished, and imperfect being; he is a social and political being; he is a rational and intelligent being striving to understand his human condition.

Religion Reduced to Ideology

Resistance to this wider notion of religion is put up both by those who identify religion itself as an alienating ideology and those who have reduced it to an orthodoxy with a *doxa* stripped of its "glory." If Man is simply *res cogitans*, even if defined as *roseau pensant* and thought is reduced to the ability to process ideas, we end up by letting religion degenerate into a system of ideas. It goes from being Man's existential and conscious path toward his destiny—whatever its interpretations may be—to meaning a set of doctrines by which this destiny is conceived. Religious faith is thus transformed into doctrinal beliefs to which Man's primacy over being is attributed. We will not be assessed—some might say judged—for our faith or works, but for our ideas. Orthodoxy will no longer be Man's true glory—truth—nor will orthopraxis be humanizing conduct—goodness; only the acceptance of some correct doctrines will be crucial. Man is reduced to a thinking machine.

The situation deteriorates when thought ceases to consider itself as the ability to evaluate the attraction of everything to its place—because the place itself has been transformed into abstract space—that is, when it ceases to be a qualitative perception of reality and is transformed into a quantitative calculation of the behavior of things. The weight that thought weighs up is the love of each thing for the place it belongs to. Love has been separated from thought.

But let us limit ourselves to underlining the old Hellenic dichotomy between body and soul and the relegation of conscious activity to the mind that is innate in the soul. Whatever thought is, it is the soul that carries out this operation, and all the body can do is, at most, offer the natural place in which the soul can be more or less comfortable. An instrumental reason only needs an instrumental body.

It is a short step from here to the "business of the salvation of the soul." Furthermore, without going to these extremes, the function of religion is confined to the so-called spiritual sphere. If the soul does not exist, evidently religion does not exist either. Those who are "tolerant" will allow religion to take care of what is spiritual as long as it does not intrude into material, political, health, nor ultimately temporal issues. Religion is relegated to the eternal and the beyond.

Here we could put forward parallel dichotomies in other cultures, like that of illusion and reality, but we will refrain from doing so because the anthropological and cosmological assumptions are different. *Sarvam sarvātmakan, quodlibet in quolibet,* everything is in relation to everything else, as more than one tradition claims. The dichotomy between the soul and the body is one of the many lethal divisions of a millenary civilization that, after having exploited the body—of slaves, workers, and women—felt relieved when it discovered (second grade) machines that could continue exploiting the body of the Earth. Myths last longer than ideas. On other occasions I have tried to describe the new mortal dichotomies of a civilization that, due to an understandable fear of monism/pantheism, has fallen into the predominant dualism of our times.[4]

Obviously, we do not deny that some religions have rebelled against this reductionism. Furthermore, the majority do not separate health from salvation, nor spiritual from physical reward. The sacramental vision of religion, like the tantric vision that is its equivalent, recognizes the value of the body for the attainment of the fullness of human life, but almost all of them have fallen under the influence of a modernity that considers rationality to be the distinctive trait of Man and, in general, have reduced reason to an illative faculty that reflects—this is true—critically on its own functioning.

In other latitudes, the dominion of a disembodied spirit has been characterized by the elitist religions that have, with benevolent condescension, kept their distance from the popular religions, those that actively make the corporeal participate in religious activity.

The separation between truth, beauty, and goodness, which reduces the first to something that corresponds to good intellectual practice, may serve as an example that we will make clear further on. Thus, truth is simply intellectual and has little or nothing to do with the other transcendentals.

Body: Beauty

It is very significant that when we speak of the body we immediately think of something material, accepting the modern scientific identification of body and matter. Celestial bodies are spoken as one speaks of the resistance of materials. In Western languages, the material body is little less than a tautology. We should remember that our guiding thread is not so much the body *in itself*—even if personally I do not believe in this—as its relation to religion, and that we must therefore leave out many other equally important problems.

The digression of the paragraph above requires an explanation. This is not a marginal confession but rather represents one of the central assumptions of this study, which aims to tackle the human problem not from an analytical or synthetic point of view but from a tridimensional harmonious vision—holistic. Thus, it does not consider the body—in itself—on the one hand and the soul—in itself—on the other, and then tries to join them in a more or less artful synthesis, but rather it attempts to approach human truth using the triple knowledge—sensitive, intellectual, and spiritual. Already we can glimpse that our method clashes with the difficulty of having to fall back on the dualistic language that today proves to be

---

[4] These dichotomies are body/soul, masculine/feminine, good/evil, believers/unbelievers, time/eternity, theory/practice, subjectivity/objectivity, God/world, Being/beings.

practically obligatory. Neither body nor soul exists in themselves. The "in itself" is neither, strictly speaking an *an sich* nor a *quoad se*, but a "self" of our minds, an in *mente* of a subjectivity that thirsts for objectivity, but this does not mean that the distinction—always mental—between the objective and the subjective does not have its raison d'être and its foundation. The classical Castilians used to say, "Lo cortés no quita lo valiente" (The two are not mutually exclusive). "Weder diz noch daz" (Neither this nor that), Meister Eckhart would say (*Sermo mysticus V*) echoing the *Upaniṣad*, which he certainly did not know: "*etad vai tad*" (this [is] certainly that; KathU II.1.3)—"on Earth as in heaven. . . ."

The Material Separated from the Spiritual

Even if the word *matter* has many meanings, we only cite two: first, the meaning of matter as the opposite of form or simply as that which is subject to what we call material things. In this way, "matter" is an abstraction, be it "first matter," "second," power, or be it also that which sets itself against life. This matter is "in itself" inert. Thus, matter approaches the notion of mass in physics. When one speaks of living matter one generally assumes that life prevails over matter. The second meaning of matter is that which opposes itself to the notion of spirit. Matter is that which is not spiritual. The material can be observed and verified while the spiritual does not seem to be directly perceptible.

The split between matter and spirit is basically cosmological. Reality is thus divided into spiritual and material. The realm of the spirit is immaterial. This cosmological dualism is subject to the distancing of the body from its own religious field, which is the problem in which we are directly interested. For the moment we just hint at this before continuing.

The Body as Sensible Appearance

In German there are two terms: *Körper*, comparable to the Latin *corpus*—maybe from a root from which the Sanskrit *kṛpā* (form, beauty) is derived, and perhaps in relation to *kr* (*karman*, to do). The body "does," delineates, and is also beautiful. But there is a second word: *Leib*—related to *Leben* (life). The first, similar to the Latin *corpus* and which translates the Greek *sōma*, makes direct reference to corpse, while the second refers to the living body. In Greek *demas*—see house, *domos*, and *demō*, meaning to build—often refers to the living corporeal form of the human being. It cannot be ignored that the word *sōma* first and more commonly refers to the inanimate body, even if later—as in the *koinē* of the New Testament—it broadens its meaning. This is the inanimate body to which the soul will give life.

These brief observations serve to illustrate that the division has ancient origins.

In a word, body is the opposite of spirit; the latter is invisible while the body is visible, as the classic dictum states: "Omne quod potest videri corpus dicitur"

(Everything that is visible can be called body). The body is appearance, what one sees, the phenomenon.

A certain predominant philosophical thought, both in the West and in most of the East, tells us that because that which appears is mutable, the body is nothing else but the more or less deceptive covering of what really is.

Melissus, disciple of Parmenides, told us that everything that exists is devoid of corporeity because, if it were corporeal, it would have parts that contradict the unity of being. "To on . . . dei . . . sōa mē echein" (Being cannot have a body).

We will briefly mention that this way of thinking that gives value to the permanent and immutable, insofar as it alone can be conceptualized, already represents the dominion of the mind, of the second eye (*oculus mentis*), over other forms of knowledge. If we are not aware of this, any defense of the corporeal will seem to be either irrationalism or a simple tendency toward a materialistic conception of reality. It should be clear that our meditation follows neither of these two paths.

What we perceive with our senses belongs to the field of aesthetics. *Aisthēsis* means sensation, perception. The verb *aisthanomai*, from *aiō*, means to perceive, to understand. *Anaesthesia* is what cannot be perceived. Incidentally, it would seem that aesthetics leans more toward hearing than sight. The invisible can be heard.

Aesthetics are certainly the realm of appearance. But more than anything, appearance is appearance because it is appearance of what appears in the appearance. Appearance is the revelation of the thing, as it covers the invisibility of the thing itself with a visible veil. It is through appearances that we can see reality.

Certain Chinese paintings offer an interesting example of this. It is enough to contemplate one of those pictures in which an entirely clothed figure is the greatest manifestation of the body. It is not a representation of an abstract figure but a living body revealed in the revelation of clothes that are not really transparent. It is the clothing of the body and not nudity that reveals corporeity. The body is not anatomy nor is it physiology. "Clothed with the cloak of modesty," is an Islamic expression from Ibn ʿArabī (*Revelations of the Mecca* 44).

Aisthēsis has always been considered a form of knowledge, but in the ancient past it did not develop as a distinct science in itself. It is interesting to note that the origin of the expression *aisthētikē epistēmē* is unknown. Alexander Gottlieb Baumgarten is attributed with having introduced the study of this science with his book *Aesthetica* of 1750/1758. The definition he gives is interesting: "Aesthetica (theoria liberalium artium, gnoseologia inferior, ars pulchre cogitandi, ars analogi rationis) est scientia cognitionis sensitivae."

Obviously, in those days, Baumgarten had to subordinate both art and aesthetics to reason and define it as a "theory of inferior knowledge" and as an "art analogous to reason."

From a general reflection on aesthetics, that which in our times is a distinct science ensued: the aesthetics of religion. Its contributions are of great value and help us to understand, for example, the Christian concept of the icon and the depths of the so-called iconoclastic disputes of the past. Later on, we add a reflection on how Indian philosophy has put this question into perspective.

The "aesthetics of religion" has not yet sufficiently dealt with what we want to underline here.

The "aesthetics of religion" has mostly studied the participation of the senses in the religious act or in religion in general. It has dealt with gestures, voices, odors, spaces, and other sensitive actions in worship and religious life. It has also studied the mutual relationship. The aesthetics of religion, in a word, deals with all the sensitive signs involved in religious manifestations, including emotions and sentiments.

If we interpret art as an expression of the sensitive, the aesthetics of religion has, up to now, been interested in the role of art in religion and the influence of religion on art, including the study of art as an *Ersatz* (substitute, replacement) for religion. The contemporary bibliography is extensive, and could not be otherwise, seeing that art and religion are intimately connected.

However, the question we are posing is not so much the participation of the corporeal in religion, but rather the aim of religion itself in the body, that is, the integration of religion into the corporeal and not only of the corporeal into the religious. The body participates in religious worship. But what has religion got to do with the body? What service does religion render to the body? Or, to paraphrase old discussions of various schools: Can we claim that *religio ancilla corporis*, or must we be content with the "ancillary" role of the body in religion?

To shed light on these dilemmas we must go back to philosophical disquisitions.

Three are the windows through which Man looks out on reality: the senses, reason, and the intellect. When we only look out of one window we risk reductionism— that is, to reduce our vision of reality and what we see, using only one organ of knowledge, whichever it may be. Materialism, rationalism, and intuitionism could be three words to describe the universal vision of the world. The three words of the ancient Western tradition to express this would be the following: *Ta aisthēta* (the sensible), *ta noēta* (the mental or rational), and *ta mysthika* (the mystical), which we have here defined as the intellectual to distinguish it from reasoning, playing on the somewhat vague distinction between *intellectus* and *ratio*. The first represents a complete intellectual experience, an intuition that includes both the objective and the subjective. The second means the vision of a congruent cohesion, an objective plausibility. Only through a three-dimensional vision can we know reality to the whole extent of human possibility. In other words, an appearance can be sensible, rational, or intellectual. These three are appearances because they show us this triple form of human knowledge. We can and we must distinguish them, but every separation deforms our vision of reality, just as every monopoly of one form over another distorts it. Basically every human experience is simultaneously sensible, rational, and intellectual, even if our conscious attention can only focus on one of the three dimensions at a time. When we become aware of something, we are already using the senses, reason, and that intuition that we have called *intellectual*, so as not to call it *mystical*. I insist: That which appears to reason is appearance just as much as that which appears to the senses, and the same can be said for that which appears to intellective intuition.

We need to recognize that the words used are ambiguous and that, over the course of the history of philosophy, they have been used in many different ways. We discover, for example, the same ambiguity in the use of the words *buddhi* and *cit* (or *citta*) in Indian philosophy, as also in Platonic, Thomist, as well as Kantian philosophy. We understand "intelligence" with the meaning with which Scholasticism defined the angels as "pure intelligences" without, however, wanting to say that the notion is synonymous to incorporeal—as understood by tradition.

It is thanks to Xavier Zubiri that the unitary aspect of human intellect was pointed out, being both sentient and intelligent at the same time: "To hear and to understand are actually two phases of something unique and unitary: two phases of the impression of reality."[5] Our meditation would like to follow this path, distinguishing, without separating, Man's reasoning activity from the intellectual domination that I have called mystical. The latter is not only conscious of sensible reality and the subject that grasps it, more or less vaguely according to each circumstance, it also perceives the connection of the subject and the object with the whole of reality—what I call *cosmotheandric intuition*.

When I hold a stick in my hand I am mainly sensitive to the wood that I am touching and seeing. On further reflection I discover the subject that touches and sees the wood. I am aware of having a sensitive knowledge of the stick in my hand. This realization—of the stick in my hand—is the fruit of the mind's eye that has opened at the same time as the eye of the senses. Without this second realization I would not know that I am holding a stick in my hand, although without the realization of the first eye, the second would be a complete hallucination. The two eyes work together. But there is more. The third eye opens when I perceive both the object (the stick) and the subject (myself) of knowledge. Not only do I realize that I am holding a stick in my hand, but also that there is a more or less complete sphere in which the object and the subject find themselves. I actually realize that neither my knowledge of the stick is complete, nor does my knowledge that I know I am holding a stick in my hand represent everything I am experiencing of the object stick and the subject that is aware of his knowledge of the stick. I also know that both the known and the knower are a particular case that I experience as such because I realize that the whole of reality is involved in the process.

What we have said has a corollary that is relative to what we want to say. The body, as that which is simply sensitive and "corporeal," is purely an abstraction of our minds; it is a purely scientific entity. The body is not only the object of sensible knowledge, because a human knowledge that is not simultaneously sensible, rational, and intellective does not exist. To realize what we perceive with our senses, they must be interpreted by our reason that, in turn, must lead us to a total—holistic—intuition of the subject and the object that we perceive. Our sensitive perception will be able,

---

[5] X. Zubiri, *Inteligencia sentiente* (Madrid: Alianza, 1980), 78.

more or less consciously, to integrate the vision of the other two eyes that are surely there. When we see a body, for example, we do not only see its beauty but we also perceive the truth and the goodness. We see that that body has life, and we realize that life is a mystery. That instruction and culture have often withered our organs of knowledge and lead us to interpret that what presents itself in the immediate to our being as pure materiality, simple formality, or paranormal phenomenon is quite different; these are the consequences generated by a hyperspecialist and positivist culture that seems only to be interested in having control and dominion of what is in front of it.

The Body as a Symbol

The great discovery attributed to Socrates, which was not accepted without resistance in his time, is what is generally called *concept*. Conceptual knowledge, a great work of reason, is what allows us to know things and say what they are. Thus, the price of this ingenious algebra is the abstraction of the singular. Plato and the followers of Aristotle both said that there is no concept of the particular. And some formulated it even more radically, saying that "science," or rather "knowledge," of the singular does not exist. Well then, the body is the space of a singularity. Each body is unique. And those very ancients had to recognize that the principle of individuation is to be found in matter. If, however, each body is unique and there is no knowledge of uniqueness, it follows that there is no scientific knowledge of the body. The body turns out to be irrelevant for the *res cogitans* that is Man; it is transformed into an abstraction, an object of modern science.

The time has come to introduce, even if briefly, what I have tried to formulate— that is, the role of symbolic knowledge.[6] The symbol is sensible. A symbol without *sensible perception* does not exist. But the symbol is also something rational. A symbol without self-awareness that acknowledges that it knows the symbol does not exist. Furthermore, the symbol is also intellectual. There cannot be a symbol if we are not aware that that which is symbolized "is" not the symbol nor "is" it not the symbol, and that it is not identical to the symbol nor can it be separated from it. A symbol cannot exist without this intuition that I have called mystical or deeply intellectual. In other words, a symbol that is not simultaneously sensible, rational, and intellectual cannot exist. However, we should not forget that the symbol is a symbol only when it is recognized as such. If the symbol needs further mediation to explain what the symbol is, only the one that does not require further explanation is really the symbol.

In other words, the symbol places itself beyond the separation between subject and object, because what the symbol symbolizes is neither beyond what is symbolized nor on this side of the symbolizer. The symbol is not a sign that refers us to

---

[6] See R. Panikkar, "Símbolo y simbolización: La diferencia simbólica—Para una lectura intercultural del símbolo," in K. Kerényi, E. Neumann, G. Scholem, and J. Hillman, eds., *Arquetipos y símbolos colectivos: Círculo Eranos I* (Cuadernos de Eranos) (Barcelona: Anthropos, 1994), 383–413; also in *Myth, Symbol, Cult* (*Opera Omnia*, IX.1).

something else. The symbol symbolizes the symbolized in the symbol itself. This is the *symbolic difference*. The symbol is not the symbolized, but the symbolized cannot be separated from the symbol; it is not the thing in itself hidden by the appearance but it is "that" which appears in the appearance when I recognize it as such. "As such" means the recognition of the appearance of what the appearance is: precisely appearance. The recognition of the symbolic appearance—this is what we are referring to—is an a-dual knowledge. One does not know the appearance as a *noumenon*, as if the appearance were the "thing in itself." The symbol is not reality—symbolized in the symbol. This would be a mistake. But it is not known as *pure* appearance either, like, for example, a simple veil that covers another thing or a simple sign that also refers to another thing. Symbolic appearance is recognized as such when, so to speak, it is recognized as the reincarnation of the invisible, as that which we are given to know of the thing because knowledge is above all our relation with the same. I can recognize the shining shell on the ground as if it were an appearance of silver just because in some way I already know silver—to give a classic Vedantic example. When a certain *vedānta* tells us that the world is *māyā*, appearance, it does not tell us that the world is mere illusion—unreal. It tells us that it is *avidyā*, that ignorance arises when symbolic knowledge disappears and we are unaware that the appearance is only appearance. That is when we do not recognize it as appearance. We have not recognized it as such and have confused it with the reality of which it is essentially appearance. We thought the shell was silver.

I insist once more on this point. The symbolized is inseparable from the symbol not because our reason is weak and, being unable to realize the distinction, cannot go "beyond" the symbol. Our reason is perfectly capable of abstracting and presenting us with the conceptual formality of the symbol. However, what the symbol means, that is, conceptualizes—the concept of that symbol—cannot be confused with what that symbol *is*. The symbol is the very incarnation of the symbolized; the symbol lies within the symbolized—to fall back on the spatial metaphor, for lack of a better one. The symbol is such when it symbolizes, and it symbolizes only when it is doing it for us—when it is a symbol for us. This is why we—our subject—cannot remain separated from it: Christian credos were called "symbols of faith" because without faith they did not symbolize anything and were transformed into mere, more or less objective, formulations. But faith is not objectifiable. It would no longer be salvific. It would be idolatry. There is no "thing" that saves.

Thus, as proved implicitly in the preceding paragraph, the symbolized neither is nor is not the symbol. This is not an irrational statement that invalidates the principle of noncontradiction. It would be a contradiction to say that A (the symbol) is and is-not A (the symbol) using the verb univocally. Let us say instead that the symbol is not the symbolized, seeing as the symbol is the symbol—symbolizer—and the symbolized is the symbolized—"that" which the symbolizing operation symbolizes. However, we will add that the symbol—symbolizer—is the symbolized because this presents us with what the symbolized is. Here we have the *symbolic difference*.

Symbolic perception requires the activity of our three organs of perception.

Their Relationship: Goodness

It is equally significant that the problem of coupling—that is, of the relationship—has been one of the greatest headaches—and heartaches—of the history of humanity. I am not only thinking of the *filioque* or of Trinitarian and Christological problems. I am also thinking of the disturbing problems of the world and God, good and evil, male and female, theory and practice, being and beings, objectivity and subjectivity, time and eternity—soul and body in our case—and more concretely, religion and body.

Both in the East and the West, for most of the reflection that has been carried out, both philosophical and theological—seeing as in most cultures they are not separated—the relation of the human body with that other aspect of the real that opens itself to reason and the intellect has always been controversial for the reasons mentioned above—that in the end are reduced to the division between *aisthēsis* and *noēsis* (that is, our subject). The body, in its singularity, does not fall under the "dominion" of reason. When Man thinks about his destiny, the sense of the universe and of life, using only reason, the corporeal does not present itself as an object of thought but as the subject of the same. The realm of ideas overwhelms with all its strength. To the mind they seem to be true reality. The thinking subject believes it is the only subject. The names of Śaṅkara and Plotinus are fairly representative, but could be placed next to those of Descartes and Hegel.

Yet matter exists and cannot be easily eliminated. Copernicus, Galileo, and Kepler, to name only three, lost interest in the thinking subject and conceived a passion for the object that presented itself to their observations: the material—in movement. Descartes justifies it thus: here the *res extensa* stands for the object and therefore is at the service of the *res cogitans*. It is therefore necessary to know matter deeply; from here onward this knowledge will obsess the interest of the Western world, with the exception of a small elite of "pure thinkers" who will earn the epithet of philosophers and will no longer be defined as scientists. Modern science will eminently be knowledge of bodies, even if these are made up of electrons, dendrites, quanta, pulsations, and units of energy. There is no irony in these words. The obsession with internal life can be as unhealthy as an excessive preoccupation with external life. The history of modern science, furthermore, often transudes a healthy air of neglect when inquiring into the difficulties the soul has in consecrating itself, and forgetting itself, to investigate the world in front of us, which we feel the need to mold for its own good and ours. In fact, the scientist dedicates himself to the study of what has been called the nature of things without intimate curiosity toward himself. For the scientist, we could say, making use of a Judaic-Christian-Islamic *theologumenon*, that the first half of the second great commandment is sufficient: "Love your neighbor." It is not necessary to "love God," and he has no time for or interest in "as yourself." The neighbor is the world.

But to retrieve cosmotheandric harmony, centuries of rational and analytical attention have been required. During the process we have briefly described, there has been a gradual division of fields: philosophy turned to thought, science to matter, and religion to the destiny of the soul—the "beyond" in general. Yet the body offers resistance because it sees itself as involved in everything. So as to stick with our theme: the human body presents religion with a problem, with which it often comes to blows.

The three attitudes that we will mention refer prevalently to the body and indirectly to religion. It is, however, evident that the task of religion consists in offering a path of salvation or liberation for Man, and, as Man is more than just soul and/or spirit, the body is directly part of the religious project. So we must discuss the attitudes that Man has toward his body.

The Alienated Body

After this brief synthesis that, despite numerous precautions and adaptations, we believe represents the predominant direction of modern-Western culture that has penetrated the whole world, it can be understood that the human body has been more or less abandoned to scientific research and that religion limits itself to cultivating the so-called spiritual values and attributes of the soul. The possible conflict that could have ensued was quickly resolved in that religion gave up the right to deal directly with the body. Despite popular resistance, the religion of the experts took refuge in the temples—and also in schools—and even there, so as to avoid "getting involved in politics," it forwent taking an interest in the corporeal except to point out its dangers and deviations, always centered on sexual activity. Religion devoted itself to the soul, "and the soul is of God alone," as the poet tells us. But, as we have mentioned more than once, the origins of this human attitude have been handed down to us since ancient times.

In what we call controversial or interrupted relations we can distinguish two attitudes that we will briefly describe.

Contempt. The body (*sōma*) is an obstacle to Man's salvation, it is a prison, it is *sema* in its twofold meaning of sign and grave. Porphyry was ashamed to have a body, and St. Paul calls it the body of death. The body has been a great cause of Man's perdition, his great obstacle. Sooner or later it must be abandoned. We should not waste time on what will come to an end, nor pay much attention to what appears. We must free ourselves of its domination over us. Corporeal mortification is essential to spiritual life. We can find examples in most of humanity's religions, especially in the so-called great religions because they, in particular, have set up a complex conceptual structure in which the body is irrelevant. The "ascetic" scorns his body.

Abandonment. Seeing as our human condition on this Earth seems to be linked to a body, and for us this Earth is transient, the best thing to do is to ignore the body, to live as if we did not have one. Considering that to oppose sex can cause all sorts of trouble, it is prudent and healthy to simply ignore it and not give it any importance. There are far more important things in this world. Also, in this case, there are endless examples. Most of so-called spiritual training follows an asexual anthropology. The less importance we give it, so much the better. In the great adventures of the spirit one must go beyond the body. The senses are a distraction, to say the least. One must concentrate on the spiritual.

In a word, there is no direct relation between the body and religion. The latter is the prerogative of the soul, of the spirit, and its home is "beyond." The "saint" sets his body aside.

The Instrumentalized Body

Yet the body continues to claim its rights, and however much Man engages in letting go of the body, it presents itself as an unavoidable fellow traveler. Therefore, the best thing will be to use it as a tool for the great aims of human life.

This exploitation can be positive or negative.

Negative. As the body is the seat of our basic instincts, it is necessary to ascetically subjugate it and keep it in check. The mortification of the body and the control of the senses is part of traditional asceticism all over the world. The body can be useful to us but it must be a faithful servant, a docile slave because it has no wisdom and it is reason that must counsel, dominate, and use the body.

Positive. One aspect of this attitude accentuates the fact that the body must be well treated, like the slaves, so that it can serve us best. We must give our "brother body" what it is due; if not, it will rebel with counterproductive effects. Nature teaches us this. There are moral doctrines that say, for example, that God attributed a certain corporeal pleasure to the sexual act because otherwise men would not have procreated. Athletic asceticism exists as does the pleasure of bodily health. *Mens sana in corpore sano.*

It is not necessary to dwell any further on this subject to explain what we mean. All are examples of the dualism of which we have spoken. Today, the question of respect, and also of love for the body, is already a religious question. "My friends, the senses" is the title of a recent book. The value of the body is not denied, and its influence on the soul is almost universally recognized. Yet all this comes under instrumentalization. It is not surprising that our era is one of tools, instruments.

On this Earth the body is an essential and precious tool, because it is with it and through it that we attain "heaven," that we can reach "the other shore." However, it is obvious that, once the other shore is reached, once the end has been achieved, the body no longer serves a purpose. The nearer Man gets to his end, his perfection, the more he will liberate himself from the burden of his body and will be able to disregard it. There are many traditions that tell us that in higher mystical states the body serves no purpose. Often liberation is understood as liberation from the body. The ultimate reality is incorporeal. God is pure spirit. Ordinary Christians mock the Muslim heaven because in it the pleasures of the senses are described. The "sage" uses his body.

The Body as a Constituent Part of Man

This is where the *novum* of what I call "sacred secularity" presents itself as a challenge both for tradition as well as for the modern era, since the former defends the dualism of a spirit that dominates and controls a body, and the latter defends another dualism in which the body has supremacy over the spirit.

Another observation to bear in mind in this oblivion of the body in religion can be found in the dominant patriarchal society of the cultures of the last two millennia, even though there are some important exceptions. The scenario would have been different if, instead of predominantly male philosophers and theologians, we had shown greater commitment to cultivating the female element. It is harder for women to abstract themselves from their bodies than for men, and they have a far more natural relationship with their bodies.

We now intend to present an a-dualistic experience of the soul-body relationship (matter-spirit) as the basis of the relationship between religion and corporeality.

In contemporary culture it is not easy to combine harmoniously the values of the spirit and those of the body, especially when one starts from inadequate premises. Human fullness requires a unity that is not the sum of respective groups of values but rather an a-dualistic harmony of everything that Man is. However, harmony in the West is more a musical than a philosophical or theological term. Without the notions of *he* (harmony), *zhong* (balance), and *li* (ritual), Chinese culture would collapse. On the other hand, the notion of harmony, despite Aristotle's intriguing Pythagorean quote (*Metaphysics* 1.5.986a2), does not seem to play an explicit role in Western philosophy. The fact that the majority of philosophical and theological treatises do not consider the notion of harmony to be important, and that most of the dictionaries I have consulted only contain this word with reference to musical technique, may serve as an example.[7]

But let us keep to the point.

Man Is Corporeal

To introduce the theme as simply as possible, we should be aware that he who asks what Man is, is already a body. The question itself is rooted and formulated in a body that asks—a body that is undoubtedly alive and also intelligent, a "sentient intelligence," as Zubiri would say. With our thought we can put forward many very

---

[7] *Encyclopaedia of Religion and Ethics*, 1913; *Die Religion in Geschichte und Gegenwart*, 1959; *Lexicon für Theologie und Kirche*, 1960; *Handbuch theologischer Grundbegriffe*, 1962; *Handbuch philosophischer Grundbegriffe*, 1973; *The Encyclopedia of Philosophy*, 1967; *New Catholic Encyclopedia*, 1967; *International Encyclopedia of Social Sciences*, 1968; *Sacramentum mundi*, 1968; *Encyclopedia Universalis*, 1984; *The Anchor Bible Dictionary*, 1992; *The New Encyclopedia Britannica*, 1993; *The Modern Catholic Encyclopedia*, 1994.

pertinent distinctions, but we cannot separate ourselves from our body while we think, and the body is as much the subject of our knowing as the "soul" can be. By saying this we become aware that we are not only body, or better, we realize that what we call body is an abstraction of our thought, just as what we have called soul is, too. We can attribute sensitive knowledge to the body and intelligible knowledge to the spirit, but this very affirmation is based on the gratuitous assumption of this attribute. The only thing we realize is that our living body feels and understands. Or, as we have mentioned before, we realize that we feel, we understand what we feel as belonging to a sentient I, and, third, we intuit that this sentient I, besides what it feels with each action, is not completely isolated or autonomous but is constitutively interconnected to everything we can call reality.

More than one philosophical current of thought already accepts that Man does not only have a body, but that he is a body. The body is not a human accident, as the most ancient Scholasticism informs us; it is the very substance of the human form.

Without dwelling further on this point, we will go on to see what it has to tell us regarding religion.

It tells us that the religious path—that is, the path Man treads on the Earth to find the meaning of his life—cannot ignore the body. If we are body, the meaning of our existence must integrate the body into our lives.

Many excessively "spiritualist" religious doctrines may object that this body is transitory or mortal and that we must not allow ourselves to be distracted from "the life above," which is the true life. To be consistent one should accept the Jainist doctrine according to which, as this corporeal and mortal life is not the true life, to let oneself die is not an act of cowardice. Perhaps the "I am dying because I do not die"[8] does not justify active suicide, but it is a strong invitation not to suffer the torment of this life for too long. The *saṁlekhanā* of the Jainist hero, that is, the voluntary extinction of the body, would thus be the aim of life on Earth: to prepare oneself to abandon the body and to abandon it when one is fairly well prepared to do so. In the meantime, one must pass through successive reincarnations until one reaches the final *nirvāṇa*—or through the necessary tests and purifications to be able to attain heaven.

The concept of the instrumentality of the body could, in a way, represent a compromise. We need to take care of the body because we need it to be able to take the mortal leap, so long as it is a disinterested servant, an obedient slave that does not lay claim to its own rights. The value of the body is purely functional. Any autonomous "pleasure" will cause us feelings of guilt and imperfection that we could use as a source of humility, as certain forms of Christian and Hindu spirituality tell us to do, to give just two examples. It is no wonder that these forms of religiousness often show an unhappy face, often even gloomy. They console us with hope for the future while they drag us across this "vale of tears." The body is an onerous burden to be borne with patience. The fullness of life is exclusively "spiritual" life. There is

[8] See Teresa de Jesús, "Poesías lírico-místicas 1," in *Obras Completas* (Madrid: Editorial de Espiritualidad, 1984), 1177.

a consistency also between these two doctrines and a likelihood of painful human experiences, although it is not clear why human suffering must be ascribed only to the body and not the soul—to continue with this dualistic language. It should be clear that we are neither painting a rosy picture of human existence nor are we denying the pain of the world, still less are we questioning the injustice and the suffering of Man's condition. We are merely saying that they all belong to Man and that we should not simply attribute them to the body. Hunger, for example, is a human suffering, not just physiological malnutrition.

The a-dualistic vision we are defending neither means nor justifies the exact opposite of a corporeal licentiousness, so to say. Perhaps the actual wisdom of words can help us. Wisdom means knowing how to relish Life, but one can only "enjoy" (*fruir*) something if one is "frugal"; "fruition" requires "usufruct." To possess the "fruit" does not permit "fructification."

I repeat: It is not a matter of giving the body what it asks for, but neither of giving the soul what it demands. What should we give them? It is not just a question of the body directing the impulses of the soul—as sexual instinct may do at times—but it is also not a question of the soul decreeing what the body should do or feel—like a hypocritical smile. The dichotomy must be overcome so that it is Man as a whole that does not find pleasure in orgies and is disgusted by purely theoretical activity. Human maturity does not consist in going from one extreme to another. Soul and body are not two parts of Man, even if a certain dualistic culture has presented him as such. Human life is one and not the sum of two lives, the material and the mental. That medicine is a meditation and moderation is once again what human experience tells us, as is summarized in the words themselves; all three derive from the same root *med*.

It is not a matter of saving the body. The crippled may enter the kingdom of heaven. Nor is it a matter of saving the soul. Prostitutes may precede the just in the kingdom of heaven. It is a matter of "saving"—so as not to get mixed up with words; Man in his wholeness must attain the aim of his life, which may be interpreted in the most diverse ways, which could or should be discussed at a later stage.

The Greeks—inspired by the scholars who spoke of "beatitude" as the aim of Man—said that the path toward this "full," or good, life does not consist in the "terrena despicere et amare caelestia" (contempt for the terrestrial and love of the celestial) of medieval Christian liturgy, nor in the *nityānityavastuviveka*, discrimination between the "temporal and the eternal" (with echoes in the Jesuit of Nieremberg),[9] almost as if *brahman* were real and the world (*jagat*) an illusion, of a certain vedānta.[10] Rather it consists in the experience of the resurrection of the flesh, "huius quam gestamus et non alterius carnis resurrectionem" (in the resurrection of this flesh that we carry now and not of another), that flesh of the here and now if we must heed the

---

[9]   See Juan Eusebio Nieremberg, *Diferencia entre lo temporal y eterno* (Madrid, 1640), an asthetic text of admirable prose, with numerous editions and translations, whose influence can be felt in Jacint Verdaguer, *L'Atlàntida*.

[10]   Śaṅkara, *Vivekacūḍāmaṇi*, 20.

Councils,[11] or in the conviction that no possible difference exists between *samsāra* and *nirvāṇa*[12] in the experience of the *jīvanmukta*, and so on.

Let us look at the positive side by quoting sources from the same traditions that we have presented negatively.

The *Vāstusūtra-upaniṣad* begins by defining knowledge of things as divine (*vāstospati*) and in the second *sūtra* refers to the *Rg-veda* VI.47.18: "rūpam rūpam pratirūpo bhabhūva . . . pratirūpam bhavatiiti viséva," that the same *upaniṣad* translates and comments on:

> Every form is the image of the original form, since this is the difference— between the two. This knowledge is divine knowledge (*divyajñāna*).

And continues declaring in *sūtra* 4 that

> From the knowledge of art springs—this—divine knowledge that is the one that leads us to liberation (*mokṣa*), which is truly the essence of artistic knowledge.

Or, even more clearly, in *sūtra* 5:

> From images faith is born (*sraddhā*), from faith, firm devotion springs, and from this, knowledge (*jñāna*) originates, which in turn leads to liberation (*mokṣa*).

Furthermore *sūtra* 7 specifies,

> When religious acts take place without corporeal images, the mind is disturbed by uncontrolled fantasies.

It is only by starting from the sensible and with the sensible that Man realizes his liberation. This is the same thing that the Christian spirituality of the icons transmits.

A text by St. Paul, interpreted and used by the tradition for other reasons, can shed light here:

> It is clear to see (*kathoratai*) that ever since the creation of the world, the invisible existence (*ta aorata*) of God and his everlasting power have been clearly seen by the mind's understanding of created things. (Rom 1:20)

It is through contemplation of the reality of the world that one knows its creator. It is the sensible things that reveal the invisible. Without the sensible, one would

---

[11] See Denz 77, 325, 485, 540, 684, 797, 854, etc.
[12] Nāgārjuna, *Mādhyamika-kārikā*, XXV.10.

not have knowledge of what falls within the sphere of the senses. Or, we could say, beauty is the path toward the discovery of what cannot be seen because beauty lies in seeing the invisible in things which have been made (*poiēma*). The invisible is seen through form. The "aorata" (invisible things) are part of "kathoratai" (clearly seen). Contemplation sees the invisible in such a way that the visible is seen as having become being (*gegonenai*), starting from the nonvisible (Heb 11:3). The two realms cannot be separated. One can see the invisible because it has become being (*gegonenai*), the visible. "It became being (*bhavati*) in every form, the original form," as the above quoted *ṛg-veda* says. Basically, all poets speak this language: form is form because it informs the informed, otherwise it would be nothing. In the same way, the informed would not exist if it were not informing the form—the formed. Not without profound intuition is *morphē* form and essence, just as *rūpa* is form (figure) and at the same time *pratirūpa*, original form.

What has been said so far introduces the following point.

The Body Is a Dimension (and Not a Part) of Reality

As the two texts we have just quoted tell us, everything is a form of divinity; appearances are actually phenomena of the divine and reveal the invisible. The nonsensible manifests in the sensible. We can and must distinguish both sources of knowledge, but we cannot separate them. We can and must distinguish dimensions—or if one prefers, levels of reality—but we cannot completely separate them. We have said that both the concept of body and the concept of soul are abstractions. One cannot abstract one from the other, just as one cannot abstract God from the world. Without the creator there would be no creation, and without creation there would be no creator, as many mystics have claimed—beyond the tautology represented by this formulation. God would not exist without the world. To the objection that there certainly could be a God without world, one would answer that this possibility only means that the concept of God does not include the concept of creator, and that one could think of a God who does not create. In this way, one could think of a world that has not been created. In both cases human reason is absolutized with no support outside of itself. It is constituted as supreme arbitrator of reality. Reason is absolutized. A beautiful formulation by Pedro Laín Entralgo says,

> For the human mind, that which is certain will always be second to last, and the last will always be uncertain.[13]

We want to get to the following reasoning: the history of humanity's religious thought demonstrates that religious experience is often considered not only different but also superior to aesthetic experience, because the former does not take corporeity into consideration and elevates itself to the status of pure spirituality from which

---

[13] P. Laín Entralgo, *Cuerpo y alma* (Madrid: Espasa Calpe, 1991), 15.

the corporeal is excluded. The supreme experience is considered to be incorporeal because we believe ultimate reality is also incorporeal.

We have already illustrated two reasons why this doctrine has been successful: the first, metaphysical, and the second, moral.

The first can be reduced to the experience of change. That which changes is unstable. That which is unstable is impermanent. Permanence is an indispensable condition for the concept, and the concept is the highest tool through which modern science approaches reality. This is where the scenario changes. We place more trust in reason than in the senses. Reason needs stability to be able to conceptualize: the senses do not. Incidentally, let us recall that this is where the great Buddhist revolution takes place: *anātmavāda*, reality, is impermanent; there is no *ātman*. But prevailing Western culture has banished Heraclitis. Is it possible to think movement? This will be Bergson's great question.

But let us continue our brief analysis. The senses bear witness to the fact that the world changes. The concept cannot have anything to do with change as such. It is "reasonable" to trust more in reason than in the senses, all the more so because reason itself often discovers sensorial deception; we see a slanting pole submerged in water as if it were broken though we know it is not. Some will deduce that the real is rational, but almost everyone, in this culture, is convinced that the rational is, at least, the most perfect—since it is permanent and overcomes the inevitable passing of time and the limitations of space. At all times and in all places 2 + 2 = 4—disregarding, for now, our criticism of logical postulates. From here to the concept of God as a perfect Being, immutable and spiritual, there are just a few steps, longer or shorter but, in any case, congruent. The material is subject to change. "God does not change," said St. Teresa. The aim of religion is to lead us to our final, permanent, real destiny.

There are three weak points in this argumentation. The first consists in a purely spatial concept of change. Bodies, in effect, can change place. But there can be a nonspatial change, as the ancients recognized, when, for example, they spoke of the passage from strength to action, and maybe this continuous change is a sign of life—and of real life. Creation, according to Scholasticism, is no change at all, however.

The second point consists in an ecstatic conception of reality. We could call it the substantivization of Being, forgetting that being, grammatically, is also a verb. The truth, insofar as it is, *cannot* attain being—becoming—it *must be* already complete. Thus, one concedes that change presupposes imperfection. That which is perfect, in fact, is *per-factum* (*per-ficere*), finished; it wants for nothing; it has no need of acquiring anything new because then it would mean that something was still missing, that it did not already have everything. And the concept of everything is that which lacks nothing. It is the Parmenidean sphere. Everything is already in place—done: from the rich root *dhē*, to put, to place. Being is already finished; thus *it is*, it does not simply "become," it reaches being (*to be it*). The flaw consists in a-critically accepting the Parmenidean assumption that denies reality to what cannot be thought—thus falling into a metaphysical tautology.

The third point consists in the notion of time as linear and in its objectivization into a channel through which pass beings who have not yet become what they really should be. Man is thirsting for eternity, as three different examples, the Upaniṣad, St. Augustine, and Spinoza, attest. However, we separate eternity, which certainly cannot be reduced to time, from temporality. Only God or the Absolute is eternal. The eternal is unchangeable, and corporeality, characterized by space, movement, and time, can never be eternal.

In a word, if Man must quench his thirst for the infinite, if Man is more than an animal, it is because he has, or is, spirit, and the spirit cannot be material. This need for the absolute that is inborn in Man cannot refrain from aspiring to an eternal, a-temporal, spiritual, nonmaterial existence—and must therefore abandon its corporeality. Death seems to be the most serious problem, but the answer, since ancient times, consists in presenting immortality as the greatest test of human dignity. And seeing as the body clearly is not, we must consequently conclude that it is the soul that is immortal.

This is all very wise and very congruent. These beliefs have persisted over the centuries in the human belief system. It would be presumptuous and irresponsible to claim they were all mistaken.

If we disagree, it is not because we are accusing them of being wrong. This hypothesis does not openly contradict these ancient and venerable beliefs; rather it reformulates them, reinterprets them, and in the end transforms them. Could it not be that *metamorphosis* is a characteristic of life? The deep intention of ancient wisdom was not that of defending its own doctrines, but rather to express in present-day language something that could not be expressed differently. Thus, for example, in no way do we presume to undermine human dignity, its thirst for the infinite, and desire for divinization; we simply say that the body is not an obstacle to all of this.

The second reason, already mentioned above, according to which pure spirituality separated from corporeality has been considered the specific field of religion, is based on human experience of the abuse that Man has committed with his body. Torture, corporeal violence, aberrations, and excessive lust, greed, sloth, war, and human withdrawal from the purely material are more than sufficient reasons why many projects for the salvation of Man have shown themselves cautious and mistrustful of the power of human corporeity, so that the more noble part of Man, his mind, seems to be able to rise above the limitations of matter.

Briefly, it would be irresponsible to try to minimize this aspect of human life and to deny the inertia of matter. We must add, however, that it does not seem right to us to deny the complicity of the soul and also of the spirit—if one prefers the tripartite division—in all this. Greed, to give an extreme example, is not of the stomach but of Man in his entirety. If the inertia of matter exists, then there is also inertia of the spirit.

It is up to our epoch to reestablish the balance and harmony between the different "components" of Man.

All this can only last if we integrate our anthropological vision into a more complete cosmovision. Our hypothesis is the following: the *saeculum*, secularity, is a definitive dimension of reality. It is the sacred secularity to which we have alluded.

With this beautiful Indo-European word, of probable Etruscan origin, we mean that the space/time/matter triad is a constituting ingredient of reality. Congruently with our a-dualist vision, when we say *dimension, ingredient, constituent element of reality*, we do not in any way state that reality can be divided into three parts, one of which is the material. The parts of a whole can be the division carried out by our mind, but neither the whole is the sum of the parts, nor are these parts like the segments of a whole. The interpretation, the *perichōresis*, the interconnection, the relational nature, is constituent. One dimension does not exist without the other. This is the cosmotheandric experience of reality.

There Is No Religion without Corporeality

We will give just one example in relation to our theme: the interdependence of the so-called transcendentals. Just by saying *interdependence* we are giving a meaning of intrinsic and constituent dependence and not simply a more or less strong interconnection. Religion, at least ideally, deals with truth, the art of beauty, and the aesthetics of goodness. Or, to put it in more philosophical and traditional terms, truth is what corresponds to the intellect, beauty to artistic taste, and goodness to volition. So, we could also say that beauty is the truth of the corporeal just as truth is the beauty of the spiritual and that goodness is really the synthesis of the two—something that seems to be related to the Greek notion of *kalokagathia*. Thus, aesthetics would not be the "science of the beautiful" as if it were the intellect—science—that establishes the rules of beauty, but it would represent human consciousness that opens itself to the manifestations of beauty seen through our triple vision. *Aisthēsis* and *logos* are inseparable.

After everything we have said, it is clear that the title of this section also means something more: that our body has a role to play in that which we call *religion*. We have already stated that religion itself has a task to carry out in the "salvation" of our body.[14] And it must do so from a religious and not simply moral standpoint.

For the sake of brevity we will give just one example. Many religions tell us that love is the most important aspect of the religious act, that love is the essence of religion. Yet it would appear that they are merely referring to an "amor Dei intellectualis," without any intention of referring back to Spinoza. So there is much talk of love, and linguistic distinctions are also made between *agapē, eros*, and *filia*, between *prema, bhakti*, and *kāma*, and so on, even if the vital sense of the words does not allow for watertight compartments. It would seem that religion must deal with love in its more sublime aspects: love of God, of truth, of justice, and in the end, of one's neighbor and, consequently, of ourselves and so on. However, it would appear

---

[14] See R. Panikkar, "Medicine and Religion," chap. 23, this volume.

that the religious—but not moral—question must respectfully or maybe modestly come to a halt when faced with the corporeal and more universal phenomenon of human love, leaving psychology or other disciplines to deal with this.

It is clear that we are referring to falling in love, which is neither merely physical attraction nor simply spiritual sympathy—bearing in mind that we use these words inadequately. Yet without the sum of the two, falling in love does not exist. I repeat that many religions tell us next to nothing in this regard, except to underline the dangers—which are obvious, if one does not overcome dualism. There is no doubt, however, that falling in love is an eminently religious act as it frees us from egoism, brings us closer to the other, and makes us more perfect. In theistic terms it brings us closer to God and in general opens us to the unknown, to the numinous aspect of existence, the unique value of being loved, and in a word, to the mystery. And it is falling in love itself that teaches how precarious the balance between the spiritual and the physical is, and how harmony is attained by not repressing either of these two dimensions. Still less is it attained by shutting them up in ourselves and slipping into what the Scholastics defined as *amor curvus*, or more simply, lust, or angelism, or even more simply, spiritualist vanity.

Falling in love shows us that the other is not an object but a you, and that my ego is not self-sufficient but constitutively "relegated" and what is more, vulnerable. In this regard, Ebner and Lévinas could be two symbolic names.

However, sublimation or overcoming can suffocate love just as much as repression or denial. And here we discover the eminently religious character of love when it attains a-duality, which can be reached neither through simple physical union nor through the mere consent of the soul. A-duality is Trinitarian. True love, both in its physical and in its spiritual aspect, is not idolatry. Love is directed neither at oneself with narcissistic degeneration, nor at the other with masochistic alienation. It is the very experience of love that opens us to the experience of a-duality. In theistic language, one would say that the divine lies in the middle. It is falling in love itself that leads us to relativize both the body and the spirit—that is, not to see them as absolutes. This is proved by the fact that love itself declines when it goes to either of these extremes, of idolizing the object of one's love or of abandoning the human condition by projecting human love toward an exclusively transcendent God and Other.

Religious instruction, in this sense, would teach us a path of love that, while going deeper on the one hand—as in being loved concretely—extends itself on the other—to the whole of reality. This requires a harmony within our being that "integrates" body and soul or, better, redeems us as much from the domination of the body as from the control of the soul, and leads us to perfect freedom, as the Christian Scripture says (Jas 1:25). "Love and do what thou wilt," says St. Augustine, which is neither licentiousness nor submission to a law; it is the experience of "amor meus pondus meum" (my love is my weight), to quote the Berber genius once again.

We can express it in another way by using traditional language. If the final aim of Man is his perfection, his union with God, his liberation, and if it is a matter of Man's destiny and not of something else, it must be Man himself who achieves his aim and not someone else who is not Man himself. If Man is not body, the sooner he liberates himself from it, the sooner he will achieve his aim. If, on the other hand, Man is body, his final aim cannot abandon the body and must, in some way, incorporate it. Salvation is not alienation. He who saves himself is Man and not something that is not human.

One of the happiest intuitions regarding this problem is the so-called *śarīra-śarīra-bhāva* by Rāmānuja, that is, the concept of the relationship between the souls and the bodies and between the supreme soul and the world. More exactly: "The living being (*jīvātmā*) has *brahman* as its *ātman*, seeing as the living being is the form (*prakāra*) of *brahman*, since the living being is the body (*śarīra*) of *brahman*."[15] This often badly interpreted doctrine is anything but pantheism. The whole world is the body of God. The whole of reality is *paramātmā, jīvātmā*, and *śarīra*: the Supreme Being, the souls (or living beings), and the world (body).

Rāmānuja's a-dualistic vision is more clearly revealed when he speaks of the actual meaning of the words. He says, "These, above all, mean the named objects in this discourse, then, through these objects, they refer to the *jīvātmā* inherent in them. Furthermore, the words themselves also denote the Supreme Being *paramātmā*, the inner guide—the inner controller or immanent energy, the *antaryāmī*—of each word—and consequently, thing."[16]

In other words, there is an immanent divinity in every being, a supreme Life that expresses itself by manifesting itself, through diverse modalities and forms, in all the bodies whose ontological support are the souls of all things, seeing as the purely corporeal is unable to exist without its animic support. The relationship between this trinity is not "democratic." With the Gītā the Hindu tradition recognizes that "I reside in all beings yet I am independent from all things."[17]

To sum up: The religious experience is the experience of reality, but this reality is corporeal, spiritual, and divine. We should not confuse the three dimensions, but neither can we separate them. Religion and body are closely linked.

Appendix: The Body in the Christian Tradition

I have been asked if the ideas set out here are compatible with the Christian conception of the body, which seems to have reduced it, in the best-case scenario, to an instrument to use that is abandoned in the higher spheres of mystical experience, and that never ceases to put us on guard against the dangers of the flesh.

We could quote any number of passages from the Christian Scriptures to prove the exact opposite, but we will limit ourselves to simply recalling the basis of the Christian tradition, without complex exegesis.

---

[15] Rāmānujācārya, *Vedārthasamgraha*, 17.
[16] Ibid., 18.
[17] See *BG* IX.4–5.

In effect, practically all the fundamental Christian dogmas reinforce everything we have just said.

In the first place the *Trinity*, which is not monotheism. If it were, the only congruent interpretation of the Trinity would be the modalism that claims that the three divine persons are simply aspects of the divine essence, which is a heresy explicitly rejected by tradition.

Nor is it tritheism that was also thematically condemned, on top of having neither meaning nor function in the theist conception of reality in which, up to now, the Christian tradition has placed itself.

So what is the meaning of the Trinity? Its meaning is intimately related to the central Christian dogma, as it has understood itself according to the same tradition, which consists in making room within theism for the *incarnation*—which is the second dogma to which we have referred.

In effect, the figure of the *avatāra*, like that of the prophet, makes complete sense, as both Hinduism and Islam have verified.

God can descend from above to restore the *dharma*—as the Gītā says—as often as he deems fit and assuming whatever form he wishes. But it is only an exterior and apparent form. The *avatāra* is truly God and only has the appearance of a creature. From a Christian point of view this is pure docetism.

God can inspire Man and also dwell in him in a special way, and make him into a prophet or the Prophet. Yet no matter how pervaded with divinity he is, the Prophet remains Man. The prophet is a man, not God.

The incarnation is not this, nor is it the "descent" of a god, nor the "elevation" of a man. The Christian Christ is both totally man and totally God. Within monotheism this statement is meaningless. Within tritheism or polytheism is it quite useless. Everything is related. The incarnation has meaning only within the Trinitarian conception of the divinity.

However, if we are sure of this, human flesh is divine, it is God, and is a constituent part—not a juxtaposition—of the same divinity. In this conception a corporeal reality that is at the same time fully divine does not produce ontological rejection. At least in one single point the distance between the divine and the human has been cancelled, despite all the hairsplitting of tradition.

Thus there is a divine flesh. Corporeity does not contradict the divine. Christ is not a minor divinity, even if we must not confuse the natures, as the Councils have decreed. But we can no more separate them. That is, our distinctions are purely mental, for as much "fundamentum in re" as they may have.

And if the vocation of the Christian is that of making himself like Christ, he must divinize himself like his model and master, creating a single body with Him, as the Scriptures themselves say. We could say that the Christian religion is the religion of the body par excellence.

We can add one more argument to avoid any doubt. Jesus was a historical person who rose from the dead. The resurrected Jesus, who continues to be a corporeal being because he is Jesus, is the Christ of the Christians, God and Man together, in which the Christian is called upon to "incorporate" himself. This *resurrection*— our third dogma—is carnal, physical, and corporeal. And this Christ, that of the Eucharist and that of the heavens, is once and for all real, without going into further considerations or explanations. The Eucharist—not the communion, as specified in ecclesiastical documents—is essential to salvation and is what confers divine life to Man, as tradition testifies.

If this is not enough to complete the Christian vision of reality in a congruent manner, there is the fourth dogma: the *ascension*. Christ does not more or less mysteriously remain on Earth and/or in the Eucharist, but ascends to heaven—a body, which, even if considered glorious, is still a body—precisely as it should be—which ascends to the bosom of the divinity and sits at His right hand with His corporeity, however much one wishes to sweeten the metaphor. Here and now, not only in a beyond that is yet to come, there is a body in the bosom of the divinity. The adventure of Jesus was not just a temporal episode in the past, it is a tempiternal event in the present. And if we have returned from the dead with him (*synēgepthēte, consurrexistis*, Col 3:1), our resurrection is here and now and we can live it out when we have it, thanks to a nonlinear experience of time and a tempiternal experience of reality. Thus the Christian vision does not postpone the ascension of Christ to the end of time.

To conclude and to reinforce what we have been saying, the ultimate dogma of the church declares that Mary was "corpore et anima ad caelestem gloriam assumptam" (taken up, body and soul, into the glory of heaven)—in other words, that it is not only a matter of ontological possibility but of an anthropological plausibility since, unlike Jesus, Mary was a human being like all of us, however many privileges she may have had.

Christian history is paradoxical: If, on the one hand, the Manichean genius of Augustine contaminated the church with corporeal scruples, on the other, this same church has been far more rigorous in condemning excessively spiritualist doctrines than more permissive and indulgent attitudes toward the rights of matter. Here we should mention the tripartite Judaic-Christian anthropology that would have allowed us to overcome Platonic dualism. But this is not our task. It is enough with what we have said.

23

MEDICINE AND RELIGION

After six thousand years of human experience—which I take here as parameters, since they span the historical period of human consciousness—the time has come to have the courage, as well as the humility, to ask ourselves the global meaning of Man's adventure on Earth. The alternatives are today inescapable: either humanity enters and embraces a new moment, which we may call posthistorical and which amounts to a mutation of human being itself, or else a minority of the human species continues to destroy the Earth, eventually provoking a cosmic abortion that will surely miscarry any further possibilities for life on this planet to flower at all.

In other words, we must bring to a close the era of specializations, which have in the past few centuries so enriched us—but at such a cost—if we are to survive as inhabitants of a living planet. *Specialization* may be defined as that activity that approaches a sector of reality according to a method so "specific" that it cannot be applied to anything else. Yet since Man cannot renounce a vision of the whole, there is always the obvious danger of extrapolation. Some will always seek to understand the whole by extrapolating a particular method beyond its specific bounds. And thus are born not only scientism, pragmatism, and historicism, but equally the purely objective or purely subjective visions of things, as well as all the many other closed compartments: in a word, the fragmentation of knowledge and of human activity.

To this tendency we may contrast the method of *concentration*, which does not divide the whole into fragments but participates in it and tries to discover points of connectedness and conjunction between various aspects of the reality under scrutiny. It is at this level of radical critique that we must take our stand. To refuse to do so would be myopic. We know all too well, however, the sensible reaction of the majority: since it seems nothing can be done to remedy the world situation, better to remain myopic than succumb to despair or cynicism. Cynicism crops up in both egoism and indifference: "Who gives a damn, anyway?" Cynicism impels us to be party to anything that promises a way out. And despair leads directly to violence, be it physical, moral, or intellectual. We lose hope because we believe ourselves to be at a dead end. And, as a matter of fact, we undoubtedly are at a dead end. Conditioned by the myth of progress, we persist in moving along that path—always more technology, more armaments, more options, more knowledge, more information, more discoveries, more political parties. . . .

Lost in the labyrinth of modernity as if on an endless highway going nowhere, it is no longer possible for us to turn back. So we remain fixated on the road ahead, incapable of seeing that only a radical transformation or metamorphosis (*metanoia*) can save us.[1] What is more, Man has not yet *repented* of this historical project that we so cynically call a human one. This is the reason the kingdom of God never comes, because it requires repentance.[2] We do not want to—or, indeed, cannot—recognize our mistakes, rectify our trajectory, change our ways. God repented of having created Man, says the Bible.[3] Noah convinced Him to renounce to his destruction. But Man has not yet imitated God: he has not yet repented of this historical project of which he is so proud. Original sin is merely this historical consciousness oriented exclusively toward the future: our first parents were victims of this very illusion of the future— "You shall be like Gods. . . ."—which promised them only that they would become what they already were.[4] Hence the murderous instinct of historical Man. St. Paul's affirmation takes on its full force here: "The wages of sin is death,"[5] which today might be translated as: death comes from Man's exclusively historical project, his flight from the present—no doubt through being ashamed of himself—to a linear future that alienates him evermore from his true nature. Will we be able, after all is said and done, to carry out a *regressus*, to find the wellspring, the creative thrust by which we may spring anew into the very life of the universe?

All this already serves as an introduction to my topic, since death stands before us as the crucial issue common to both medicine and religion. All this is prologue, and necessary background today more than ever, if we are to approach a topic as vast and arduous as that of medicine and religion.[6]

Colligite quae superaverunt fragmenta—"Gather up the leftovers," says Christ after the multiplication of loaves and fishes.[7] This Gospel injunction does not just mean that we must gather up the material goods left over from the "first world's" feast, but rather that we must make use of the experience and knowledge acquired over the course of these millennia to direct not merely the destiny of history but also the very adventure of reality. These are the only coordinates that to me seem adequate for the present historical moment.

This text has three parts. In the first, we present our thesis; in the second, we call upon the authority of the oldest human documents; and finally, in the third, we draw out some consequences from the first two.

---

[1] See R. Panikkar, *Técnica y tiempo: La tecnocracia* (Buenos Aires: Columba, 1967).

[2] See Mk 1:15, etc.

[3] See Gn 6:6–7.

[4] See Gn 3:5.

[5] Rom 6:23.

[6] The work of A. von Harnack, *Medizinisches aus der Kirchengeschichte* (Leipzig: Hinrichs, 1892), is still a goldmine of information with regard to the Christian tradition. See also the excellent book by H. Schipperges, *Der Garten der Gesundheit* (Munich: Artemis, 1985).

[7] See Jn 6:12.

The Relationship between Medicine and Religion

For the sake of clarity, we shall be unfolding our one thesis as a triptych with three panels, or, you might say, introducing it with three comments, two negative and one positive, before arriving at a final formulation.

*1.   Failing to distinguish between medicine and religion cripples
      the former and distorts the latter.*

While there is surely an intimate and unbreakable relationship between medicine and religion, confusing them does no service to either.

To be sure, medicine does resemble the practical, corrective, and immediate aspect of religion. While religion aims essentially at the ultimate well-being of Man, medicine seeks primarily to remove immediate obstacles to human well-being. One must attend to concrete problems lest they remain unresolved. In the final analysis, original sin or that of my parents' may indeed be the ultimate cause of my toothache, but I should not on this account neglect poor diet or dental hygiene or any of the other more immediate causes of my malady. In other words, medicine simply cannot develop unless you *concentrate* your attention on the immediate symptoms of illness. I say concentrate attention on the problem, not specialize in the area. But I shall not now go on about *truth and method*.[8] It is fairly obvious that without such concentrated attention, medicine could scarcely ever come into its own.

It should also be obvious that when religion interferes indiscriminately in the second causes that prevent human beings from reaching fullness of life, disrupting the ontonomy of the means,[9] it becomes a merely technical sort of cure that forgets that human fulfillment is multidimensional and much more complex. Possibilities

---

[8]   See the important work of Hans-Georg Gadamer, *Truth and Method* (New York: Crossroad, 1985).

[9]   [*Ontonomy* is one of the basic concepts of Raimon Panikkar's thought. It is the *nomos tou ontos*, the intimate and constitutive *nomos* of each being, a contribution "to the mutual understanding and fertilization of the diverse fields of human activity and domains of the being, which allows for growth (*ontonomic*) without breaking the harmony." This concept can be central in the sphere of thought (scientific, philosophical, theological-spiritual . . .), and in the political and economic spheres, as well as any other sphere of life. We must avert both the independence that is separated and disconnected from the particular domains of the being (*autonomy*), as well as the predominance of one dominion over another (*heteronomy*), in order to arrive at a harmonious integration of the diverse parts in the whole (*ontonomy*). The person is the reality that achieves ontonomic order, since he or she is "the conjugation of all pronouns." In addition to speaking of the phase of heteronomy that took place in antiquity and the Middle Ages—an attitude that could also be defined as *theonomic*—and of the *humanistic* critique that led to the attitude of autonomy, our author speaks of *ontonomy* as a new notion of the relationship between creature and God. For a more in-depth explanation of the concepts of heteronomy, autonomy, and ontonomy, see *Myth, Symbol, Cult* (Panikkar, *Opera Omnia*, IX.1).]

for salvation are to some extent commensurable with the predicament of personal health. To push the point to an extreme: Human beings may achieve a fullness of life—although not easily—that is to say, they may achieve a *certain* plenitude, even in a hospital or a concentration camp. The human person's final destiny is not restricted to her state of health. A sick person, within certain limits, can also obtain salvation, even if this is understood as personal fulfillment—which is always relative—although she may not enjoy the full psychosomatic functioning of her organism. Magic is the great temptation of religion, and the abuse of power the great trap into which religion and medicine alike may fall.

2.   *Separating medicine and religion has been degrading for the former and alienating for the latter.*

Reviewing the history of medicine and of religion, we have to recognize that their rumored divorce has proceeded so slowly and incrementally that it is still far from being finalized.[10] From the institutions of ancient Egypt to the offices of today's psychiatrists, the medical profession has always retained its sacred aura.[11] There is no absolute break in continuity between the shaman or medicine man, the priest-as-medical-doctor of old, and the modern-day psychologist, or doctor-as-spiritual-director.[12] The ecclesiastical organization of medicine down the ages seems to be a human invariant.[13]

Let us proceed step by step:

- *Medicine without religion does not heal: it is no longer medicine.*
Here as elsewhere, we must first come to some agreement on the meaning of words. We have to ask ourselves just what an authentic medicine might be. We should say, sadly and parenthetically, that we are referring here mainly to Western medicine, which, as do all the natural sciences, persists in the colonialist syndrome of believing itself to be culturally neutral and therefore universal.[14] In point of

---

[10] See Werner Leibbrand, *Der göttliche Stab des Äskulap. Vom geistigen Wesen des Arztes*, Salzburg: O. Müller, 1939), where the author presents a certain theology of medicine from a historical basis (esp. 17).

[11] "The physician is the most prominent among members of the generally recognized professions. He is seen by the public as possessing a higher standard than any other professional" (Eliot Freidson, in *International Encyclopaedia of the Social Sciences*, ed. D. L. Sils [New York: Macmillan, 1968], 10:105).

[12] See the instructive observations of a Freudian psychoanalyst who does not want to renounce his Indic tradition, and his description of medicines in contemporary India: Sudhir Kakar, *Shamans, Mystics and Doctors* (Boston: Beacon, 1982).

[13] See Ivan Illich's caricatured but nonetheless realistic description in *Limits to Medicine—Medical Nemesis: The Extrapolation of Health* (London: Marion Boyars, 1976).

[14] According to a World Health Organization statistic from 1967, 70 percent of

fact, this syndrome is taking over the world.[15] Contemporary medicine, despite its scarcely negligible iatrogenic effects, does cure some sicknesses.[16] Less often does it cure the sick, and almost never the human being—which is exactly what it claims to do. Never have there been so many sick people as there are today—and you cannot say that they all existed in earlier times, but never realized it until they were nearly dead. A sick person is not merely an object. A sick person not diagnosed as such is not sick. What we have accomplished in our times—and again, very relatively, since human life can hardly be gauged only in solar years—has been to increase longevity and reduce infant mortality, thanks mainly to hygiene.

Nowadays, the mechanistic model of medicine and of the medical doctor as a mechanic for the human machine, responsible for keeping it up and running, has fallen from favor in principle, but in practice still stands as the dominant model, despite all the palliatives and precautionary measures.[17] Even admitting that modern medicine reestablishes health, Man still wants to be healthy for something.[18] If one forgets that "something," medicine loses its way and even

---

the professors of medicine in Africa were non-African, and indigenous medicines were systematically spurned. See "Medical Education," in *Encyclopaedia Britannica*, vol. 27, 1974, as a good example of contemporary Western-style medicine presenting itself as a universal science.

[15] Most treatises on modern medicine are blatant examples of monoculturalism and ethnocentrism, which would today be unacceptable in a treatise on history, art, or philosophy. As if Europe—and its North American colonies—were the unique efficient depository of "medical science," everything else seems to be presented as no more than sorcery, magic, or simple quackery. Here again, medicine only imitates modern physics, but while the latter has the right to postulate its axioms, the starting point of medicine is the real human being and not a complex of postulates. See, as an example of the coexistence of a certain praxis of Western medicine with aboriginal traditional theories—which, in spite of everything, remain very much alive throughout the African continent—Janice Reid, *Sorcerers and Healing Spirits: Continuity and Change in an Aboriginal Medical System* (Oxford: Pergamon, 1983).

[16] See the definition of "human illness" given by our learned historian of medicine: "Illness is a painful way of living of [*sic*] man, a reaction to an occasional alteration or to a permanent state of his body which render [*sic*] impossible the temporal realization of his personal destiny (lethal sickness), impedes or hampers occasionally that realization (curable illness), or limits it painfully and definitively (residual or cicatricial illness)" (P. Laín Entralgo, *Estudios de historia de la medicina y de la antropología médica*, vol. 1 [Madrid: Escorial, 1943], 329). The author indicates in a note that the "reactional" way of living can be an organic, individual, or personal reaction.

[17] The following assertion is still current in the Western medical conception: "The Greek spirit of rational inquiry may be considered the starting point of medical education because it introduced the practice of observation and reasoning regarding disease" ("Medical Education," *Encyclopaedia Britannica*).

[18] See, for example, C. G. Jung, who advocates precisely a more comprehensive medicine. *Das Grundproblem der gegenwärtigen Psychologie, Gesammelte Werke*, vol. 8 (Zürich: Rascher, 1967), 404.

its own identity.[19] The purpose of medicine is the healing of Man. But what does healing mean?

A single example will suffice to show us the degradation of a medicine that pretends its autonomy but is in fact enslaved to an external system that dominates it. Seeking autonomy, medicine has become heteronomous: its nature and function are dictated to it from outside itself; indeed, it is generously paid to put itself at the service of a particular society.

For the great majority of modern medical institutions, health consists in keeping people on the job. Declaring somebody "back on the job" is synonymous with declaring them cured. To be able to hold down a job is the sign of a healthy man, which implies, indeed, that to be human means to be an employee, and to be an employee means an economic slave to an enterprise foreign to any ideals of the people employed there. We must distinguish carefully between "work" and "labor."[20] Man is a worker, an artist, a creator, and co-creator in all the fields of the real, a *Homo artifex* but not necessarily an employee, a laborer.[21] The degradation of human activity from being creativity, art, study, science, to being work, mere physical and mental effort for someone else's benefit, to a mere indirect means of "earning a living" (as if life had to be earned), is part of the curse attached to original sin: "It is by the sweat of your brow that you will eat your bread,"[22] instead of eating in the joy of a shared *agapē*. Creative activity is Man's destiny and vocation, not "full employment."[23] Creativity is not a sin or the fruit of sinfulness, nor need it be painful. It is ironic to note that the less a modern state claims to be Christian, the more it seems to believe in the biblical curse. "Spain is a Republic of laborers from all classes," said the Preface to the Republican Constitution of 1931. In the USSR, having a job was considered a duty and not merely a right. In certain countries of *Western* Europe, the unemployed do not even have the right to cultivate the garden of a relative.

The syllogism is simple. Human activity is considered no more than a good job: Man is no more than an employee. In order to be employed, one must be healthy; ergo, health consists in being employable. Medicine is that technique that gives back to the system employable human beings who will keep at the never-ending job of maintaining the smooth functioning of its mechanisms.

---

[19] C. G. Jung, *Psychotherapie und Weltanschauung*, in *Gesammelte Werke*, vol. 16 (Zürich: Rascher, 1967), 89.

[20] See R. Panikkar: "L'émancipation de la technologie," *Interculture*, no. 85 (October–December 1984): 22–37. Other authors, such as Hannah Arendt, had already made this distinction.

[21] Generally, all terms that refer to work contain this note of fatigue or pain. It is rewarding to consult dictionaries of synonyms.

[22] See Gn 3:17.

[23] That is what could be added to the otherwise excellent book by Gregorio Marañón, *Ensayos sobre la vida sexual*, 4th ed. (Madrid: Espasa-Calpe, 1969), 24.

Medicine has become merely the means modern society uses to keep the ranks of its employees filled.

I am not criticizing here the notion of Man as *Homo faber*, although this may not be his most appropriate definition.[24] My critique aims rather at the confusion between labor, which is an alienating activity, and praxis, or *technē*, art as a constitutive activity that springs from the very nature of Man. The critique takes aim at *Homo laborans*, not at *Homo faber*, and still less at *Homo creans*.

Let us now see what most traditional medicines understand by health.

Here, the criterion of health is not the capacity for labor but the capacity to enjoy.[25] It is when people are in a permanent state of sadness—in the Christian tradition *acedia* was considered a capital sin—that they are considered sick: when they can no longer enjoy life, when they are overcome by *taedium vitae* (boredom), or by the pandemic malady of modern society, or by depression, when they have no gusto, no "taste" for food or for life, when they can no longer bear pain because they no longer know how to enjoy life.[26] It is not when your organism functions smoothly like a perfectly regulated machine that you are healthy, but when you are in harmony with yourself and with the universe that you enjoy *beatitudo* (happiness), which is Man's goal, even if only in a proleptic way.[27] Infirm indeed is the human being incapable of *delectatio, ānanda* (bliss). Joy has, however, too often been suspect in certain puritanical milieus, although this runs counter to the most authentic Christian tradition.[28]

Again, I repeat: Medicine without religion loses its raison d'être. Why cure Man? So that he can again become cannon fodder? It is no coincidence that modern medicine has made so much of its progress on battlefields.[29] *Intelligenti pauca!*

---

[24] Let us recall here H. Bergson's views in favor of the definition of Man as *Homo faber* and the pertinent critique by M. Scheler.

[25] The Greeks, on the other hand, were very aware of the danger of seeking pleasure for itself. See Plato's warning (*Symposium* 187) against illness derived from pleasure—in order to experience pleasure without getting sick.

[26] See my little book *La joia Pasqual*, with a Prologue by Lluís Duch (Montserrat: Publicacions de l'Abadia de Montserrat, 1988), recently published in the trilogy *La gioia pasquale: La presenza di Dio e Maria* (Milano: Jaca Book, 2007), where I comment on the gospel message of joy. See 1 Jn 1:3, etc.

[27] See the monumental work in five volumes of J. M. Ramírez, *Obras Completas*, vol. 2, *De hominis beatitudine*, ed. V. Rodríguez (Madrid: C.S.I.C., 1972), which, while of Thomistic inspiration, transcends the limits of a purely scholastic anthropology.

[28] See the first distinction of Raymond Llul, *Libre de Contemplació*, vol. 1, book 1, who treats joy as a fundamental attitude of the believer: "perquè, qui s'alegra de les coses finites, gran sorpresa fóra que no s'alegrés de les coses infinites" (*Obres Essencials* [Barcelona: Selecta, 1960], 2:108).

[29] From this point of view, the articles on Medicine in *Encyclopaedia Britannica* (1974) seem worrisome and manifest a high degree of unconscious colonialism.

Now, for the second part.

- *Religion without medicine does not save: it is no longer religion.*

From its side, religion detached from medicine ceases to be what every religion has always claimed to be: a source of joy; it must then postpone happiness, the proper goal of Man, to a beyond disconnected from the present moment. Religion separated from medicine becomes an alienating force that, to be sure, can take refuge in "the business of saving" disincarnated souls or in the expectation of a heaven projected into a lineal future, but which loses its earthly value—and even its raison d'être—since it can no longer save real Man in the flesh. Religion then degenerates into a series of norms that Man must follow if he doesn't wish to be chastised, or fall into a fate that he must accept willy-nilly, consoling himself, maybe, with some idea of a better future. Even in the best of cases, religion then comes to no more than medicine for that other world, at the price of neglecting this one.

If that other world, removed from this one, is all that counts, then the sooner we get out of this "bad inn,"[30] this "vale of tears," the better—"I'm dying because I do not die."[31] Religion no longer acknowledges, then, medicine's true function of curing and relegates it in practical terms exclusively to the task of relieving pain—insofar as pain is not considered salvific. Let's admit that we are facing here what amounts to sickly attitudes, due precisely to the divorce of religion and medicine.[32]

I am not trying to defend a naturalistic conception of religion. Sacrifice is essential to religion: change, exchange (*commercium*), even rupture of planes, death and resurrection, the immolation of contingency, or however we choose to call it. Religion is precisely answer, new life, transformation of basic structures—that is to say, cure, health. An unhealthy salvation, a salvation that is not at the same time health, is not salvation, even if we still have to explain what authentic health is, which obviously cannot limit itself to being good physiological functioning.

To repeat: Religion without medicine dehumanizes itself, becomes cruel and alienates human beings from their very life on this Earth; religion without medicine itself becomes pathological.

Let us move on now to the third, and positive, aspect of this thesis.

3.   *The relationship between medicine and religion is ontonomic.*

We intend neither to subordinate medicine to religion, nor religion to medicine. Their relationship is neither autonomic nor heteronomic. Religion and medicine are not totally independent, one from the other, but not dependent, one upon the

---

[30]   See Teresa de Jesús, *Camino de Perfección*, C.V. cap. 40.9; in *Obras Completas* (Madrid: Editorial de Espiritualidad, 1984), 808.

[31]   See Teresa de Jesús, *Poesías lírico-místicas*, 1; in ibid., 1177.

[32]   We must avoid the methodological error of a *katachronic* interpretation of past attitudes. Even spiritualities that today would seem only sickly and unacceptable can have a positive interpretation in other contexts.

other, either. As in politics or the sciences, such perspectives have repeatedly proven themselves harmful. The relationship here is ontonomic. Religion and medicine are neither dependent nor independent, but intradependent; they are interconnected because they are parts of the whole.[33]

An ontonomic relationship refers to the *nomos* of the *on*, that is, to the internal regularity of any being in its constitutive relationship to the whole of which it is a part. Medicine and religion are thus two faces of the same reality: the first develops the art of attaining and retaining health (defined according to diverse traditions); the second emphasizes the ultimate character of this human fulfillment or well-being, and the means to it. At the deepest level, ontonomy is the structure of a-duality.

The following reference will allow us to be clear. It is better to enter the kingdom of heaven one-armed or blind than to be thrown out of the kingdom of life with an unscathed body.[34] There is a hierarchy of values, and neither the eye nor the hands constitute the essence of the person. It is better to suffer a stomachache while loving one's neighbor—thus achieving eternal life—than it is to hate one's neighbor while enjoying good digestion—accompanied by good siestas. But the one who truly loves stands a better chance of having a healthy stomach than the one who hates. There is as direct a relationship—although not immediate—between love and the proper functioning of the body as there is between hate and functional disorders. We are touching here on the problem of holiness and sickness, and the psychology of mysticism. No need to expand on this, but we can say that physical health is not always synonymous with psychic health, nor the latter with salvation, although a religious life requires equilibrium between soul and body. Of what value was it for the blind man of the Gospel to have had his sight restored if this had no consequence for the kingdom of heaven?[35]

Once we are aware that the relationship here is ontonomic, we see that we are concerned neither with a religious medicine, one conditioned or dictated by "religious" considerations, nor with a "medical" religion, one seeking merely to cure the human "composite." Or rather, in both these expressions the use of the words "religion" and "medicine" is already improper. If we reject autonomy (dualism), we also repudiate heteronomy (monism).

Let us cite a central example to save us the trouble of lengthier disquisitions: death. It is unconvincing to say that death pertains to religion and life to medicine, namely, that medicine helps us attain the good life on this Earth and religion helps us make a good death. Religion must by its very nature participate in life, in the same way that medicine must by its very nature concern itself with death. When they confront death, religion and medicine encounter one another; but they find themselves equally astounded before a mystery. Each is equally aware of the

---

[33] See in this vein E. K. Ledemann, *Mental Health and Human Conscience* (Amersham: Averbury, 1984), and J. Needlemann, *The Way of the Physician* (San Francisco: Harper & Row, 1985), among others.

[34] See Mt 18:8–9.

[35] See Mt 12:22.

importance of having tasted life in depth, and both are aware of the importance of knowing how to die well: that is, not falling into the banality of a mere extinction of physiological functions. Both find themselves face-to-face with something radically incomprehensible. Death as a phenomenon eludes direct consciousness because it represents a threshold of discontinuity incommensurable with all that precedes it and all that might follow. There is no experience and no science of death, only belief and hope in its meaning. Death is an infirmity of consciousness: it is not possible to be conscious of death, since death itself is loss of *con-sciousness*—the dead are no longer with us—even if it may be an awakening to a superior knowing (*scientia*).

And yet, neither medicine nor religion can avoid meeting death, be it to put it off, eliminate it, or transform it. We confront here the mystery of time and of tempiternity, the hidden key to human existence.[36] But let us for now let this mystery be, and move on to a concrete and final formulation of the thesis.

Overcoming the Estrangement between Their Guiding Concepts

The situation here is similar to the famous disputes between reason and faith, nature and grace, wave and particle theory, the chicken and the egg, that in fact represent problems wrongly put, which one must step back from in order to resolve. We find ourselves once again with the *regressus* that rejects the idolatry of progress. So often do we lack the eye of the artist or the reflection of the philosopher, stepping back to find a new perspective! At bottom, this requires us not to be attached to the past, to the already done, to the inertia of being. There is a link between Taoist freedom, Hindu detachment, Buddhist indifference—to cite only three instances—and the fundamental attitude I am seeking to describe. It is written that the spirit renews all things,[37] and this implies detachment from all that is outdated, and acceptance of the process of death and resurrection. The new is not what is chronologically posterior—like summer coming after winter—or what is spatially distant—like some exotic product on the market. The new is neither the "latest model," nor a variation on an old theme. The new here symbolizes the creativity of Being, the very vitality of reality. It is the appearance of what was unthought, because it was supposed to be unthinkable; it is the liberation of Being from thinking. This is the very character of freedom.[38]

The fact that we lack words to describe what we would say is, on the one hand, awkward; on the other hand, it confirms the novelty of what we are trying to express. This would be neither synthesis nor reconciliation between medicine and religion.

---

[36] See R. Panikkar, "El presente tempiterno. Una apostilla a la historia de la salvación y a la teología de la liberación," in *Teología y mundo contemporáneo: Homenaje a K. Rahner*, ed. A. Vargas-Machuca (Madrid: Cristiandad, 1975), 136.

[37] See Rev 25:5, etc.

[38] See the chapter "Hermeneutic of Religious Freedom: Religion or Freedom," in Panikkar, *Myth, Faith and Hermeneutics* (New York: Paulist Press, 1979), 419–60.

We cannot shake off past millennia. It is not a return to the past, not even to the best of what traditional religiosities offer, though none of that should be neglected or underestimated. It is a cross-fertilization of the new and the old—as the Gospel said[39]—between the traditional notions of medicine and religion, as well as between these and our contemporary vision.

Two exogenous words may well help explain this fundamental human attitude. Were I to limit myself to defending "a religiousness for our times" or a "contemporary spirituality," as so many others do, we would still be pinned to the old grids and would do scant justice to the present situation. Let us not forget that having superseded the vision of prehistoric Man, we now take our leave of historical existence and glimpse the dawn of a new cosmic mutation. Of the two words that will help us describe this attitude one is Greek, *eudokia*, and the other Sanskrit, *dharma*. One will easily understand why we drop the word *religion*, as does the New Testament,[40] not only due to past associations, but also because here the question is precisely how to move beyond the supposed dualism, the rift between medicine and religion, without suppressing the ontonomy existing between the two in the process. I do not claim to give a religious meaning to medicine—that would merely be a conservative defense of religion—or to discover a hygienic or medico-scientific meaning for religion— that would merely be a conservative defense of medicine. The two words I propose would symbolize the fruit of their encounter. It should be obvious that I am using these words as simple indicators of a fundamental attitude.

Allow me a sociological remark. All too often we meet people disappointed by medicine! Just as often we meet entire segments of society disenchanted with religion. To prescribe them a new medicine or preach them a new religion is stale and unconvincing. New medicines are not very effective, and new religions amount to no more than sects of little momentum. What we do need is a new attitude toward life, the instauration of a new way of life. Simple reforms do nothing but prolong the agony of a sick civilization—hence the need for new words: to express the novelty of new experience.

On the other hand, to "erase it all and start from scratch" is naïve, if not impossible; one cannot ignore history or simply return to the past. One must connect with tradition. This is why I use words that already exist in distinct traditions, confident in the strength of the mutual fecundation of which I have spoken.

Our contemporaries, thirsting for both health and salvation, cannot content themselves with a response limited to simple iconoclastic critiques of the status quo. We must seek points of conjunction. The disenchantment of ordinary people in our latitudes is now something quite palpable. Restorations are no longer convincing. Innovations do not succeed in implanting themselves. Hence my vision of the fecundation, the cross-fertilization, as well as the justification for the two words I now introduce, which are both old and new at the same time.

---

[39] See Mt 13:52.

[40] The word *religio* (*thrēskeia*) is used only a few times in the Vulgate and generally with a meaning different from the modern meaning of religion. See Ac 26:5; Col 2:18; Jas 1:26–27. Sometimes the New Testament *eusebēs* is translated as *religious*; see Ac 10:2.

• *Eudokia*, wedding goodwill to well-being (contentment), with all its connotations and derivatives, could serve to express this fundamental attitude.

The prefix *eu* indicates positivity, well-being, joy, nobility. And the verb *dokēo* means not only to appear but also to judge, hope, believe, as well as to be better, to surpass, to have dignity. The deep meaning of *eudokia* harmoniously combines the individual aspect of pleasure, happiness, and satisfaction with the social aspect of concord, consent, recognition, acceptance, and hence also justice, with a third dynamic dimension of willing, desiring, selecting, "opting," deciding.

We are all familiar with the evangelical phrase, peace to *anthrōpois eudokias*, generally translated as "Men of good will" or, rather more exactly, as people in whom favor resides, in this case divine favor.[41]

Without now entering into linguistic details, we can say that the vital field of this word connotes the following: that fundamental attitude of goodwill, decision, and aspiration that responds in a positive manner to what comes from outside—transcendence—and which, by accepting it, assimilates it and discovers in it fullness and personal happiness. In a way, *eudokia* harmoniously unites freedom and happiness; it represents the fruit of a harmony between what we have been—nature—and the effluvia that reach us: by accepting them we transform them in order to come to be—what we *are* truly, what we are called to be.... The word *dignity* (*dignus*), which has the same root, could very well summarize that attitude, without forgetting that it also means elegance and even beauty (*decus*). "Vere dignum et justum est, aequum et salutare" (It is truly meet and just, right and for our salvation), proclaims the Introit of the Christian Latin Rite, playing with four adjectives related to this very notion of *eudokia*,[42] which stands for the harmonious marriage of immanence and transcendence. In this our dignity resides.

When medicine and religion fecundate one another, they give rise to *eudokia* as a fundamental human attitude that does not ignore yet goes beyond the dichotomies between individual and society, between this world and the world to come, between internal and external, between knowledge and will.[43]

• *Dharma* is a key word for the entire Indic and probably Asiatic conception. It is related to the Vedic notion of *ṛta* and to the medieval Latin notion of *ordo*, as also to the Greek concept of the universe as *kosmos*.[44] Its etymology gives us the root *dhr*, which means to hold, keep, maintain in cohesion.[45] *Dharma* is what keeps people together in harmony, says the Mahābhārata.[46]

---

[41] See Lk 2:14.

[42] The root of the Indo-European verb *dek* indicates to take, to accept, and hence, to honor (see the Sanskrit, *daśasyati*, to venerate), and also to consecrate (see the Sanskrit, *dikśa*, consecration, initiation). See the Greek, *doxa*, opinion, glory, etc.

[43] See the Coptic Gospel of Thomas 22.

[44] See J. Miller, *The Vision of the Cosmic Order in the Vedas* (London: Routledge & Kegan Paul, 1985), and my Preface.

[45] The Indo-European *dher*, to maintain (oneself), to lean, to sustain (oneself). See the Latin, *firmus*, and the numerous Sanskrit derivatives, from *dharāna* to *dhruva*, etc

[46] See Karna-pārva 69.59; Śānti-pārva 109.14, and also 266.12–13.

The idea implies a social order tied to the four stages of life, *āśrama-dharma*, and a cosmic order to which the individual must adjust beyond all other moral conflict, as brilliantly taught by the Bhagavad-gītā.[47] Whoever perturbs this order harms himself. *Dharma* is the very texture of the universe. It is the web whose knots are the people themselves.[48]

In contemporary India, in the languages derived from Sanskrit, the word *religion*, usually translated by *dharma*, also means duty, right, custom, law, justice, morality, norm, virtue, merit, conduct, character, doctrine, harmony. *Dharma* is also the degree of reality each thing has, and so forth.[49] Human beings exist in the measure to which they recognize their *svadharma*, which amounts to one's personal and specific appropriation of the universal *dharma*. *Dharma* is that which maintains each being in its place within the universe.

I introduce these two words to suggest a triple movement beyond modernity: first, moving beyond *individualism* (medicine and religion limited to the individual); then, beyond *anthropocentrism* (medicine and religion limited to Man); and finally, beyond *dualism* (medicine for health in this world, religion for salvation in the next, etc.). Besides, *eudokia* and *dharma* express a direct relationship with all humanity, on the one hand, and with the whole universe, on the other. The universal harmony of the Chinese or the Greek, the Christian mystical body of Christ, the African anthropocosmic spirituality are all very close to this attitude I am trying to describe here and which I have elsewhere called the *cosmotheandric intuition*.

It may be that *Homo religiosus* has always been *eudotic* and *dharmic*, as the shaman or medicine man has also wanted to be. In any case, we must go beyond the reductionisms that presume to limit everything to the individual or even to Man.

At best, medicine and religion would be only partial remedies, each in its own field. What we need is a creative hermeneutics that allows us to step over these barriers, without setting off blindly on a course where we can no longer take our bearings.

The words *medicine* and *religion* have suffered such erosion that they no longer serve either to express their original meanings, or to communicate a vision of the world that integrates both the contributions of other cultures and the impact of modernity. Today the word *religion* suggests primarily the idea of an institution rather than the deepest human dimension. The word *medicine* suggests technology and institutionalization, a far cry from the art of maintaining and obtaining that human fullness to which human beings cannot but aspire during this lifetime.[50]

The second part will help us see these things more clearly.

---

[47] See *BG* III.35; XVIII.47 on *svadharma*, but especially the solution to Arjuna's inner conflict from the beginning.

[48] See my definition of the person as a knot in the web of relationships in "Karma and the Individual," *Myth, Faith, and Hermeneutics* (New York: Paulist Press, 1979), 376–81.

[49] See my chapter "Algunos aspectos de la espiritualidad hindī," in *Historia de la Espiritualidad*, ed. B. Jimenez Duque and L. Sala Balust (Barcelona: Flors, 1969), 4:436–40, for more details and for bibliographical references.

[50] The Greek expression *technē iatrikē* was translated into Latin as *ars medica*, and thence to the German *Heilkunst* (and *Heilkunde*).

The Truth of the Thing

In keeping with the parameters and perspectives adopted above, we must now have recourse to the most trustworthy documents of all in this field: that which defines itself as the "science of truth," namely, etymology.[51] For it is in words that the deepest and oldest experiences of humankind are crystalized. Each word is a world, and each linguistic root is the seed of an entire universe of discourse. We shall realize this as we analyze the three following notions. We have not yet said what medicine is, although we have implicitly criticized a certain notion of it. *Medicine* refers to medicating, and it is through this door we shall enter to consult the wisdom of the words themselves. In English, healing and health stem from the root *hoelan* (*haal*), whence also derive the English words *whole, hale, wholesome,* and indeed, *holy.* In Spanish, medicine refers to *salud* (in French: *santé*), which refers directly to *salvación* (in French, *salut*; in English, salvation), which would seem to be the specific task of *religion.* Hence our analysis, even if very succinct, of these three groups of words.

Medication, Meditation, Measure

What does the word *medicine* have to say about itself? Medicine, medication (in French, *médecin*), and all other derivatives come directly from the Latin *medeor* (*mederi*) which means to treat, to cure, to medicate. Let us remember that if in Castilian Spanish medicine is the science or art that aims at curing *enfermedades,* that is, weaknesses (*infirmitates*), lack of vigor or of strength (see the Greek *asthenes, astheneia*), in most of the Romance languages "medicine" seeks to cure *maladies* (French), *malalties* (Catalan), *malattie* (Italian)—although the word *infirmo* also exists—that is, "the bad *habitus*" (*male se habens*), without forgetting the sarcastic irony of the Catalan, which calls poison *metzina* and the one who poisons *emmetzinador*: medication transformed into its contrary.[52]

This already outlines the field where medicine and religion run up against one another in their struggle against evil.[53] But it is an intelligent struggle.

In Sanskrit, the physician is called *vāidya,* the one who knows, who sees. The root *vid* means to know and is related to the Latin *videre* and to the French *voir.* Today, the *doctor* by antonomasia, that is, the learned man, the one who knows, and even

---

[51] *Etymos* means true, real, and it is generally opposed to *pseudos,* false, untrue. *To etymon* means the true meaning of a term. See *eteos* with the same meaning and the verb *etazō,* to examine, etc. In their respective dictionaries, P. Chantraine, contrary to J. B. Hofmann, is doubtful about this term's relationship with the Sanskrit *satya* (truth), from *sat* (being).

[52] This meaning already appears in Latin. See Ps. Quintilian, *Declamationes* 15.4; Tacitus, *Annales* 12.67.1, etc., in *Thesaurus Linguae Latinae,* 7.531.28ff. and 7:535.1ff., at the words *medicamen* and *medicamentum,* which often equally mean *auxiliis magicis.*

[53] The German *Krankheit,* from *krank,* also means weak, skinny, small, and is related to the Latin *aegrotus* and *infirmus.* The etymology of the English illness (ill) is uncertain (evil, sic).

more who teaches (*docet*), is the physician—not the philosopher or the theologian. Similarly, the German *Arzt*, which comes from the late Latin *archiater*, and that from the Greek *arch-iatros*, chief medical man (court physician).[54]

Another Sanskrit word is *cikitsaka*, from *cikitsa*, to cure, derivative of *cit*, to perceive, to be aware, to know. The doctor is the one who cures and does so because he knows; he is the one who has knowledge, the sage.[55] One cures therefore by knowledge, not by intervention—as an experiment.

But there is more. The iterative of *medeor* (*mederi*) that we have seen above is *meditor*, whence *meditate*, *meditation*. Medicine is therefore a *meditation*. And if Plato defines philosophy as a *meditatio mortis*, Ayurvedic medicine defines itself etymologically as a *meditatio vitae*, a science of life: *āyur-veda*.[56] Authentic meditation is the great medicine. Let us not forget that we are now pursuing our "meditation" on "medicine and religion."

The essence of medicine is not objective knowledge, in the modern sense of the word, but precisely *medicatio* and *meditatio*, that is, existential participation in the systole and diastole of reality, which is the authentic meditation: to care for reality itself by participating in it, by virtue of that participative knowledge or cognitive participation that is love. We can see that as we get close to authentic religiousness, we take our distance from all official religion, and the closer we get to medicine, the farther we are from the hospital!

But what constitutes this medicine that is meditation and hence loving knowledge? If we follow the leading thread of the Indo-European root, we notice that besides treating, curing, and meditating, *med* also means to measure, as indicated in the Spanish *medir*. Medicine is hence also a measurement, reflexive and thought out, that judges. The Latin *judex*, judge, becomes in Latinised Osque[57] *meddix* (originally *meddiss*), from that selfsame root *med*.

---

[54] The medical doctor's authority is also reflected in the words *medoma*, in Homeric Greek *medeō* (to cure, take care of), meaning the chief. From *mēdomai* (meditate, reflect) comes also *mēstor* (the counselor). See its feminine *klytaimēstra* (converted into Clytemnester), the one who takes decisions (Benveniste).

[55] "The foundations of medicine are knowledge of nature, human knowledge, and skill," wrote Viktor von Weizsäcker in 1943 in "Die Grundlagen der Medizin," in *Diesseits und Jenseits der Medizin* (Stuttgart: Koehler, 1950), 49. We may recall the gigantic figure of Paracelsus in sixteenth-century Europe. See the collective work by H. Dopsch et al., ed., *Paracelsus* (Salzburg: Pustet, 1993), published on occasion of the fifth centenary of Paracelsus's birth.

[56] *Carata-samhit ā* 1.30.20. See, on the other hand, most of the current definitions synthesized in *Diccionario de La Real Academia Espanola* (1984 edition): "Ciencia y arte de precaver y curar las enfermedades del cuerpo humano" (Science and art of preventing and curing ailments of the human body). Hermogenes, in his *Programa de Salud*, CEDEL (Girona: Viladrau, 1984), 27, rightly asks himself if one should not better define medicine as "the art and science of health."

[57] The Osci were an indigenous people of Italy who kept their own language until the first century.

In Persian and in the Avesta, the medical man is called *vi-mad*. Here again, one finds the root *med* and the prefix *vi*, which suggests distantiation and probably authority. The "doctor" therefore also judges: he is *judex*. But, on the other hand, the authentic judge is also a doctor. And both meditate. In Irish, *midiur* (from the Latin *medeor*) means "I judge."[58]

Here we are touching a point crucial to the entire Indo-European culture of the last three millennia or more. There are two ways of exercising this human intellectual activity that we call thinking: one consists in measuring and expresses itself through the root *men* (*man*) and its derivatives: *mantra, mānana, manu, manyate, manas, mimāmsā*, and so on; in Greek, *memona, mimneskō*, and so on; in Latin *memento, memini, moneo*, and so on. The root *mē* (*m-e-t*) means, in fact, to think, in the sense of measuring. That is where the Sanskrit word *manas* comes from, and the English *mind*, and the Latin *mens-mensis*, the month. Hence also the English *moon*, because it is a means of measuring time. Moon in German is called *Mond*. *Meto* means the year: measure. *Meti* means prudence or, as we still say today, moderation. See also the Indo-European *menot* (genitive *meneses*). The Latin is *metior* and the Greek, *metron*. Plato names the right measure: *metrion*.

The other is our root *med*, which also means thinking and measuring, but in another way.[59] While the first way established bounds and milestones in order to measure quantitatively (Pokorny), to measure through instruments, the second way measures through moderation (Benveniste), that is, by being *modestus*, the one who is full of moderation (Benveniste), *massvoll, bescheiden* (Pokorny). This measure is that of the judge; it conforms itself to a determined order because it believes, as the Bible says, that "omnia in mensura, et numero, et pondere disposuisti" (you, however, ordered all things by measure, number, and weight).[60]

The Septuagint translates *metron, arithmon, stathmos*, but the meter here is obviously not quantitative, nor the number mathematical, nor the weight gravitational. It is a matter of acknowledging the cosmic order, *ṛta*, which makes the world a *kosmos* and not a *chaos*. "The measure of Man is that of the angel," says the Apocalypse.[61] Hence this very root *med* also means to govern and includes the legal sense already indicated. *Modo* means "the proven measure which re-establishes order in a troubled situation."[62]

A cure is not the result of a quantitative experiment, but the reestablishment of an order that has been perturbed.

---

[58] See the remarkable chapter about *med* and the notion of measure in E. Benveniste, *Le Vocabulaire des institutions indo-européennes* (Paris: Minuit, 1969), 2:4.

[59] One must underscore that for Plato (*Philebus* 66a), the most important among the five goods of life is precisely *to metron* (measure); in second place comes proportion, symmetry; and only in third reason (mind, intelligence); followed by the arts and sciences; and finally, in fifth place, pleasure.

[60] Ws 11:20.

[61] Rev. 21:17.

[62] Benveniste, *Le Vocabulaire des institutions indo-européennes*, 2:129.

As I say, the tension represented by these two roots has determined the fate of the West. For Man is a thinking being, even a "thinking reed," to cite Pascal, or a *res cogitans*, according to Descartes, but thinking may mean many things.[63] It can mean to *measure*, that is, to go through experiments with reality by knowing its quantitative aspects, or else it may mean to *moderate*, that is, to enter into the experience of what is by judging it according to a superior paradigm. Thinking, in brief, can mean *men*, to measure, calculate, or *med*, to meditate, reflect. The first experiments, the second experiences. The first gives birth to the natural sciences, the second to the humanities, the *humaniora*.[64]

The modern West, following Galileo and Descartes among others, has opted for the quantitative measure for calculation. Thus, a person who calculates is seen as prudent. Prudence, *sōphrosynē*, that is, "the healthy state of mind and body" (Bailly), has degenerated into calculation rather than *moderation*.[65] To think is to calculate. Science is calculation. One must expose the quantitative side of everything. Thus, medicine consists of clinical analyses. Computers govern finance—anachronistically called *economics*—and along with the latter, politics. Contemplation is a luxury; art, a pastime. Small matter into whose hands the means of production fall, those of the state or those of the most intelligent. It is always about the means of production.[66]

Indo-European culture—limiting ourselves to this one—knew, before its rhythms were ruptured by acceleration, another form of thinking as the *morphē*, the form proper to human life. It is a sovereign form of thinking that does not measure, but moderates; it is a knowledge that does not intervene, but hopes, and which, while hoping, observes and loves. The quantitative can be calculated; the qualitative must be tasted: it needs an appreciator, not a calculator.

The issue is not whether to opt for mere mathematics, forgetting that for Pythagoras, numbers were the *archai* of things.[67] Nor is it simply to give in to sheer technique, forgetting that for Plato *technē* was first of all the art of living.[68] We do

---

[63] Heidegger's assertions are well known: "Most thought-provoking (*das Bedenklichste*), in our thought-provoking time is that we are still not thinking"; furthermore, "Science does not think." See M. Heidegger, *Was heisst Denken?* in *Vorträge und Aufsätze* (Pfullingen: Neske, 1967), 2:4.

[64] One must recall that classical studies on humanities were called *studia humaniora*—that is, a comparative adjective to denote that these studies led to or made possible a more humane stage for Man.

[65] Let us not forget that it is the same root *saos*, *sōs*, salvation, to be healthy, strong.

[66] "So that Man today becomes a slave to progress, . . . so that production is incomparably more important than the product, . . . predominance given to haste . . . stimulates more than the pleasure of the product. . . . Who will enjoy so many accumulated goods? When?" writes García Morente, *La filosofía de Kant* (1917; Madrid: Espasa Calpe, 1975), 126. The "so that" refers to the Kantian impact on modern society.

[67] See Aristotle, *Metaphysics* 1.5 (985b.25–26).

[68] See Ortega's beautiful text: "The value of art has been greatly exaggerated in recent times. Without wishing now to depreciate it, I will however remark that the supreme art is the one that makes of life itself an art. Painting and music are certainly delectable: but

not have to choose between *men* or *med* in an exclusive way. Our task is to bring about a positive and fruitful symbiosis in which *bios* goes beyond theory and praxis and discovers *zōē*, that other Life that perdures down the ages.[69]

This, then, is medicine according to the very meaning of the word: *medication, meditation, measure*. In other words, medicine is *medication* when it comes through an external influence, be this transcendence or a more skillful hand; it is *meditation* when it comes through internal growth and interior knowledge of a personal situation; it is *measure* when it comes through respect for the modest—keeping within measure—order of things and conservation or recuperation of this harmony, which, when all is said and done, constitutes reality. Let us now see how close or far we are from religion.

Salvation, Health, Confidence

If medicine includes the three components we have just described, religion also displays these three attributes. As before, we shall let ourselves be guided by the wisdom of words. But after the reflections above, we may now be a bit briefer.

The Latin *salus*, the state of the one who is *salvus*, is called in Greek *sōtēria*. The word means salvation, health, to salute (greet), and consequently, security. There is a Sanskrit root that means vigor, power, strength. Its first meaning is found in the Sanskrit word *sarva*: full, complete, intact, and from there, whole. In French, *salut* means the action of being saved or the action of saluting (greeting). The Spanish equivalent, *salud*, means health or the action of saluting (greeting). The German *heil* also means salvation and health. Until the third century, to save and to salute (greet) kept their link: *salvare, salutare*. The idea of salvation and even of redemption, and from this, forgiveness, has also played a role in the history of *sōtēria*. The savior king does more than save; he forgives. Salvation is to make whole again, complete. The primary meaning of the German word *ganz* (*Ganzheit*) is also that of *heil*, to be saved and to be healthy in order to be complete, to have *genug*, enough of what is needed. Saved is the one who is safe and sound, that is, *unverletzt, vollständing*, secure, protected.

This root puts us in mind of *holos totus*, complete, "holistic," and is related to the Latin translation, *omnis*, of the sanskrit *viṣvaḥ*. The connection between *sollus* and *solidus* is interesting. What is solid is complete; it has no holes, it is intact. *Insanus* in Latin means not merely a sick person, but an insane person.

---

what are they as compared to a delicately chiseled friendship, to a polished and perfect love? The *supreme form of life is conviviality*, and a conviviality that one would tend to be like a work of art would be the peak of the universe," in J. Marias, "Ortega ante Goethe," Cuaderno 4 of the Fundación Pastor de Estudios Clásicos (Madrid, 1961), taken up again in Cuaderno 22 *Estudios sobre el humanismo clásico* (Madrid, 1977), 54.

[69] No need here to relate the three Greek words for "life," *bios, zōē, psychē*, with the three Sanskrit words *jīva, prāṇa, ātmā* (*bhūtatmā*).

In Castilian Spanish, unhealthy people (*malsanos*) are more than sick; they are bad (*malos*). The Indo-European word for healthy is formed by *kal* (*kali, kalu*), which also means beautiful. Let us recall the Greek *kallos*, beauty, and the Sanskrit *kalyāṇa*, beautiful, salutary.

Thus, medicine and religion both seek to save Man, in the sense already mentioned: to make him complete, whole. Religion seeks, besides, to give him the *confidence* that saves him. This is why faith is required. But can we be content with this dichotomy between a medicine that saves the body and a religion that saves the soul? Can we admit that medicine tries to reestablish health in this world, and religion to establish salvation in the other world? We must refute this dualism without in the process falling into monism. This is what we have called ontonomy and *advaita*. Even were we to permit this lethal dichotomy to stand, medicine and religion would not thereby cease to have an intrinsic and constitutive relationship. Despite all the necessary distinctions, Man is a unity and cannot be saved if he is divided into many pieces. It is impossible to perform an autopsy on a living being; not only because it would kill, but also because it would lose its raison d'être.

Thus there is no health without salvation, nor salvation without confidence. There can be a healthy organ and a provisional salvation. Confidence is not a certitude based on objective knowledge. Its basis is not objects but reality. Our confidence is cosmic, or rather, cosmotheandric. In brief, there is no individual salvation. Salvation is the harmonious equanimity between my being and my life, which is to say, between Being and Life. The whole is distinct from and anterior to the sum of its parts. The problem rears its head when we think only by measuring and not also by moderating. Then the laws of logic lose their link with the laws of the heart. Then sentiment is no longer what unites knowledge and love.[70] What makes science possible—its fundamental postulate—but is not found in other cultures—which give priority to thinking rather than measuring—is what is called "the uniformity of natural laws." Repetition is its criterion of truth. Yet confidence is not certainty. But this would take us too far.

Religion, Relinking, Reelection

It is well known that there exists no universal word to indicate what we call religion, not even in the Indo-European linguistic world. What we have said previously will allow us now to be even more brief.

---

[70] See my *F. H. Jacobi y La filosofía del sentimiento* (Buenos Aires: Sapientia, 1948); J. Bofill, "Para una metafísica del sentimiento," in *Obra filosófica* (published posthumously; Barecelona: Ariel, 1967), 107–61 (previously appeared in *Convivium* 1, no. 1 [1956], Universidad de Barcelona, 1950, 19–53, and no. 3 [1957], 3–36). See also the works of Th. Haecker, *Metaphysik des Fühlens* (Munich: Kosel, 1950), and O. F. Bollnow, *Das Wesen der Stimmungen* (Frankfurt, a.M.: Klostermann, 1941 [5th ed., 1974]), to which can now be added the work of B. Bebek, *The Third City* (London: Routledge & Kegan Paul, 1982).

Paradoxically, the very success of the word *religion* to indicate the entire complex of myths, beliefs, symbols, and actions that claim to lead Man to his final destination has been the cause of its limitation and, in a certain sense, its discredit.

The origins of the word are much more humble. Grammatically, it is probable that *religio* comes from *re-legere*—according to Cicero's interpretation—that is, to gather, collect, even if philosophically Lactantius's interpretation has been preferred, which tends toward *re-ligare*—that is, what unites, links, Man to his divinity. Recently, Xavier Zubiri speculated on the relinking of Man.[71] The word has had illustrious advocates.[72] One also knows St. Augustine's interpretation, which makes of *religio* a derivative of *re-eligere*, Man's effort and choice to unite himself anew with God, in order to restore the link broken by original sin.

Without entering into further considerations, not even discussing whether true religion is what unties and unbinds us—that is, what gives us freedom—we can deduce from the entire linguistic complex above that there is something in human beings—be it inside or outside of us, or maybe both inside and outside us—that we need in order to be safe and sound. Man is an incomplete being. Faith is our capacity to be more—better—than what we are. Medicine and religion are, at worst, two institutions and, at best, the expression of a human dimension that must be fulfilled, cured, saved, redeemed, must reach its completion, however relative this may be, even if it entails renouncing such a dream.

Our purpose here is sufficiently complete if we underscore the intimate relationship between these two notions and draw some conclusions from this.

The Call to Harmony

I have already said that I do not wish to go back to a magical conception of things, or to let diverse spheres meld into an uncritical indistinctness. The issue here is not nostalgia for the primitive chaos but overcoming the current fragmentation of life triggered by the cancerous specialization of modern civilization. It is a matter of reestablishing harmony between all the dimensions of the real, that very harmony that pre-Socratics, Taoists, and Vedantins, among others, have sung and celebrated in such deep and eloquent words.

We shall start with an example regarding religion: the loss of its medicinal function, which is to say, of meditation. We are concerned with discovering the internal harmony of the person. And we cannot forget that the traditional name for this art is medicine.[73] This we shall follow with an example regarding medicine: the loss of its religious function, which is to say of health as salvation. Here we are concerned

---

[71] See X. Zubiri, *Naturaleza, Historia y Dios*, 4th ed. (Madrid: Editora Nacional, 1959), 309–40.

[72] See detailed facts in W. C. Smith, *The Meaning and End of Religion* (1962; New York: Harper and Row, 1978), in *Toward a World Theology of Religions*, ed. L. Swidler (Maryknoll, NY: Orbis, 1987), 118–53.

[73] See Plato, *Symposium* 187c.

with discovering the external harmony of the person. Let us not forget that the traditional name for this art is music.[74]

We shall conclude by referring to a traditional medicine, which might well serve as stimulus for the cross-fertilization we have been foreshadowing all along.

Personal Experience

I want to speak about an experience of which most all of us are capable, but few of us know. It is said that at forty, we are responsible for what our faces look like. But there is more to it. Our health depends as much on the extrinsic causes that condition it, as it does on our own innate disposition—our deepest being, beyond the scope of a "free" will conditioned by external stimuli.

The functioning of my body is directly linked to the functioning of my soul—to speak more traditionally. No maladies are only somatic or exclusively psychic. Meditation is not solely a recourse for peace of the soul or intellectual clarity; it is also a solace for the body. Put another way, there is no Eucharist without bread—that is, no salvation without food, no salvation without health.[75] *Annam Brahman*, say the *Upaniṣad*. *Brahman* is food.[76] When parents tell their children that their teeth will fall out if they lie, they are indeed exaggerating, but the saying still holds a great truth. The errors of our life do contribute to the degeneration of our body. It is true that the error may be that of a neighbor who broke our teeth with his fist, or an arm, or a leg by hitting us with his car. But even here, there is interdependence.

The miracles of Christ are less the acts of a miracle worker proving his mission than the direct effect of medicine and religion upon each other, that is, of the link between health and salvation. The sick, the infirm, and the miserable get well because they are saved. Christ does not manipulate things, nor is he exclusively concerned with the beyond. His cures are the very symbols of salvation, say the Gospels. That is why they require faith—that is, confidence, surrender, purity of heart, the whole power of our being. In a word, we are the artisans of our own destiny, not so much by a detached will as by the integral power of our being. Such a power does not come solely from ourselves, but must be received and transformed by us.[77] To do so,

---

[74] Ibid. The passage is worth quoting: "Now, in all this, conciliation is now introduced by music (*mousikē*), as it was a little while ago by medicine (*iatrikē*), music being the one which realizes love and concord (*erōta homonoia*) between opposites. In other words, music is, in its turn, in the realm of harmony and rhythm (*armonia, rythmos*), the science of the phenomena of love (*erōtikōn epistēmē*)."

[75] See the expression *pharmakon athanasias* (medicine of resurrection) for the Eucharist; Ignatius Antioch, *Epist. ad Eph.* 20.2 (*PG* 661), quoted in R. Panikkar, "La Eucaristía y la Resurrección de 1a Carne," in *Humanismo y Cruz* (Madrid: Rialp, 1963), 345, etc., for other similar texts.

[76] See *CU*, VII.9.

[77] Many of Christ's parables echo this theme.

we must really know ourselves, as the Delphic Oracle demanded.[78] But as Chuang-Tzu (Zhuangzi) reminded us, "Man does not see himself in troubled waters, but in tranquil waters."[79] The acknowledged word for this existential self-knowledge is meditation. "We turn into whatever we meditate," says the *Śatapatha-brāhmaṇa*.[80] "This is eternal life," says Christ, "that they know you, and the one whom you have sent."[81] This knowledge is no simple intellectual perception but an identification, an incorporation, one could say, into the theandric reality of which that very text speaks.

Meditation is not spiritual narcissism or an uncritical shutting in upon oneself. It is, to the contrary, that activity of the spirit beyond the mental realm that yet does not repress the mind, but indeed assumes it. Hence the importance of "knowing how" to meditate, which is not quantitative or calculating thinking but fully participating in reality itself, as much objectively as subjectively. It begins with thinking well and clearly about the reality that surrounds us, starting with our bodies, but it ends up at the very limits of the universe.

The best medicine is, therefore, meditation, that is, the harmonic reintegration of the real. Entering anew into the ebb and flow of the Trinitarian *perichōresis*, so to speak, entering into the *choreia*,[82] into the dance of the whole of reality, reestablishing harmony through the very power of the Spirit: "Sana quod est saucium [. . .] rege quod est devium"[83] (heal that which is wounded [. . .] make right that which is wrong).

Within the Judeo-Christian tradition, there formerly existed what was called the custody of the heart (*phylakē kardias*), or again, guarding the mind (*tērēsis noou*), a practice based on a more or less literal exegesis of a saying from the book of Proverbs: "Omni custodia serva cor tuum, quia ex ipso vita procedit" (Keep watch over your heart, since here are the wellsprings of life).[84] What concerns us here—besides the reminder that *leb* (*lebāb*) in Hebrew means the intellectual as well as the volitional and spiritual center of Man—is the admonition that we take our life into our own hands and become responsible for the forging of our destiny.

It is not for me to speak here of techniques of meditation—Oriental or otherwise—or of the importance of mental illness, or the emergence of psychology as a branch of medicine. I wish only to recall the most simple and basic trait. I have

---

[78] *Gnōthi seauton.*

[79] See chapter 5, "Inner Chapters: Superabundant and Authentic Virtue," in *Chuang Tsu: Inner Chapters*, trans. G. F. Feng (New York: Vintage Books, 1974).

[80] *SB*, X.5.2.20: *tam yatha yathopaseta tad eva bhavati.*

[81] Jn 17:3. Note, with regard to note 76, the word here is *zōē* and not *bios*. See, on the other hand, the testimony of Pavel Florensky (who died in 1943, after eleven years of deportation in Siberia): "Nevertheless, one must not confuse the suprarational character of spiritual life, *zōē*, that slavophiles spoke of . . . and the irrational character of *natural* life, as a biological phenomenon, *bios*" (*La colonne et le fondement de la verité*, trans. from Russian by C. Andronikof (Lausanne: L'Age d'Homme, 1975), 388.

[82] See Plato, *Timaeus* 89–90.

[83] *Veni Sancte Spiritus*. Hymn of Latin liturgy on the Feast of Pentecost.

[84] Pr 4:23.

called it the medicinal function of religion, and for me it consists in reaching the internal harmony of the person. The word I would for the moment use presumably indicates the best possible medication, but it is so dear—and so efficacious—that it cannot be bought, not even at the price of one's will: *peace.*

Whoever is at peace is healthy and joyous; she fears nothing and no one; she does not fear death, and especially does not unconsciously desire sickness so as to solve other problems, nor does she involuntarily conjure up war through her insecurity and anguish. Peace is internal and external; it is the peace of the spirit but also the peace of the heart, the peace of personal life, at once intimate and public, social and political peace. Peace does not build walls, which, as Plato remarked early on, lead neither to a healthy city nor to a healthy life.[85] Peace is received, given, reached, and even merited; it is the fruit of a deep Heraclitian *eris* (struggle).[86] But peace is not won by force. If I have vanquished my body, my spirit will not be at peace; if my soul has been vanquished, my body will take revenge; if we win, sooner or later you will take revenge or your children will; if we subjugate the Earth, it will not leave us in peace; if peace does not reign in the family, my stomach ailment will reappear; if we have no peace on Earth, illnesses will be unceasing and humans will not be saved—that is to say, healthy. Peace is not the fruit of victory; as long as there are victors and vanquished, the good do not triumph. Peace is nobody's triumph. Victory brings triumph, not peace. Peace is the fruit of meditation. It is a fruit of the Spirit, says the Christian tradition. Medically speaking, microbes should not be killed, says Ayurvedic medicine.[87] An a-dualistic medicine does not situate good and evil, health and illness, at the same level. The latter should not be vanquished but transcended, eliminated, perhaps displaced. Or rather, the very concept of illness is an abstraction and, worse yet, an objectified abstraction.

We have said that religion must be medicine and that this medication is meditation. But I must insist that a meditation that does not heal is not really meditation but escapism from reality. Yet the real is not exclusively the temporal or the object of experimental verification—or falsification. The primary function of meditation is probably to liberate us from temporal strictures. To meditate means to enter tempiternal existence by superseding the absolutization of time. Meditation heals us from temporal anguish and, hence, from "the terror of history" (Eliade). One does not meditate *for* anything, for the future or for whatever. This is why meditation is traditionally considered a gift, since it is beyond the power of will. To want to meditate as if one were taking a pill falsifies the very meaning of meditation. The one

[85] *De legibus,* 778–79. The whole passage is worthy of attention. See the incisive commentary by Bebek, *Third City,* 213ff., who reinterprets Plato in the line of a *philosophia perennis,* as has so rarely been done.

[86] See Heraclitus, *Fragm.* 8, etc.

[87] It is worth quoting what a contemporary authority has said on the topic: "All medicines and therapies, including preventive measures prescribed in Āyur-veda, aim at conditioning the tissues and not killing the invading organisms" (Bhagawan Dash, *Fundaments of Ayurvedic Medicine* [Delhi: Bansal and Co., 1978; reprinted in 1984], xii.

who truly meditates discovers the transhistorical dimension of reality and, hence, no longer lives propelled toward the future. You live because you live, and not even to go on living. Life is not the racing of time; it only rides upon time, so to speak, piercing the temporal crust to discover the domain of the tempiternal.[88] Living is an activity at once transitive and intransitive.

Heterostasis

The Chinese, Indic, and African cosmologies are not the only ones to homologize Man to the universe; Greece has also called Man a microcosm.[89] The destiny of the universe plays itself out in each human being. "On Earth as in heaven," says the Gospel, thus symbolizing the repercussions of eternity in the passing of time; the Christian Scholastics spoke of the specular character of human being that, like the mirror, reflects the whole universe. The spirituality of orthodox Christianity could be telescoped into its notion of the divine icon that Man is, whose function consists in giving the divine image all its splendor. Modern physics teaches us anew that everything is a function of everything else, that time is like a field where each point is a function of all the others, that the evolution of the universe plays itself out in each atom, and so on.[90]

At this level of abstraction, such an insight seems sublime and is generally accepted. But problems arise as soon as one comes down to more concrete levels.

Let us try to do so, keeping to our theme of medicine and religion. And in order to avoid even medical abstraction, let us not worry about whether the medical doctor would be equally disposed to cure the soul or even the sick society—since

---

[88]   See R. Panikkar, "Le Temps circulaire: Temporisation et temporalité," in *Temporalité et alienation*, ed. E. Castelli (Paris: Aubier, 1975), 207–46.

[89]   The idea of Man as a world in miniature is attributed to Philo of Alexandria by Stephan Palos in his *Chinese Art of Healing* (New York: Herder and Herder, 1971), 24. Wolfson, the great specialist on Philo, says, however, that this analogy is attributed by him to some anonymous philosophers who "declared that man is a small world and alternatively the world a great man" (*Quis rerum divinarum heres sit* 31.155). Such an idea is implicit in Heraclitus's notion of the world as "the greatest and most perfect man" (*De migratione Abrahami* 39.220) and in that of Man as a "small heaven" (*De opificio mundi* 27.82). On that analogy, see Plato, *Timaeus* 30d; 44d; and Aristotle, *Phys.* 8.2 (252b.26–27). See H. A. Wolfson, *Philo*, 4th ed., revised (Cambridge, MA: Harvard University Press, 1968), 1:424–25. On Man as *macranthrōpos* and its theological use, see the works of the great theologian of the Mystical Body, Emile Mersch, especially *Le Christ, l'Homme et l'Univers* (Paris: Desclée de Brouwer, 1962), 13.

[90]   Suffice it to cite the names of David Bohm, *Wholeness and the Implicate Order* (London: Routledge, 1980, 1981); R. Sheldrake, *A New Science of Life* (London: Blon and Briggs, 1981), etc. It is significant to note that one of the priorities of the Ecumenical Council of Churches coincides with this type of problem between religion (philosophy) and science.

Man is also a community. I shall, rather, allow myself to present a hypothesis that may perhaps offend medical sensibilities.

To say that illness is a lack of human and even cosmic harmony is only to repeat what most human traditions have said and believed.[91] If we add that there is a relationship little less than ontological between the house as human habitat and the body of Man, we are only reminding ourselves that even for Cervantes and Fray Luis de León, the word *vivienda* means the house, the material construction, as well as the lifestyle, the way of life.[92] The link is so close that in numerous Indo-European languages, one and the same verb expresses the fact of being alive and of inhabiting. Thus, in Castillian Spanish one could say, "Yo vivo porque *vivo* (habito) en mi *vivienda* (casa) con mi *vivienda* (con mi propio estilo de vida)" (I live because I inhabit my home according to my own way of life).

It is interesting to read in the history of religions that the cosmos is not just an exterior envelope, some sort of Newtonian space into which human beings are inserted,[93] but this insight has no more bearing on scientific activity, or in our case on the practice of medicine, than a traditional religious sermon. God and religion should not meddle in serious scientific work, it is gravely asserted. History abounds with bitter undue interventions, and Miguel Servet is unfortunately not an exception. It should by now be sufficiently clear that I reject suffocating heteronomies as well as lethal autonomies. Neither monism nor dualism will do here, but only the a-dualism of ontonomy. All this by way of presenting my hypothesis.

One of the reasons for the cancer presently decimating peoples from the industrialized world lies precisely in the loss of social and cosmic homeostasis that characterizes modernity. By modernity I mean the technocratic complex that rules the destiny of the contemporary world and that dictates the rhythms of our daily life, as well as those of its thought forms. No need to remind anyone that cancer is characterized by the loss of the self-regulating function of a precise group of cells in the living organism. Once they lose their capacity for self-limitation, no exogenous homeostasis is capable of checking their anarchic proliferation.

Modern technology—which means much more than merely applied science—is based upon acceleration and multiplication—building thousands of kilometers of roads, manufacturing tons of metal alloys, and pumping lakes of liquid fuels would scarcely make sense if it all went into producing only a single car—it generates a

[91] "The Greeks were not alone in viewing disease as a manifestation of disharmony in man's overall relation to the universe." *Medical Care (Ethno-Medicine)*, in *International Encyclopaedia of the Social Sciences.*
[92] One example will suffice: "Y así, por esta razón, es vivienda muy natural y muy antigua entre los hombres" (And thus, for this reason, it is a natural and very ancient custom among men), *Los nombres de Cristo* (Pastor), in Fray Luis de León, *Obras completas* (Madrid: B.A.C., 1957), 1:466.
[93] See M. Eliade, "Der heilige Raum und die Sakralisierung der Welt" (The sacred space and the sacralization of the world), in *Das Heilige und das Profane* (The sacred and the profane) (Hamburg: Rowohlt, 1957), 35ff.

consumer society, demands the present-day rhythm of life, destroys the cyclical conception of time, and, in brief, magnifies the principle of the *ever more*, the quantitatively ever more. There is no longer any intrinsic, that is ontonomic, limit to the race for money, power, acceleration, growth, development, efficiency, productivity. The only existing limits are reduced, so to speak, to artificial customs tariffs, whether these are imposed due to moral considerations or fear of one's neighbors. Even the arms race, unanimously considered an unacceptable economic burden on the peoples of the world, can no longer limit itself.

Our culture has lost its homeostasis. Yet we still ask ourselves about the origin of cancer and wonder how it is that peoples who have not yet been caught up in the technological maelstrom have lower incidences of cancer. We have forgotten that the Earth is a living organism, and that we are in the process of breaking its equilibrium. Just a few centuries ago, belief in a world soul or *anima mundi* was practically universal. Everything affects everything else, not only on the physical plane, like the acid rain that strips forests or the *Concorde*, which, in order for a few people to save a few hours, burns energy that took centuries to accumulate in the womb of the Earth. Everything affects everything else on the psychic and spiritual plane as well. One cannot be naturally healthy in a megalopolis, which is why we require artificial medications. For the megalopolis is neither an image of the universe nor a humane habitat adopted by Man and attuned to the needs of body and soul. No harmony is possible. So one may readily understand why the soul feels imprisoned in the body, just as the body is imprisoned in the city. There is no flux, no *commercium*, no harmony. Man has excommunicated himself from the Earth. This is why we need the artificial medicine of technology and the entire complex of protective measures we have been obliged to invent. We seek "certainty" based on ourselves (ever since Descartes), and we end up obsessed with national security, again based on ourselves. Undoubtedly, all that I have been saying about medicine and religion is now more easily understandable. How can we even imagine what an electroencephalogram of Jesus of Nazareth might mean, or the psychoanalysis of Confucius, or the Buddha's cholesterol level? I can understand scientific curiosity, but you will acknowledge with me the total absurdity of such experiments.

It is telling to observe how today's vast cancer research industry somehow always gets bogged down in the study of its own means, in the very objectivity of its data. At best, it turns to sociology or even social psychology, but as far as I know, it has not yet perceived the cosmic and theological dimensions of the problem.[94] We have lost natural self-limitation because we have eliminated it from our lives and from the environment in which we live. We have artificially provoked the cancer of matter by fissioning the atomic nucleus. The atomic reaction comes from destroying the homeostasis that maintains things within their proper limits. "The sun does not overstep

---

[94] See the theory of Dr. Hamer according to A. Vogel, *Gesundheits Nachrichten* 42, no. 7 (1985): 103–5, according to which cancer is principally a sickness of the soul (up to 70 percent), due to conflicts within the life of the individual. Neurobiological experiments realized with some of his collaborators seem to confirm his results—otherwise obvious.

its measure," says one of the Fragments of Heraclitus.⁹⁵ Man, however, trespasses his own limits. This is precisely the meaning of *hybris*: the human desire to be more than human.⁹⁶ According to the Bible, human pride consists in wanting to be *like* God, and presumably before the time is ripe—thus rupturing the rhythms—not in seeking *theosis*, divinization: the desire to be God is not alienating since God is understood to be more interior to Man than Man is to himself (*intimior intimo meo*).⁹⁷

The sun does not trespass its *metra*; it keeps to its measure because it follows a circular orbit. Modern civilization has shrugged off the cyclical conception of time in its own prehistory and in other cultures; it has preferred a rectilinear progress, and its thirst for the infinite has now become carcinogenic. Where is medicine and where is religion? Our affliction, as Plato⁹⁸ put it and the New Testament echoed,⁹⁹ is *pleonexia*, insatiable appetite, the desire for the absolutized *more*, literally, "the desire to (always) have more."¹⁰⁰ Cancer is the response of our organism resonating with the pleonectic civilization we have constructed.¹⁰¹ "Medicine is governed by that God" of Love, as Plato said once upon a time.¹⁰² By *eros*, that is, and not by the quantitative proliferation that is Mammon, the God of avarice or *pleonexia*.¹⁰³

In other words, cancer is a subproduct of what could be called the *technocratic imperative*. Our civilization, due precisely to the technocratic complex, has fallen victim to this imperative, which is neither moral, nor human, nor cultural but technocratic. We could formulate it this way: *If it can be done, it must be done.* If it is possible to fly faster, one must do it; if it is possible to transplant an organ, to modify a gene, to split an atom, to count faster, to produce more . . . it must be done, and as soon as possible. *Technocracy* recognizes no *ontonomy*, no self-regulation, no homeostasis. Only an external compulsion, some exogenous factor—state power, dictatorship, exterior pressure . . .—can oblige one not to make actual all that is now possible. Potentiality no longer has any ontological status, so to speak; it is just an intermediary and provisional step toward the present. "You shall be *like* Gods!"; but not a God who limits himself, who makes himself flesh and blood in a given place and time, but an unlimited, absolute, supreme God. The correlate in our own

---

⁹⁵ *Fragm.* 94 (Diels): "Ēlios gar ouch hyperbēsetai mētra." Ἥλιος γὰρ οὐχ ὑπερβήσεται μέτρα.

⁹⁶ In spite of Heraclitus's warning itself (*Fragm.* 40) and of the Bible: "Altiora te ne quaesieris" (Do not try to understand things that are too difficult for you; Si 3:21).

⁹⁷ See Augustine, *Confessions* 3.6.11, etc.

⁹⁸ See *De legibus* 1.782c; *Republic* 572b, etc.

⁹⁹ See Mk 7:22; Lk 12:15; many texts of St. Paul; and also 2 Pet 2:3, 14.

¹⁰⁰ From *pleon* and *echō*. The German translates most properly and literally as *Mehrhabenwollen*.

¹⁰¹ Note that we are speaking not of a causal scientific relationship but rather of a real concatenation, as is the case with astrology.

¹⁰² Ἥ τε οὖν ιατρική, . . . , πάρα διά του θεού τούτου κυβέρνατα (Plato, *Symposium* 186e).

¹⁰³ See Mt 6:24; etc. "You cannot be the slave both of God and of money," etc.

organism is cancer.

This correlation does not exist merely between the carcinogenic development of society and the human body. It also manifests itself in the hypertrophy of the calculating function in the human mind. Thinking has become practically synonymous with calculating, reckoning, measuring, according to one of the two meanings we examined earlier. It is not by chance that calculators and computers proliferate like cancer cells. Let us calculate ever more, with ever greater speed and accuracy! The "accuracy" of one's thought is, of course, measured by external verification, which is to say not by internal intelligibility, or by the transparency attained, but merely by the appearance "in re" of what has already been "thought" (calculated). Repetition, not uniqueness, is the criterion of truth. "Verification," as it is impudently called, is not the discovery or manifestation of how things are, but simply the external notation of a previously calculated repeatability. This way of thinking also lacks homeostasis. Paradoxically, one could say that number has no measure.

Although little meditated upon and even less practiced, one recalls the description of medicine given by the medical doctor Eryximachus in Plato's *Symposium:* "Medicine is then, to put it briefly, the science (of the rhythmic fluctuations) of love, of what the body loves with regard to filling and evacuating; and the one who can distinguish between beneficial love and harmful love may claim to be a physician in the fullest sense of the word."[104]

It may now be clearer why we spoke of *eudokia* and *dharma*.

The Voice of Tradition

For traditional healing arts, the relationship between medicine and religion presents a wholly different character, less because the concept of that relationship is different, but because the notions of medicine and religion are different. It is often erroneously asserted, for example, that the relationship between medicine and religion in India is different from that in the West, without any recognition that it is the very notions of medicine and religion that diverge. It is not a matter of another philosophical conception, but the fact that the very notion of philosophy does not exist or that it is radically other.

Allow me to broach the topic of the traditional medicine of India, limiting myself to what is most elementary and at the same time most fundamental.

When one enters into the culture of India, one is first struck by the error of the cliché that presents it as highly spiritual philosophico-mystical speculation, with scarcely any concern for the concrete and empirical issues of human life on Earth.[105]

---

[104] *Symposium* 186c.

[105] See S. Dasgupta's long chapter, "Speculation in the Medical Schools," in *A History of Indian Philosophy* (Cambrdige: Cambridge University Press, 1952), 2:273–436, in which he defends devoting so many pages to medicine in a philosophical treatise precisely so as to correct the error we are here considering. Not only is medicine the first of all natural

The *Caraka*, one of the two classical treatises of medicine, written by the author of the same name, asserts that the *Āyur-veda* is a *Veda* alongside the four classical Vedas, and more than an *upānga* or appendix to the *Atharva Veda*, since it offers the foundations for the "good life" in this world and the next. As we have already said, the word *Āyur-veda* means "life science," and its specific purpose, as described at the beginning of *Suśruta Samhitā* (I.1.1), consists precisely in "curing illness, protecting health, and prolonging life." There are four kinds of life: happy (*sukha*), unhappy (*duḥka*), good (*hita*), and bad (*ahita*). Medicine takes all four into account. *Mokṣa*, liberation or salvation in the broadest sense, is the aim sought by both medicine and religion. It is, moreover, the aim of all science and all human activity.

But this liberation does not have to negate earthly life. Quite to the contrary, the Āyur-veda wants to save Man by helping him to recover health.

The descriptions of a happy life (*sukham āyuḥ*) are very realistic and of great beauty. It is a life without illness, whether physical or psychic, full of energy, of intelligence, beauty, success, strength, and pleasure, and it is acknowledged by other men. The good life is that human fullness that includes friendliness to all beings, right conduct, pleasure in action, personal harmony, vitality in every realm, an agreeable and happy life. Happiness, says the Caraka, is not liberation from this life, but the freedom to live it fully. The sick person, once again, is not the *in-firmus* but rather someone incapable of enjoying life. This same definition of medicine goes on to say: "*āyur vedayati iti āyur-vedah*" (*Āyur-veda* is what instructs us about life) (*Caraka* I.30.20.) The *Suśruta* (I.1.14) gives us two interpretations of the latter: "that by which life is examined (known)," or "that by which life is reached."

Health means equilibrium, harmony between the three factors (*dhātu*): *vāyu* (air), *pitta* (bile), and *kapha* (lymph, phlegm), as well as the five elements. When the proportion is right (*svamāna*), there is health. The purpose of the Āyur-veda is to attain *dhātu-samya*, harmony between all the factors that compose human life. What counts is the equilibrium between the diverse constituents, not that they are good or bad. Everything that exists is good, although the proportions can be noxious.

I underscore the importance of this vision. It is not a question of eliminating evil by destroying the toxic factors or elements, but rather of reestablishing their equilibrium through a return to the right proportion. Everything in the universe exercises its function.

The cause of illness is twofold: bad diet and sins. Each has its remedies, but there is a relationship between the two kinds of causes. When these causes are specified, it all comes down to an examination of the various rhythms involved. Thus, the three principal causes are the senses, the climate, and the spirit. The senses can operate in an excessive way—too much noise, light, food—or deficiently, or falsely. The climate can be too hot or cold. Finally, one can overuse intelligence, which brings one to abuse the senses and thus to *adharma* (sin, transgression, disorder).

---

sciences cultivated in India, one must even revise all the modern divisions.

The Ayurvedic conception is very far from being magic. It believes in the possibility of restoring harmony between the material and the spiritual, between the individual and the collective, between this world and the other. The three things wished for are life, the good life, and eternal life. The *Āyur-veda* intends to collaborate toward that equilibrium.

Epilogue

I have spoken often here of mutual fecundation. Mere restoration would not be a convincing resolution. The fecundation is twofold: first, between the different cultures of the world. The colonial mentality, whose distinctive trait is the belief that a single culture possesses universal values, is presently an indefensible anachronism. Neither medicine nor religion can today mean what they have meant for the past century in Europe.[106] To persist in dictating the meaning of key words for present-day culture, or in unilaterally formulating human categories, is an unacceptable enterprise. Second, the cross-fertilization must also take place, as I have already indicated, between the archaic-traditional and the scientific-modern. The present study would like to be a modest contribution in this direction.

---

106   See V. von Weizsäcker, *Der kranke Mensch: Eine Einführung in die medizinische Anthropologie* (Stuttgart: Koehler, 1951); Akhilananda, *Mental Health and Hindu Psychology* (Boston: Harper and Row, 1951); W. Warnach, *Die Welt des Schmerzes* (Pfulligen: Neske, 1951).

EPILOGUE
Religions Are Called to Conversion

1.   Religions are called to conversion, not to make propaganda for conversion.[1]

The task that we set for ourselves is nothing less than the conversion of religions. Religion is considered to be both the vehicle and the tool for the conversion of Man, but periodically it needs to convert itself back to its own character and religious goal. The conversion of religions becomes especially important as they increasingly appear to be forgetting their true origin—which is also the goal toward which they strive—devoting themselves to the consolidation of dogmatic statements, reinforcing their identity, and consolidating their institutional bodies. The times in which we are living are a demonstration of the fact that we now find ourselves in this predicament and that religions deserve nothing more than the bad reputation that they have acquired.

---

[1] What appears reproduced here are the guidelines written by Panikkar for the "Spirit of Religion" project, which he worked on actively and with great enthusiasm during the last three years of his life, as a living testimony of the subject matter of this volume, which appeared a few months after his passing. This project was conceived as the natural development of a life dedicated to the study of that which is universal in each one of the religious itineraries and the traditions that sustain them; a study developed not through the fusion or superposition of practices, teachings, experiences, and doctrines, but rather through a respectful and attentive approach to the diverse institutions and possibilities of which religions are testimony. The underlying idea was to form a group of people from different religious sensibilities and experiences (Hindu, Buddhist, Taoist/Confucianist, Christian, Jewish, Islamic, Australian aboriginalist, and Mayan) to meet periodically to spend a period of time together, sharing daily life in all of its aspects, and to savor, thanks to this closeness, the religious testimony of the other. The main instrument of this mutual and friendly gathering was the interchange of texts that each member considered particularly significant in their own tradition and apt to indicate to others the heart of their own religious message.

2.   Religions do not hold a monopoly over religion, over the religious sense of life.

The conversion of religions is possible because religions do not have a monopoly on religion: religiousness is inherent in Man and in the human spirit, which religions can sustain and are one of its possible vehicles. Therefore it is a good idea to start by clarifying what we actually mean by religion in our context. The various etymological reconstructions of the word give us the definition of gathering, "binding together." This function manifests itself on various levels: the reconstruction of the dynamic union of body, mind, and spirit; reuniting one with the other, me, and you; reconnection of Man with Nature; restoration of contact with the Mystery; and redirecting human beings to the threshold of the afterlife. The function of religion is one of liberation insofar as it binds, reconnecting, and then unbinds, thus liberating.

3.   Identity is not ideological but symbolical.

I make a distinction between identity and identification, understanding by identity the discovery of the unique and inimitable nature of each one of us, the face that is revealed on encounter, without prejudice toward the other. By identification I mean that reference to belonging that may give support and certainty, and that may even substitute our authentic face with a predetermined mask. Rather than a confrontation between doctrines, religious dialogue is the language of the symbol. While doctrine is based on "objective" reference to the ideology that upholds it, the symbol is not objective but regards relationship: it is the relationship between the symbol itself and that which is symbolized that comprises its expressive power. To be effective, the symbol needs to be believed in: a symbol that is not believed in no longer represents that which it symbolizes, but becomes merely a sign devoid of meaning. Thus, one should not consider the symbol to be absolute, but it is the principle of pluralism and the language of the mystic. Pluralism means that there is a plurality of meanings, each of which allows access to the orientation symbolized—for example, many religions use the morning star as a symbol of the clear light that dawns, at the same time establishing diverse modes of belief with that symbol. When religion loses its own mystical aspect it tends to become an ideology, and the language in which it is expressed changes from symbolical to logical. Symbolic language is manifold and relational while logical language is unequivocal and refers to the self.

4.   We must search for harmony among religions, not their unification.

The aim of our coming together and our project is harmony among religions, not their unification. It is not a matter of coming up with an all-comprehensive religion, but rather to create harmonious relations based on reciprocal recognition. Furthermore, the religious path, if it is authentic and sincere, shows those who follow it, whatever their reference may be, that faith is a risk: the risk of fully trusting something that is not based on anything guaranteed. If faith were a certainty, it would negate itself insofar as it is faith, that is to say, faithful abandonment and a risky leap. It thus implies a relationship of insecurity, in terms of assessing a risk. Faith is certain; it is not a probability, and therefore it does not belong to the order of guaranteed certainties. The obsession with safety fostered by our modern society leads us to a state of paranoia in our search for certainty. Faith cannot be used as a shield or a weapon; it entails openness and being available.

*

On the other hand I would like to stress that a further step needs to be taken, a step that is difficult but absolutely necessary: it is a matter of posing uncomfortable questions first to ourselves and then to others. This means revealing the shadow that lies within our own religious tradition, because if this critical operation is not carried out, the risk of "self-referentialism" and complacency is too high. As we said earlier, religions need conversion; they need transformation. Without deep-reaching critical revisiting, no authentic transformation can take place. Religions, even those that have been "revealed," are elaborations that cannot escape the laws of change. Therefore, the elements that today need transformation must be identified because they are no longer in tune with human sensitivity. This is the most difficult task because one tends to seek refuge in religious vision and doctrine, which actually serves the purpose of rousing us from our certainties and egocentric convictions. In our turn we must then "rouse" our own religion so that it can access its liberating function again.

Religion is a process and not a heritage of unchangeable doctrines and teachings: as a process it must adapt to the times in which it manifests itself. The spirit of religion is exactly that of grasping the relationship between the ideal and reality, between the here and the beyond. To adapt to the times does not mean to adapt to circumstances in a pragmatic and opportunist manner but rather to be able to renew one's expressive language, sensitivity, and way of life. The relationship between tradition and reality is more important than ever in the times we are experiencing, where it is ever more obvious that the frames of reference that were valid up to yesterday are no longer relevant, and that the risk of inflexibility arising from fear of renewal is increasingly strong in all the religious traditions and the hierarchies that express them.

Thus, the theme of transformation becomes both unavoidable and complex.

*

Themes for Reflection

1.   *We must not see our own religion as absolute.*

The religious process does not consist in reducing everything to our own religious reference as if it were a scheme through which we can interpret reality. On the one hand, it is important when giving one's own testimony to refer to that which we call our own religion by examining our own experience in the light of the tradition to which we refer. On the other hand, having a mystical attitude that means not using our religious categories as a filter in our understanding of the other is just as important, simply to understand the other without using our own religion as a paradigm for interpretation. Here again we are faced with the difference between relativity and relativism: It is not a matter of putting everything on the same level in a neutral way but of seeing the relativity of all points of view without making one of them absolute, even if it is our own.

2.   *However open a dialogue may be, it does not mean abandoning one's own religion.*

The distinction between identity and identification that we mentioned above is of vital importance. Often it is thanks to the encounter with another that attitudes that are not authentic are revealed by the mirror in which we are obliged to see ourselves through the eyes of the other, with which he or she sees us.

3.   *Dialogue is a process, not an exercise in juxtaposition.*

This is easy to say and almost obvious but much harder to put into practice. The drift of a syncretism of convenience is always on the lookout. The outcome of dialogue is unpredictable, but it is never a confused jumble of elements.

4.   *To conduct an authentic dialogue there is no need whatsoever for a common denominator.*

On the contrary, diversity is radical, which is just what it should be: dialogue and encounter become significant through the radical nature of diversity. The aim is not to merge all differences in a single idea in which those engaged in the dialogue can identify more or less perfectly. Nor must we come up with universal cultural concepts to which everyone must sooner or later refer to, but rather to connect with a human invariant that can be elaborated differently by all. A universal religion does not exist, and it is not something we should aspire to. Perhaps there is a human religiousness, a religiousness inherent in Man that is nourished by difference, one that requires reciprocal dialogue on the foundation of that common instance. Dialogue is ontic because it refers to and addresses bare reality, which, however, can only be indicated and found through ontological hermeneutics.

5.   *The following three corollaries appear to be indispensable.*

  • An authentic knowledge of other religions is indispensable; if the effort to achieve this knowledge is authentic, the other, perhaps surprisingly, will be able to recognize him- or herself in my description, and in turn, correct it: Dialogue moves forward.

  • Dialogue is a process of continuous conversion. We are talking about a religious process and not a technique that aims at achieving a result.

  • The atmosphere surrounding dialogue is one of love, of knowledge based on love.

GLOSSARY

abba (Aramaic): Father; as Jesus called God.

Abgeschiedenheit (German): "detachment"; an expression coined by Eckhart in his treatise *On Detachment*; represents one of the central points of his mystical conception, implying both an active and a passive attitude.

abhavyatva (Sanskrit): the inability to attain liberation; used in Buddhism and Jainism.

abhimāna (Sanskrit): vanity, presumption, deceit, attachment.

Abhinavagupta (*Abhinavaguptācārya*) (Sanskrit): a tenth-century Śivaite mystic.

Abhiṣiktānanda (Sanskrit): monastic name of Henri Le Saux (1910–1973), a Hindu-Christian monk who sought to synthesize both traditions in his work and his life.

ācārya (Sanskrit): teacher of *Veda*, spiritual guide who imparts initiation. The term is anterior to *guru*.

acosmism: doctrine that denies reality and/or the value and ultimate sense of the world (*cosmos*).

actio (Latin): activity, action.

adam (Hebrew): man, the first man, as prototype, according to the Bible. Only later it became a man's name. Etymologically related to "red" and "earth," "ground."

ad-extra (Latin): outward.

ad-intra (Latin): inward.

advaita (Sanskrit): nondualism (*a-dvaita*). Spiritual intuition that sees ultimate reality as neither monistic nor dualistic. The recognition that the merely quantitative problem of the one and the many in dialectical reasoning does not apply to the realm of ultimate reality. The latter, in fact, possesses polarities that cannot be divided into multiple separate units; not to be confused with *monism*.

advaitin (Sanskrit): followers of *advaita*, who profess *ātman-brahman* nonduality.

agapē (Greek): love.

Agni (Sanskrit): the sacrificial fire and the Divine Fire, one of the most important Gods or divine manifestations, the mediator or priest for Men and Gods.

agnihotra (Sanskrit): the daily fire sacrifice performed morning and evening in all homes of the high castes, which consists of an oblation of milk sprinkled on the fire.

agnostic: a recently coined philosophical position that claims that there is no such thing as certain knowledge, especially with regard to God and ultimate questions.

agōn (Greek): fight, struggle, battle; the agonic sense of life.

agora (Greek): public square where the townsfolk gathered and held meetings in ancient Greece.

aham (Sanskrit): "I"; first person pronoun. *Aham* as ontological principle of existence is generally distinguished from *ahaṃkāra* as a psychological principle.

aham asmi (Sanskrit): "I am"; a formula of spiritual creation or *mahāvākya*, deriving from the *Bṛhadāraṇyaka-upaniṣad*.

ahaṃkāra (Sanskrit): the sense of the ego.

ahiṃsā (Sanskrit): "nonviolence," respect for life, not killing and not wounding, not desiring to carry out violence against reality. A moral and philosophical principle based on ultimate universal harmony. The root *hiṃs*- from *han*- means "to wound," "to kill." This is not exactly a Vedic notion; it appears only a few times in the *Upaniṣad*; it was developed in Jainism and Buddhism.

Ahriman (Persian): principle of darkness and evil, according to Mazdaism; a noun deriving from Angra Mainyu (evil spirit), used by Zoroaster.

aiōn (Greek): cosmic time, eternity; also a period of life.

aisthēsis (Greek): perception, sensitivity, sense, knowledge.

ākāśa (Sanskrit): air, sky, space, ether, the fifth of the primordial elements (*mahābhūtāni*), which is the element of sound. It is all-pervading and infinite, and therefore often identified with Brahman.

aliud (Latin): the other, neutral.

alius (Latin): the other (other I).

amerimnia (Greek): absence of anxiety.

'am ha'aretz (Aramaic): "people of the earth," lower classes, the disinherited, the poor, the untouchable, the ignorant, those who do not know the *Torah*.

amplexus (Latin): embrace.

amṛta (Sanskrit): immortal, imperishable (*a-mṛta*); refers mainly to the Gods; noun, neutral: immortality, absence of death, and nectar of immortality, *soma*, the sacred drink (ambrosia).

anakephalaiōsis (Greek): summary of all things (in Christ); used by St. Paul.

ānanda (Sanskrit): joy, bliss (cf. *sukha*), the delights of love, and especially the highest spiritual bliss; *sat*, *cit*, and *ānanda* represent three possible attempts at defining *brahman* or absolute reality.

anātman (Sanskrit): absence of *ātman*, of the substantiality of an individual ontological Self.

anātmavāda, nairātmyavāda (Sanskrit): mainly Buddhist doctrine of the insubstantiality of the *ātman* or Self.

anātmavādin (Sanskrit): follower of the doctrine of *anātman*.

anima mundi (Latin): soul of the world; as an analogy of man, the earth is conceived as the body of expression of a planetary Consciousness or Soul.

animus-anima (Latin): masculine (in the woman) and feminine (in the man) image or characteristic, as psychologically thematized by C. G. Jung.

anitya (Sanskrit): impermanence.

antarikṣa (Sanskrit): that which is "between," the space of air between the sky and the earth, atmosphere, intermediate space (cf. *dyu* and *pṛ thivī* as two other terms for *triloka*).

anthrōpos (Greek): man, in a general sense.

anubhava (Sanskrit): direct experience, knowledge deriving from immediate spiritual intuition.

apatheia (Greek): impassibility, indifference, calm, imperturbability (complete liberation from all emotional stress produced by the events of life).

apokatastasis pantōn (Greek): restoration of all things at the end of the world, or of a period of time, according to Christian Scripture.

aporia (Greek): difficulty that prevents one from going beyond reason, dead end.

arhat (Sanskrit): ascetic, saint, the highest and most noble figure of Theravada Buddhism.

asat (Sanskrit): nonbeing; denial of being; as opposed to *sat*, being.

asparśayoga (Sanskrit): yoga without intermediary, without mental content, stopping of the mind, "nonmind."

āśrama (Sanskrit): state of life, the four traditional periods in the life of the "twiceborn": student (*brahmacārin*), head of family (*gṛhastha*), inhabitant of the forest (*vānaprastha*), and itinerant ascetic (*saṃnyāsin*). Also the hermitage of a monk and, therefore, the title of an ascetic. Also indicates a spiritual community, generally under the direction of a *guru* or spiritual teacher. Also refers to a stage in human life.

asura (Sanskrit): spiritual, incorporeal, divine. In *Ṛg-veda* the highest spirit, God (from *asu*, life, spiritual life). Varuṇa is considered an *asura*. Later the meaning changes completely and *asura* (now analyzed as *a-sura*, or "non-God") takes on the meaning of demon or evil spirit constantly opposed to the *deva* (*Brāhmaṇa*).

atha (Sanskrit): here, now, furthermore; particle translated according to context.

ātman (Sanskrit): principle of life, breath, the body, the Self (from the root *an*, to breathe). Refers to the whole, undivided person and also to the innermost center of man, his incorruptible nucleus, which in the *Upaniṣad* is shown to be identical to Brahman. The Self or inner essence of the universe and man. Ontological center in Hinduism, which is negated in Buddhism.

ātmānātma-vastuviveka (Sanskrit): discernment between real and unreal.

ātmavāda (Sanskrit): doctrine that accepts the existence of the Self, the *ātman,* as the essential, incorruptible center of being.

ātmavādin (Sanskrit): follower of the *ātman* doctrine.

ātmavid (Sanskrit): he who knows the Self (*ātman*), who has fulfilled his innermost being.

atyāśrama (Sanskrit): the state beyond the four traditional states of a man's spiritual being (cf. *āśrama*), which transcends them in complete spiritual freedom.

Aum (Sanskrit): cf. Oṃ.

autarkeia (Greek): self-sufficient.

avatāra (Sanskrit): "descent" of the divine (from *ava-tṛ,* descend), the "incarnations" of Viṣṇu in various animal and human forms. Traditionally, there are ten *avatāra: matsya* (the fish), *kūrma* (the tortoise), *varāha* (the wild boar), *narasiṃha* (the lion-man), *vāmana* (the dwarf), Paraśurāma (Rāma with the axe), Rāma, Kṛṣṇa, Buddha, and Kalkin at the end of time. In general, any personal manifestation of the Divinity, descended into this world in human form; descent as antonomasia.

avidyā (Sanskrit): ignorance, nescience, absence of true and liberating knowledge, often identified with *māyā* and a cause of illusion and delusion.

āyus (Sanskrit): vital force, vitality, life, temporal existence, the length of life granted to man. Cf. Greek *aiōn,* aeons.

bandhu (Sanskrit): bond, connection, relation, friendship, friend.

Bhagavad-gītā (Sanskrit): The "Song of the Glorious Lord," the "Song of the Sublime One"; a famous ancient Indian didactic poem included in the *Mahābhārata* (often called the "New Testament of Hinduism"), the most well-known sacred book in India.

bhakti (Sanskrit): devotion, submission, love for God, personal relationship with God, devotional mysticism. One of the paths of salvation through union with the divinity.

bhakti-mārga (Sanskrit): the path of love and devotion, one of the three classical spiritual paths (cf. *karma-mārga, jñāna-mārga*).

bhārata-nāṭyam (Sanskrit): divine dance.

bhāṣya (Sanskrit): commentary.

bhikṣu (Sanskrit): he who begs for food and leaves home, the monk.

bios (Greek): existence, biological life, length of life.

bodhisattva (Sanskrit): the enlightened one. In particular, in Mahāyāna Buddhism, he who, having attained liberation on earth, makes a vow to help all other beings attain liberation before they enter *nirvāṇa*.

Brahmā (Sanskrit): the creator God (cf. the "Trinity," later Brahmā, Viṣṇu, Śiva). It is not important in the *Veda* but in later periods it inherits many of the characteristics of Prajāpati.

brahmacārin (Sanskrit): student of Brahman, i.e. of *Veda*; novice who lives a life of chastity and purity. He who lives in the first of the four *āśrama*.

brahmacarya (Sanskrit): life of a student of Brahman, also of the chastity and education of Brahman. The first of the four *āśrama* (cf. *gṛhastha, vānaprastha, saṃnyāsa*).

brahman (Sanskrit): prayer, sacrifice, the inherent power in sacrifice; the Absolute, the ultimate reason underlying all things; in the *Upaniṣad* it is identified with the immanent Self (*ātman*). Also, one of the four priests who perform the sacrifice or the clergy in general.

Brahma-sūtra (Sanskrit): traditional Hindu text; one of the bases of the Vedānta.

Bṛhadāraṇyaka-upaniṣad (Sanskrit): one of the most ancient and important *Upaniṣad*.

buddhakāya (Sanskrit): lit. "body of Buddha," universal solidarity, the behavior of the Buddha.

buddhi (Sanskrit): the highest faculty of the intellect, also comprehension, thought, meditation.

cakra (Sanskrit): center of energy in the subtle body of man (related, perhaps, to each plexus); lit. "wheel."

capax Dei (Latin): capacity of the soul to perceive and receive God.

cela (Sanskrit): disciple.

cenobitic: relating to the monastery (*cenobium*).

Chāndogya-upaniṣad (Sanskrit): one of the most ancient of the *Upaniṣad*, which deals with the mystic value of sound, song and the identity of *ātman-brahman*.

chara (Greek): grace, joy, cheerfulness.

circulus vitiosus (Latin): "vicious circle," bad reasoning, which states what is still to be proven.

circumincessio (Latin): compenetration of the three Persons of the Trinity. Corresponds to the Greek *perichōresis*.

cit (Sanskrit): root noun (from the root *cit-*, to perceive, to comprehend, etc.), meaning "consciousness, intelligence." One of the three "characteristics" of Brahman (cf. *sat, ānanda*).

civitas Dei and *civitas terrena* (Latin): "city of God" and "earthly city"; theory formulated by Augustine (354–430), according to which there are two citizenships or "states."

cogito (ergo) sum (Latin): "I think (therefore) I am."

coincidentia oppositorum (Latin): coincidence of the opposites.

colloquium salutis (Latin): dialogue of salvation.

complexio omnium (Latin): integration of all things.

comprehensor (Latin): one who truly comprehends; one who already possesses the beatific vision, the fulfilled man.

compunctio cordis (Latin): repentance, heartfelt sorrow, the essential attitude of monastic spirituality.

consecratio mundi (Latin): consecration or sanctification of the world; the secular is sacralized, contemplated in its sacred dimension.

contemptus saeculi (Latin): contempt for all that is temporal and worldly.

conversatio (Latin): dialogue, conversation between the members of a community; the human relationship, especially political, based on words.

conversio (Latin): change or transformation, generally religious; one of the translations of *metanoia*.

conversio morum (Latin): change in customs, way of living.

cosmotheandric: the nonseparation between World, God, and Man.

creatio continua (Latin): "continuous creation"; doctrine of the continuous creative force of God in the sense of the preservation of the universe and universal government.

Christianity: religiosity based on the experience of Christ.

darśana (Sanskrit): from the root *dṛś*, to see, to observe; hence vision, sight; philosophy, *Weltanschauung*. In a religious context it means the vision of a saint or God, hence also meeting, audience, visit.

Dasein (German): being here; real, existing man; a term used mainly by M. Heidegger; human existence.

deva (Sanskrit): connected with *div*, sky, light (Latin *divus, deus*), celestial, divine. Also God, divinity, heavenly being, cosmic power. The *deva* are not on the same level as the one God (sometimes called also *deva*, in the singular, or *īśvara*) or the absolute (Brahman). They are powers that have different functions in the cosmos. Subsequently, the human sensory faculties are also called *deva* in the *Upaniṣad*.

Dhammapāda (Pāli): collection of 426 Buddhist verses of the Pāli canon.

dharma (Sanskrit): cosmic order, justice, duty, religious law, religious and social observances transmitted by tradition; "religion" as a collection of practices and laws. That which holds the world together. One of the four "human purposes" (cf. *puruṣāsartha*).

dharmakāya (Sanskrit): mystical body of *dharma* in Mahāyāna Buddhism.

dhyāna (Sanskrit): meditation, contemplation.

diachronic: that which extends through time.

diakonia tou logou (Greek): ministry of the word.

diatopic: that which extends through space.

digambara (Sanskrit): ascetic of the Jain religion who walks naked as a symbol of detachment and purity.

dīkṣā (Sanskrit): initiation; the preliminary rites; consecration of one who performs the sacrifice, such as that celebrated, for example, at the beginning of the *soma* and leads to a "new birth." Out of the context of sacrifice *dīkṣā* is the initiation of the disciple by the *guru* into *saṃnyāsa*, the life of the errant monk.

dipsychos (Greek): one who has a double soul.

discretio (Latin): discernment, discretion, prudence.

docta ignorantia: classic term used by Nicolaus Cusanus to denote supreme innocence, ignorance of one's own knowledge.

doxa (Greek): glory.

dualism: vision of a basic split within the being into two principles, each irreducible to the other, particularly spirit and matter, soul and body.

duḥkha (Sanskrit): disquieted, uneasy, distress, pain, suffering, anguish (lit. "having a poor axle hole," i.e., that which does not turn smoothly), a basic concept in Buddhism and Hinduism. Opposite of *sukha*.

Dulosigkeit (German): absence of all reference to any "you."

dvandva (Sanskrit): pair of opposites, e.g., cold and heat, pleasure and pain.

dvija (Sanskrit): one who is born a second time into the life of the spirit, the initiated.

dynamis (Greek): power, energy, capacity.

ecclesia (Latin): church, assembly, reunion.

eidetic: relating to knowledge; from *eidos*, idea.

eidos (Greek): idea, form, appearance.

ekāgratā (Sanskrit): concentration in one spot; hence simplicity and purity.

ekam (Sanskrit): one; generally the primordial oneness, the origin of all, later identified with Brahman.

enstasis (Greek): entering fully into one's self: through concentration and meditation one attains a state of absolute identification (absorption) with the contemplated object, with the Self.

epektasis (Greek): dilatation, expansion, extension; man's trust in his divine destiny, according to St. Gregory of Nyssa. Hope.

epistēmē (Greek): science.

erōs (Latin): love.

eschatology: from the Greek *eschaton*, which refers to the ultimate, both in relation to time (the last things that will happen, the end of this life), and in ontological importance (the ultimate reality).

exclusivism, inclusivism, pluralism: terms indicating an attitude toward non-Christian religions, which (a) considers the latter as being excluded from the salvation of Christ, (b) absolutizes the salvation of Christ by granting a place to non-Christian religions, and (c) recognizes that the different visions of the world are mutually irreducible.

esse sequitur operari (Latin): being follows action.

extasis (Greek): ecstasy, "outside of itself."

extra ecclesiam nulla salus (Latin): "outside the church there is no salvation."

fanum (Latin): temple, sanctuary. Cf. *pro-fanum*.

fides quaerens intellectum (Latin): "faith seeking understanding."

fuga mundi (Latin): escape from the world; an attitude indicating a departure from the things of this world to focus on a world beyond that is considered the "true" world.

Gautama (Sanskrit): family name of prince Siddhartha, who became the Buddha.

Gītā (Sanskrit): cf. *Bhagavad-gītā*.

gnōsis (Greek): saving knowledge, liberating wisdom. Cf. *jñāna, prajñā*.

gopī (Sanskrit): shepherdess full of love and devotion for Kṛṣṇa; symbol of the soul united with the divine being.

guhā (Sanskrit): cave, grotto, secret place (human heart).

guṇa (Sanskrit): the three qualities or attributes of being: *tamas*, darkness; *rajas*, desire; *sattva*, being.

guru (Sanskrit): cf. *ācārya*; usually refers to one who has attained fulfillment.

hamartia (Greek): sin.

haplotēs (Greek): simplicity, naïveté; *h. kardias*: simplicity of heart.

hara (Jap.): center, place of vital energy in man; area of the belly.

hen (Greek): one, unit.

hermeneutics, hermeneutic: "the art of interpretation"; the theory and method of understanding and interpreting writings.

hiraṇyagarbha (Sanskrit): "the golden germ," a cosmological principle in the *Veda*, later identified with the creator (*Brahmā*).

holistic: that which considers reality in its entirety.

homeomorphic: that which performs a similar function.

homeomorphism: theory used in comparative religion to discover functional equivalence in two or more religions.

humanum (Latin): the basic human; that which is specific to all humanity.

hypomonê (Greek): patience, perseverance.

ihāmutrārthaphala-bhoga-virāga (Sanskrit): renouncement of the reward for good deeds done.

inclusivism: cf. *exclusivism*.

Indra (Sanskrit): the great divine warrior who wins all battles in favor of his worshippers, both against opposing clans (*dasyu* or *dāsa*) and against demons such as Vṛtra and Vala. His virile power is irresistible and is the *soma* that provides him with the energy needed for his mighty exploits. He is the liberator of the compelling forces; he releases the waters and the light. His weapon is the *vajra*, the lightning bolt.

Īśā-upaniṣad (Sanskrit): one of the shortest of the *Upaniṣad*, which deals with the presence of the divine in all things.

Īśa, Īśvara (Sanskrit): the Lord, from the root *īś-*, to be lord, to guide, to possess. Although a generic term for Lord, in posterior religious systems it is more often used for Śiva than for Viṣṇu. In the Vedānta it is the manifested, qualified (*saguṇa*) aspect of Brahman.

itivuttaka (Pāli): "so I have heard"; traditional form of passing on the teachings of Buddha and the heading of a text in Buddhist writings.

Jainism: post-Vedic ascetic tradition organized by Mahāvīra (fifth to fourth centuries BC), path of purification emphasizing the importance of *ahiṃsā* (nonviolence). Religion slightly anterior to Buddhism.

jīva (Sanskrit): living being (from *jīv-*, to live); the soul in its individuality, as opposed to *ātman*, the universal soul. There are as many *jīva* as individual living beings.

jīvanmukta (Sanskrit): "liberated while alive and embodied," the highest category of the holy or fulfilled person who has reached the destination in this life and, therefore, in the human body; he who has fulfilled his *ātman-braham* ontological identity; he who has reached his own being, becoming totally integrated.

jñāna (Sanskrit): knowledge (from the root *jñā-*, to know), intuition, wisdom; frequently the highest intuitive comprehension, the attaining of *ātman* or *brahman*. *Jñāna* is the result of meditation or revelation. Cf. *jñāna-mārga*.

jñāna-mārga (Sanskrit): the path of knowledge, contemplation, and intuitive vision; one of the three classic paths of spiritual experience, generally considered superior to those of *karman* and *bhakti*, although many *bhakta* regard *jñāna* as merely as form of *bhakti*.

jñānavādin (Sanskrit): person who claims that supreme knowledge (*jñāna*) is in itself sufficient for liberation. Actions barely count.

kaivalya (Sanskrit): isolation, solitude, detachment; one of the spiritual states of supreme freedom.

kalpa (Sanskrit): a period of the world, a cosmic time of variable length.

kāma (Sanskrit): the creative power of desire, personified as the God of love; one of the *puruṣārtha*.

kāraṇa (Sanskrit): cause.

karma, karman (Sanskrit): lit. "act, deed, action"; from the root *kṛ*, to act, to do; originally the sacred action, sacrifice, rite, later also moral act. The result of all actions and deeds according to the law of *karman* that regulates actions and their results in the universe. Later also connected with rebirth, it indicates the link between the actions carried out by a subject and his destiny in the cycle of deaths and rebirths.

karmakāṇḍin (Sanskrit): refers to those who emphasize the importance of the action, in occasions of ritual, for salvation/liberation.

karma-mārga (Sanskrit): the path of action; one of the three classic paths of spirituality (cf. *bhakti, jñāna*). In the *Veda* it refers to sacrificial actions viewed as the way to salvation; later includes also moral actions, or all actions that are performed in a spirit of sacrifice.

katachronism: interpretation of a reality or doctrine with categories that are extraneous or posterior.

kāya (Sanskrit): body.

kāyotsarga (Sanskrit): the abandoning of all bodily activity; spiritual exercise in which even the possession of one's body is renounced.

kenōsis (Greek): annihilation, emptying of oneself, overcoming of one's ego.

keśin (Sanskrit): "long-haired" (*keśa*), he who has long hair, ascetic, monk.

kleśa (Sanskrit): affliction, impurity of the soul.

koinōnia (Greek): community, communion.

kosmos (Greek): order, the ordered universe, the wholeness of the world.

Kṛṣṇa (Sanskrit): *avatāra* of Viṣṇu (lit. "the black one") and one of the most popular Gods. He does not appear in the *Veda*, but he is the revealer of the *Bhagavad-gītā*. He is the divine child and the shepherd God of Vṛndāvana, the incarnation of love and the playful God *par excellence*.

kṣetra (Sanskrit): "field," both in a metaphorical and literal sense. Knowledge begins with the distinction between the field and he who knows the field, i.e., between the world (as the object) and the knowing subject.

kunamnama (Sanskrit): rigid, inflexible; the feminine form *kunamnamā* also indicates a feminine divinity.

kurukṣetra (Sanskrit): the battlefield where the war of the *Mahābhārata* was fought and where Kṛṣṇa revealed the *Bhagavad-gītā* to Arjuna.

lama: head of Tibetan Buddhism.

laukika (Sanskrit): natural, worldly, temporal.

leit-ourgia (Greek): activity of the people, liturgy.

līlā (Sanskrit): divine game, the world as the amusement of God. This concept is not Vedic but Purāṇic.

liṅga (Sanskrit): characteristic feature of Śiva; phallus.

lingua universalis (Latin): universal language.

locus theologicus (Latin): the proper and legitimate place of theological activity.

logos (Greek): word, thought, judgment, reason. In the New Testament Christ as the word of God (Jn 1).

loka (Sanskrit): "world," open space, place, kingdom. Cf. *triloka*.

lokasaṃgraha (Sanskrit): the "keeping together, maintaining of the world" by the wise man and the saint through the sacred or liturgical action (concept of *Bhagavad-gītā*).

madhyama (Sanskrit): central position, middle.

madhyamamārga (Sanskrit): the middle path taught by Buddha.

Mahābhārata (Sanskrit): epic poem that tells the legendary story of the Indian people and expounds its prescriptive values.

mahātma (Sanskrit): "great soul." Name of the founder of the Jain religion (fifth to fourth century BC).

mahāvākya (Sanskrit): "great saying." Refers to great expressions of the *Upaniṣad* that express very concisely the content of the experience of the Absolute.

Mahāyāna (Sanskrit): "great vehicle." Branch of Buddhism established in India two thousand years ago.

maithuna, mithuna (Sanskrit): union, mating, copulation both in a sexual and metaphorical sense.

Maitreyī (Sanskrit): wife of the sage Yājñavalkya. Was considered a "knower of Brahman."

manas (Sanskrit): mind in its broadest sense, heart, intellect, the internal organ that is the seat of thought, comprehension, feeling, imagination, and will. In Upaniṣadic anthropology *manas* is one of the three constituent principles of man (cf. *vāc, prāṇa*).

maṇḍala (Sanskrit): lit. "circle." Mystic representation of all reality; a pictorial illustration of the homology between the microcosm (man) and the macrocosm (the universe). Also a book of the *Ṛg-veda* (a "circle" of hymns). The *Ṛg-veda* is made up of ten *maṇḍala*.

mantra (Sanskrit): prayer, sacred formula (from the root *man-*, to think), sacred word, a Vedic text or verse. Usually only the part of the *Veda* consisting of the *Saṃhitā* is called a *mantra*. As it is a word of power it may also take the meaning of magic formula or spell.

Manu (Sanskrit): the father of humanity, the man par exellence; also the first priest to establish sacrifices.

mārga (Sanskrit): road, path, way.

martys (Greek): martyr; one who gives testimony for his own life, even through death.

maṭha (Sanskrit): monastery.

mauna (Sanskrit): silence, practiced by the silent itinerant monk; cf. *muni*.

māyā (Sanskrit): the mysterious power, wisdom, or ability of the gods, hence the power of deceit, of illusion. In the Vedānta it is used as a synonym of ignorance and also to indicate the cosmic "illusion" that shrouds the absolute Brahman.

mederi (Latin): to heal, to treat.

metanoia (Greek): transformation, change of mentality or heart, conversion; going beyond (*meta*) the mental or rational (*nous*).

metron (Greek): measure, meter.

mikrokosmos (Greek): the entire reality reflected or concentrated in the individual; "man as *mikrokosmos*" refers to man as compendium of the cosmos.

mokṣa (Sanskrit): ultimate liberation from *saṃsāra*, the cycle of births and deaths, and from *karman*, ignorance, and limitation: salvation. Homeomorphic equivalent of *sōteria*.

monism: from Greek *monon*, unique; concept by which all things are traced back to a single active principle.

monos (Greek): one, unique.

monotropos (Greek): alone, solitary, he who lives in one place only.

morphē (Greek): figure, form, apparition.

mu (Jap.): nothing, nonbeing.

mumukṣutva (Sanskrit): derivative form of the root *muc-* (cf. *mokṣa*); desire for salvation, and yearning for liberation, the necessary prerequisite for embarking on the path of liberation.

muni (Sanskrit): a silent monk, ascetic; an ecstatic. One who practices *mauna*, silence.

mythos (Greek): the horizon of presence that does not require further inquiry.

Nachiketas (Sanskrit): name of a young brahman who descends into the realm of Yama and discusses ultimate questions with him (in the *Kaṭha-upaniṣad*). Some have interpreted his name as "he who does not know," i.e., the novice, the seeker.

nāda (Sanskrit): sound, original vibration in the emanation of the word; an important concept in Tantric cosmology.

nāma-rūpa (Sanskrit): "name and form," the phenomenic world that constitutes the *saṃsāra*.

neti neti (Sanskrit): "not this, not this" (*na iti*), i.e., the negation of any kind of characterization of the *ātman* or *brahman* in the *Upaniṣad*; pure apophatism.

nirguṇa-brahman (Sanskrit): Brahman without attributes and qualities, the unqualified, transcendent Absolute.

nirodha (Sanskrit): halt, destruction.

nirvāṇa (Sanskrit): lit. "the going out (of the flame)," extinction. The word does not refer to a condition, but indicates liberation from all dichotomy and conditioning, whether it be birth and death, time and space, being and nonbeing, ignorance and knowledge, or final extinction including time, space, and being; the ultimate destination for Buddhism and Jainism.

nirvikalpa (Sanskrit): certain, beyond doubt.

nitya (Sanskrit): the eternal, permanent, real.

nitya-anitya-vastu-viveka (Sanskrit): discernment between permanent (eternal) and temporal things.

nomos (Greek): custom, rule, law.

nous (Greek): mind, thought, intellect, reason.

ob-audire (Latin): to listen, to obey.

Ohrmazd (Persian): or Ahura Mazdā; God of light and truth in the Medo-Persian religion and that of the *Avesta*.

oikonomia (Greek) science of the management of household affairs (of the human family). Stewardship of the human *habitat*, home economics.

Oṃ (Sanskrit): the sacred syllable, formed by three letters A-U-M. Also means "yes," "so be it" (*amen*). Used also at the beginning and end of every recitation of sacred writings and is believed to have a mystic meaning. The highest and most comprehensive symbol of Hindu spirituality, which is also used as a *mantra* in Buddhism. Manifestation of spiritual energy, which indicates the presence of the Absolute in the world of appearance.

on (Greek): participle of the verb "to be" (*einai*); being, that which is higher, entity, that which exists.

ontonomy: intrinsic connection of an entity in relation to the totality of Being, the constitutive order (*nomos*) of every being as Being (*on*), harmony that allows the interdependence of all things.

operari sequitur esse (Latin): "acting follows being."

orthodoxy and *orthopraxy*: "correct doctrine" and "correct action."

pan (Greek): all, everything.

Pantokratōr (Greek): the Sovereign of all; designates Christ and also God.

paramahaṃsa (Sanskrit): "sublime swan," i.e., the supreme soul, a liberated person who enjoys complete freedom, a class of ascetics.

pāramārthika (Sanskrit): ultimate level, ultimate reality, true reality.

paredra (Greek): female companion.

parigraha (Sanskrit): tendency to possess, hoarding.

parousia (Greek): the return, the presence, the second coming of Christ.

pars in toto (Latin): the part in the whole.

pars pro toto (Latin): the part that represents the whole.

pati divina (Latin): passive attitude of man toward the "touches" of the divine; synonym of mystic experience.

penthos (Greek): repentance, sadness.

perichōresis (Greek): notion of the early Church Trinitarian doctrine describing the interpenetration of divine persons. Corresponds to the Latin *circumincessio*.

phainomenon (Greek): phenomenon, that which appears, that which shows itself.

phaneros (Greek): bright, from *phanos*, light.

plerōma (Greek): fullness, the full, complete.

pluralism: cf. *exclusivism*.

polis (Greek): the city-state of ancient Greece.

politeuma (Greek): belonging to the social body, political unit. Cf. *conversatio*.

polysemic: having several meanings.

Prajāpati (Sanskrit): "Lord of creatures," the primordial God, Father of the Gods and all beings. His position is central in the *Brāhmaṇa*.

prajñā (Sanskrit): understanding and awareness, consciousness, wisdom. Cf. *gnōsis*, *jñāna*.

pramāṇa (Sanskrit): means for attaining valid knowledge.

prāṇa (Sanskrit): vital breath, life, the breath of life, the vital force that holds the body together. In the *Upaniṣad* one of the three constitutive principles of the human being (cf. *vāc, manas*). It is made up of five types of breath (*prāṇa, apāna, vyāna, samāna, udāna*). The cosmic equivalent of *prāṇa* is *Vāyu*, air, wind.

prasthānatraya (Sanskrit): term referring to the three principle texts of the Vedānta (*Upaniṣad, Bhagavad-gītā,* and *Brahma-sūtra*).

pratiṣṭhā (Sanskrit): foundation, support, base.

pratītyasamutpāda (Sanskrit): Buddhist doctrine of the "conditioned genesis" or "dependent origination," which claims that nothing exists for itself but carries within itself the conditions for its own existence, and that everything is mutually conditioned in the cycle of existence.

primum analogatum (Latin): the point of reference for every analogy.

pro-fanum (Latin): pro-fane; outside the temple (*fanum*).

psychē (Greek): soul, psyche, heart, animated being.

pūjā (Sanskrit): worship, reverence, adoration. The concept is more closely related to the *bhakti* cult than the Vedic cult.

purohita (Sanskrit): priest, liturgy.

Puruṣa (Sanskrit): the Person, the spirit, man. Both the primordial man of the cosmic dimension (*Ṛg-veda*) and the "inner man," the spiritual person existing within man (*Upaniṣad*). In the Sāṃkhya it is the spiritual principle of reality (cf. *prakṛti*).

quaternitas perfecta (Latin): the perfect quaternity.

qui/quid pro quo (Latin): substitution of one thing for another; error consisting in the mistaking of one person (*qui*) or thing (*quid*) for another.

rāhib (Arabic): instructor, teacher, monk.

Rāmāyaṇa (Sanskrit): Indian epic poem.

ratio (Latin): reason.

res cogitans / res extensa (Latin): thinking thing / extended thing, division of reality, according to Descartes.

res significata (Latin): signified thing.

Ṛg-veda (Sanskrit): the most ancient and important of the *Veda* texts.

ṛṣi (Sanskrit): seer, sage, wise man; the poet-sages to whom the *Veda* were revealed. Regarded as a special class of beings, superior to men and inferior to the Gods. According to one tradition there were seven *ṛṣi*, probably the seven priests with whom Manu performed the first sacrifice and the seven poet judges in the assembly. Their identification with the names of ancient seers and with the stars of the Ursa Major occurred later (*Brāhmaṇa*).

ṛta (Sanskrit): cosmic and sacred order, sacrifice as a universal law, also truth; the ultimate, dynamic, and harmonious structure of reality.

Saccidānanda (Sanskrit): Brahman as Being (*sat*), Consciousness (*cit*), and Bliss (*ānanda*).

sadguru or *satguru* (Sanskrit): eternal teacher, teacher archetype, universal *guru*.

sādhaka (Sanskrit): one who practices a spiritual, yoga discipline.

sādhana (Sanskrit): spiritual practice or discipline.

sādhu (Sanskrit): straight, leading straight to the goal, good, just. A good person, renunciant, monk, or ascetic.

sādhvī (Sanskrit): female ascetics in Hinduism and especially Jainism; feminine form of *sādhu*.

saeculum (Latin): the human age, era, century; also spirit of the day.

saguṇa-brahman (Sanskrit): Brahman with quality, corresponding in the Vedānta to *Ūśvara*, the Lord.

śaivasiddhānta (Sanskrit): religion, philosophical/religious school pertaining to Hinduism; dominant Śivaism in Tamil Nadu.

śakti (Sanskrit): energy, potency, divine power, the creative energy of God. The active, dynamic—feminine—aspect of reality or of a God (generally of Śiva). Personified as the goddess Śakti, consort of Śiva with a creative function.

salus (Latin): health, salvation.

śama (Sanskrit): calm, tranquility, method of mental appeasement.

samādhi (Sanskrit): state of deep concentration, compenetration, immersion, perfection (enstasy); the last of the yoga stages; also the tomb of a saint.

saṃgha (Sanskrit): the (monastic) community of those who follow the path of the Buddha.

saṃnyāsa (Sanskrit): renunciation, the fourth stage of life spent as an errant monk (from *saṃnyas-*, to suppress, to renounce, to abandon).

saṃnyāsin (Sanskrit): renunciant, ascetic; pertaining to the fourth stage or period of life (*āśrama*), to some the superior stage.

sampradāya (Sanskrit): tradition, religious system and community that follows a tradition.

saṃsāra (Sanskrit): the impermanent phenomenic world and the condition of identification with it, the temporal existence, the cycle of births and deaths, of conditioned existences; state of dependence and slavery.

saṃskāra (Sanskrit): "sacrament," rites that sanctify the various important stages and events in human life. Also karmic residues, physical impressions left over from previous lives, which in some way influence the individual existence of a person.

samudaya (Sanskrit): origin.

Śaṅkara (Sanskrit): eighth-century Hindu philosopher and teacher; one of the most famous exponents of nondualist Vedānta.

śānti (Sanskrit): peace, tranquility, quiescence. The closing *mantra* of many prayers and oblations.

śānti-mantra (Sanskrit): introductory invocation or prayer of an *Upaniṣad*, which is generally common to all the *Upaniṣad* of the same *Veda*. Recited at the beginning and usually also the end of an Upaniṣadic reading, although not actually part of the text.

sarvam duḥkham (Sanskrit): "all is suffering," a classic Buddhist statement.

śāstra (Sanskrit): precepts, orders, rules, authoritative teachings; body of traditionally authorised texts.

sat (Sanskrit): essence (present participle of *as-*, to be), existence, reality. Ultimately, only the Brahman is *sat*, as pure Being is the Basis of every existence. In the Vedānta one of the three "qualifications" of the Brahman (cf. *cit*, *ānanda*).

Śatapatha-brāhmaṇa (Sanskrit): "*Brāhmaṇa* of one hundred paths," the most complete and systematic of the *Brāhmaṇa*.

satori (Japanese): experience of enlightenment in *Zen*.

satyāgraha (Sanskrit): active nonviolence of those who live for the truth.

satyasya satyam (Sanskrit): true truth, true reality, the being of the existent.

schola Domini (Latin): school of the Lord.

secularity, secular: of this world, being-in-time, being-in-the-world (from Latin *saeculum*).

semper maior (Latin): always greater.

septuaginta (Latin): "the Seventy" (translators); translation of the Hebrew Bible into Greek, carried out in the third to first centuries BC in Alexandria.

simplicitas cordis (Latin): simplicity of heart.

śiṣya (Sanskrit): disciple (cf. *guru*).

Sitz im Leben (German): vital setting, context.

Śiva (Sanskrit): propitious, gracious, pleasant, benevolent. He who is of good omen; in the *Veda* it is Rudra who is known to the *Śvetāśvatara-upaniṣad* as Śiva, one of the most important Gods of Hindu tradition. He is the destroyer of the universe (cf. also *Brahmā, Viṣṇu*), and also the great *yogin* and model of ascetics. His consort is Pārvatī or Umā.

Śivaism, Śivaita (Sanskrit): one of the two great families of the Hindu religion, whose God is Śiva.

sobrietas (Latin): sobriety, moderation.

sola fides (Latin): "the one faith," the response of Scholasticism to philosophically unsolvable theological questions; the central doctrine of Luther.

soma (Sanskrit): the sacrificial plant from which the juice of the *soma* is extracted through elaborate rituals, hence the sap or drink of immortality (*amṛta* is another name for *soma*); a divinity ("Soma the king"). *Soma* was used ritually for entering a higher state of consciousness. Later it also took on the meaning of "moon."

sōma (Greek): body.

sophia (Greek): wisdom.

sōteria (Greek): salvation, liberation, redemption.

śraddhā (Sanskrit): "faith," the active trust (in Gods or in the rite itself) required in every act of worship; confidence (in the teachings of the *Veda*). In the *Ṛg-veda* (X.151), *śraddhā* is invoked almost as a divinity.

śrāddha (Sanskrit): rite of homage to deceased relatives; offering to ancestors generally made by the son of the deceased and repeated on certain occasions. Consists in oblations of food to the ancestors and a meal for relatives and priests.

stūpa (Sanskrit): sacred place or sacred mountain in Buddhism.

sui generis (Latin): "of its own kind."

sukha (Sanskrit): happiness, pleasure, joy, bliss.

śūnya, śūnyatā (Sanskrit): void, vacuity, nothingness, the structural condition of reality and all things; represents the ultimate reality in Buddhism (cf. *nirvāṇa*).

suṣupti (Sanskrit): deep, dreamless sleep; one of the four states of consciousness, along with wakefulness, dreaming, and the state of conscious enlightenment.

sūtra (Sanskrit): lit. "yarn, thread of a fabric." Short aphorism in a sacred text that generally cannot be understood without a comment (*bhāṣya*). The literature of the *sūtra* is part of the *smṛti* and is conceived to be easily memorized.

Śvetaketu (Sanskrit): son of Gautama; in the *Chāndogya-upaniṣad* a famous disciple of Uddalaka, to whom is imparted the highest teaching on the *ātman* and the *brahman*, which ends with: *tat tvam asi* ("that is you").

Śvetāśvatara-upaniṣad (Sanskrit): one of the principles of the last *Upaniṣad*, frequently cited in the Vedānta, which tends to personify the supreme principle (Brahman) and identify it with the God Śiva or Rudra.

symbolon (Greek): symbol.

syneches (Greek): continuous, uninterrupted, persevering, solid: that which keeps something in cohesion.

Taboric light: the light that illuminated Jesus in the transfiguration; this light may be regarded as the visible character of divinity, the energy or grace by which God allows himself to be known; Man may receive this light.

taṇhā (Pāli): thirst; thirst for existence; origin of all suffering, according to Buddhism. Cf. *tṛṣṇā*.

Tantra (Sanskrit): lit. weave, weaving, loom; religious system not based on the *Veda*, consisting in secret doctrines and practices that give access to hidden powers; accentuates the interrelation between body and soul, matter and spirit; the development of special powers. The Tantric tradition has practically permeated the entire spiritual tradition of Asia. The basic assumption of all Tantric practices is the interrelation between body and spirit, matter and soul, *bhukti* (pleasure) and *mukti* (liberation).

tao (Chinese): "way," a central concept in Chinese philosophy, especially Taoism.

Tao-te Ching (Chinese): "the book of the way and its power," a fundamental work of philosophical Taoism in China, attributed to Laotzi (sixth century BC), historically demonstrable from third century BC.

ta panta mataiotes (Greek): all (is) vanity.

tapas (Sanskrit): lit. heat; hence inner energy, spiritual fervor or ardor, austerity, ascesis, penitence. One of the forms of primordial energy, along with *kāma*.

tat (Sanskrit): demonstrative pronoun: "that." Opposite of *idam* (this), refers to Brahman. When isolated, it refers to the ultimate reality without naming it.

tat tvam asi (Sanskrit): "that is you," an Upaniṣadic expression meaning that *ātman* is ultimately Brahman. One of the four Great Sayings (*mahāvākyāni*) of the *Upaniṣad*, as taught to Śvetaketu.

theandric: "divine-human" (from Greek *theos* and *aner*).

theanthropocosmic: "divine-human-cosmic" (from Greek *theos*, *anthropos*, and *kosmos*).

technē (Greek): art, ability, handicraft.

theōreia (Greek): theory; originally in the sense of "contemplation."

ṭīkā (Sanskrit): commentary, generally of the *sūtra*.

tīrthaṅkara (Sanskrit): line of great sages/saints in Jainism.

tonsura: preparatory religious rank for receiving the minor orders in Christianity; special haircut as a distinctive mark of the clerical status that distinguishes it from the secular and signifies separation from the world.

triloka (Sanskrit): the "triple world," totality of the universe, consisting in three realms: earth, atmosphere, and sky, or earth, sky, and the nether regions (later called hell); the inhabitants of the three worlds are Gods, men, and demons.

tṛṣṇā (Sanskrit): thirst; cf. *taṇhā*.

tvam (Sanskrit): you (personal pronoun, second-person singular).

tyāga (Sanskrit): renunciation, abandonment of possessions and attachments.

umma (Arabic): the community of believers; church.

Ungrund (German): bottomless, without foundations, abyss.

Upaniṣad (Sanskrit): fundamental sacred teaching in the form of texts constituting the end of the *Veda*; part of the revelation (*śruti*) and basis of posterior Hindu thought.

upekṣā (Sanskrit): equanimity, detachment, benevolence.

utrumque (Latin): the one and the other.

vāc (Sanskrit): word; the sacred, primordial, and creative Word; sound, also discourse, language, the organ of speech, voice. Sometimes only the *Ṛg-veda* and other times all the *Veda* are referred to as *vāc*.

vairāgya (Sanskrit): estrangement, renunciation, indifference; one of the requisites of the spiritual path.

vānaprastha (Sanskrit): inhabitant of the forest, hermit; the third stage of life or *āśrama*, when the head of family withdraws into solitude, with or without his wife, after having fulfilled his earthly duties.

Varuṇa (Sanskrit): one of the main Gods of the *Veda*; Varuṇa is king, commander, and supervisor of the moral conduct of men. He is Lord of *ṛta*, cosmic and moral order. He is often invoked together with Mitra. Due to his close association with water he later became known simply as a God of water, the Lord of the ocean.

vāyu (Sanskrit): air, wind, personified as a God in the *Veda*.

Veda (Sanskrit): lit. knowledge (from the root *vid-*, to know); the sacred knowledge incorporated in the *Veda* as the entire body of "Sacred Scriptures" (although originally they were only passed on orally). Strictly speaking, "*Veda*" refers only to the *Saṃhitā* (*Ṛg-veda, Yajur-veda, Sāma-veda, Atharva-veda*); generally, however, *Brāhmaṇa* and *Upaniṣad* are also included. In the plural it refers to the four *Veda*.

vedanā (Sanskrit): sensation, feeling.

Vedānta (Sanskrit): lit. end of the *Veda*, i.e., the *Upaniṣad* as the climax of Vedic wisdom. In the sense of Uttaramī māṃsā or Vedāntavāda, a system of Indian philosophy (Advaita-vedānta, Dvaita-vedānta, etc.) based on the *Upaniṣad*, which teaches a spiritual interpretation of the *Veda*; one of the last schools of Hindu philosophical thought, of which the most renowned representatives include Śaṅkara, Rāmānuja, and Madhva.

viator (Latin): traveller, novice, aspirant, disciple.

vidyā (Sanskrit): knowledge, wisdom, also branch of knowledge; a section of a text in the *Upaniṣad*.

vihāra (Sanskrit): monastery, generally in Buddhism; Buddhist or Jain temple.

vinaya (Sanskrit): collection of moral rules and practices in Buddhism.

viveka (Sanskrit): discernment, discrimination.

Vivekacūḍāmaṇi (Sanskrit): "jewel/diadem of discernment," an important work of the Advaita-vedānta, written by Śaṅkara, which deals with the distinction between true reality and the phenomenic world.

vrata (Sanskrit): vow, religious observance.

vyāvahārika (Sanskrit): "relating to earthly matters, to mundane life," i.e., the earthly way of seeing, the practical perspective; the relative level.

wu wei (Chinese): "nonaction" in Taoist philosophy.

xeniteia (Greek): the state of being a stranger.

yakṣa (Sanskrit): spiritual, semidivine, supernatural being; beings belonging to a higher level than the physical.

Yama (Sanskrit): the "twin" of Yamī, the first man and the first to pass through death and obtain immortality; hence the predecessor of men on the path of death and he who commands in the realm of the dead. Later became the personification of Death and the Lord of the nether regions.

Yamī (Sanskrit): the sister of Yama, with whom she forms the first couple of humans on the earth. Although her brother attempts to commit incest with her, she (according to some texts) does not yield.

yang (Chinese): the solar, celestial, masculine aspect in the yin-yang polarity.

yin (Chinese): the lunar, earthly, feminine aspect; complement of *yang*.

yoga (Sanskrit): from the root *yuj-*, to yoke, to join, to unite, to prepare, to fix, to concentrate; union; method of mental, physical, and spiritual union;

concentration and contemplation, which also uses bodily posture (*āsana*), breathing control (*prāṇāyāma*) and spiritual techniques. Yoga appears to be an extremely ancient Indian practice that was developed into a system by Patañjali (*Yoga-sūtra*) and made to correspond to the philosophical system Sāṃkhya. Yoga as a method has become a fundamental factor in practically all religions of Indian origin.

yogin (Sanskrit): the ascetic, one who practices self-control, a follower of the path of yoga.

zen (Japanese): from the Sanskrit *dhyāna* (deep meditation); school of Buddhism that claims to be the purest and most direct path to enlightenment (*satori*, *nirvāṇa*).

INDEX OF ORIGINAL TEXTS IN THIS VOLUME

Introduction contains a reviewed part of "Have Religions the Monopoly on Religion?," *Journal of Ecumenical Studies*, XI, no. 3 (1974): 515–517.

Religion and Religions. — The functional, essential and existential concurrence of religions. A philosophical study on the dynamic and historical nature of religion, from an unpublished text. Religione e religioni. Concordanza funzionale, essenziale ed esistenziale delle religioni. Studio filosofico sulla natura storica e dinamica della religione. Presentation by Card. Franz Köning, Morcelliana, Brescia 1964.

"Meditation on Melchizedek," originally "Meditación sobre Melquisedec," *Nuestro Tiempo*, no. 102, (1962): 675–695. Published in Italian in *Maya e Apocalisse – L'incontro dell'induismo e del cristianesimo* (Abete, Roma, 1966), cap. 9. Translated from Spanish by Carla Ros.

"The Invisible Harmony: A Universal Theory of Religion or a Cosmic Confidence in Reality?" *Interculture*, no. 108 (1990): 45–78.

"The Religion of the Future or the Crisis of the Concept of Religion," originally "La Religione del futuro o la crisi del concetto di religione. La religiosità umana, Civiltà delle macchine," XXVII, no. 4/6 (1979): 166–171. Translated by Roger and Yakshi Rapp and Mary Eastham.

"Every Authentic Religion is a Way to Salvation," in *Hinduism and Christianity* (Student World: Geneva 1962), pp. 304–323.

"Nine Ways Not to Talk about God," *Cross Currents* 47, no. 2 (1997): 149–153, originally "Novenario sobre Dios," *El Ciervo*, XXXIX, no. 489 (1991): 9–10.

"Are There Anonymous Religions? The Name and the Thing," in *The Notion of 'Religion' in Comparative Research: Selected Proceedings of the XVIth Congress of the International Association for the History of Religions*, Rome 3–8/IX/ (L'Herma: Roma 1990), pp. 889–894.

God in Religions, originally *Dios en las religiones* (Misión Abierta: Madrid 1985), 5–6. Translated by Carla Ros.

"Aporias in the Comparative Philosophy of Religion," *Man and World*, XIII, no. 3–4 (1980): 357–383.

"The Ambiguity of the Science of Comparative Religions. Noēma and Pisteuma,) in S. Painadath & Leonard Fernando (eds.), *Co-worker for Your Joy: Festschrift in honour of George Gispert-Sauch*, (ISPCK: Delhi 2006): 25–36.

"Philosophy of Religion in the Encounter of Cultures," in *Contemporary Philosophy: A Survey*, (ed. R. Klibansky, 1968).

"The Scandal of Religions," originally "L'escàndol de les religions," *Diàleg entre les religions. Textos fonamentals* (Trotta: Madrid, 2002), pp. 167–175. Translated by Carla Ros.

"The Challenge of the Study of Religion," *The Teillard Review*, XXV, no. 3 (1990).

"Reflections on Religion and Europe," originally "Que religión para Europa?," *La vanguardia* (14 de julio 1991): 30.

"Religion and the Body," originally "Religión y cuerpo," in *Estética y religión, El discurso del cuerpo y los sentidos* (eds. Amador Vega, J.A. Rodríguez Tous, Raquel Bouso), "Revista de Filosofía," (1998), pp.11–48. Translated by Clarissa Balaszeskul-Hawes.

"Medicine and Religion," *Interculture*, no. 125 (1994): 1–39, originally "Medicina y Religión," *Jano*, XXI, no. 737 (1994), pp. 12–48.

Index of Names

Aaron, 140, 148
Abel, 140, 148
Abraham (Abram), 138–39,
140–41, 142, 144, 147
Adam, 141, 142, 143, 147–48
Aeschylus, 181n29
Ambrose, Saint, 140
Anastasius, Saint, 141
Aṅgirasa, 83
Anselm of Canterbury, Saint, 224
Aquinas, Thomas, 46, 49,
116, 141, 263, 329
Aristotle, 5, 156, 162, 172,
177n3, 181n28, 250, 259,
317, 330, 335, 370n89
Assaglioli, Roberto, 270n9
Augustine, Saint, 39n1, 141, 286,
322, 341, 343, 346, 366
Aurobindo, Śrī, 114

Bahm, A. J., 238n14
Bailly, J. S., 363
Baumgarten, Alexander Gottlieb,
327
Beethoven, Ludwig von, 319
Bellarmino, Roberto, Saint, 321
Benveniste, E., 362
Berdyaev, Nicolas, 283
Bergson, H., 353n24
Berkeley, G., 221
Bermejos, D., 313
Bernard of Clairvaux, Saint, 314
Boas, H., 268n5
Boethius, 154
Boff, Leonardo, 313

Bonaventure, Saint, 141, 143
Boniface VIII, 314
Boutin, Maurice, 178n10
Bruno, Giordano, 313
Buddha, 12, 111, 114, 142, 151,
195–96, 372

Caesar, 180
Caffarena, J. G., 238n13
Carnap, R., 221
Cassius Dio, 180n25
Catherine of Genoa, Saint, 243
Cervantes, Miguel de, 371
Chantraine, P., 360n51
Charlemagne, 314
Christ, 14–15, 16, 48, 83, 113,
138, 140, 142, 144–48, 158,
165, 195, 196, 209, 211–16,
230, 299, 316, 319, 345–46,
348, 368. See also Jesus
Chrysostom, John, 141
Chuang-Tzu (Zhuangzi), 179, 368
Church, A., 221
Cicero, 39n1, 303, 322, 366
Clement of Alexandria, Saint, 140
Comte, Auguste, 312
Confucius, 142, 224, 372
Constantine, 314
Copernicus, 332
Coser, Lewis A., 238n12
Curran, C., 313
Cusanus. See Nicolas of Cusa

Dash, Bhagawan, 369n87
Demosthenes, 178n12

About the Author

An international authority on spirituality, the study of religions, and intercultural dialogue, Raimon Panikkar has made intercultural and dialogical pluralism one of the hallmarks of his research, becoming a master "bridge builder," tireless in the promotion of dialogue between Western culture and the great Oriental Hindū and Buddhist traditions.

Born in 1918 in Barcelona of a Spanish Catholic mother and an Indian Hindū father, he is part of a plurality of traditions: Indian and European, Hindū and Christian, scientific and humanistic.

Panikkar holds degrees in chemistry, philosophy, and theology, and was ordained a Catholic priest in 1946. He has delivered courses and lectures in major European, Indian, and American universities.

A member of the International Institute of Philosophy (Paris), of the permanent Tribunal of the Peoples (Rome), and of the UNESCO Commission for intercultural dialogue, he has also founded various philosophical journals and intercultural study centers. He has held conferences in each of the five continents (including the renowned Gifford Lectures in 1988–1989 on "Trinity and Atheism").

Panikkar has received international recognitions including honorary doctorates from the University of the Balearic Islands in 1997, the University of Tübingen in 2004, Urbino in 2005, and Girona in 2008, as well as prizes ranging from the "Premio Menéndez Pelayo de Humanidades" for his book *El concepto de naturaleza* in Madrid in 1946 to the "Premio Nonino 2001 a un maestro del nostro tempo" in Italy.

Since 1982 he has lived in Tavertet in the Catalonian mountains, where he continues his contemplative experience and cultural activities. There he founded and presides over the intercultural study center Vivarium. Panikkar has published more than fifty books in various languages and hundreds of articles on the philosophy of religion, theology, the philosophy of science, metaphysics, and indology.

From the dialogue between religions to the peaceful cohabitation of peoples; from reflections on the future of the technological society to major work on political and social intelligence; from the recognition that all interreligious dialogue is based on an intrareligious dialogue to the promotion of open knowledge of other religions, of which he is a mediator; from his penetrating analysis of the crisis in spirituality to the practice of meditation and the rediscovery of his monastic identity; from the invitation of *colligite fragmenta* as a path toward the integration of reality to the proposal of a new innocence, Panikkar embodies a personal journey of fulfillment.

Among his most important publications with Orbis are: *velo della realtà* (2000); *L'incontro indispensabile: dialogo delle religioni* (2001); *Pace e interculturalità. Una riflessione filosofica* (2002, 2006); *La realtà cosmoteandrica. Dio-Uomo-Mondo* (2004); *L'esperienza della vita. La mistica* (2005); *La gioia pasquale, La presenza di Dio and Maria* (2007); *Il Cristo sconosciuto dell'induismo* (2008).